IELTS

ACADEMIC ESSAYS FROM THE PAST EXAMS

DR. KIRANPREET KAUR MAKKAR
(MBBS, DGO - Makkar Hospital, Phagwara)

ER. INDROOP SINGH MAKKAR
(MS in IE & OR Pennsylvania State University, USA)

Published by: Makkar Publishing House
#SCF15, Phase- 7, Mohali, Punjab - 160062
M: 9646044322 | O: 9872461083
www.makkarielts.com | ravielts@gmail.com

Published By: Makkar Publishing House

Revised Edition 2023

First published in India by makkarIELTS 2017

Written by: Kiranpreet Kaur Makkar & Indroop Singh Makkar

Contributions: Ravpreet Singh, Deepa Makkar

Cover Illustration: Ravpreet Singh

Printed By: Chandigarh Publishing House, Sector 41, Chandigarh

ISBN: 978-93-5267-635-4

PREFACE

This book is meant to help the average student crack the IELTS essay. Over 17 years of my IELTS coaching experience has taught me a lot about what all would help the students do better in the writing module of the IELTS. In the past 2 years the live online classes with students from all over the world, I learnt that the simpler the essay, the easier it becomes for the student to grasp and so most of the essays have been rewritten in a much simpler format.

The IELTS essay has to have a plan. Time spent on the plan, is time well invested. A plan is surely going to produce an essay, which works. A crisp, but brief and to-the-point introduction and conclusion, and two to three well planned paragraphs with relevant topic sentences, is all that is needed for the IELTS essay.

This book has 430+ essays seen in the actual IELTS exams, most of which have been repeated many times. Valuable contributions have been made to the content of the book by Indroop Singh Makkar (Head of Makkar IELTS Centres, Phagwara), Deepa Makkar (incharge website www.makkarielts.com), Ravpreet Singh (Head of Phase 3B2 and Phase 7 Mohali Centres) and Dilmohan Singh (Head of Mohali Centre 104 Sector). This book would not have been possible without their efforts.

Hope you enjoy going through the essays in the book.

Kiranpreet Kaur Makkar

General Introduction

The IELTS essay is the second part of the writing section of the IELTS test. It requires you to write an academic essay with the **minimum word count of 250, within a period of 40 minutes**. There is no limit to the maximum word count. This part takes up 2/3rd of the overall score of the writing section.

Each essay is marked with 4 different criteria, which share an equal proportion of the overall band score.

Category	What it means is that the examinee
Task Response	1. Answers the question fully and relevantly 2. Gives a position or opinion 3. Gives and develops ideas
Coherence and Cohesion	1. Organises the writing, showing progression 2. Makes the sentences and parts fit together 3. Organises paragraphs well
Lexical Resource	1. Use a range of words 2. Uses those words accurately
Grammatical Range and Accuracy	1. Uses a range of grammar 2. Uses that grammar accurately

One important point to understand is that you need to achieve all the descriptors to achieve the matching IELTS band score. All the descriptors are connected, and you must look at them all.

IELTS Writing Task 2: Band Descriptors (6-9)

Source: www.ielts.org

	Task Response	Cohesion and Coherence	LR – Lexical Resource	GRA– Grammatical Range and Accuracy
Band 6	- Address all parts of the task although some parts may be more fully covered than others - Present a relevant position although the conclusions may become unclear or repetitive - Present relevant main ideas but some may be inadequately developed/unclear	- Arrange information and ideas coherently and have is a clear overall progression - Use cohesive devices effectively, but cohesion within and/or between sentences may be faulty or mechanical - Use referencing clearly or appropriately, although at some places there may be flaws - Use paragraphing, but not always logically	- Use an adequate range of vocabulary for the task - Attempt to use less common vocabulary but with some inaccuracy - Be able to communicate, although you may have some errors in spelling and/or word formation (but they should not impede communication)	- Use a mix of simple and complex sentence forms - Be able to communicate, although you may make some errors in grammar and punctuation (but they rarely reduce communication)
Band 7	- addresses all parts of the task - presents a clear position throughout the response - presents, extends and supports main ideas, but there may be a tendency to overgeneralize and/or supporting ideas may lack focus	- Logically organize information and ideas; and have a clear progression throughout - Use a range of cohesive devices appropriately although there may be some under-use or over-use - Present a clear central topic within each paragraph	- Use a sufficient range of vocabulary to allow some flexibility and precision - Use less common lexical items with some awareness of style and collocation - may produce occasional errors in word choice, spelling and/or word formation	- Use a variety of complex structures - Produce frequent error-free sentences - Have good control of grammar and punctuation but may make a few errors
Band 8	- Sufficiently address all parts of the task - Present a well-developed response to the question with relevant, extended and supported ideas.	- Sequence information and ideas logically - Manage all aspects of cohesion well - Use paragraphing sufficiently and appropriately	- Use a wide range of vocabulary fluently and flexibly to convey precise meanings - Skilfully use uncommon lexical items but there may be occasional inaccuracies in word choice and collocation, and you have only rare errors in spelling and/or word formation	- Use a wide range of structures - Write a majority of error-free sentences - Make only very occasional errors or inappropriacies
Band 9	- Fully address all parts of the task - Present a well-developed response to the question with relevant, extended and supported ideas.	- Use cohesion in such a way that it attracts no attention - Skillfully manage paragraphing	- Use a wide range of vocabulary with very natural and sophisticated control of lexical features; rare minor errors occur only as 'slips'	- Use a wide range of structures with full flexibility and accuracy, with rare minor errors occurring only as 'slips'

Common Essay Questions

Four different types of IELTS Essays

1. Opinion essays
    - Opinion 1 – Agree/Disagree.
    - Opinion 2 – Is this a positive or a negative development.
    - Opinion 3 – Do you think the advantages are more than the disadvantages.
2. Discuss essays
3. Problem and solution essays
4. Direct question essays

Makkar IELTS YouTube channel (https://www.youtube.com/user/MakkarIelts) and website https://makkarielts.com has videos on attempting all of these essay types.

General things to know about any type of IELTS essay

The key to writing a good IELTS essay is uniformity throughout the essay. The introduction, the body paragraphs and the conclusion should convey the same thing.

The three elements of an essay

1. Introduction
2. Body Paragraphs
3. Conclusion

Introduction has two elements - Essay topic paraphrasing and thesis statement. So, to write a good introduction you need to write one sentence to introduce the topic, which can be done by paraphrasing the question and the second sentence to answer the question.

Body Paragraphs have three elements – Topic sentence, points and supporting points.

Conclusion – It Is the repetition of the opinion/thesis but in a different way.

Linking Words for IELTS Essay

Linking words, sometimes called as cohesive devices, discourse markers or transitional words are one of the most important parts of the IELTS Writing module as they bring overall structure and flow to your essay.

Most of the students pursuing IELTS exam, know these words as Firstly, Secondly, Furthermore, However, etcetera. But, once the students become aware about them, they tend to either overuse these words or use them inappropriately. So please make sure, that the linking words are used judiciously in your essay in order to get a high band score for Coherence and Cohesion.

Following is a list of the linking words that you can use in your essay, categorized according to the use.

- **Sequencing** - Firstly, Secondly, Next, Then, After, To begin with, First of all
- **Addition** - And, also, Furthermore, What is more, Moreover, Additionally, To further strengthen this view, another point/fact/factor is
- **Contrast** - In comparison, On the other hand, In Contrast, On the contrary, Admittedly, However, Although, Having said that, That said
- **Comparison** - Also, equally, similarly, likewise, compared with
- **Adding examples** - For example, For instance, To illustrate, To cite an example, To exemplify
- **Result** - So, therefore, As a result, thus, because, consequently, owing to this
- **Highlighting** - In particular, especially, mainly, particularly, above all
- **Restating** - In other words, Put more simply, rather, in simple terms
- **Conclusion** - To sum up, To conclude, To summarise, In conclusion

Useful phrases:

- Not only... but also
- This coupled with (to state an additional related point)
- Undoubtedly, Without a doubt, Indubitably (To state a fact)
- To state further points supporting the same view/point:
- Moreover, Furthermore, What's more, In addition, Additionally, To further strengthen my viewpoint, another point/fact/factor is
- To state opposite view/points:
- In contrast, By contrast, On the other hand, However, Having said that, That said

To state an advantage regardless of a fact or evidence: Despite this, Nevertheless, Nonetheless, Notwithstanding.

INDEX

29.	Temporary jobs	Advantages more than disadvantages	Job
30.	People change their career and place of residence several times during their lifetime.	Positive/negative development	Job
31.	An increasing number of people change their career during their work life. What are the reasons for this?	Reasons and Positive/Negative	Job
32.	Doctors, nurses and teachers should be paid more than sports and entertainment celebs.	Agree/Disagree	Job
33.	Celebs earning more than politicians	Positive/negative development	Job
34.	Some countries have a law to limit working hours for employees. Why?	Positive/negative development	Job
35.	In some countries, it is illegal for companies to reject job applicant for their age.	Positive/negative development	Job
36.	Nowadays, some workplaces tend to employ equal numbers of men and women workers	Positive/negative development	Job
37.	There should be a quota for women in high level jobs.	Agree/Disagree	Job
38.	Benefits of requiring young people to serve the army. Is community work a good alternative?	Direct question	Job
39.	Rich countries should not employ skilled labour from poor countries,	Agree/Disagree	Job
40.	People aim to achieve a balance between their work and lives, but few people achieve it	Problem/solution	Job (20/7/19)
41.	Many people leave their country to work abroad and take their family with them.	Advantages more than disadvantages	Job
42.	Youth unemployment.	Problem/solution	Job
43.	Employers should give at least 4 weeks holiday to employees	Agree/Disagree	Job
44.	Increased use of technology – young vs old workers	Agree/Disagree	Job
45.	Time spent in travelling to work can be reduced by apartments in place of parks	Agree/Disagree	Job
46.	Students should learn academic subjects and NOT cookery, dressmaking and woodwork.	Agree/Disagree	Education
47.	Increasing usage of computers and mobile phones has had a negative effect on reading and writing skills.	Agree/Disagree	Education
48.	Now a lot of people in college are doing academic study. We should encourage them to learn vocational sl ill	Agree/Disagree	Education
49.	To be successful, you need a university education, whereas others say it is not true.	Discuss	Education (22/2/2020)
50.	Should healthy eating and importance of healthy food, taught in schools OR by parents.	Discuss	Education
51.	Some say history has nothing or little to tell us, but others think it can help us better understand the present.	Discuss	Education
52.	Schools are spending more time in traditional subjects like history etc. They should rather spend more time in teaching skills that can help them find a job.	Agree/disagree	Education
53.	Local history vs world history	Agree/disagree	Education
54.	Government should invest more money in teaching science than other subjects	Agree/Disagree	Education
55.	Should teenagers concentrate on all school subjects OR on the subject they are best at.	Discuss	Education

56.	University students should not focus on one subject and learn a range of other subjects.	Agree/Disagree	Education
57.	Unpaid internships - How beneficial for the student as well as the company or institution?	Direct question	Education
58.	Fewer people today write by hand using a pen, pencil or brush. Reasons.	Positive/negative development	Education
59.	It is unnecessary to teach children about the skills of handwriting.	Agree/Disagree	Education
60.	Traditional skill of letter writing vs technology	Agree/Disagree	Education
61.	School starting age should be 4 OR 7	Discuss	Education
62.	Should teachers teach students what is right and wrong OR should only teach academics	Discuss	Education
63.	It is better for children to learn foreign language at primary school than secondary school.	Advantages more than disadvantages	Education/ language
64.	The advantages of English as a "global language" will outweigh the disadvantages.	Agree/Disagree	Education/ language
65.	It is better to teach language students in small classes, OR big classes	Discuss	Education/ language
66.	A foreign language should not be mandatory at school	Agree/Disagree	Education/ language
67.	Teaching a foreign language to primary school students is essential in some countries.	Advantages more than disadvantages	Education/ language
68.	Should governments spend on saving languages with few speakers from dying out OR is it a waste of financial resources.	Discuss	Education/ language
69.	We should invent a new language for international communication.	Advantages more than disadvantages	Education/ language
70.	In order to learn a language well, we should learn about the country as well as the cultures and lifestyles of the native people.	Agree/Disagree	Education/ language
71.	Some languages are increasingly spoken in different countries, while the usage of others is rapidly declining.	Positive/negative development	Education/ language
72.	Computer translation vs human translator	Agree/Disagree	Education/ language
73.	Fast food restaurants and supermarkets give money to schools to promote their products.	Positive/negative development	Education
74.	Distance learning cannot bring the benefit as much as attending college or university.	Agree/Disagree	Education
75.	Once children start school, teachers have more influence than parents on their intellectual and social development.	Agree/Disagree	Education
76.	Gap year	Advantages more than disadvantages	Education
77.	In a Gap year is working better or travelling	Discuss	Education
78.	Students today can access information online, so libraries are not necessary.	Agree/Disagree	Education
79.	Public libraries should provide books and Not expensive hi-tech media	Agree/Disagree	Education
80.	Should government should establish free libraries in each town. OR is it a waste of money	Discuss	Education
81.	Mathematics and philosophy should be optional rather than compulsory.	Agree/Disagree	Education
82.	International student exchange would be beneficial for all school students.	Advantages more than disadvantages	Education
83.	Teachers are better than internet or TV	Agree/Disagree	Education

84.	In which areas are computers more important and in which areas are teachers important?	Direct question	Education
85.	Some people think typical teaching of a teacher and students in the class will not exist by the year 2050.	Agree/Disagree	Education
86.	What do you think are the main functions of a university?	Direct question	Education
87.	Government paying university fees. Are the advantages more than disadvantages	Advantages more than disadvantages	Education
88.	Higher education can be funded in three ways	Direct question	Education
89.	More money should be spent by government on free-time activities.	Agree/disagree	Education
90.	It is neither possible nor useful for a country to provide university education to a high proportion of young people.	Agree/disagree	Education
91.	The best way to remove poverty in developing countries is to provide 6 years of free education to all children so that they can read, write and use numbers.	Agree/disagree	Education
92.	Universities should make it easy for poor to study at.	Agree/Disagree	Education
93.	Rote learning plays a role in many education systems.	Advantages more than disadvantages	Education
94.	Should we encourage our students to evaluate and criticize teachers OR will it result in a loss of respect and discipline in classroom.	Discuss	Education
95.	Schools should reward students who show the best academic results, OR reward students who show improvements.	Discuss	Education
96.	Studying literature is important for individual character building OR is a waste of time.	Discuss	Education
97.	It is important for children to take lessons outside classroom	Agree/disagree	Education
98.	Home-schooling OR going to school	Discuss	Education
99.	It is not necessary for adults to receive education in class. Self-study is better	Agree/disagree	Education
100.	Should courses of performing arts, be funded by government OR through other ways	Discuss	Education
101.	More and more people are competing for a place to study in universities. Why?	Positive/negative development	Education
102.	Schools should teach pupils according to their academic abilities, OR have pupils with different abilities study together.	Discuss	Education (22/6/19)
103.	What should education consist of for the development of individuals and the wellbeing of societies.	Direct question	Education
104.	Main purpose of schools is to turn the children into good citizens and workers, rather than to benefit them as individuals.	Agree/disagree	Education
105.	In some countries, university students live away from home while studying.	Advantages more than disadvantages	Education
106.	Financial support from the government should be provided for scientific research rather than research for less useful subjects.	Agree/disagree	Education
107.	Not enough students are choosing to study science subjects at university. Why? Effects?	Cause/effects	Education
108.	Should schools and teachers be provided to rural children OR should computers and internet be provided.	Discuss	Education
109.	Do students only need to get primary education to solve unemployment, OR is secondary education is necessary.	Discuss	Education

110.	Should government decide which subjects students should study at university, OR students should be allowed to apply for the subject they prefer.	Discuss	Education
111.	The best way for children to learn to read is by using online materials. OR printed materials should be used.	Discuss	Education
112.	Schools should stop using books for teaching children as they find them boring, and use film, TV and computer instead.	Agree/Disagree	Education
113.	Children should be encouraged to watch TV both at home and school	Agree/Disagree	Education
114.	Everyone should stay in school until they reach the age of 18.	Agree/Disagree	Education
115.	Groups study. OR study alone. Benefits of each study method. Which one do you think is more effective?	Direct question	Education
116.	Students should learn more practical courses like computer, OR should they learn more about theoretical	Discuss	Education
117.	Students are pushed to hard work when they are young.	Positive/negative development	Education
118.	Out of all school subjects, which one is the most important and which one is the least.	Direct question	Education
119.	Universities should accept equal numbers of male and female students in every subject.	Agree/Disagree	Education
120.	Full time university students spend most of the time studying. They should be doing other activities too.	Agree/Disagree	Education
121.	Many people who leave school hold a negative attitude towards learning.	Problem/Solution	Education
122.	The authorities such as the government decide the subjects and lesson contents. Teachers should make the choice.	Agree/disagree	Education
123.	Nowadays sending children to boarding school is becoming popular. Why?	Positive/negative development	Education
124.	Secondary school students should study international news as one of their subjects. OR this is a waste of valuable school time.	Discuss	Education
125.	In schools and universities, girls tend to choose arts subjects, while boys choose science subjects. Why? Should the trend change	Reasons and direct question	Education
126.	Do students benefit from going to private secondary schools. OR not.	Discuss	Education
127.	More and more students choose to go to another country for their higher education.	Advantages more than disadvantages	Education
128.	Children find it difficult to concentrate on or pay attention to school. Reasons. Solutions	Problem/Solution	Education
129.	In many countries, sport and exercise classes are replaced with academic subjects. Why and its effects	Reasons and direct question	Education
130.	We have three important parts of education: reading, writing and math. Some people think every child will benefit from a fourth skill added to the list: computer skills.	Agree/Disagree	Education
131.	Some people think that schools should concentrate on academic classes, because they are helpful for future career. And they think music and sports classes are not useful.	Agree/Disagree	Education
132.	Some people believe that reading stories from a book is better than watching TV or playing computer games for children.	Agree/Disagree	Education
133.	The only way to protect the environment is at an international level.	Agree/Disagree	Environment

134.	Climate change and its effect on business	Discuss	Environment
135.	Despite warnings why people do not limit energy use.	Problem solution	Environment
136.	Environmental problems are too big for individuals to be solved OR individuals can solve problems with government action.	Discuss	Environment
137.	Why global steps to save environment have failed	Problem/solution	Environment
138.	Is industrial growth necessary to solve poverty, OR is it leading to poverty and should be stopped.	Discuss	Environment
139.	Is economic development necessary to reduce poverty OR it should be stopped to stop damaging the environment.	Discuss	Environment
140.	Governments should focus on reducing environmental pollution and housing problems to prevent illness and disease	Agree/Disagree	Environment
141.	The best way to solve the world's environmental problem is to increase the price of fuel.	Agree/Disagree	Environment
142.	The natural resources such as oil, forests and fresh water are being consumed at an alarming rate.	Problem/solution	Environment
143.	Companies and private individuals, or governments should pay the bill of pollution.	Discuss	Environment
144.	Technology causes environmental problems. The solution is everyone accepts a simpler way of life, OR technology can solve these problems.	Discuss	Environment
145.	Most countries do not recycle their waste like paper, glass, and aluminum cans. Reasons?	Reasons/Solutions	Environment
146.	The amount of noise people make has to be controlled strictly. OR people should be free to make as much noise as they wish.	Discuss	Environment
147.	Noise pollution. Causes and solutions	Problem/solution	Environment
148.	In some cities, government has imposed a congestion tax during rush hours.	Positive or negative development	Environment
149.	Instead of preventing climate change we should find a way to live with it.	Agree/disagree	Environment
150.	Household waste e.g. food packaging is increasing day by day.	Reasons/Solutions	Environment
151.	In some countries the use of alternative sources of energy are encouraged,	Positive or negative development	Environment
152.	Nuclear energy is a better choice for meeting increasing demand. Do you support its use	Direct question	Environment
153.	International community must act immediately to ensure all nations reduce consumption of fossil fuels e.g. gas and oil.	Agree/disagree	Environment
154.	Should government strictly control the supply of fresh water	Discuss Version 1	Environment
155.	Should government strictly control the supply of fresh water	Discuss Version 2	Environment
156.	The main benefit of international cooperation is in protection of the environment, OR is in the world business.	Discuss	Environment
157.	The increased demand for oil and gas has made it necessary to locate these sources in remote areas. (Against drilling)	Advantages more than disadvantages	Environment
158.	Vehicle-free day - private vehicles banned while the public transport is permitted	Advantages more than disadvantages	Environment
159.	Nowadays, people always throw the old things away when they buy new things and do not repair. Why? Effects?	Cause/Effect	Environment
160.	We have developed into a "throw-away" culture	Agree/disagree Solutions	Environment

161.	To solve the problem of traffic congestion government should provide free public transport 24 hours a day, 7 days a week.	Agree/disagree	Environment
162.	Should government spend on speed of public transport or on its cost and environment	Discuss	Environment
163.	Some countries are spending a lot to make it easier to use bicycle. Why? Is it the best solution	Reasons/Solutions	Environment
164.	Throwaway society – getting rid of old things to buy the new	Advantages more than disadvantages	Consumerism
165.	Consumerism and damage to environment	Reasons and solutions	Consumerism
166.	Consumer goods are cheaper to buy.	Advantages more than disadvantages	Consumerism
167.	Everyone in the world want to own a car, a TV and a fridge.	Advantages more than disadvantages	Consumerism
168.	Who should have the responsibility to reduce the amount of packaging of goods. Manufacturers or customers	Discuss	Environment
169.	Brand consciousness	Positive/negative development	consumerism
170.	The best way to improve road safety is to increase the minimum legal age for driving	Agree/disagree	Environment
171.	The only way to improve the safety on our own road is to have stricter punishment for driving offenders.	Agree/disagree	Environment
172.	Should governments spend money on building train and subway lines to reduce traffic congestion OR build more roads	Discuss	Environment
173.	The number of people using bikes as main transport mode is decreasing, even though it is so beneficial. Why? How people can be encouraged to use more bicycles?	Reasons/solutions	Environment
174.	In some cities people are choosing cars instead of bicycles, while in other cities riding bikes are replacing cars. Why? What is better?	Direct question	Environment
175.	The high volume of road traffic is a problem. Reasons/solutions	Reasons/Solutions	Environment
176.	The unlimited use of cars may cause many problems. What are those? Solutions	Problem/solution	Environment
177.	Some people claim that there are more disadvantages of the car than its advantages.	Agree/disagree	Environment
178.	Some people think the government should pay for increasing roads, while others think the car owners should pay for it.	Discuss	Environment
179.	Small town-centre shops are going out of business because people tend to drive to large out-of-town stores. it may result in an increase in the use of cars.	Advantages more than disadvantages	Environment
180.	Large shopping centres and shopping malls vs small shops.	Positive/Negative	Globalisation
181.	It is more important to plant trees in towns and cities than to build more houses.	Problem/solution	Environment
182.	The key to solving environmental problems is for the present generation to sacrifice their convenient life	Agree/Disagree	Environment
183.	Living with nature important for physical and mental well-being	Reasons/solutions	Environment
184.	Climate vs economy – impact on human life	Discuss	Environment
185.	Cultural traditions may be destroyed when used as money-making attractions OR it it the only way to save these traditions.	Discuss	Tourism
186.	When visiting other countries, how can visitors learn about culture and tradition of other countries? Why do some people	Direct question	Tourism

	learn about culture and tradition of foreign countries while other people do not?		
187.	Some people believe that air travel should be restricted because it causes serious pollution and uses up the world's fuel resources.	Agree/disagree	Environment
188.	Air travel can only benefit the richest people in the world.	Agree/disagree	Environment
189.	International travel makes people prejudiced rather than broad-minded.	Problem/solution	International tourism
190.	People have to spend more and more time to travel from their homes for jobs and study.	Reasons/solutions	Travel
191.	It is now possible for scientists and tourists to travel to remote natural environments such as the South Pole.	Are advantages more than disadvantages	Tourism
192.	Children from wealthy countries are doing unpaid work in poor countries. Why? Who gets more benefit, the community or them	Direct question	Tourism
193.	It has become easier and more affordable for people to travel to other countries.	Is this a positive or negative development	Tourism (18/5/19)
194.	Tourists should accept social and environmental responsibility OR tourists should not accept any responsibility at all.	Discuss	Tourism
195.	Visitors to others countries should imitate local customs and behaviours. OR host country should welcome cultural differences.	Discuss	Tourism
196.	People moving to a new country should accept new culture rather than living as a separate minority group	Agree/disagree	Tourism
197.	Foreign visitors should be charged more than local people when they visit the cultural and historical attractions in a country.	Agree/disagree	Tourism
198.	Foreign visitors should be charged more than local people when they visit the cultural and historical attractions in a country.	Agree/disagree	Tourism
199.	The traditional life style of local people in developing countries is attracting and increasing the number of tourists to the countries, which has the effect of preventing local people changing to modern ways.	Agree/disagree	Tourism
200.	Not necessary to travel abroad as we can see places on TV and Net	Discuss	Tourism
201.	Not necessary to travel abroad as we can see places on TV and Net	Agree/disagree	Tourism
202.	Mainly tourists, but not local people, visit museums and historical sites. Why? Solutions.	Reasons/solutions	Tourism
203.	It is easy to apply for and be given a credit card.	Advantages more than disadvantages	Money matters
204.	More and more people do online shopping. Why? What is the effect on shops and communities?	Reasons /Effects	Money matters
205.	Some people think that personal happiness is directly related to economic success. OR happiness depends on different factors.	Discuss	Money matters
206.	Some people believe they should keep all the money they have earned and should not pay tax to the state.	Agree/disagree	Money matters
207.	Is paying taxes is enough to contribute to the society. OR being a citizen involves more responsibilities.	Discuss	Money matters
208.	Some people say that it is the responsibility of individual to save money for their own care after they retire.	Agree/disagree	Money matters
209.	As well as making money, businesses should also have social responsibilities.	Agree/disagree	Money matters
210.	Developing countries are happy with economic growth but developing are not. Why? What lesson we learn from it?	Direct question	Rich Poor essay

211.	The best way to produce a happier society is to ensure that there only small differences between the richest and the poorest	Agree/disagree	Rich Poor essay
212.	Range of technology available to individuals today is increasing the gap between poor and rich. OR it is having an opposite effect.	Discuss	Rich Poor essay
213.	The gap between the rich and the poor is becoming wider. What problems can the situation cause and give the solutions?	Problem/solution	Rich Poor essay
214.	Government should not give aid if they have unemployed and homeless in own country.	Agree/disagree	Rich Poor essay
215.	Rich countries should give other types of help to the poor countries than the financial aid.	Agree/disagree	Rich Poor essay
216.	Charity organizations should only offer help to people of their own country. OR these organizations should give aid to people in great need wherever they live.	Discuss	Rich Poor essay
217.	Does success in life depends on hard work and determination, OR on other factors like money and personal appearance	Discuss	Money matters
218.	Whether or not someone achieves aim in their life is mostly a question of luck.	Agree/disagree	Miscellaneous
219.	Most important thing about being rich is that it gives you the opportunity to help the poor.	Agree/disagree	Rich Poor essay
220.	Famous people's support towards International aid organizations draws the attentions to problems, OR do celebrities make the problems less important.	Discuss	Rich Poor essay
221.	We need to give aid to all poor countries. OR we should not give international aids to countries with corruption in their system.	Discuss	Rich Poor essay
222.	Some people think that giving aids to the poor countries has more negative impacts than positive ones.	Agree/disagree	Rich Poor essay
223.	Individuals and countries cannot help everyone who needs help in the world, so they should only be concerned about their own communities and countries.	Agree/disagree	Rich Poor essay
224.	Charities and organisations have to publicize their activities by setting up a number of days Why do they do so? What are the effects?	Cause/effects	Rich Poor essay
225.	Economic progress is the only way to measure a country's success, OR there are other factors. Which is more important	Direct question	Money matters
226.	Should parents be punished if children do crime	Agree/Disagree	Juvenile delinquency
227.	Crimes increasing among teenagers	Problem solution	Juvenile delinquency
228.	Juvenile criminals should be punished as adults	Agree/Disagree	Juvenile delinquency
229.	Should juvenile delinquents do community work or be sent to prison	Direct question	Crime – Prison or community work
230.	Educating prisoners is the best way to reduce crime	Agree/disagree	Crime – Prison
231.	People afraid to leave home because of crime. Can something be done or nothing	Discuss	Crime –can anything be done
232.	People not safe within the home or out.	Problem/solution	Crime –Problem solution
233.	Security measures in urban areas	Advantages more than disadvantages	Crime – security measures

234.	Ex-prisoners are the best to talk to students about the danger of committing a crime.	Agree/disagree	Crime – ex-prisoners
235.	Education is better than prison to curb crime	Agree/disagree	Crime – prison vs education
236.	Long term prison OR alternative measures to curb crime	Discuss	Crime – Longer term in prison
237.	Why criminals reoffend	Problem/solution	Crime - Prisons
238.	Proper function of prisons is to punish criminals and life in prisons should be hard.	Agree/disagree	Crime - prisons
239.	Nothing can be done to prevent crime.	Agree/disagree	Crime
240.	Criminal cases in the law courts are shown on the television, so that public can watch.	Advantages more than disadvantages	Crime (4/1/20) China
241.	Armed police encourages violence	Agree/disagree	Crime
242.	Should public have guns or not	Discuss	Crime
243.	Newspapers have influenced people's ideas and opinions. Reasons for this?	Positive or negative development	Media
244.	Although people are reading news through internet, newspapers still remain of value.	Agree/disagree	Media
245.	News media nowadays have influenced people's lives in negative ways.	Agree/disagree	Media
246.	Social media is used by people	Advantages more than disadvantages	Media
247.	Should we believe the journalists? What qualities should a good journalist have?	Direct question	Media
248.	Celebrities complain about the way media publicize their private lives. Some people say should accept it as part of their fame.	Agree/disagree	Media
249.	Nowadays young people are admiring media and sports stars, even though they do not set a good example.	Positive or negative development	Media
250.	Exposure to international media has a significant impact on local cultures. What do you think has been the impact?	Advantages more than disadvantages	Media
251.	Recent advancements in technology have made the TV screen so live that people do not feel to go for any live performance	Agree/disagree	Media
252.	Most of our information comes from the Internet nowadays. A large part of the information we get is incorrect.	Agree/disagree	Media
253.	Radio is the best way to get news, OR TV is better for this purpose.	Discuss	Media
254.	People watch foreign films much more than local films. Why? Should the government help to local film industries?	Direct question	Media
255.	The number of TV programs is growing. Some people say that it is good, while others say it affects the quality of TV programs	Discuss	Media
256.	Some people think that 24-hour transmission is positive, while others believe it is negative.	Discuss	Media
257.	People are using the Internet to do their tasks rather than doing in person.	Advantages more than disadvantages	Media
258.	More and more people are using computers So, printing of books, magazines and newspapers should not be done.	Agree/disagree	Media
259.	We can see more disasters and violence shown on TV. Causes and effects on the individual and the society?	Cause/effect	Media
260.	The government should control the amount of violence in films and on television in order to decrease the violent crimes in society.	Agree/disagree	Media
261.	Some people say that the media should be strictly controlled.	Agree/disagree	Media

			13/02/2020
262.	Many people regard films as less important form of art than literature and painting.	Agree/disagree	Media
263.	In many countries, government spent a large amount of money on improving internet access. Why? is it the most appropriate use of government money?	Reasons/Direct question	Media
264.	The news reported in the media focuses on problems and emergencies rather than the positive developments is harmful.	Agree/disagree	Media
265.	News have no connection to people's lives, so then it is a waste of time to read and watch television news programs	Agree/disagree	Media
266.	Do violent films and videogames have negative effects on people and should be banned. OR they are just relaxation sources.	Discuss	Media (9/3/19)
267.	Children are facing more pressures nowadays from academic, social and commercial perspectives.	Causes/solutions	Family/children
268.	In many parts of the world, children have more freedom than in the past.	Positive or negative development	Family/children
269.	Some people think that nowadays children have too much freedom.	Agree/disagree	Family/children
270.	Children are taught to push themselves to try and be better than their classmates, rather than work together for everyone's profit.	Are advantages more than disadvantages	Family/children
271.	Competitiveness among people	Positive or negative development	Family/children
272.	Team activities vs solo activities	Agree/disagree	Family/children
273.	The parents expect children to spend long time in studying both in and after school and have less free time.	Positive or negative development	Family/children
274.	Should children obey rules or do what their parents and teachers want them to do, OR children controlled too much cannot deal with problems well by themselves.	Discuss	Family/children
275.	Should parents organise free time activities for children. OR children should be free to choose what they do in their free time.	Discuss	Family/children
276.	Parents should encourage their children to spend less time studying and more time doing sports/physical activities.	Agree/disagree	Family/children
277.	Today, children spend a lot time playing computer games and less time sports. Why?	Positive or negative development	Family/children
278.	Studies suggest that children spend more time watching TV than they did in the past and spend less on doing active or creative things.	Reasons/solutions	Family/children
279.	Is watching TV is bad to children in every way. OR TV has positive effects on children as they develop to grow up.	Discuss	Family/children (1/2/2020 India)
280.	Many children between 7 and 11 spend too much time watching television and/or playing video games. Effect on children, their families and society?	Effects/solutions	Family/children
281.	There is a general increase in anti-social behaviour and lack of respect for others.	Reasons/solutions	Family
282.	Young people know about international pop and movie stars but know very less about famous people from the history in their own country. Why?	Reasons/Solutions	Family/Young people
283.	In most of the societies, the role of mother and father differs. Reasons and future roles	Reasons/direct question	Family

284.	Playing computer games is bad for children, OR it is positive on the way children develop.	Discuss	Family
285.	In some cultures, the old age is valued more, while in some the youth is more valued.	Discuss	Family
286.	In some parts of the world, it is becoming increasingly popular to try to find out about the history of your family. Why?	Positive/negative development	Family/history
287.	The most important decision that young people have to follow is what career to choose.	Agree/disagree	Family
288.	Many people think young people should follow traditions, others argue that young people should be free to be individuals.	Discuss	Family
289.	Investing on youth is the best investment. How to invest?	Agree/disagree and direct question.	Family
290.	Old generations often hold some traditional ideas on the correct way of life, thinking and behaviour. OR it is not helpful for the young generations to prepare for modern life	Discuss	Family
291.	Some people think that we must return to the older and more traditional values of respect for the family and the local community in order to create a better world to live in.	Agree/disagree	Family
292.	In some countries around the world men and women are having children late in life.	Reasons/effects	Family
293.	Figures show that some countries have an ever-increasing proportion of the population who are aged 15 or younger. current and future effects of this trend	Direct question	Family
294.	More and more adults are living with their parents after graduating from college, universities or even after finding a job.	Advantages more than disadvantages	Family
295.	Some working parents believe other family members like grandparents can take care of their children, OR are childcare centers better	Discuss	Family
296.	In recent years the family has changed as well as family roles. Why?	Reasons/ Positive or negative development	Family
297.	Many elderly are suffering from loneliness and lack of fitness.	Reasons/solutions	Family
298.	Old people like to live in retirement homes.	Positive or negative	Family
299.	Friends and family do not have time to look after their elderly	Problem solution	Family
300.	It is suggested that all mothers and fathers should be required to take childcare training courses.	Agree/disagree	Family
301.	When families have a meal together it is considered social activity. Do you think eating together is important to people in your country?	Direct question	Family
302.	Parents have the most important role in a child's development. However, others argue that other things like television or friends have the most significant influence.	Discuss	Family
303.	Is crime because of genes OR can we prevent children from becoming criminals.	Direct question	Nature/Nurture
304.	Some people say that every human being can create art (e.g. painting), others think only the people born with the ability can create art	Discuss	Nature/Nurture
305.	Inborn characteristics have more influence on our personality and development than any experiences.	Direct question	Nature/Nurture
306.	Leadership skills – Natural or can be learnt	Discuss	Nature/Nurture

307.	Children who grow up in families, which are short of money are better prepared with the problems of adult life than children who are brought up by wealthy parents.	Agree/disagree	Family
308.	In many countries today there is insufficient respect to old people. What are the reasons? What problems might it bring to society?	Reasons/effects	Family
309.	Some people think parents should read or tell stories to children, while others think parents need not do that, as children can read books, watch TV or movies by themselves.	Discuss	Family
310.	In some countries more people choose to live alone or by themselves in recent years.	Reasons/Positive negative	Family
311.	In some countries young people are not only richer, but also safer and healthier than ever before. However, they are less happy.	Reasons/solutions	Family
312.	It is expected that there will be a higher proportion of old people than young people in the future in some countries.	Is it positive or negative	Family
313.	Peer pressure	Advantages more than disadvantages	Family
314.	Society is based on rules and laws. If individuals were free to do whatever they wanted to do, it could not function.	Agree/disagree	Family
315.	People have often failed in making ideal society.	Direct question	Family
316.	In the modern society individuals are becoming more dependent OR are becoming more independent of each other.	Discuss	Family
317.	Lifestyle affecting family relationships	Advantages/Disadv antages	Family
318.	Society governed by female leaders will be more peaceful.	Agree/disagree	Miscellaneous
319.	People are surrounded by advertising, which has an increasing effect on our lives.	Advantages more than disadvantages	Advertisements
320.	Advertising discourages people from being different individuals by making us all want to do the same and look the same.	Agree/disagree	Advertisement
321.	A large amount of advertisements nowadays are now targeted at children. Many people say this has negative effects on children and should therefore be banned.	Agree/disagree	Advertisement
322.	There is an increasing amount of advertising directed at children.	Discuss	Advertisement
323.	Consumers are faced with increasing numbers of advertisements from competing companies.	Effects/solutions	Advertisement
324.	Overeating is as harmful to people's health as smoking. So, the advertisements of certain food products should be banned as the ads of cigarettes are banned.	Agree/disagree	Advertisement
325.	Advertising encourages consumers to buy in quantity rather than promoting quality.	Agree/disagree	Advertisement
326.	If a product is good people will buy it. So advertising is unnecessary	Agree/disagree	Advertisement
327.	Because of the global economy, many goods produced by other counties have to be transported for a long distance.	Advantages more than disadvantages	Globalisation
328.	Everyone in the world is wearing same brands and watching same TV and movies.	Positive/negative development	Globalisation
329.	As we are facing more and more problems, which affect the whole planet, good relationships between different countries are becoming more important than ever before.	Agree/disagree	Globalization
330.	Many different countries have most shops and products as the same. Some consider it a positive development, whereas others consider it negative.	Discuss	Globalisation

331.	Should countries invite foreign companies in order to develop economies. OR whether countries should invest in their own companies instead?	Discuss	Globalisation
332.	Multicultural societies, where people of different ethnic groups live together can bring more benefits than drawbacks to a society.	Agree/disagree	Globalization
333.	These days the number of companies operating at multinational level has increased. To what extent are they responsible for the local communities in which they are located?	Direct question	Globalisation
334.	The spread of multinational companies and the increase in globalization produce positive effects for everyone.	Agree/disagree	Globalization
335.	The speeding up of life in many areas such as travel and communication has negative effects on society at all levels—individual, national and global.	Agree/disagree	Globalisation
336.	Increasing business and cultural contact between countries brings many positive effects. OR causes loss of national identities.	Discuss	Globalisation
337.	People are eating a lot of foreign food instead of locally produced food.	Advantages more than disadvantages	Food
338.	Traditional foods are being replaced by international fast foods. This is having a negative effect on both families and societies.	Agree/disagree	Food
339.	Some say the way to ask people to eat less fast food is to educate them, while others say education does not work.	Discuss	Food
340.	In many countries, people buy imported food rather than food produced locally. Why do people do that? How can people be encouraged to eat locally produced food?	Direct question	Food
341.	Demand of food increasing	Problem solution	Food
342.	GM foods and factory farming	Discuss	Food
343.	GM foods are good or bad	Discuss	Food
344.	Government needs to encourage sport and art for school students, than funding supporting professional sports, arts	Agree/disagree	Sport
345.	Government should increase the number of sports facilities; OR other measures to improve health.	Discuss	Sports
346.	Should national sports teams and individual men and women be financially supported by the government. OR should be funded by non-government sources	Discuss	Sports
347.	Sport is becoming a business and professionals and big companies are getting involved in sporting events.	Is it positive or negative	Sports
348.	Some people think sports and games are important for society, while others believe they should be taken as leisure activities.	Discuss	Sports
349.	Some people think Holding International games has positive effects while others argue it is a waste of money.	Discuss	Sports
350.	Youth should be banned from participating in sport competitions.	Agree/Disagree	Sports
351.	Government should ban dangerous sports, such as skydiving and rock climbing.	Agree/Disagree	Sports
352.	Do the fittest and strongest individuals and teams always succeed in sports. OR success in sports depends on mental attitudes.	Discuss	Sports
353.	Male sports vs female sports	Positive/negative	Sports
354.	Health clubs and gyms for health care, OR just walking and climbing stairs	Discuss	Health
355.	Why people are walking less	Reasons and solutions	Health

356.	Should healthcare be free or should people pay themselves	Reasons and solutions	Health
357.	Should healthcare and education be free or should people pay themselves	Reasons and solutions	Health
358.	Some people say that the public funds should be spent on promoting healthy living than on the treatment of people who are ill.	Agree/disagree	Health
359.	Nowadays, people are consuming more and more sugar-based drinks. Why? Solutions.	Reasons/Solutions	Health
360.	Should government should make laws regarding nutrition and healthy lifestyle, OR is it a matter of personal choice and personal responsibility.	Discuss	Health
361.	Some people still continue doing unhealthy habits	Reasons and solutions	Health
362.	People should look after their health for society they live in or for personal benefits.	Agree/Disagree	Health
363.	Government should give priority to health care OR spend on other important priorities.	Discuss	Health
364.	Football supporters behave violently.	Reasons and solutions	Sports
365.	Everyone should become vegetarian	Agree/Disagree	Health
366.	Should government subsidize healthy food OR set tax on unhealthy food.	Discuss	Health
367.	Overeating has become a bigger problem in the world than hunger.	Reasons/Solutions	Health
368.	Now the machine is very complex, a lot of difficult work to be automated.	Advantages more than disadvantages	Technology
369.	Computers will become more intelligent than human beings. Some people find it a positive development while others think it is negative	Discuss	Technology (7/3/2020)
370.	There are social, medical and technical problems associated with the use of mobile phones. What are these?	Advantages more than disadvantages	Technology
371.	Anyone can use a mobile phone to answer/make work calls or home calls at any place 7 days a week.	Are advantages more than disadvantages	Technology
372.	Mobile phones should also be banned as is smoking.	Agree/Disagree	Technology
373.	Mobile phones should be banned in public spaces	Agree/Disagree	Technology
374.	People do not entertain as before because technology has made them less creative.	Agree/Disagree	Technology
375.	Communication technology has more disadvantages than advantages.	Agree/Disagree	Technology
376.	People can work and live anywhere because of communication technology and transport.	Old book	
377.	People work at home and study at home with the development of computer technology.	Positive or a negative	Technology (23/2/19)
378.	Because of mobile phones and the Internet people are losing face to face communication.	Agree/Disagree	Technology
379.	Development of technology has made our life more complex, and the solution is to live a life without that technology.	Agree/Disagree	Technology
380.	Earlier technological developments more effective then recent ones.	Agree/Disagree	Technology

381.	Technological progress in the past century has its negative effect, despite its remarkable contribution.	Agree/Disagree	Technology
382.	People in 21sr Century have better life than past	Agree/Disagree	miscellaneous
383.	What ways could mobile phone and the Internet be useful to old people? How to encourage them to use this new technology?	Direct question	Technology
384.	Access to internet is necessary to lead a full life? Give your opinion	Opinion	Technology
385.	Socialise online or in-person	Advantages more than disadvantages	Technology/Communication
386.	Spoken communication vs written	Agree/Disagree	Technology/Communication
387.	Space research makes little difference to our daily life.	Agree/Disagree	Space research
388.	Money should be spent researching on other planet to live	Agree/Disagree	Space research
389.	We should protect only those animals, which are useful to humans.	Agree/Disagree	Animals
390.	Should we protect these animals from dying out, OR concentrate on problems of humans.	Discuss	Animals
391.	Too much attention and resources are given to protect wild animals and birds.	Agree/Disagree	Animals
392.	It is too late to do anything about animal and plant extinction. OR effective measures can still be taken	Discuss	Animals
393.	Why do people do so little about animal and plant extinction	Problem/Solution	Animals
394.	Some people think we can exploit animals / others do not think so.	Discuss	Animals
395.	No longer necessary to use animals for food or use animal products.	Agree/Disagree	Animals
396.	Animal Experimentation should be done OR not	Discuss	Animals
397.	Should government provide assistance to all kinds of artists OR is it a waste of money.	Discuss	Arts
398.	More spending on theatres and sports stadiums than on medical care and education.	Agree/disagree	Arts
399.	Spending on art OR on health and education	Discuss	Arts
400.	Arts vs science. What can arts tell us about life that science and technology cannot?	Direct question	Arts
401.	Is music only entertainment or has other roles	Discuss	Arts
402.	Government should spend money on paintings and statues to make cities better	Agree/disagree	Arts
403.	Should museums be free or ticketed	Discuss	Art/Museums
404.	Museums and art galleries will not be needed because of internet computer.	Agree/disagree	Art/Museums
405.	Should museum only educate OR entertain	Discuss	Art/Museums
406.	Museums and art galleries should concentrate on local works, not showing the cultures or artworks from other countries. To what extent do you agree?	Agree/Disagree	Art/Museum
407.	New buildings should be built with traditional style to preserve their culture.	Agree/disagree	Buildings/architecture
408.	It is more important to have public parks and sports facilities than shopping centres in new towns.	Agree/disagree	Buildings/architecture
409.	Architects should not worry about beautiful building and only focus on the purpose	Agree/disagree	Buildings/architecture

410.	Vertical cities vs horizontal	Discuss	Urban/rural
411.	Government should spend on new buildings, such rather than renovating old buildings.	Agree/disagree	Buildings/architecture
412.	Living in big cities is becoming difficult or easier.	Discuss	Urban/rural (19/1/19)
413.	Life in the large cities is becoming worse.	Problem solution	Urban/rural (12/12/19)
414.	Problems of big cities? Should small towns be encouraged?	Problem solution	Urban/rural
415.	The movement of people from agricultural areas to cities to work can cause serious problems in both places. What?	Problem solution	Urban/rural
416.	Only government action can solve severe social consequences caused by housing problems.	Agree/Disagree	Miscellaneous
417.	Urban planning – segregation of shops, offices houses in separate areas.	Advantages more than disadvantages	Urban/rural
418.	Some cities have no controls on the design, construction of homes, offices.	Advantages more than disadvantages	Urban/rural
419.	All towns and cities should have large public outdoor places like squares and parks.	Agree/Disagree	Urban/rural
420.	Some buildings, such as offices and schools have open-space design instead of separate rooms. Reasons?	Positive or negative development	Buildings/architecture
421.	Should businesses move to rural areas to solve transport and accommodation problems?	Advantages more than disadvantages	Miscellaneous
422.	Why individuals and countries to think about the future, rather than focus on the present?	Direct question	Miscellaneous
423.	Governments should provide free housing for everyone who cannot afford it.	Agree/disagree	Miscellaneous
424.	Shopping habits depend more on the age group they belong to than other factors.	Agree/disagree	Miscellaneous
425.	People do not know their neighbours	Reasons and solutions	Miscellaneous
426.	Intelligence is the most important quality for a leader.	Agree/disagree	Miscellaneous
427.	Similar clothes and things show that people like to copy one another	Agree/disagree	Miscellaneous
428.	Ambition – Its importance. Is it positive or negative	Direct question	Miscellaneous
429.	Influence of politicians versus scientists	Discuss	Miscellaneous
430.	In which areas we have made progress, and in which areas we still need progress	Direct question	Miscellaneous
431.	Economic development (ED) causes loss of social values. Do pros of ED outweigh cons	Are advantages more than disadvantages	Miscellaneous
432.	The governments, and not private companies should do scientific research.	Agree/Disagree	Miscellaneous
433.	21st Century – do you share the optimistic view	What changes you would like to see	Miscellaneous
434.	Cosmetic surgery – reasons	Positive or negative development	Miscellaneous
435.	Net diagnosis vs visiting a doc	Reasons/positive./ negative	Miscellaneous
436.	Music – universal language	Agree/disagree	Arts
437.	Children should aim to be the best at what they are doing, while others believe it is not necessary for them.	Discuss	Family/children

438.	Film production is not limited to large companies, nowadays anyone can produce films because of digital technology	Positive or negative development	Arts
439.	it is good for a country's culture to show imported foreign films and TV programmes. Others think that it is better to produce these locally.	Discuss	Arts

1. *The increase in people's life expectancy means that they have to work till older age to pay for their retirement. One alternative is that people start to work at a younger age. Is this alternative a positive or a negative development?*

Due to longer life span, many people are being forced to work past their retirement age. So, some people consider joining the workforce from a younger age as a solution. I believe it is not only beneficial for people but also for the society.

From the individual perspective, the first advantage of starting work at a younger age is that people can save more money and thus have financial security in the later stages of life. This ensures that they are not obligated to work during older age, when most people are already suffering from health ailments. Secondly, young people have fewer financial and family obligations than older workers, and thus they are able to prioritise their careers. For example, they might be able to move from one city to another for a promotion, while it might be quite challenging for employees with a family. As a result, they are able to climb the career ladder faster leading to significantly higher pay packages by the time they retire.

In addition, starting a career early, means that people have the option to switch careers in later stages of life, as they would be still comparatively younger. This might not be possible past a certain age in life. Finally, companies are also willing to train and invest in younger employees, who are likely to stay with them for a longer time, as compared to older ones. In other words, people have chances of securing better jobs early in their life.

That main advantage from a societal perspective is that in general younger employees are fitter and more productive as compared to their older counterparts. Moreover, starting the career earlier means, people are established by the time, they have families and thus they are able to devote more time to their children's upbringing. This can in part address issues like smoking, drinking and drug abuse in teenagers and also rising juvenile delinquency.

In conclusion, I would like to reiterate that starting a career early is certainly a better alternative to working older as it would be advantageous both for the people and the society as well.

Plan followed:
Intro: Positive development
Para1: Advantage of starting work early
Para 2: Another advantage
Para 3: Final advantage
Conclusion

2. *Interviews form the basic selection criteria for most large companies. However, some people think that an interview is not a reliable method of choosing whom to employ and there are other better methods. To what extent do you agree or disagree?*

It is undeniable that most companies rely on interviews for hiring new employees, but some people believe that this dependence on interviews is wrong and other alternatives should be preferred as they are better. I believe that interviews are a reliable method, and the other methods cannot be considered more effective.

There are many reasons why interviews are suitable for hiring new employees. Firstly, by the interview the recruiters can get an idea about the personality and social skills of the potential employees. In interviews, there is face-to-face interaction, and the candidates have to answer impromptu questions, from which personality traits can be judged. Also, by asking some case study type questions, employees can judge traits like ability to handle pressure, confidence and ability to think outside the box.

In addition, although there are many other methods for hiring, none of them could be considered superior to interviews. One of other common methods is the written test, which is good to judge the theoretical knowledge of the person. However, this method cannot give a good idea about the personality of the candidate. By contrast, through interviews, employers can judge both the knowledge and temperament of the potential employee. Moreover, the written test is fallible to cheating as sometimes candidates can take outside help.

Another selection process is group discussion, which is good where a major job requirement is conversational and persuasion skills, such as in sales jobs. They are really not suited for technical jobs because these are not customer oriented. On the other hand, interviews hold good for any type of job as the interviewer can frame questions to test the particular skills they require.

To conclude, I would like to reiterate that preference for interview for hiring among employers is justified as interviews have advantages over other commonly adopted methods.

Plan followed:
Intro:
Para 1: Why interviews are suitable
Para 2: Why written test is not superior to interview
Para 3: Why group discussion is not superior to interview
Conclusion:
Written by: Indroop Singh

3. *Most employers nowadays put increasing emphasis on social skills. Some people believe that social skills are important in addition to good qualifications for job success. To what extent, do you agree or disagree?*

It is believed by some that to be a successful employee, a person needs social skills besides subject knowledge. While I agree that requirement of social skills in jobs has increased considerably, I also believe in certain jobs a person can contribute effectively even if he lacks social skills.

The main reason why social skills are considered critical for most jobs today is that they make worker coordination easier and lower training cost. In other words, today, most tasks at the workplace require teamwork and employees with social skills are better able to interact, exchange information or even trade tasks at the workplace. Such employees are able to utilize each other's strengths at job and this enables them to adapt more easily to changing circumstances as well.

In addition, social skills are gaining more relevance because non-social skill jobs are gradually getting automated. Even jobs based on mathematical and analytical reasoning are getting automated, but computers and machines still cannot simulate human interaction. Finally, in most cases, to be successful at one's job one needs to be able to lead others effectively, delegate tasks and resolve any interpersonal conflicts that arise. This is only possible if the person possesses social skills like good communication, empathy and the ability to listen to others.

However, the growing importance of social skills does not mean a person cannot succeed without them. There are many jobs today that require little person to person contact, teamwork or collaboration. For example, software development, which involves writing code is much more about technical knowledge and reasoning. Similarly, there are data entry jobs, which are based on knowledge about database software like Oracle and MS Excel.

In summary, although it is easy to understand why social skills are given a lot of importance, certain professionals can thrive even without social interaction.

Plan followed:
Intro: Partial view
Para 1- Why social skills are critical
Para 2 – Why social skills are gaining importance
Para 3 – Some jobs in which social skills are not needed for success
Conclusion: Reiterate
Written by: Indroop Singh

4. *Some employers think that formal academic qualifications are more important than life experiences and personal qualities when they look for an employee. Why is it the case? Is it a positive or negative development?*

Some recruiters give more value to a college or university degree than personal attributes and experiences. This essay will look into the reasons that can be attributed to this phenomenon. In my opinion, it is a negative development.

There are two main reasons why some employers consider a college degree more valuable than life experiences and the individual's quality traits. Firstly, due to the increasing competition, to get into a good university or college in itself is very challenging. Academic qualifications also prove to the employer that the individual has worked hard and mastered specialist skills. Secondly, there is no way for employers to reliably check if the qualities and life experiences on the curriculum vitae are real or fake. By contrast, formal academic qualification can be easily verified with a college degree.

However, focusing only on the degree and ignoring a person's experiences and skills is negative development. To begin with, it deprives the company of talented, experienced candidates who might not have an academic degree, but are actually competent in completing or getting work done. In addition, experienced candidates can be productive from the very beginning, while recent graduates take time adjusting to a formal working atmosphere and this may impact the productivity of the company.

Another drawback is that it has been seen that when recruiters focus largely on candidates' technical skills, it results in hiring employees who have the intellect to succeed but lack the social skills required to work effectively. This results in interpersonal conflicts and in effect, a stressful workplace environment. Finally, it is easier for companies to provide technical training, if the candidate lacks such knowledge, but it is very difficult, if not impossible, to develop personality traits like adaptability, integrity and reliability at this stage of life.

In summary, it is understandable why employers give importance to academic qualifications, but I believe ignoring experience and personality traits can hurt the company's productivity and work environment.

Plan followed:

Intro: This essay shall look into the reasons for this. In my opinion it is a negative development.
Para 1- reasons why employee gives importance to academics
Para 2 – why negative development
Para 3 – why negative development continued
Conclusion: restate opinion

5. *It is suggested that all young adults should undertake a period of unpaid work, helping people in the community. Does it bring more benefits or drawbacks to the young people?*

It is considered by some that all youth in the community should work voluntarily for the benefit of the community. Although making the youth do unpaid work for the community can have certain disadvantages, I consider that its benefits far outweigh its drawbacks.

Undoubtedly, doing unpaid work for the community would be beneficial for the youth in many ways. Firstly, by helping the elderly, the sick and the disabled directly, or participating in charitable activities like raising funds or offering free consultation, young people will certainly gain and accumulate some valuable first-hand experience. The second benefit would be that it would make them feel more connected to the society. There would be a sense of ownership for the society among the youth for the community as they work for its betterment.

Finally, volunteering provides a natural sense of accomplishment. Youth's role as a volunteer can also give them a sense of pride and identity. It would make the youth feel better about themselves and in turn make them more self-confident. The better they feel about themselves, the more likely they are to have a positive view of their life and future goals.

However, there may be some disadvantages if the young provide free service helping people in need. For example, it may conflict with their normal study or work if not arranged well. In addition, youth might feel burdened and forcing them might create a feeling of resentment among the youth rather than create a feeling of self-confidence and accomplishment.

To conclude, I believe that youth undertaking some voluntary community work would be very beneficial despite the few drawbacks.

Plan followed:
Intro: its pros far outweigh the cons
Para 1: Young people would accumulate valuable experience and feel connected to society
Para 2: Young people would get a sense of accomplishment
Para 3: Disadvantages
Conclusion: More benefits than drawbacks.

Written by: Indroop Singh

6. Nowadays, older people who need employment have to compete with younger people. What problems does this cause, and what are the solutions?

It is undeniable that a growing number of the elderly are facing competition from the youth in the workplace. This situation is causing challenges for both – the older and the younger workforce, but some steps can be taken to alleviate these problems.

On the one hand, the competition among the young and the old workers can have troubling effects on the senior workers. They might find it daunting to keep up with the latest advancements in technology. For example, in the manufacturing industry, the use of advanced machines is quite common, which could be tough for older workers to operate. Companies also prefer to hire young workers, because they believe that senior employees could lead to a decline of productivity and efficiency of the enterprise.

On the other hand, the young graduates may also feel unmotivated and frustrated as the senior job candidates have rich experience because of which they outshine young adults. Some employers prefer to recruit older people with higher work experience rather than those who have just graduated from the university. Without a decent job and salary, it is extremely difficult for young people to make a living, as a consequence of which, some of them might resort to crime to fulfil their desires.

These problems can certainly be solved by some policies of the government and steps at individual level. To begin with, the government can encourage self-employment for fresh graduates, so that the older workers are not laid off. Further, the governments should allocate more money to pensions, which can basically guarantee that older people do not have to look for jobs. Finally, the elderly should plan ahead for their retirement and enjoy their retired life, instead of competing for the limited job vacancies.

To sum up, competition between both age groups for the jobs will continue to be more intense, but some steps at government and individual level can help to lessen the severity of the situation.

Plan followed:
Intro: Problem solution essay intro
Para1: Problems to elderly and companies
Para 2: Problems to youth
Para 3: Solutions
Conclusion:

7. Nowadays, more and more young people hold important positions in the government. Some people think that it is a good thing, while others argue that it is not suitable. Discuss both these views and give your opinion.

Some people believe that having important government positions in the hands of the youth is advantageous for society, whereas it is believed by others that only seasoned and experienced people should be in charge. In this essay, I will discuss both perspectives. I believe that for good governance there should be both, the young and old in important positions.

On the one hand, there are many reasons why some people are in favour of young people holding the positions of power. The first reason is that young people have a fresh perspective, which gives them a unique ability to come up with creative solutions. The young people are not constrained by deep-rooted societal norms and thus can come up with ideas that elderly people cannot think of. Secondly, young people can better relate to problems facing the youth and thus they can represent them in government. In other words, government decisions can better address youth problems, if there are young people in politics.

On the other hand, the main reason given by those who think that it is not proper to give the reins of the nation in raw hands is that the young are impatient and lack experience. Governments need to take a lot of crucial decisions with large implications and the young politicians might take rash decisions which may have severe consequences for the country. In addition, they say that politics is very complicated and young people are too immature to understand its nitty-gritties.

I believe that youth participation in politics and government is certainly beneficial, but at the same time there should also be experienced leaders in government. The young can bring in fresh solutions and provide better addressal of youth related issues like employment, university fees and so on. However, the import of such decisions also means that there needs to be people with experience to guide the youth.

Summing up, while I support the active participation of youth in policy making and execution, I also believe it must be complemented with age and experience.

Plan followed:
Intro: Discuss essay intro
Para 1: One view
Para 2: Other view
Para 3: Own view
Conclusion:

Written by: Indroop Singh

8. *Today, the life expectancy of people is much higher than before. Some people think that older people should continue to be involved in the workforce. To what extent do you agree or disagree?*

It is true that longevity has led to an increase in the ability of people to work for longer years and therefore some people hold the opinion that the older people should retire later in life. Although extended employment may lead to certain problems, I believe that the elderly people should be retired at a later age if they are interested.

There are many reasons why extended employment for the elderly should be an option. Firstly, looking at it from a country's economic point of view, increasing the retirement age would help decrease the government's burden of ensuring benefits such as senior citizen discounts, healthcare benefits and pension for the elderly. Not only this, it would also increase the tax revenues for the government. Secondly, working longer would ensure that the elderly will not have to struggle after retirement and would be able to live more comfortably as they would have more funds saved up.

Finally, working till a later age will be very beneficial to the elderly, at an individual level. They will not need to depend on anyone for their needs. Also, they'll be busy and involved in work, which will help to tackle the problems of loneliness and depression among them. These days the family members do not have the time to spend with the old members of the family, which leads the elderly to feel isolated. Increasing the retirement age will, to a great extent, reduce this problem.

However, this prolonged employment among the old can also lead to certain problems. To begin with, it may make it challenging for the youth to secure jobs as they would lack the valuable experience that the senior citizens possess. In addition, the old people would not get time to spend on their hobbies or spend time with their grandchildren. They could be utilizing this time in travelling and pursuing their interests and hobbies, which they couldn't because of their hectic work life.

Overall, while transitioning to a later retirement would not come without a cost, its benefits are far too many to disregard it as an option for the elderly.

Plan followed:
Intro: Agree with concession to problems
Para 1: Benefit of extended working
Para2: Benefit of extended working
Para3: Problems of extended working
Conclusion

Written by: Indroop Makkar

9. *In some countries, a few people earn extremely high salaries. Some people think that this is good for a country, while others believe that the government should control salaries and limit the amount people can earn. Discuss both sides and express your opinion.*

Some people believe that it is beneficial for any nation if a few top-level employees make much more money than lower-level employees, whereas others argue that there should be a cap on salaries so that the difference in salaries of employees is not too pronounced. In this essay, I will discuss both viewpoints. I believe that having a cap on salaries would be unfair and counterproductive.

On the one hand, there are many reasons why some believe that a few individuals earning high salaries is good for the country. Firstly, high salaries incentivize people to work harder. In other words, if the people at the top are earning considerably more money, the other employees would work harder to get promoted to get the same salary. Secondly, the higher-level executive officers have to deal with a lot of pressure, and they are responsible for not only their actions but also of those under them. So, high salaries are justified.

On the other hand, those who believe that governments should limit the salaries, give the following reasons. From the company's point of view the main reason is that substantial pay disparity without any justification generates feelings of unfairness, leading lower-paid employees to shrug off their responsibilities. From the society's point of view, it would reduce wealth inequality in the society and prevent the rich from gaining unfair control over resources.

I believe that high salaries are an acknowledgment of a person's hard work, talent and experience. Capping salaries would lead to many talented people leaving the country for better salaries abroad. In addition, the ability to earn high salaries also creates a level playing field because people know if they are willing to work hard and put in their efforts, they can reach any level of success.

To sum up, extremely high salaries are justified and there should not be a limit on it. A system which values hard work and rewards ability, ultimately prospers.

Plan followed:
Intro: Disagree
Para 1: First argument
Para 2: second argument
Para 3: Own view
Conclusion

Written by: Indroop Singh

10. *It is a good thing if senior management workers in a company get a much higher salary than other workers in the same company. Do you agree or disagree?*

It is believed by some that there are benefits to senior management being paid substantially more than lower-level employees. I also consider that paying significantly higher compensation to senior executives is not only justified but also beneficial for the company.

There are many reasons why higher salaries to executives and CEO's is actually beneficial. To begin with, I believe that as pay differences between job levels increase, the value of receiving a promotion also rises. In other words, if the person above is making a lot more money, the other employees would work harder to get promoted to get the same salary. This in turn would increase the company's overall productivity.

Secondly, the higher salaries are justified because today's senior management's role is much broader than simply running the company. For example, today public relations skills need to be significantly better, as the cost of even a minor slip-up can be catastrophic. Similarly, due to globalisation, supply chains of companies are spread out across countries and knowledge needed to deal with them is unending. In fact, the mental stress and challenges that senior level executives face today in itself is reason enough for the high salaries they are paid.

Additionally, the higher-level executive officers have to take accountability for not only their actions but also of all employees under them. To cite an example, recently the principal of school in Delhi was fired for the untoward actions of a teacher towards one of his students, even though the principal was not directly involved and had no knowledge about it. Thus, higher salaries to executive officers are not unwarranted.

To sum up, although some people may consider the high salaries to top level management to be unfair, I find them not only acceptable but also well deserved.

Plan followed:
Intro: Completely agree
Para 1: Advantages of higher pay of top executives
Para 2: Higher pay justified
Para 3: Higher pay justified
Conclusion:

Written by: Indroop Makkar

11. *The leaders or directors of organizations are often older people. But some people say that young people can also be a leader. Do you agree or disagree?*

When a company has to select someone for an executive position, mostly the senior employees are considered. Some individuals hold the opinion that youngsters can be as good leaders as the older employees. I believe that leadership has nothing to do with age and in some regard, youth are even better than the old at leading businesses.

There are many qualities that make young people more apt for leadership and management positions. Firstly, they have the entrepreneurial spirit and risk-taking attitude, which is absolutely necessary for companies to grow. In other words, businesses today need leaders who are ready to move ahead and are willing to accept and make changes. This is perhaps why many floundering businesses are back on the path to success, with the passing of the baton to a young heir.

Secondly, youth leaders are more in sync with the mindset of the current generation and are thus able to attract and retain young talent better. Due to digital transformation and increasing automation, leaders today need to be comfortable in technology and there is no doubt that youth leaders have an edge over the previous generation in this regard. Technology not only helps in being innovative but also is a major part of public relations today.

Finally, leadership is about qualities like communication skills, ability to listen to others, ability to motivate others and ability to handle stress. None of these qualities are dependent upon age. In fact, even some children in schools possess these traits. So, disregarding youth from leadership positions just because of their age is not only unjustified but also detrimental for any company's future.

To sum up, I believe that there is no logic to associate leadership with age and the young can even prove better than the old, if given the opportunity.

Plan followed:
Intro: Completely agree
Para1: How young leaders are better
Para 2: How young leaders are better
Para 3: Leadership not dependent upon age
Conclusion: Reiterate opinion

Written by: Indroop Singh

12. *In many countries, women are allowed to take maternity leave during the first month after the birth of the newborn. Do you think the advantages of maternity leave outweigh the disadvantages?*

Nowadays, there are laws which allow the women to take leave for a certain time period after pregnancy in most of the countries. While I agree that there might be some negative consequences of such laws, I consider their benefits to be far more than their drawbacks.

On the one hand, there are many benefits of maternity leave. Firstly, childbirth and pregnancy is a very difficult period for women both mentally and physically. They need a proper break to recover after this period and maternity leave provides that. In fact, research has shown that without a leave, women have increased risk of health complications. Secondly, the first few months are very crucial in the development of children. They need proper care and attention from the mother during this period and this period is also important to form a strong bond between the mother and child. Finally, raising a child can be very expensive. For example, parents need to spend on diapers, baby formula, medicines and clothes etcetera. A paid maternity leave assures financial stability during this period.

On the other hand, there are also a few drawbacks of maternity leave. One drawback is that it might hamper the employment of women at workplaces. Many times employers are reluctant to hire women because they do not want to pay for maternity leave later. Another drawback is that maternity leave may slowdown the career progression of women. To elaborate, when women go on maternity leave, they might lose the chance of promotions. Even after coming back, they might not be considered for a promotion as it is thought they would not be able to prioritize their work.

To sum up, the disadvantages of maternity leave are negligible as compared to the advantages. That is why some countries have taken a step forward and allowed maternity leave to women after childbirth.

Plan followed:
Intro: Agree
Para 1: Advantages
Para 2: Disadvantages
Conclusion:
Similar essay: Mothers generally stay home to take care of their children after pregnancy. Do you support the opinion that these mothers should be compensated for by the government?

Written by: Indroop Singh (20/5/2022)

13. *Some people believe that women should play an equal role as men in a country's police force or military force, such as the army, while others think women are not suitable for these kinds of jobs. Discuss both views and give your opinion.*

It is believed by some that women should be allowed to work at par with men in the police and armed forces, whereas others argue that women are not appropriate for such jobs. This essay intends to analyse both perspectives. I believe that opposition to entry of women into security services is deeply unjustified.

On the one hand, there are many reasons why people support equal participation of women in the armed forces. Firstly, people are heading towards an egalitarian society and therefore, women should have the same right as men to choose their profession. Restriction on women entry also deprives the army of the capabilities of talented women soldiers and officers. Secondly, armed forces and police forces across the world are troubled by falling retention and recruitment rates and women entry can address this problem.

On the other hand, those who are against women in the police or army jobs give their reasons as follows. The main reason is that such jobs require masculine traits like aggressiveness and strength, and as women lack such physical characteristics, they are not suited for such jobs. Another reason is that such jobs entail prolonged periods of deployment and uncertain working hours, which women would not be able to justify as they also have the onus of looking after the home and children.

I strongly support women's entry into the armed forces and the police. To begin with, physical strength can be increased by effective workouts and muscle training. Women who join such jobs do undergo rigorous training and are no less than men when they are on the job. In addition, women are more effective in some delicate circumstances than men. For example, they are able to build interpersonal relationships with locals in conflict zones and thus are better at gathering intelligence.

Summing up, denying women entry into police forces and armed forces is not only an injustice to them, but it is also depriving the security forces of women's special abilities.

Plan followed:
Intro: Discuss essay intro
Para 1: One view
Para 2: Other view
Para 3: Own view
Conclusion:

Similar essay: In many countries, women are able to join the armed forces just as men. Some people say that only men should be members of the army, navy or air force. Do you agree or disagree?
Written by: Indroop Singh

14. *Some people say that no one should do the same job forever, while others believe that doing the same job is beneficial for the individual, company and society. Discuss both views and give your opinion.*

It is believed by some that people should change jobs often, whereas others argue that it is beneficial for people to stick to one job for life, grab a pension and retire. This essay intends to discuss both perspectives. While I believe that frequent job-hopping is not good, a job change, once or twice in one's whole career span is acceptable.

On the one hand, those who favour changing jobs every few years, give their reasons as follows. Firstly, changing jobs can help a person to develop new skills and get different types of experience. For example, when people change jobs, they are pushed out of their comfort zone and they are pushed to learn new routines. Secondly, it keeps things interesting and prevents work from becoming boring and monotonous. It is also an opportunity to figure out which type of employers and company culture suit people the best.

On the other hand, there are many reasons why some people support sticking to a single job forever. The main reason is that it increases job security in today's time, when job uncertainty is at an all-time high. Employers are not only more likely to retain workers who have been working longer but they are also hesitant to hire people, who have a history of changing jobs frequently. Sticking to one job also helps in better work-life balance. In other words, with time people become more comfortable with their work responsibilities and thus they are able to devote more time to their personal life.

While I believe changing jobs once or twice in a career span is certainly beneficial, I also believe that frequent job hopping can be detrimental. Apart from the benefits mentioned above, the varied experience from working in different positions and companies makes people more adaptable and flexible. It also makes them more valuable to employers and thus they earn higher paychecks. However, if people change their jobs too often, employers start questioning their loyalty. So, people should avoid changing jobs too frequently.

To sum up, an occasional job change is understandable, but hopping from one job to the other every year or two, is surely not good for the employees and employers both.

Plan followed:
Intro: Discuss essay
Para 1: Advantages of job-hopping
Para 2: Advantages of sticking to one job
Para 3: Own view
Conclusion:

Written by: Indroop Singh

15. *The world of work is changing rapidly. Working conditions today are not the same as before and people no longer rely on taking one job for life. Discuss the possible causes for these changes and give your suggestions on how people should prepare for work in the future.*

It is irrefutable that the work scenario is changing at a fast pace. This essay shall delve into the possible causes for these changes and suggest ways to prepare for work in the time to come.

There are a number of reasons for the lack of job security. The first reason is increasing automation at the workplace. In other words, more and more jobs are being done by machines and thus a lot of people are losing their jobs to these robots and machines. Secondly, technology is changing rapidly and thus people's skills and knowledge are becoming outdated very quickly. Employers tend to hire new employees with the required knowledge rather than spend on training the older employees.

Finally, due to globalisation, companies are no longer bound by geographical boundaries in hiring decisions. For example, today many Indians are working for American IT companies. Companies are also shifting their manufacturing operations overseas to countries like China and Vietnam to cut on costs and this further reduces job security. As a result, many people in the developed world are facing unemployment.

There are various steps that people can take to better prepare for the changing work conditions. To begin with, people should be flexible, and they should be willing to relocate to foreign countries if their companies are relocating to cut on costs. In addition, people should work on updating their skills and knowledge regularly, so that their skills are never obsolete. Finally, I think people should try to have multiple sources of income or develop their hobbies as a source of livelihood, so that they are financially stable even if they lose their primary job.

Summing up, although there is no doubt that jobs are less secure than the past due to various reasons, I believe individuals can prepare for this by being flexible, regularly updating their skills and having alternative income sources.

Plan followed:

Intro: This essay shall delve into the possible causes for these changes and suggest ways to prepare for work in the time to come.
Para 1: First cause
Para 2: More causes
Para 3: Suggestions
Conclusion:

Written by: Indroop Singh

16. *Some businesses find that their new employees lack in basic interpersonal skills such as the lack of ability to work with colleagues as a team. What are the causes and suggest possible solutions? Also provide relevant examples from your experience.*

It has been seen that sometimes new company recruits lack basic soft skills and cannot get along well with their colleagues. There are many reasons why new recruits lack basic interpersonal skills, but this situation can be rectified with suitable measures.

The main reason for the new employees being deficient in basic interpersonal skills is that when it comes to recruiting strategies, hiring decisions often focus largely on candidates' technical skills and expertise, with relatively little attention to soft skills. Another reason is that education today lays emphasis on technical and theoretical knowledge rather than soft skills. So group activities, team projects and extra-curricular activities that develop social skills are not given much importance in schools. To add to it, most companies also do not spare the time and effort to develop these soft skills in their employees.

There are many ways to rectify this situation and make sure that new hires do not lack such abilities. Firstly, employers should give importance to these social traits while hiring. Interviews can include questions and scenarios that focus on social skills. Interviews can be followed by group discussions and luncheons to assess candidates' interpersonal skills. Social skills can also be assessed using standardized questionnaires, such as personality tests.

Secondly, companies can develop these skills in their employees after hiring. One way is to organise meetings to practice public speaking and discuss their problems, in an environment where they can feel safe. Companies can also organise team retreats, where new and old employees can have a fun time together and build a better rapport with each other. Finally, the education system needs to incorporate more group activities and projects. Education cannot be solely about competition among students, there is growing need to develop social skills among children from the very beginning.

Summing up, it is irrefutable that many new employees face the problem of lack of interpersonal skills due to certain factors. Nonetheless, this can be handled successfully by elaborate interviews before recruitment, training after recruitment or by increasing group activities in schools and colleges.

Plan followed:
Intro: This essay shall delve into the causes of this phenomenon and suggest some ways forward
Para 1: Reasons for this phenomenon
Para 2: solutions
Para 3: more solutions
Conclusion
Written by: Deepa Singh Makkar

17. *Many employees may work at home with modern technology. Some people claim that it can benefit only the workers, not the employers. Do you agree or disagree?*

It is believed by some that telecommuting is beneficial for the employees and does not hold any advantage for the business owners. While I agree that the option to work from home benefits the employees immensely, the advantages to employers are also significant.

There are many advantages of telecommuting to employees. To begin with, it saves time and money as employees do not need to commute to the office physically. Time is also saved, as teleworkers do not have to spend time getting ready for work. Another benefit is that workers can look after minor family commitments like dropping the child to school etc. Although most of the work done by teleworkers is monitored, still a few minutes can be snatched at times. All this helps a lot in maintaining a better work-life balance.

On the other hand, employers are also benefited in many ways. Firstly, less office space is needed as the workers are working from home. It is a fact that land prices are exorbitant, and it is very expensive to build large offices or to rent them. Thus, it is substantially cheaper to permit employees to work from home. Secondly, businesses which allow the option to work from home enjoy better employee satisfaction, and therefore are better able to retain talented employees.

Besides this, it has been observed that telecommuters take less sick leave and other leaves. They do not have to take a whole day off for a minor family commitment, such as looking after a sick family member. Finally, telecommuting is the only option that keeps businesses running during emergencies like the recent corona pandemic.

To sum up, I reiterate my opinion by saying that telecommuting is beneficial for both employees as well as employers. It would be wrong to say that employers are not benefited.

Plan followed:
Intro: disagree
Para 1: advantages of telecommuting to employees
Para 2: advantages to employers
Para 3: More advantage to employers
Conclusion: telecommuting benefits both workers as well as employers

Similar essay: More and more companies are allowing employees to work from home. Do you think this is a positive or negative development?

Written by: Indroop Singh

18. *There are some motives for people to work. Some people think money is the most important. Do you agree or disagree?*

There is no doubt that people work for different reasons, but it is believed by some that money is the most important reason to work. While I agree that money is important, many other factors are much more important than money.

The main reason why money is vital is that it is the means to achieve the basic standard of living. Everyone today wants to live comfortably, and money makes this possible as it helps to pay for goods and services. Money is also important because today social status in life is majorly dependent upon money. Almost everyone would refuse to work if they were offered no money.

However, nowadays employees care about other factors considerably more. The first factor is a sense of meaning and purpose. In other words, people today want to feel that they are contributing to society and making a difference to the world. The recent corona pandemic has amplified this feeling even further. The second factor is the feeling of appreciation for hard work. It is basic human nature to want others to acknowledge and appreciate our efforts and hard work. Financial remuneration can never be equated to employer recognition and appreciation.

Another factor which employees value over money is the opportunity to learn and grow. This is perhaps the reason why many employees leave their jobs for even lower paid jobs because they feel they have nothing new to learn at their old jobs. Last but not least, it is about well-defined career progression. Most people have an ambition beyond earning a high salary and if they see no hope of fulfilling their ambitions, sooner or later they lose their passion to work.

In conclusion, although money is an important motivation for work, it is certainly not the prime motivation.

Plan followed:
Intro: Partial view
Para 1: Importance of money
Para 2: Other factors more important than money
Para 3: Other factors more important than money
Conclusion: Reiterate opinion

Written by: Indroop Singh

19. *The best way to learn about other cultures is to work in multinational organisations. Do you agree or disagree?*

It is believed by some that multinational companies have given the employees an exposure to different cultures. I believe that although working in a multinational organisation is a good way to understand and learn about another country's culture, it cannot be deemed as the best method.

There is no doubt that working in a large MNC presents some opportunities to learn about other cultures as employees deal with colleagues, businesses and clients from different parts of the globe. For example, in some cultures it is normal to address clients and bosses by their first name, whereas in others it is considered disrespectful. Similarly, countries like Japan and Germany are sticklers for punctuality and people are expected to arrive on time for meetings but in other cultures being a few minutes late is acceptable.

Having said that, working in an MNC is definitely not the best way to learn about a culture and there are better ways than it. One way to experience and understand other cultures is to actually travel to those countries and live their lifestyle. Travelling lets one experience all aspects of a culture like food, language, customs, festivals etc. However, in an MNC, employees are restricted to just corporate aspects of a culture. Also, travelling lets you meet people from different work backgrounds and not just the corporate world.

There are other ways that are more fun and effective in learning about other cultures. For example, watching a foreign language movie, trying a new ethnic food recipe from another country and learning a foreign dance form online. These methods are stress free and entertaining, whereas corporate culture is so stressful that people do not get time to learn about other people's cultures.

To reiterate, working in an MNC is definitely a good way to know about another culture, but it is certainly not the best.

Plan followed:
Intro: Partial view
Para 1: Why MNCs are good to learn other cultures
Para 2: How travelling is better than MNC
Para 3: Other methods better than MNCs
Conclusion:

Written by: Indroop Singh

20. *Many people say that companies should give importance to their employees, whereas others say that they should give importance to customers. Discuss both and opine.*

It is believed by some that business organisations should prioritise employees, while others hold the view that the primary motive of companies should be to look after customers. In this essay, I will discuss both the perspectives. I personally believe that both customers and employees should be given equal importance.

On the one hand, the main argument of those in favour of putting employees first is that employees work harder when they are happier. In other words, a company's productivity is directly proportional to its employee happiness. Another reason is that customer satisfaction ultimately depends upon employees. Employee-customer interactions set the tone for a positive or negative customer experience. In a way, when employees are not happy at work, their interactions with customers suffer, and this can have serious repercussions for a business.

On the other hand, there are also certain reasons why some people believe in prioritizing customers. Firstly, the success of any organisation depends largely on its customer base. More customers means more revenue, which ultimately means more profits. This is why organisations today are spending crores of rupees on customer acquisition and retention. Secondly, happy and satisfied customers create a positive brand image for the company and a good brand image is paramount to success in today's competitive era.

I believe that the happiness of both – employees and customers has to be in balance as both are interdependent. Organizations have to realize that their customers will only be happy if the people servicing their customers are happy. Similarly, if a company cannot retain customers and earn profits, it cannot pay its employees well or provide them bonuses. Thus, employee satisfaction is also dependent upon customer satisfaction.

To conclude, I believe that both customers and employees should be the equal in priority for all companies and companies cannot afford to ignore either.

Plan followed:

Intro: Discuss essay intro
Para 1: Why some people say Employees first
Para 2: Why some people say customers first
Para 3: Own view
Conclusion:

Written by: Indroop Singh

21. *Adult youths are often called up for working for the development of communities. Some people say they should work voluntarily, whereas others say that they should get paid. Discuss both views and give your opinion.*

Some individuals hold the opinion that the young people should work for their communities without any remuneration, whereas others say that they should be paid. In this essay, I will discuss both viewpoints. I believe that paying the youth would increase their compliance to give their time for community work.

On the one hand, the most important reason why some say that the youth should be paid for their services to the community, is that it would increase their willingness to work. In other words, when the youth are paid, they would work with more passion and enthusiasm. A little remuneration would also cover the expenses they incur like commuting costs. Another benefit is that it would reduce their need to find a part-time job and they would be able to focus on their university studies in the remaining time.

On the other hand, those who say that the youngsters should work voluntarily for the community, give their reasons as follows. Firstly, if they are paid, they would not develop social responsibility and would consider it as a part time job rather than as their duty. Secondly, volunteerIng provides substantial non-monetary benefits. For instance, young people can also develop business contacts during such opportunities, and this can enable them to secure a good job in the future.

I believe that the young people sacrifice a lot in working for the community and thus not paying them would be unfair. For example, they could spend this time building their skills and applying for jobs. Also, spending the little leisure time that they get in helping the community would steal from them the pleasures of exploring their individuality. Thus, a little remuneration is certainly justified.

To summarise, the youth need to be paid if they do community work. A little compensation for their time would motivate them to work with more zeal.

Plan followed:
Intro: Monetary incentives should be there
Para 1: First view
Para 2: Second view
Para 3: own view
Conclusion

Written by: Indroop Singh

22. *Although countries with long average working hours are economically successful, this often has some negative social consequences. To what extent do you agree or disagree?*

It is believed by some that while long working hours have led to prosperity and economic development, this has also impacted society negatively. I agree that economic success resulting from longer time spent at the workplace comes at a price of strained relationships with friends and families, poor health, and may also contribute to higher unemployment.

There are numerous drawbacks of working more hours per week. First of all, working long hours takes a toll on employees' health. This is because when employees work long hours, they do not get time to exercise and relax. An unhealthy lifestyle increases the risk of heart disease, diabetes and stress related illnesses. Being chronically overworked can also cause psychological problems, like nervous breakdowns and depression.

Another problem of working long hours is that employees do not get enough time for socializing and family life. The main impact is on the upbringing of children and many sociologists believe that there is strong correlation between parental involvement and a child's emotional well-being and self-esteem. Also, many couples blame their long working hours for troubles in the relationships and many single people cite it as the reason for their inability to find a partner and settle down.

Finally, companies that require longer work hours will employ less people in total. More number of people working less hours, is surely better than fewer people working more hours. The consequent unemployment is definitely detrimental for society in the long run as it can lead to increase in problems like crime and bankruptcy.

In conclusion, it is clear that despite the economic benefits, the detrimental effects of long working hours on the society are too big to be ignored and thus countries must take steps to limit working hours.

Plan followed:
Intro: Agree
Para 1: Disadvantage – employees' health at risk
Para 2: Disadvantage – no time for socializing and family
Para 3: Disadvantage - unemployment
Conclusion:

Written by: Indroop Singh

23. *Research has shown that spending much less time in office can reduce the use of energy (for example, electricity, gas). Thus, some companies close for some days a week. Do the advantages of this development outweigh the disadvantages?*

People have begun to realise that energy consumption can be checked by reducing the time spent by employees in offices. Therefore, many companies have adopted strategies like reducing the number of days in a workweek. While I believe there are certain drawbacks of this trend, the advantages are far more.

There are many advantages to the employers of closing offices for some days a week. Firstly, it leads to a substantial reduction of office expenses in terms of electricity consumption, water usage and fuel costs. Secondly, the reduced workweek improves the productivity of employees and thereby compensates for the hours lost. This makes them go back to work the next day with added zeal and enthusiasm. Finally, companies offering such working conditions are more attractive for potential employees.

Similarly, reduction in the working days can benefit the employees immensely. To begin with, this extra day off could give them the much-needed time for themselves and their families. So, this would not only be beneficial for family relationships but also for people's mental health as they would be able to relax and reduce their work stress. Workers can also join some physical activity on these days, and this can help address problems like obesity and back ache caused by a sedentary work environment.

On the other hand, this shortened workweek can also have certain negative effects. Primarily, it may affect the work-output and reduce the earning of employees especially those who work on daily wages. Additionally, considering the competition faced by the companies and the targets they have to achieve within the given deadlines, this policy could have detrimental effects on the companies' performances.

To sum up, although there are minor disadvantages to this system, shorter workweeks can have benefits to individuals and companies themselves, and so it is certainly a worthwhile proposition.

Plan followed:
Intro:
Para 1: advantages of this policy
Para 2: More advantages
Para 3: Disadvantages
Conclusion:

Written by: Indroop Singh

24. *If some people get a chance to choose between life without work and spending most of the time working, then they would choose not to work. Agree or disagree?*

It is believed by some that people would choose not to work if given a choice. I think even if people are financially secure, they would choose to work because work provides more than just a living.

There are many reasons why people would not choose a life without work, even if given a choice. To begin with, work provides people with an inner creative joy and saves them from the dullness and boredom of life. It puts their energies to proper use and keeps their mind and body active. Idleness is more tiresome, and many people may hate their job, but they are more miserable doing nothing.

Furthermore, work also gives people a sense of meaning and purpose. In other words, people today want to feel that they are contributing to society and making a difference to the world. Having a sense of purpose makes them feel that what they do matters and thus brings them happiness and satisfaction. For example, many people work for non-profit organisations like food pantries and animal shelters, that do not pay much, but give people a chance to help others.

In addition, for some people work is about respect and status in society. There are many people who turn down jobs with greater financial reward for those with greater status. Finally, relying on someone else for money can be never as satisfying as working to earn one's own livelihood. This is the reason even heirs to rich billionaires work despite having enough money to live their whole life in luxury.

To sum up, work is an important part of life for a lot of reasons that go beyond just earning a living. Therefore, I disagree that most people would not work, even if they had a choice.

Plan followed:
Intro: Disagree
Para 1: work keeps busy
Para 2: work gives satisfaction
Para 3: work gives respect
Conclusion: Reiterate your stand

Written by: Indroop Singh

25. *Some people think job satisfaction is more important than job security, while others think that people cannot be expected to enjoy a job and having a permanent job is more important. Discuss both views and give your opinion.*

Some people hold the opinion that job satisfaction is more important than a secure job, while others argue that it is not realistic to expect job satisfaction, and thus it is beneficial to have a permanent job which is secure. This essay intends to analyze both viewpoints. I personally consider that job satisfaction is short-lived and hence, employees should prioritize security over satisfaction.

On the one hand, there are many reasons why some people prioritize job satisfaction. Firstly, job satisfaction is very important from the perspective of work life balance. If people are not happy with their jobs, they would be stressed and unhappy in their personal lives too. Secondly, job satisfaction means that people work more efficiently and productively and this ensures that companies value them more and reward them with bonuses from time to time.

On the other hand, the main reason given by those who favour job security is that it ensures better productivity. If people are not worried about being laid off any time, they would be able to relax and give their best at work. Another reason is that job security ensures financial stability. Financial stability means that the employees have a comfortable family life, free from worries of debts and loans and thus they are able to concentrate better at work.

I believe that people's expectations from their work will keep growing, and hence job satisfaction can only be temporary, and they may be disappointed when their further desires fail to fulfil. It can also happen that once people get job satisfaction, they may become less ambitious, which may be detrimental for themselves and their work. In comparison, job security can ensure that the employees dedicate their energy into work with little worries from being fired due to their mistakes.

In conclusion, I would argue that the quest for job satisfaction is never-ending and employees should care more about a secure job.

Plan followed:
Intro:
Para 1: One view
Para 2: Other view
Para 3: Own view
Conclusion: Job security is more important

Similar: ***Nowadays people think that the most important thing in life is job satisfaction. Without excellent career life is meaningless. To what extent do you agree or disagree.***
Written by: Indroop Singh

26. *Some people think young people should be free to choose their job, but other people think they should be realistic and think more about their future. Discuss both views and give your opinion.*

Some people believe that the youngsters of today should choose a job they like, whereas others believe that they should be practical and give more importance to a secure job with their future in mind. In this essay, I will discuss both viewpoints. believe that job security is important but going for a job which gives pleasure yields more benefits.

On the one hand, the main reason given by those who say that the young people should have the freedom to do the job of their choice, is that people who are satisfied with their jobs do better at work. They get higher salaries and climb up the career ladder more quickly than those who are not happy with their jobs. Secondly, people spend a great deal of their time in the workplace. This means that if they are not happy with their job, they are also unhappy with their personal life. It could stress them out and lead to many health problems.

On the other hand, there are reasons why some people claim that the young people should focus more on a secure job. Firstly, they believe that the youngsters do not have the maturity to think far and so may end up in a job which may not have any security or any future. They are also against the job-hopping attitude of the youth of today. They believe that the young people should do a stable job. The young people of today are hasty in joining or leaving a job and may end up in long periods of unemployment, which would ultimately add to their stress.

I personally believe that if the youngsters of today want to experiment in life and walk on the untrodden path, there is no harm in letting them do so. After all, they are better informed about the newer job openings, because the power of technology is in their hands. They may face hurdles, but it is all part of growing up. If they do well, they can be in that job for life, but if they do not, they could always settle down in any job which could give them job security.

In conclusion, it is clear that if a person chooses a career that one loves the chances of success are pretty high and job security would eventually follow.

Plan followed:
Intro:
Para 1: First view
Para 2: Second view
Para 3: Own view
Conclusion: Job satisfaction is more important

Written by: Indroop Singh

27. *As most people spend a major part of their adult life at work, job satisfaction is an important element of individual wellbeing. What are the factors that contribute to job satisfaction? How realistic is the expectation of job satisfaction for all workers?*

There are many factors which influence an individual's job satisfaction directly or indirectly. In the following paragraphs I intend to delve into the factors that contribute to job satisfaction and discuss how practical it is for workers to expect job satisfaction.

The most important factor contributing to an individual's job satisfaction level is good salary and benefits. Competitive pay that matches a job's demand and skill set makes employees feel valued. Individuals also feel satisfied when their career path is filled with opportunities to learn, grow and earn promotions. Another factor that keeps employees happy and satisfied is a good relationship with supervisors and colleagues. For example, having a boss who praises their good performance and listens to their opinions makes employees feel important.

In addition, a healthy and comfortable work environment contributes to an employee's job satisfaction. Employees like working in places that are free from stress, harassment and discriminatory practices. Physical features of the workplace like proximity to home, cleanliness, good lighting and comfortable seating also makes employees satisfied. Last but not least, the feeling that the work done by them is meaningful and has a positive impact on society brings satisfaction to individuals.

Admittedly, it is difficult for all employees to become satisfied with their job completely. Firstly, there are many factors that lead to job satisfaction and it is not practical to expect everything in one job. For example, job satisfaction is dependent on rapport with bosses and colleagues and their behaviour is not in the hands of the employee. Secondly, expectations of individuals change throughout their career span. What satisfies an individual in the beginning of their career may not give them the satisfaction a few years down the lane. Sometimes they are unable to find new jobs and so get stuck in jobs that make them unhappy.

To sum up, job satisfaction depends on many factors like pay, work environment and relationship with colleagues. It is difficult to meet all these requirements and hence, expecting job satisfaction for everyone is unrealistic.

Plan followed:

Intro:

Para 1: Pay, promotions and relationship with boss, colleagues

Para 2: Work Environment, nature of work

Para3: why it is difficult for all employees to become satisfied with their job completely

Conclusion: there are many characteristics of a good job and it is not practical to expect work satisfaction

Written by: Indroop Singh

28. *In many countries, good schools and medical facilities are available only in cities. Some people think new teachers and doctors should work in rural areas for a few years, but others think everyone should be free to choose where they work. Discuss both views and give your own opinion.*

Some people opine that teachers and doctors, who are fresh out of college, should work in villages for a few years, whereas others believe that the choice of where to work should be left on these professionals. Both views will be discussed in this essay. I believe that professionals can be lured to work in rural areas through incentives and forcing them would be counterproductive.

On the one hand, there are many reasons why some people say that fresh teachers and doctors should work in rural areas for a few years. Firstly, it is undoubtedly true that rural areas lack trained professionals, and this could be a solution to provide quality healthcare and education in such areas. Secondly, it would enable the teachers and doctors to get a wider range of training and experience. For example, rural physicians come across a broader scope of illnesses, as people in rural areas lack access to specialty healthcare facilities.

On the other hand, those who are against this compulsory policy of making fresh teachers and medical specialists to work in villages for some time, give their reasons as follows. To begin with, forcing fresh graduates to work in rural areas might create resentment in them and this would directly affect their performance. Another adverse effect may be that fewer and fewer students would choose such careers, and so in the long run there would be a shortage of such professionals.

In my opinion, governments should try to attract new graduates to rural postings through incentives like loan waivers and higher salaries as it is the only solution to the dearth of professionals in such areas. It would also be beneficial for these professionals as they would learn more, and thus enable them to perform their duties better. However, forcing recent graduates by making it obligatory would not be a good solution.

To sum up, it could be said that sending doctors and teachers to rural areas would be an ideal situation, but it should be achieved through incentives and not coercion.

Plan followed:
Intro: Discuss essay intro
Para1: Advantages of having teachers and doctors work in rural areas
Para 2: Compulsory policy may have some negative effects
Para 3: Own opinion
Conclusion:

Written by: Indroop Singh

29. *Some people tend to take temporary jobs (they only work for few month of year), for they have time to do other things. Do the advantages outweigh the disadvantages?*

In recent years, it has become very common for people to take temporary jobs so that they can spend time on their hobbies and other activities. While I consider that temporary jobs have certain disadvantages, their benefits definitely outweigh the drawbacks.

The main advantage of temporary work is that it is relatively easy to get. If the candidate's credentials match the temporary job requirements, he might be called upon to fill the position. Secondly, doing temporary work gives a candidate the much-needed work experience. Most companies require two to three-year experience, which puts recent graduates at a loss.

Another benefit of doing temporary work is that if a vacancy becomes available within the company, one can apply, and chances are that he might be asked to stay on with the company on a full-time basis. Furthermore, by going from company to company, a temporary worker gets a lot of exposure of different kinds of environments. By learning to work with different kinds of people, a temporary worker can sharpen his people skills.

On the other hand, there are some drawbacks of temporary jobs. First, a temporary job does not have job security and one may be fired any time. Second, one also does not get the perks and benefits that regular full-time employees get. For example, full term employees get health insurance, paid leave or retirement plan, which temporary employees do not get. In addition, many temporary workers feel isolated and not well respected by other employees. Finally, there may be long gaps in one's employment from time to time.

Summing up, disadvantages of temporary jobs are far less than the advantages. For some people, a temporary job is just temporary until they find something full-time, while for others it is a way of life.

Plan followed:
Intro: the pros definitely outweigh the cons
Para 1: Advantages
Para 2: More advantages
Para 3: Disadvantages
Conclusion: disadvantages of temporary jobs are far less than the advantages

30. *An increasing number of people change their career and place of residence several times during their lifetime. Is this a positive or negative development?*

In recent years it has become very common for people to change their career and place of living many times during their life. While there are a few disadvantages of this trend, the advantages are far more.

Undoubtedly, there are some drawbacks of changing job and place of living. The first disadvantage is that there is risk involved. If a person changes jobs or residence, then he has to face new challenges and adjust with new people. There is always a risk that he may not find things very smooth sailing and may have to suffer emotional and physical stress.

However, there are some strong benefits that can come from a career change. One of the major benefits is the pay hike which is usually there with a career change. Secondly, a person may finally discover a career, which gives him the maximum job satisfaction. He may get to do something interesting, which would also give him personal satisfaction. Moreover, those who have a wide range of career experiences will also have less chances of suffering from unemployment. For instance, if they lose one job, they can seek out jobs in different career fields, as opposed to one career field.

Similarly, there are also many advantages associated with the change of residence, which comes along with a career change. Change of surroundings and new exciting experiences are useful for self-education and development of a person. Besides, these changes usually bring positive emotions, which help to fight stresses and have overall good effect on health. It is also very beneficial for the person's family, as this change gives them the opportunity to make new friends, enjoy new cultures and experience new climates. In other words, it adds spice to life.

Summing up, I reiterate my opinion by saying that although changing careers and place of residence several times during a lifetime may bring a few challenges in life, on the whole it is a positive development.

Plan followed:
Intro: This situation is largely a positive one.
Para 1: Disadvantages
Para 2: Advantages of career change
Para 3: More advantages
Conclusion: reiterate opinion

31. *An increasing number of people change their career during their work life. What are the reasons for this? Is this a positive or a negative development for the society?(23/2/22 CBT)*

It is irrefutable that more and more people are willing to switch careers during their working life. There are several factors responsible for this phenomenon. However, I believe this trend is detrimental for the society.

There are some strong motivations behind the decision to switch careers. The first reason is undoubtedly money. The cost of living has increased dramatically in the last few decades and there are many careers, which are not as lucrative as in the past. There is also no questioning the fact that money is the main motivation for work today as people are much more materialistic than the past. Sometimes, changing job profile is also done to increase one's skillset and to open the doors for new job opportunities. Secondly, people are very impatient today and they easily get bored doing the same thing every day. Changing careers is a means to break the monotony of life. In other words, a change in career can be a liberating experience for some people. They change jobs for self-fulfilment and job-satisfaction, which they might have lacked in their previous job.

However, I believe that when people change their vocation, it often affects the society adversely. The main drawback is for the businesses in the society. A large amount of money is spent on training and educating employees, but all this money gets wasted when individuals change jobs. It not only impacts companies' profits, but also the development of the society as it affects the taxes the companies can pay to the government. Another major impact is on the community spirit and social bonding. People who change careers seldom form close bonds with their colleagues. Also, a change in career is often associated with a change in residence, which means it negatively affects the social bonds with the neighbours. Hence, it is not surprising that the societies are becoming more and more selfish and self-centred today.

In conclusion, I would like to reiterate that although there are many reasons why people change careers, the trend affects the communities negatively.

Plan followed:
Intro: Several factors responsible for this. Negative for the society
Para 1: Reasons
Para 2: Negative effects on the society
Conclusion: Reiterate Opinion

Written by: Indroop Singh

32. *Some people say that professional workers such as doctors, nurses and teachers, who make greater contribution to society should be paid more than those people in the field of sports and entertainment. To what extent do you agree or disagree?*

The high incomes of celebs in the field of sports and entertainment have always been a matter of dispute. I believe that actors and sportsmen also contribute equally to our society, so I disagree that doctors, nurses and teachers should be paid more.

The main reason why the contribution of people working in sports and entertainment is no less than educators and medical professionals is because they provide us entertainment and inspiration. They are role models for society and people follow them and listen to them. Art and entertainment is as much a human need as food, clothing and shelter. These celebs also bring name and fame to our country. They spread our culture through their art. Therefore, their high earnings are very well deserved.

Secondly, these actors and sportsmen face a lot of competition and have to work really hard to be successful in their careers. Their schedules are really tight and their jobs are both mentally and physically demanding. They have to follow a strict diet and exercise regimen to stay in shape. Injuries in case of athletes and a series of unsuccessful movies or shows for actors can end their careers. Also for most celebrities and sportspersons the high earning phase is short lived, so the comparisons in pay are not justified.

Finally, these celebs completely sacrifice their personal life and freedom. They cannot enjoy the common things of life like the common man does. They are always followed by the paparazzi, and their children also always need security. Most of the things published about them in magazines are false or highly exaggerated and this causes a lot of controversies and disturbances in their personal lives. This is too much of a price to pay, and so the high salaries they receive are not unwarranted.

Summing up, people in the field of sports and entertainment, well deserve their high incomes. Their services to the society are as important as the services of doctors, teachers and nurses.

Plan followed:
Intro: disagree
Para 1: Points in favour of higher salaries for celebs
Para 2: More points
Para 3: Another point
Conclusion: Reiterate opinion

Written by: Indroop Singh

33. *In some countries, celebs earn more than senior politicians. What are the reasons? Is this a positive or a negative development?*

The earning of celebrities is substantially more than that of high-ranking politicians. In this essay I will put forth the reasons for this discrepancy. I believe that it is a negative development overall.

There are many reasons why celebs earn a lot more than politicians these days. The main reason is that they have talent and they work extremely hard to keep up that talent. Even among the talented, very few get the celebrity status. The second reason is that celebs have very short career spans. For example, a sportsperson or a film star earns a maximum 15-20 years. They earn till they work, and once they are out of work their earning sees a full stop. They do not get any pension like in other professions. In addition, they have stressful lives and have to remain away from their families for weeks or months at a stretch.

The big difference in the earning of politicians and celebs is negative because of many reasons. First, because of less pay, many politicians shirk work. More pay would produce more attentive public servants. Secondly, high salaries would work as anti-corruption measures. For example, in Singapore the prime minister earns $1.7 million a year, which is four times more than the salary of the US president. These high salaries in Singapore, apart from decreasing corruption, are also seen to attract the best talent, who would otherwise go into finance or computing. High salaries have seen these politicians more eager to represent their constituents' interests.

Moreover, politicians also sacrifice their personal lives just as celebs do to serve the public. They have no time for themselves and their families and at times have to remain away for days at a stretch. They are also always surrounded by the paparazzi and cannot enjoy life like a common man. Their career span as a politician is also very small and they need security as their lives are at a risk from anti-social elements. Therefore, these politicians should be paid more, as they are also no less than any other celebs.

To sum up, there are many reasons why the celebs are earning a lot more than politicians. I believe this discrepancy is negative on the whole.

Plan followed:
Intro:
Para 1: Reasons why celebs earn more
Para 2: Why it is a negative development
Para 3: More reasons
Conclusion:

34. *Some countries have introduced a law to limit working hours for employees. Why is this law introduced? Do you think it is a positive or a negative development?*

There are countries in the world, such as the USA, Canada, Australia and many more, where a person cannot work for more than 40 hours a week. In the following paragraphs, I shall discuss why this law was introduced. I believe it is a positive development.

The main reason this law was introduced is to protect the economic rights of the workers and prevent worker exploitation. It is seen that in places where there is no such law, employees are made to work long hours for little pay. Furthermore, exhausted employees are more likely to make mistakes and this can result in injuries. Long work hours also put a strain on family relationships and affects employees' mental and physical health.

In my opinion having a law for limiting work hours is a positive development. To begin with, it would help workers maintain a better work life balance and give them the much-needed time for themselves and their families. So, this would not only be beneficial for family relationships but also for people's mental health as they would be able to relax and reduce their work stress. Workers can also find time for physical activity and this can help address problems like obesity and back ache caused by a sedentary work environment.

In addition, having a limit on working hours also helps solve the problem of unemployment. More people working for a fixed number of hours is better than fewer people working more hours. Finally, having a limit on the working hours improves the productivity of employees and thereby compensates for the hours lost. The employees get time to recharge their batteries and this makes them go back to work the next day with added zeal and enthusiasm.

Summing up, this law was imposed for the benefit of employees and I believe it is advantageous for employees, employers and the society at large.

Plan followed:

Intro: This essay shall discuss why this law was imposed. It is a positive development
Para 1: why this law was imposed
Para 2: why it is a positive development
Para 3: why it is a positive development
Conclusion:

Written by: Deepa Singh Makkar

35. *In some countries, it is illegal for companies to reject job applicant for their age. Is this a positive or a negative development?*

In recent years, many countries have implemented laws against age discrimination while hiring. I believe age discrimination has negative effects not only for the old and young people but also for the economy and society as a whole. So, I definitely consider such law to be a positive development.

There are many reasons why I consider that companies should be prohibited from discriminating on the basis of age. Firstly, it creates a feeling of incompetence among the old and young. It creates a sort of inferiority complex amongst them. In other words, after repeatedly being rejected on the basis of age, the older and younger people start feeling dependent, non-contributing members of the society. This feeling in turn gradually affects their productivity as well.

Secondly, older people who are not able to secure a job due to age discrimination might be forced into an early retirement. This would mean not only a loss of productivity from an economic point of view but also a greater social security burden on the state in the forms of pensions for a longer time. This problem would become even worse with increasing life expectancy and an in general Increase in the old age population.

Finally, age discrimination is a big loss to the economy as it is a direct loss of experience that old people have accumulated over years. Undervaluing their hard-earned experience is also disservice to the old generation. Moreover, age discrimination would ultimately prevent potentially talented candidates from applying for jobs and thus companies lose by having a smaller pool of candidates to choose from.

In conclusion, I would like to reiterate that laws against age discrimination are a welcome change and such laws are beneficial for the whole society.

Plan followed:
Intro: It is a positive development
Para 1: Reasons why it is positive
Para 2: More reason
Para 3: Final reason
Conclusion: reiterate opinion

Written by: Indroop Singh

36. *Nowadays, some workplaces tend to employ equal numbers of men and women workers. Do you think it is a positive or negative development?*

Traditional male dominated workplaces are decreasing nowadays, and some workplaces are giving jobs to equal numbers of men and women. Although there may be a few drawbacks of this situation, the advantages are much more.

Admittedly, having a quota for men and women may have some negative impacts. To begin with, having a fixed quota would mar the chances of both deserving men or women. People should be chosen for jobs based on their skills, qualification and character, and gender should not come in the way of the selection process. In addition, those who tend to discriminate against women would find some other ways to discriminate, such as by underpaying the women at the same posts as men.

However, a more equal mix of men and women in the workforce not only boosts national economies, but also increases job satisfaction and performance in workplaces. Not only do men and women feel better when working together, but they also seem to perform better. Those working in gender-balanced groups have less absenteeism and so more turnover, compared to those in settings dominated by females or males.

Secondly, gender diversity at management level spurs innovation and creativity as men and women bring different perspectives about solving problems. Moreover, the different perspectives from men and women enable the companies to serve customers' from both the genders more effectively. Last but not least, more employment opportunities for women would lead to financial independence for women and this in turn would lead to women empowerment.

Summing up, the trend of employing an equal number of men and women in the workplace is a positive development overall, despite the few negatives.

Plan followed:

Intro: it is a positive development
Para 1: Why negative
Para 2: Why positive
Para 3: Why positive
Conclusion: Reiterate opinion

37. *Men are placed in most high-level jobs. Some people say that the government should encourage a certain percentage of these jobs to be reserved for women. Do you agree or disagree?*

Some people believe that the government should make companies reserve some leadership roles for women as these kinds of jobs are mostly dominated by men. While I agree that having more women at high ranks is beneficial for companies, reservation is not the solution and this equality should be brought about in a more organic way.

There are many benefits of hiring women at high-level positions. Firstly, having women at senior positions lessens gender discrimination in recruitment, earnings and promotions. In other words, women at high ranks can ensure a better work environment for women at low ranks. Secondly gender diversity at management level spurs innovation and creativity as men and women think about and solve problems differently.

However, reservation is not the right way to ensure equal representation of men and women in high-ranking positions. Forcing companies to hire, promote and appoint women could negatively affect businesses. Management is about making important decisions and an undeserving candidate may seriously hamper a company's growth and progress. Reserving a few seats for women may also result in negative discrimination against deserving men that are more qualified for a job.

Instead, this glass ceiling preventing women from reaching to the top should be resolved by encouraging a change in traditional mindset. This typical stereotypical thinking leads to the belief that women are primary caregivers for their children and spouses. Even if women work, they are still expected to take care of household duties and this creates the feeling that they can never devote the time needed for work in management positions. The change should come from an early age by teaching children equality and that would go way farther in empowering women than forced reservation.

Summing up, women in leadership roles help companies but forcing companies to allocate these jobs to women is not the best way to address this imbalance. Rather it is a question of changing mindsets, so that those who deserve to be at the top, will earn it and be appropriately appointed.

Plan followed:
Intro: Disagree. Imposing quota is not the solution
Para 1: how women at high ranks benefit companies
Pats 2: why reservation is not the solution
Para 3: Better solution to fix this issue
Conclusion: Reiterate opinion

Written by: Deepa Singh Makkar

38. *In some countries it is compulsory for all young people to join the armed forces for some time. What are the benefits of requiring young people to serve the army? Does participation in community work qualify as an alternative?*

Military service is voluntary in most of the world. However, it is compulsory in some countries like Mexico and Iran. Although conscription has many benefits, I believe community service is also a good alternative.

There are many advantages of conscription. First of all, young people can raise their physical fitness and enjoy better health. They also develop a sense of team spirit and improve abilities to get along well with others. They learn to cope with problems independently, and gain self-confidence. What is more, they expand their social circle, as people from different corners of the country are together in the army camps. This can prove an invaluable asset when they return to civilian life.

Furthermore, a few years in the army teaches young people to be efficient, disciplined and excellent time managers. They are highly respected by the civilians. Some of them may join the army permanently if they like that life. It is also considered a positive point when they look for other jobs. It also instils a sense of patriotism among the youth.

However, despite all these benefits, its mandatory nature is arguable. Many young people cannot cope with the high level of stress in the army. That's why community service is suggested as an alternative in most countries. By doing community service young adults develop skills, gain work experience and explore career options. They can also acquire practical knowledge through community service.

Summing up, military service is helpful only when it is voluntary. Mandatory military service does not suit all young people, whereas community service benefits every young person. Therefore, community service is better than military conscription.

Plan followed:
Intro: Balanced approach
Para 1: Advantages of military conscription
Para 2: More advantages of military conscription
Para 3: Advantages of community service
Conclusion: Compulsory military service is not good. Community service is better.

39. *Rich countries should not employ skilled labour from poor countries, as poor countries need the workers more. Do you agree or disagree?*

Some people hold the opinion that rich countries should not depend on workers from poor countries. However, I believe that rich countries should employ laborers from poor countries as this is not only beneficial for the developed countries but also the poor countries and their workers.

There are undoubtedly benefits of hiring skilled workers from poor countries for the industrialised nations. Firstly, the migrant workers bring their entrepreneurial and cost-effective methods with them to rich countries, benefitting their economies immensely. Secondly, many developed countries are facing a skilled labour shortage and hiring employees from developing countries is the only way to save their economy from stagnation or recession.

Developing countries also reap the benefits when openness to foreign employment is embraced. When rich countries require skilled labour from developing countries, a demand is created in these poor countries, which leads to the development of their internal infrastructure such as good educational institutes. For example, when many IT professionals were hired by the United States in the late 20th Century, there was a big growth in the Indian tech-related education sector. Moreover, these workers bring back the cosmopolitan culture of developed countries and this leads to change in traditional thinking in poor countries.

Finally, migration benefits the skilled workers and their families as well. To begin with, in their home countries, their skills are wasted due to lack of job opportunities. On the contrary, in developed countries, they are not only able to find suitable jobs but also earn enough to send some of their earnings back to their families. These workers also learn new work-related skills and are able to use it to find better jobs when they return to their own countries.

Summing up, rich countries should employ skilled labour from poor countries as both these countries and the workers are benefitted and it is a win-win situation for all.

Plan followed:
Intro: Disagree.
Para 1: Advantage to developed countries
Para 2: Advantage to developing countries
Para 3: Advantage to skilled workers
Conclusion:

Written by: Indroop Singh

40. *People aim to achieve a balance between their work and lives, but few people achieve it. What are the causes of this problem? How to overcome it?*

It is true that most people fail in the quest to achieve work life balance despite trying very hard. There are many reasons for this imbalance, but a few steps can be taken to achieve work life balance.

The main reason for the inability to achieve a work life balance is that jobs have become stressful and competition at work forces people to work harder and longer than others. Technology has also made everyone more reachable and this constant connection to work has reduced the time people get to relax at home. Another culprit for this lack of balance is the materialistic society of today. People care more about the luxuries of life than spending time with loved ones. Finally, higher cost of living has forced some people to work more and take on second jobs.

There are many steps people can take to lessen their workload and achieve a healthier work life balance. Firstly, people need to set realistic and manageable goals at work. Prioritizing important tasks and eliminating or delegating other tasks will not only save time but also make people feel more accomplished. Secondly, individuals should consider asking employers for flexible work hours and telecommuting options. This would increase their productivity and give them more time to spend with families at home.

In addition, a healthy lifestyle is essential to cope with stress and to achieve work-life balance. People need to start eating well, include physical activity in their daily routines and get enough sleep. Furthermore, when people come home from work, they must learn to switch the office button off and instead do relaxing hobbies that take their mind off work like reading, gardening, hiking etc. Last but not least, downshifting, which means reducing one's standard of life for an improved quality of life, would result in more spare time and reduced workloads.

To sum up, heavier workloads create a work life imbalance but certain strategies can help people rectify this situation.

Plan followed:
Intro:
Para 1: Reasons why we do not achieve a perfect work-life balance
Para 2: Solutions: realistic goals, flex hours
Para 3: Solutions: healthy lifestyle, downshifting
Conclusion:

41. *These days many people leave their country to work abroad and take their family with them. Do you think benefits of this outweigh disadvantages in terms of family development?*

It can be commonly seen that when people move to other countries for employment, their families also accompany them. While there might some negative consequences of this on family, I would argue that it is far more beneficial.

There are many obvious benefits of going abroad to work along with family. To begin with, individuals have more bonding with family. The family relationship would not be weakened by distance. Some couples finally end up in divorce, as one or both of them cannot endure the long-term separation. Secondly, many people feel homesick and lonely and therefore cannot adjust in the foreign country and return home thereby missing the golden opportunity of working abroad.

Finally, the children, especially who are in young ages, need the care from both parents. Childhood is a crucial phase of life and comes only once. If children are deprived of one parent's love it may have a considerable impact on their psyche. Therefore, working abroad with family can provide complete love and care to the children. What is more, children too are benefited from international exposure.

On the other hand, there are some problems of working abroad with families. To begin with, living with family members abroad means more expenses. A single person can share room with someone in the initial stages, but a complete family needs a proper house. What is more, all the members face stress of adaptation to alien surroundings. Parents themselves feel culture shock and therefore cannot help their children.

Summing up, there are both advantages and disadvantages in any choice of this issue. Personally, I believe that people should decide according to their specific circumstances. If there are financial constraints, then it is better to go alone initially. However, the family should be called as early as possible.

Plan followed:
Intro: Advantages more than disadvantages
Para 1: Advantages
Para 2: More advantages
Para 3: Disadvantages
Conclusion:

42. *In many countries more and more young people are leaving school but unable to find jobs. What problems do you think youth unemployment causes for individuals and the society? What measures should be taken to reduce the level of unemployment among youngsters?*

Youth unemployment has become an issue of grave concern. This essay shall highlight the effects of youth unemployment on individuals and society and suggest some solutions to mitigate the problems.

Unemployment has profound effects on the young people. Firstly, it affects their psychological and social development. Having completed their graduation, young people are eager to be in control of their lives, which can only be possible if their dependence on their parents for their financial needs is not there. They are frustrated with their lives. Some may even develop suicidal tendencies or become drug addicts.

On the societal level also, there are many effects. There is increased crime in the society which has a very detrimental effect. Young people are energetic and if their energy is not channelized in the right direction then definitely violence and crime is there in the society. Poverty, which is the result of unemployment, also leads to many problems like diminished health standards. So, on the whole, the society suffers.

The solutions are not simple. Education system should be reformed. There are many people without jobs and many jobs without suitable people. So, students should be encouraged to take up those courses, which have no dearth of jobs. Government can also provide subsidies to those firms that take on unemployed people. Government can set up industries based on agriculture and also set up cottage industries such as those of carpets, mats and soaps. Finally, government can encourage self-employment by giving loans to young people who want to be entrepreneurs.

Summing up, youth unemployment is a serious issue and should be dealt with on a war footing as there are a lot of detrimental effects on the individual and society.

Plan followed:

Intro:

Para 1: Effects on young people

Para 2: effects on society

Para 3: Solutions

Conclusion: youth unemployment is a serious issue and should be dealt with on a war footing.

43. *Employers should give staff at least four weeks holidays a year to make employees better at their jobs. To what extent do you agree or disagree with this statement?*

It is irrefutable that work stress has increased a lot in the past few years. Hence, some people opine that employers should give workers a month of holidays in a year at least. I believe this is certainly a good idea and it would not only benefit the employees but also the employers.

There are many reasons why such an initiative would benefit the employees. Firstly, it has been seen that due to long working hours and lack of holidays, many employees are under a lot of stress. In fact, in recent times work stress has been a major cause of suicides as well. A month of holidays would enable people to recharge their batteries and to refresh themselves. Secondly, it would give people time to spend with families and go on vacations and pursue their hobbies. Many companies are facing attrition because employees are unable to balance their personal life and their professional life and thus such a step would go a long way in reversing this trend.

Furthermore, companies and firms would also be benefitted by such a change. To begin with, companies which offer holidays would be more attractive to job seekers. In other words, such initiatives would help companies recruit better talent. Another advantage would be increased work efficiency and productivity. Regular yearly breaks would reduce stress and thus, help employees to concentrate better at their work. Lastly, I believe that if employees feel cared about and important, it would also improve customer satisfaction as customer satisfaction depends largely upon employee moods and their working conditions.

In conclusion, I would like to reiterate that I am strongly in favour of the idea of employers giving four weeks of holidays to their employees, since it would benefit the employees as well as the employers.

Plan followed:
Intro: Agree
Para1: How it would help employees
Para 2: How it would help employers also
Conclusion: Reiterate opinion

Written by: Indroop Singh

44. There is increased use of technology in the workplace. Some people find that it is good for young people's prospects of gaining a job and harder for old people. To what extent do you agree or disagree?

It is undeniable that technology is a major part of the workplace nowadays. However, many individuals are of the opinion that although technology has increased the employability of youngsters, it has made it harder for old people to compete for jobs. I certainly agree with this notion.

The main reason why I consider that technology has given youth an edge over the old in regard to jobs is that the youth of today have been using technology since their childhood. They are very comfortable with it, while the old have to spend time and make efforts to learn it and even after spending time it is very hard to reach the same level of affinity that youth have with technology.

Furthermore, there is also a perception among employers that the old-aged candidates are not adept with technology and thus hiring them would either mean lower productivity or extra expenditure to train them. This perception may be wrong but it does create a barrier and senior job seekers need to make special efforts in interviews to prove that they are comfortable handling technology.

Last but not least, technology is not constant. The technology keeps changing and thus there is a need to relearn and to adjust continuously. It is also human nature that the ability to adapt and to change decreases with age. In other words, young people are easily able to make changes and learn new things, while it takes time for the old generation to do the same. Not only that some old people try to resist change, rather than to adapt themselves and this further makes employers avoid hiring them.

In conclusion, I would like to reiterate that while the coming of technology in the workplace has benefitted the youth, it has made it all the more challenging for the old.

Plan followed:
Intro: Agree
Para 1: 1st reason
Para 2: 2nd reason
Para 3: 3rd reason
Conclusion: Reiterate opinion

Written by: Indroop Singh

45. *Some people think that the best way to reduce time spent in traveling to work is to replace parks and gardens close to the city centres with apartment buildings where commuters can live. To what extent do you agree or disagree?*

To reduce the commuting time to workplace, some people consider that parks and gardens in proximity to the city centres should be converted into apartments. I believe that such a change would not reduce the travelling time, and on the contrary would create more problems.

There are many reasons why I believe that replacing parks with apartment buildings would not reduce the travelling time. Firstly, the main reason for long travelling times is not the long distances but actually traffic congestion. Building apartments near to city centres would worsen the situation by adding even more cars on the roads. Secondly, many people like to live far away because of the noise and overcrowding near the city centres and building new apartments would increase this problem even more. In other words, it would be very hard to convince people to move into such apartments.

Moreover, taking such a drastic step would bring its own set of problems. To begin with, the abundance of buildings made up of asphalt and concrete in cities creates the urban heat island effect. This makes urban neighbourhoods noticeably warmer than other nearby areas. Additionally, removing trees in parks and gardens would add to air pollution, which can increase the risk of certain cancers and have adverse effects on children, the elderly and anyone with underlying respiratory problems.

Last but not least, parks provide space for neighbourhood residents to interact with each other and meet new people. They're also great spaces for events and for people to engage in recreational activities. This allows people to develop a sense of community. Hence, converting parks into apartments would adversely impact people's quality of life and their sense of community.

In conclusion, I reiterate that converting parks and gardens in the city centres would not be a step in the right direction, and would lead to more serious problems.

Plan followed:
Intro: Disagree
Para 1: Why travelling time would not be reduced
Para 2: Problems created by removing parks and trees
Para 3: More such problems
Conclusion: Reiterate opinion

Written by: Indroop Singh Makkar

46. *Students in school should learn academic subjects and pass exams. Other skills such as cookery, dressmaking and woodwork can be learnt well from family and friends. Do you agree or disagree?*

It is believed that school curricula should only focus on academic subjects, and domestic sciences such as cooking, sewing and carpentry should be learnt at home. While academic subjects are important, there are countless advantages of having craft education classes in schools.

Undoubtedly, academic subjects are very important. Firstly, the basic knowledge of academic subjects such as maths, life sciences, social sciences and languages makes children well-informed citizens of tomorrow. Secondly, the competition today is very stiff, and students have to excel in academics to secure a seat in a good university or college. It is also a well-known fact that academic subjects taught at school enable students to be competent in the future work place.

However, for the holistic development of children, the non-academic subjects are as important. Firstly, craft education improves the intelligence level of students. Recent researches claim that there is a direct correlation between hand eye coordination and the development of the brain. So, students do better in other subjects also. Also, students can learn maths through real life applications. They need math when they are measuring, designing and planning their projects.

Moreover, craft education takes away gender stereotypes. Both boys and girls learn how to knit and sew and cook. Both boys and girls learn how to woodwork and hammer and use power tools. Secondly, making something is often a slow and tedious process, which teaches students to concentrate and focus. This helps students who have problems with sitting still and listening in class. Finally, if such subjects are there in schools, students can adopt them as career options after school and start earning early on in life.

To sum up, cooking, woodworking, dressmaking etc. are important subjects, which need to be taught along with academic subjects to children at a younger age. Children need to see the practical applications of their education. These skills cannot be taught at home.

Plan followed:
Intro: disagree
Para 1: Why academic subjects are important
Para 2: advantages of craft classes
Para 3: More advantages
Conclusion: Reiterate view

47. *Some people think that increasing communication usage of computers and mobile phones by young people has had a negative effect on their reading and writing skills. To what extent do you agree or disagree?*

It is believed by some that both writing and reading skills have suffered a setback, due to computers and smartphones. While this modern communication technology has led to a deterioration of reading and writing skills, I believe that if used judiciously these effects can be reversed.

To begin with, modern day technology has an overall negative effect on students' writing skills because it encourages cyber slang, which involves using shortcuts, alternative words, or even symbols in an electronic document. When children start using abbreviations, such as 'lol', 'C U L8R' and 'bcoz' in academic writing, they start forgetting the actual words and their spellings. Moreover, the autocorrect feature fixes their mistakes, so they do not even realize that they have written something wrong. Students find it difficult to get rid of these habits.

Similarly, the influence of electronic media on the reading habits of pupils has become an issue of concern. Students now spend more hours browsing the net, playing games on their handsets and writing non-stop SMS's to their contacts. Students are rarely interested in reading for pleasure and enjoyment, and instead they read only to pass examination. Lack of reading culture among our youth nowadays, has greatly affected the quality of graduates being produced.

I believe these gadgets have come to stay and their negative effects on their reading and writing skills can be revoked with their sensible usage. For example, the kindle has aroused the interest of many youngsters to read. I personally own a kindle, and ever since I started using it, I have started reading more. I carry it with me always and I snatch time to read a few pages of any book I have downloaded in it.

To sum up, I reiterate that the communication technology of today is definitely hampering the reading and writing skills. The onus is on the parents and teachers to teach children the right ways to use this technology, so that its negative effects are minimized.

Plan followed:
Intro: Agree
Para 1: negative effects on writing
Para 2: negative effects on reading
Para 3: Own view
Conclusion:

48. *Now a lot of people in college are doing academic study. We should encourage them to learn vocational skills (for example, to become plumbers and electricians). Do you agree or disagree?*

A majority of the youngsters, nowadays, go for tertiary education. It is suggested by some people that they should go in for some vocational training to start earning soon. While vocational education has its own value, I firmly believe that university education has an edge over vocational education.

Undoubtedly, vocational education can be completed in much less time than college or university education. Therefore, young people can start earning money early and can become independent, and can afford their own house or start a family. Young people who decide to find work, rather than continue their studies, may progress more quickly. They have the chance to gain real experience and learn practical skills related to their chosen profession. This may lead to promotions and a successful career.

However, I believe that it is more beneficial for students to continue their studies. Firstly, academic qualifications are required in many professions. For example, it is impossible to become a doctor, teacher or lawyer without having the relevant degree. Another advantage of graduating from a university is that it gives a person more choices when it comes to choosing a job. Most employers are more impressed by a candidate who has a degree than they would be by one who only has high school qualifications. University graduates also tend to earn higher salaries than those with fewer qualifications.

Furthermore, the job market is becoming increasingly competitive, and sometimes there are hundreds of applicants for one position in a company. Young people who do not have qualifications from a university or college are not able to compete. What is more, those who work in the construction work or as car mechanics will always have to work under those who have civil and mechanical engineering degrees.

To sum up, for the reasons mentioned above, it seems to me that students are more likely to be successful in their careers if they continue their studies beyond school level.

Plan followed:
Intro: discuss essay intro
Para 1: Advantages of stepping into the job market before university education
Para 2: Advantages of university education
Para 3: Advantages of university education
Conclusion: University education is definitely better

49. *Some people think that to be successful, you need to get a university education, whereas others say it is not true. Discuss both ideas and give your own opinion.*

Some individuals opine that tertiary education is an essential prerequisite of success, whereas others oppose this view. This essay intends to analyse both perspectives. I believe in some fields, university education is compulsory for success, but in other areas, experience and soft skills are the key to success.

On the one hand, there are many reasons why some people believe that success depends on tertiary education. Firstly, a university education is essential if a person wants to have a career in a profession such as law, engineering, teaching, or medicine. What is more, it opens more doors for future employment. Also, the university is a great place to develop a network of friends who may later become business associates or partners. So, definitely, in this respect, university education can help a person get success.

On the other hand, those who say that success can be achieved without going for higher education, give their reasons as follows. To begin with, they cite the examples of many people who have made it big without going to college. For instance, Henry Ford never graduated high school but owns one of the largest automobile manufacturing companies, Ford Motor Company. Secondly, people with some talent, but no education can be successful too. To illustrate, many successful sports persons and celebrities are not even high school graduates.

I believe that university education is essential for success in academic related jobs because it is nearly impossible to become a doctor, a lawyer or an engineer without a college degree. At the same time, I believe when it comes to business or marketing it is about experience and soft skills. Moreover, this is the age of entrepreneurship where many people want to start their businesses and I think success here depends upon innovative ideas and creativity much more than a paper degree.

To conclude, it can be said that the attributes needed to become successful in today's world do not necessarily depend on a university degree. However, in academics, a university degree is needed to get success.

Plan followed:
Intro: Discuss essay template
Para 1: How university education can get success
Para 2: How success can be achieved without a university degree.
Para 3: Own view   Conclusion:
Written by: Indroop Singh
***Similar past essay**: Some people believe that studying in a college or university is the best way for students to prepare for their future career. But others think they should leave school as soon as possible to develop their career through work experience. Discuss both these views and give your own opinion.*

50. *Many people believe that healthy eating and the importance of healthy food should be taught in schools. Others say that parents should teach their children about healthy food and diet. Discuss both views and give your opinion with relevant examples.*

Some people opine that parents should apprise children about a healthy diet, whereas others say that it should be on the teachers to teach students about healthy eating. This essay intends to analyse both perspectives. I believe that in today's scenario, both teachers and parents have to share this task pro-actively.

On the one hand, there are many reasons why some people believe that teaching children about healthy eating should be a parent's job. Firstly, parents can start developing healthy eating habits in children even before they start school. Children's eating patterns start early and these starting years are a good opportunity for the parents to teach good eating habits that remain with children when they get older. Secondly, parents can set up a good example and make better nutritional choices like swap sugary beverages with fresh juices.

On the other hand, there are reasons why some people contend that teachers are in a better position to teach students about healthy eating. To begin with, some parents themselves are not much aware of nutritious foods and diet. Teachers can in fact teach them too through their children. Moreover, some parents are busy with their hectic jobs and this added responsibility can add more stress to their lives.

I believe, neither teachers nor parents can shrug off their responsibilities and say it is not their job to teach children about healthy eating. Teachers are considered experts and so children are more likely to listen to their teachers. At the same time, if parents do not reinforce the healthy habits taught in schools, then children are likely to ignore them and eventually forget about them.

To sum up, talking about wholesome diets to children is very essential in today's times and both teachers and parents must do it together to leave an imprint on the minds of children.

Plan followed:
Intro:
Para 1: Why Parents: start early, role models
Para 2: Why teachers: parents are not aware, parents are busy, children listen to teachers more.
Para 3: My opinion: both have an equal role
Conclusion:

Written by: Deepa Singh Makkar

51. *Some people think history has nothing or little to tell us, but others think that studying the past history can help us better understand the present. Discuss the two views and give your own opinion.*

Some individuals are of the opinion that studying the past history is useless today, but others believe it is very essential to know history to better understand the present. I intend to discuss both sides of the argument in this essay. I believe that there is a lot to gain through the study of history and it is far from useless.

On the one hand, the main reason given by those opposed to the study of history is that the past was very different from the present, and people cannot apply that knowledge to the present. For example, they say that the French Revolution and the Freedom Struggle of India have no need to be learnt because those situations will never arise again. They say that instead of digging in the past, people should focus on the present and the future.

On the other hand, there are reasons why some believe that the study of history is of value even today. Studying the past history can enable us to better understand what is going on around us. For example, the relevant knowledge of history would tell us how people progressed and reached where they are today. Secondly, history can serve us as a guide because of which people would not repeat the mistakes of yesteryears. People also get inspiration from the great men of the past through history.

I believe that the study of history is imperative for everyone, even for professionals, such as architects and accountants. They would be better in their professions if they know something about the history of architecture or that of accountancy. What is more, even if the freedom struggle and the French Revolution would not come again, this knowledge makes people realize the importance of liberty and self-governance. So, studying the past can never be a waste of time.

To sum up, studying the past history can not only deepen and widen people's knowledge, but also help them develop the power of analysis. Thus, people are able to look at what is happening at present from a historical perspective and better understanding.

Plan followed:
Intro: Discuss essay intro
Para 1: One view
Para 2: Other view
Para 3: Own view
Conclusion: Study of past history is very important

Written by: Indroop Singh

52. *Schools are spending more time in traditional subjects like history etc. They should rather spend more time in teaching skills that can help them find a job. To what extent do you agree or disagree?*

It is believed by some that job-oriented courses, such as communication skills and business courses should be given more importance than. While it is important to focus on subjects which can secure a good job in future, subjects such as history are also very important.

On the one hand, subjects such as business studies and communication skills can secure good jobs and are very important. Eventually, all students will encounter the world of business, whether they work in urban or rural areas. Then there are subjects such as the social and life sciences which can help students to become doctors, lawyers or engineers. Therefore, the importance of these subjects cannot be undermined.

However, the field of history is also important for many reasons. Firstly, history throws an insight Into how the society, technology and government worked way back then, to understand how it works now. So, it teaches how to approach the future. Secondly, by studying history one can pursue a career in a wide array of fields such as politics, journalism and law.

Finally, studying history helps students to be better citizens. For example, even though situations like the freedom struggle of India will never come back, history tells about the suffering and sacrifice which went behind the freedom and they will learn to appreciate the freedom they are enjoying today even more. Finally, students learn to understand other people. They learn about other cultures and how they affect their own.

To conclude, although subjects which can help to develop a career are important in today's scenario, it is as important for students to learn history.

Plan followed:
Intro: disagree that subjects such as history should be given lesser importance
Para 1: Importance of the study of business and communication skills
Para 2: Importance of the study of history
Para 3: More importance of history
Conclusion: Reiterate your opinion

53. *It is more important for school children to learn local history than world history. To what extent do you agree or disagree?*

It is believed by some that studying local history is more advantageous for children than studying world history. While the knowledge of local history is important, the study of world history is as important.

On the one hand, there are profound advantages of teaching local history to the students. To begin with, this information is relevant to the students' own surroundings. It touches children with their roots. The study of local history helps them become better voters and more effective members of any type of society. Secondly, local history fills the young minds with a sense of patriotism. For instance, it is through history alone that an Indian child comes to know of the various deeds performed by such patriots as Guru Gobind Singh, Rani Lakshmibai, Bhagat Singh, Gandhiji, etc. By reading their great lives and deeds, the child can easily be inspired to emulate them. A proper teaching of history can prepare the way for sober nationalism.

On the other hand, the study of world history cannot be undermined in today's era of globalization. All major civilizations of the world have common roots, which point to the basic unity of mankind. The cultures of different countries have contributed in one way or the other to the total heritage of mankind. One of the important aims of history is to point to this basic unity. History is one subject that can promote international understanding in the best possible way. It can destroy prejudices existing among nations, and it can also help develop unity among nations. Global history people understand how other cultures affect their own. It also encourages them to develop a greater appreciation for multicultural influences within their own communities as well.

To sum up, it can be reiterated that the study of history is important in toto, but local history must be taught before teaching the history of the world.

Plan followed:
Intro: Agree
Para 1: Importance of local history
Para 2: More importance
Para 3: World history importance
Conclusion

54. *Some people think that the government should invest more money in teaching science than other subjects to make progress. Do you agree or disagree?(29/12/22 CBT India)*

It is believed by some that government should spend more resources on imparting science education. While I believe that science is important, the study of arts and humanities is probably more important than ever and so these subjects should be given as much importance as is given to science.

Undoubtedly, the study of science is essential. Science is the study of the world around us. By learning science students learn all about the world that they live in, such as how things work, what living things there are, how things happen, etc. Science helps them to become less gullible. There is a lot of wrong information on the television, the Internet, and in rumours. If children learn the truth by learning science, they will not fall for all those hoaxes and superstitions.

However, studying the arts and humanities can help students become better scientists. For example, recent studies of cognitive development show that studying music at an early age can strengthen a child's later grasp of science. Secondly, people need some spark and beauty in their lives that only the study of arts can bring in. This is particularly important in an era dominated by science and technology.

Furthermore, the study of arts is needed to preserve our culture and tradition. Similarly, the study of social science helps the students to know the importance of democracy, freedom and rights and how to live in society. It develops moral and social values. It also develops the all-round personality of the students, and makes them responsible and well-informed citizens of society.

In conclusion, I reiterate my opinion that governments should not devote less funds to the arts and humanities. These areas of study augment and enhance learning in science, as well as help to preserve the richness of our culture and tradition.

Plan followed:
Intro: Disagree
Para 1: advantages of studying science
Para 2: advantages of studying arts and humanities
Para 3: More advantages
Conclusion: Reiterate opinion

55. *Some people believe that teenagers should concentrate on all school subjects. However, others believe that teenagers should focus on the subject that they are best at or that they find the most interesting. Discuss both these views and give your own opinion.*

It is believed by some that teenagers should be made to study all subjects, whereas others say that they should be given the choice of studying subjects of their interest. I intend to analyze both viewpoints in this essay. I personally believe that focusing on all school subjects is beneficial for the young minds.

On the one hand, there are many reasons why some people hold the opinion that students should be given the opportunity to choose their own classes. Firstly, the students will probably be more enthusiastic about their study and will have more motivation to learn and come to school. If students are forced to study all subjects, they can easily lose interest in education. Secondly, it reduces stress among the students as they have fewer subjects to worry about and they can find time to relax with some extracurricular activities like dance, sports, drama etc.

On the other hand, those who think that students should study a broad range of subjects, give their reasons as follows. To begin with, most subjects are related to each other in some way or the other, so it is important that students learn a little bit of all basic subjects like maths, English, science. For example, a basic knowledge of mathematics is needed to excel in computer languages. It also helps to keep the student's options open and gives them the opportunity to develop interests in subjects they thought were not interesting before.

I believe that students should study all subjects at school level. At college level, students can select the subjects of their choice and explore them further. At school level the student may not know what his real interests are. They are dependent on their parents and teachers to help them make decisions about the subjects they should choose, so giving them that option does not make sense. Moreover, skills learnt through various subjects help students gain general knowledge and have a better understanding of how the world works.

To sum up, teenagers should learn all subjects as they are not mature enough to know their real interests at school level and exposing them to different subjects makes them more knowledgeable.

Plan followed:
Intro: Disagree *Para1: Why teenagers should not be forced to study all subjects*
Para 2: Advantages of studying a range of subjects *Para 3: Own view: More advantages*
Conclusion: Reiterate opinion
Written by: Deepa Singh Makkar
Similar essay: *In some countries, secondary schools aim to provide a general education across a range of subjects. In others, children focus on a narrow range of subjects related to a particular career. Discuss both views. For today's world, which system is appropriate?*

56. *University students often focus on one subject. However, some people think that universities should encourage students to learn a range of other subjects. To what extent do you agree or disagree?*

It is believed by some that students pursuing tertiary education should study a range of subjects instead of focusing on one. While studying one subject has a few benefits, I believe that studying more than one subject is needed in today's scenario.

Admittedly, studying only one subject at university would make the student a master in that field and he would stand a better chance of getting a high-paid job in that field. As it is, students have the basic knowledge of all subjects from their secondary education, and now it is time for them to study one subject on the basis of which they want to develop their career.

However, the main advantage for students of studying a number of subjects is that is that if they do not get a job in their field, they will be able to get any job related to their other subjects. They will not suffer unemployment. Moreover, a well-rounded education is very important in today's time. For example, excellent communication skills are very important while looking for a job. For that the student needs a basic English class, and a doctor specializing in MRI scan, needs to have a good knowledge of physics, such as magnetism etcetera.

Another advantage is that learning a range of subjects can add spice to the students' studies. Students may be fed up with study when they concentrate on one subject constantly. Finally, it is well known that most of the subjects are linked to each other, to some extent. With a range of knowledge, students will definitely become more creative and innovative in the field they specialize in. Clearly, the students with all-round knowledge have an apparent advantage over those specializing in only one subject.

To conclude, I reiterate my opinion that studying a variety of subjects is beneficial to the university students. By doing so, not only can the students better themselves, but also become adaptable and flexible in the increasingly challe nging and competitive world.

Plan followed:
Intro: Agree
Para 1: advantage of studying one subject
Para 2: learning a range of subjects can add spice to the students' studies
Para 3: More advantages of a range of subjects
Conclusion: Reiterate opinion.

57. *In some countries, schools arrange work for students without any payment, so that students get experience. Do the advantages of this trend outweigh the disadvantages?*

In some parts of the world, unpaid internships are a part of education programs to get students valuable experience. While there are a few drawbacks of unpaid work, I believe its advantages are far more.

On the one hand, the main advantage of students working in companies for free, as part of their course, is that they gain valuable hands-on work experience. They get the opportunity to apply the skills learnt in the classroom to the real world and also learn soft skills like communication and time management. This gives them a competitive edge over others and helps them in securing jobs after graduation. In addition to this, internships give students an opportunity to build professional networks. A network can offer valuable advice and career guidance and connect students with other professionals in their field.

Unpaid internships also benefit the employers in several ways. It gives them an opportunity to test-drive the talent and evaluate how an individual would fare in an actual workplace. They can always hire the interns who show good progress when performing duties assigned by them. In this way employers can convert interns to full-time employees seamlessly, which reduces or eliminates any training-related costs. Also, employers can use internships as a way to introduce their brand to the up-and-coming generation. This helps them gain visibility and hire the best talent.

On the other hand, unpaid internships also have a downside. Firstly, some companies offer unpaid internships just for PR reasons and do not actually need interns. They make unpaid interns do small irrelevant jobs like copying documents, making deliveries or fetching coffee which is a waste of their time. When companies pay their interns, they are more committed to their professional development. Secondly, unpaid interns decrease employment opportunities as some employers prefer to have unpaid interns permanently than hire full time staff to cut their operational costs.

To sum up, I believe the benefits of unpaid internships to students and employers are enough to disregard their few disadvantages.

Plan followed:
Intro:
Para 1: Advantages to students
Para 2: Advantages to employers
Para 3: Disadvantages
Conclusion:

Written by: Indroop Singh

58. *Fewer and fewer people today write by hand using a pen, pencil or brush. What are the reasons? Is this a positive or negative development?*

Writing by hand using a pen, pencil or brush has come under a serious threat. This essay intends to discuss the reasons of this phenomenon. I firmly believe that this is a negative development.

The decline in handwriting is mainly because in the competitive era of today people need to be able to reach many people and edit documents quickly. Business matters require speed and clarity for reaching a wide audience. Secondly, the tablets, smartphones and laptops have come within the pocket of most individuals. Earlier these gadgets were expensive and only the upper strata of society could afford them. Finally, these gadgets have aided teaching as the teacher can see the students' work while they are actually working on the exercises. In place of the blackboard, a projector displays the image of the tablet from the teacher.

Despite the various reasons of digital writing, I believe the slow death of handwriting is a negative development. Research shows that when children learn how to write, they also learn how to express themselves. Handwriting is so much more than simply putting letters on a page; it is a key part of learning to communicate. Writing is almost as important as speaking, as a medium for communicating thought.

Moreover, handwriting is a complex skill that affects cognitive development of children. When they write, they build hand-eye coordination and practice fine motor skills. Good handwriting can lead to better grades, too. Studies show that pre-kindergarten children with fine motor skills scored higher years later in reading and math than those with poor handwriting. In short, there's a direct link between writing skills and academic success.

To conclude, the traditional methods of writing with a pen, pencil or brush are dwindling because of the ease, which technology is bringing in, but this is indubitably a negative occurrence.

Plan followed:
Intro:
Para 1: Reasons for the death of handwriting
Para 2: Why it is negative
Para 3: Why it is negative
Conclusion:

59. *Some people say that in our modern age it is unnecessary to teach children about the skills of handwriting. To what extent do you agree or disagree?*

A common opinion is that with the increasing role computers play in our society, handwriting is no longer an important skill to learn at an early age. Unfortunately, this opinion is misguided. I firmly believe that handwriting is very important even in today's time of technology. A number of arguments surround my opinion.

The main reason why handwriting is important is that it is a form of communication. When children learn how to write by hand, they also learn how to express themselves. Handwriting is so much more than simply putting letters on a page. It is a key part of learning to communicate. Writing is almost as important as speaking, as a medium for communicating thought. For this reason, writing which is difficult to decipher, can be likened to stammering speech.

Moreover, handwriting is a complex skill that affects cognitive development of children. When they write, they build hand-eye coordination and practice fine motor skills. Good handwriting can lead to better grades, too. There's also a direct link between writing skills and academic success. Studies show that elementary school children with good handwriting skills scored higher years later in reading and math than those with poor handwriting.

Furthermore, handwriting proficiency inspires confidence. Once it is mastered, children can move on to focus on the subject, rather than worry about how to form letters. Finally, handwriting aids memory. For example, if a person writes a list or a note — then loses it — he is much more likely to remember what he wrote than if he just tried to memorize it.

In summary, handwriting skills are very essential even today. Apart from being a tool of communication, it helps the brain develop, it can improve grades and confidence and also aids memory.

Plan followed:
Intro: Disagree
Para 1: Writing is a method of communication
Para2: Handwriting improves grades
Para3: Improves confidence and memory
Conclusion: reiterate opinion

60. *With the increase in the use of mobile phones and computers, fewer people are writing letters. Some people think that the traditional skill of writing letters will disappear completely. To what extent do you agree or disagree? How important do you think is letter-writing?*

It is irrefutable that in today's era of modern technology, many people struggle to produce letters and often avoid writing letters altogether. While I agree that technology has impacted the traditional skill of writing letters, I do not agree that this skill will die completely as it is still very important.

Admittedly, modern technology has reduced the need of traditional letters. Firstly e-mails are much faster and cheaper than the traditional letters. That is why these days people are much more likely to email someone than write a letter. In addition, business communications have become more informal than in the past. As a result, a less formal style of writing is more acceptable. Other forms of communication such as text messaging have reduced the need to write letters even more.

However, there are times when there is no alternative to writing a letter. Letters are generally more formal and carefully composed than emails. Letters provide a written record, so they are better in the case of official complaints or legal matters. Also, traditional letters are more suitable for occasions when they are likely to be kept and re-read by the recipient, such as letters of thanks or condolences, as these have sentimental value.

Letter writing is a very important skill to learn because the impact of the hand written message has a more lasting impression on the recipient than any other form of communication technology can offer. In addition, hand written letters are lasting memories. For example, my father has a bunch of hand written letters which his grandfather wrote to him when he was in college. He has carefully put them in a file and shows them to us as a prized possession. Even though these letters may be written on computers rather than by hand, one should still learn and practise this skill.

To sum up, there are fewer times when we need to write letters than in the past. However, I feel there are still some important occasions when a letter is the most appropriate form of communication and so the traditional letter will not die in the foreseeable future.

Plan followed:
Intro: Disagree
Para 1: Why the traditional letter writing skill is declining
Para 2: Instances where the skill of letter writing is still important
Para 3: Importance of letter writing
Conclusion:

61. *Some think that children should start school as early as possible, while others believe that they should start school at the age of seven. Discuss both views and give your own opinion.*

It is believed by some that children should begin their formal education at a very early age, whereas others opine that the age of seven years is the best for young people to commence education. This essay intends to analyse both perspectives. I believe that parents should make the choice according to the situation of the family.

On the one hand, there are many reasons given by people who advocate sending children to school at an early age. Firstly, children who begin to study at a very early age have more chances to succeed in the future. Such children get a head start in learning, which definitely gives them an advantage in their later school years. Secondly, if children remain at home till 7 years, they waste time in unproductive activities but in school they are purposefully engaged in activities that stimulate their minds.

On the other hand, the main reason given by those who say that children should begin schooling at the age of 7 is that playing and communicating with parents is very important. Childhood comes but once in life and should be spent as much as possible with parents. Also, in their early age children need more exercise, because at this age the development of their body is a very essential aspect. The stress of school and homework stifles the growth of many children. As it is, there are many years of schooling for children even if they start at seven.

I believe that if families are nuclear, and both parents are working, then it is better to start sending children to school at an early age. Otherwise, parents will have to leave the child under the care of a nanny. One parent may even have to quit their job to take care of the child. However, if at least one of the parents is able to stay home and spend time with the child then delayed schooling is the better option.

To conclude, both approaches have their own sets of merits. Parents have to see what suits them best and decide accordingly.

Plan followed:
Intro: Discuss essay intro
Para 1: why some people say that a very early age is better to start school
Para 2: Advantages of later age (7 years)
Para 3: Own opinion
Conclusion: Give opinion

62. *Some people think that teachers should be responsible for teaching students to judge what is right and wrong so that they can behave well. Others say that teachers should only teach students academic subjects. Discuss both views and give your opinion.*

Some people believe that teachers should be concerned with only academics whereas others think that teachers should also teach manners and etiquettes to children. In this essay I intend to discuss both perspectives. While teaching academic subjects is the prime duty of teachers, teaching moral values should also be taken up by the teachers.

On the one hand, those who say that teachers should only concentrate on teaching course material, argue that competition is stiff and if children lag behind in curriculum, they will never be able to catch up with their counterparts in other parts of today's global village. As it is teachers find it difficult to complete the syllabus in the given school hours. If they have to impart moral education also, it would be an added burden on them. Also, they believe that moral values should be taught early on and parents can do it before the children start going to school.

On the other hand, the main reason why some people think that teachers should impart moral values also is that parents are busy with their hectic jobs and do not get enough time to spend with their children. So, it is the teacher's responsibility to assist in developing desirable characteristics like honesty, kindness, responsibility, creativity etcetera. in children. Moreover, students always try to imitate their teacher's actions, so teachers do not need to spend extra time or effort and can impart moral education by just being good role models. For example, teachers can set a good example by being punctual to class and having all their lessons prepared.

I believe that teachers can convey many good things to parents and society through students. For example, in Nepal, where illiteracy rate is very high, teachers convey many valuable messages such as personal hygiene through students. In such areas, teachers are playing a much greater role than just being academicians. Also, earlier children used to stay in joint families and had elders to guide them right. Now, nuclear families are common and both parents working means that teachers need to become friends, philosophers and guides for their students.

In conclusion, I believe that teachers have a much bigger role than just covering the academic syllabus.

Plan followed:

Intro: Discuss essay intro
Para 1: One view – teachers should teach only academic subjects
Para 2: Other view
Para 3: Own view
Conclusion: teachers have a much bigger role than just being academicians.
Written by: Deepa Singh Makkar

63. *Some people think it is better for children to begin to learn a foreign language at primary school than at secondary school. Do you think the advantages of this trend outweigh the disadvantages?*

It is commonly believed that teaching foreign language to children in primary schools is more beneficial than at secondary school. Although there are drawbacks of starting foreign language classes so early, I believe the advantages are far more.

There are many reasons why learning a foreign language at primary school is better than learning it at secondary school. Firstly, young minds are more receptive and they easily remember and retain the knowledge during these years. In other words, just like students pick up their mother tongue with ease, they can also learn their foreign language easily if they start learning it at an early age.

Secondly, primary school goers are not afraid of making mistakes, whereas senior students often have a fear of making mistakes when they are speaking in a new language. This fear is one of the biggest barriers for a person in their efforts to speak freely. Last but not least, early years are considered the best time to learn a foreign language because there is less burden of other subjects. Children can spend more time learning the language as they are learning less new things alongside.

Admittedly, there are some negative effects of adding a foreign language to the primary school curricula. The main argument is that it may waste precious time that students can spend on understanding and building foundational knowledge about subjects like maths and science. Another drawback is that learning the mother tongue and the foreign language may make it confusing for the students and may also hamper the development of the first language too.

To sum up, although there are a few drawbacks of making children learn foreign languages from primary schools, I believe it is certainly better than starting in secondary school.

Plan followed:

Intro: Advantages are more
Para 1 – Advantages of teaching foreign language to primary school students
Para 2 – More advantages
Para 3 - Negatives of teaching a foreign language in primary school.
Conclusion: Reiterate opinion

Written by: Indroop Singh

64. *The advantages brought by the spread of English as a "global language" will outweigh the disadvantages. To what extent do you agree or disagree with this view?*

There is no doubt that more and more people across the world are speaking English and it is becoming a common language. While I agree that there would be a few drawbacks of the increasing use of English as a global language, its advantages would certainly outweigh the drawbacks.

Admittedly, the spread of the English language would not come without its problems. To begin with, many people see the spread of English as nothing but the increasing domination of the western world. It could be opposed by those who want another language to be the global language. Esperanto is a language whose supporters want it to be an international language. They say that it is an invented language and not based on any culture. They say that if governments promote the use of English as a global language, it might speed up the death of many cultures. Language and culture are interrelated and thus the death of a language is ultimately the end of the culture.

However, there would be several advantages of people resorting to English for communication across the world. First, it would be accepted by so many people who already know this language. More non-natives than natives already speak English and thus, it would be an easily accepted transition. Secondly, English is easier to learn than any other language. Unlike other languages, for example, English has only 26 alphabet, which are combined to make words and sentences. In my opinion, it is one of the few languages which can be learned by all age groups.

Finally, its spread would bring about many economic benefits as it would lead to increased trade and commerce across the world. A major hindrance to the spread of business and trade is the language barrier and universalization of English would be a major impetus to the world economy. Its transition to a global language would also be the least expensive. For example, most websites are in English, and governments across the world would save huge amounts needed to translate them. Even the automatic translators available online, work best for English.

To conclude, the transition of English into an international language would certainly result in loss of diversity, but I still consider it to be a positive development for its advantages.

Plan followed:
Intro: Agree
Para 1: Disadvantages of English as a global language
Para 2: Advantages
Para 3: More advantages
Conclusion:
Written by: Indroop Singh

65. *Some people say that it is better to teach language students in small classes, whereas others think the number of people does not matter. Discuss both sides and give your own opinion.*

Some people opine that small classes are better for language students, while others say that large classes are better for teaching languages. In this essay, I shall discuss both views. I believe that for a language class to be effective, it should neither be too big, nor too small.

On the one hand, advocates of smaller classes cite a host of benefits. First, teachers can pay more attention to fewer students. They can employ numerous innovative classroom strategies that a smaller class makes possible, and at the same time have more discipline in the classroom. This gives more time for teachers to focus on instruction than classroom management. Secondly, smaller groups can enjoy better peer interaction. This is because everybody knows everybody. Everybody knows if someone is absent or off-track, and the smaller groups help the low-performing students achieve better.

On the other hand, there are reasons why some people are in favour of bigger classes. Primarily, if class size is made smaller, many new and inexperienced teachers are put into the job, which reduces the efficiency of teaching. Therefore, with fewer, but more experienced teachers, there is more effective teaching in bigger classrooms. Moreover, students learn independence and self-motivation, because teachers do not have time for one-on-one interaction with students. Finally, students learn to work in groups, because group work becomes a necessity in large classrooms.

In my opinion, classes need to be balanced in size for students to gain the most out of them. If the class size is too small, there is not enough competition for students to work hard, and in addition students do not develop the habit of working independently without the teacher's guidance. By contrast, if the class size is too big, it is difficult to ensure speaking practice, which is an essential part of language learning.

To sum up, in deciding the class size, the key for teachers and administrators is to strike a balance between too many students and too few students.

Plan followed:
Intro: Discuss essay intro
Para 1: Advantages of smaller class size
Para 2: Advantages of bigger class size
Para 3: Own opinion
Conclusion:

Written by: Indroop Singh

66. People believe that not all school children have the natural ability to learn a new language. This means it is not right to force all school children to study a foreign language. Do you agree or disagree?

Some people believe that foreign languages should not be compulsory for all school students as all the students do not have the cognitive ability to learn a language. While forcing mentally slow children to learn foreign languages can have certain problems, I still believe that schools should teach at least one foreign language to every student.

Admittedly, there could be certain drawbacks of forcing foreign language on young children. Firstly, if they are forced, they would become stressed. This would affect their other studies as well. Second, they would not concentrate, so it would be waste of time and money. They would also slow down the learning speed of other children. Therefore, forcing children to learn foreign language can be disadvantageous.

However, there is a range of benefits of teaching foreign language to school students. To begin with, now there is a lot of competition and companies prefer candidates who are multilingual. So, learning foreign language at the young age may be difficult, but it would be very beneficial in the long run. It would also open education opportunities for these children in other countries and getting an education overseas can be beneficial for children in many ways.

Moreover, it has been seen that multilingual children perform better than monolingual children in academics. So, teaching foreign language might improve performance of these children in other subjects. Furthermore, forcing might also create some interest and these students will then put more efforts in learning the language and overcome their mental limitations.

In conclusion, I would like to reiterate that although forcing a foreign language on children might cause certain negative effects on children's learning, I still cannot support the idea that foreign language should not be taught to weak students.

Plan followed:
Intro: Although forcing a foreign language may have some drawbacks, a foreign language must be taught in schools
Para 1 - Drawbacks of teaching a foreign language
Para 2 – Benefits
Para 3 – More benefits
Conclusion: Reiterate opinion

Written by: Indroop Singh

67. *In many countries, teaching a foreign language to primary school students is essential. Do you think the advantages of teaching a foreign language to young learners outweighs the disadvantages?*

It is true that today learning a foreign language is considered a necessity in many parts of the world. While I believe that there might be some drawbacks of teaching young children a foreign language, the benefits achieved are far greater.

On the one hand, there are many benefits of learning a foreign language at an early age. Firstly, bilingualism and cognitive development go hand in hand. In other words, children who are bilingual or multilingual have better IQ than those who are monolingual. Thus, multilingual children perform better academically than monolingual children. Secondly, people who have developed the ability to think in different languages and move from one to the other become much better multi-taskers.

Finally, it is a well-known fact that language and culture are inextricably linked. Therefore, children who learn another language also become aware of another culture and their outlook of life broadens. They are more accepting of people from other cultures and they are less likely to face a culture shock when moving to another country. Besides making them broad indeed, this also improves their employability. Globalization and the increasing spread of multinational companies means that being multilingual is not just an option, but a necessity for job seekers.

On the other hand, there are also a few drawbacks of including foreign language in the primary school curriculum. The main drawback is that it wastes valuable time that students can spend on mastering the basics of subjects like maths and science. In addition, some people also feel that it makes it confusing for children to learn two language subjects at a time and due to this students find it hard to master their mother tongue as well.

To sum up, despite the drawbacks of teaching children a foreign language, I think that it is very essential for children.

Plan followed:

Intro –the pros of teaching a foreign language to young learners outweigh the cons
Para 1 – Advantages of teaching foreign language to primary school students
Para 2 – More advantages
Para 3 - Disadvantages
Conclusion: Reiterate opinion

Written by: Indroop Singh

68. *Some people think governments should spend money on measures to save languages with few speakers from dying out completely. Others think this is a waste of financial resources. Discuss both views and give your opinion.*

It is believed by some that efforts should be made to save dying languages, but others think it would be a waste of money. In the following paragraphs, I will discuss both perspectives. I believe that languages are much more than a way of speaking and their death would be an immense loss.

On the one hand, the main reason why some want to save a dying language is that language is directly related to culture and traditions. If languages die, people's ability to understand the culture and traditions of the people that spoke it, also dies. Another reason is that languages are an accumulation of knowledge. For example, with the death of a language, information about the medicinal value of plants and habits of local animals becomes lost as well.

On the other hand, the first reason for those opposed to saving a dying language is that the link between culture and language is overstated. For example, being Punjabi does not mean speaking Punjabi. Certainly, a culture can prosper and thrive without its language. Secondly, they say that there are many other important problems in the world and the money spent on saving these languages could be better spent on addressing other problems like unemployment, poverty and so on. In other words, death of a language does not impact human lives in the same way as other issues.

I believe there is an urgent need to save languages. Besides being important from a cultural standpoint and being a storehouse of knowledge, languages being shared with only a few other people is a sense of community and identity. Moreover, if the languages are preserved, there would be an option to revive them later if some group is interested, but if they are not preserved today, they would be gone forever.

To conclude, it could be said that the death of languages would leave an unfillable void and every possible effort should be made to save them.

Plan followed:
Intro:
Para 1 – One view
Para 2 – Other view
Para 3 – Own view
Conclusion: Repeat opinion

Written by: Indroop Singh

69. *Some people think that we should invent a new language for international communication. Do the benefits of this outweigh the problems?*

Some individuals propose to invent a new international language to help people from different parts of the world communicate with each other. While there are a few advantages of inventing a new language, I believe the disadvantages are far more.

Admittedly, there would be some advantages of having one international language. To begin with, trade and travel would be better because language barrier would not be there. People would understand each other better and all the misunderstandings because of communication would go. This would also result in more peaceful and tolerant societies. Also there would be no grudges in the minds of anyone as it would be an artificial language and not related to any culture.

However, there would be many disadvantages of inventing a new international language. Firstly, adopting a new common language could lead to the loss of cultural diversity. Language and culture are interrelated so using one international language could lead to the death of other languages and ultimately the end of cultures. If one language is spoken in the whole world, it would be a dreary and dismal place to live in.

Secondly, the new language may be divided into dialects, and so the whole purpose of having one language would be lost. For instance, in Punjab, a small state of India, the mother tongue Punjabi has two dialects, which are quite different from each other. So it would be unrealistic to expect one language without different dialects in the whole world. Finally, many people might not accept a new language because it would be artificial and not based on any culture. People would also have to spend time learning the grammar and the words of the new language. Therefore, promoting a new language would be difficult and require a lot of time and effort.

To sum up, although inventing a new common language has a few benefits like easy trade and travel, it is disadvantages would be too many to consider it as a tool for international communication.

Plan followed:

Intro: I personally see more disadvantages than advantages of inventing a new language.
Para 1 – Advantages of new international language
Para 2 – Disadvantages
Para 3 – More Disadvantages
Conclusion: inventing a new language for the international communication is not a good idea

Written by: Indroop Singh

70. *In order to learn a language well, we should also learn about the country as well as the cultures and lifestyles of the people who speak this language. To what extent do you agree or disagree with this opinion?*

It is believed by some that learning a foreign language thoroughly requires the knowledge of that country and the lifestyle of its people. While it is possible to learn a foreign language without such knowledge, I strongly agree that in order to learn a language 'well' one must also know the way of life and the culture of those people.

Admittedly, a language can be learnt by learning its words, grammar and sentence construction. That is why some successful language learners have never learnt about the culture and lifestyle of the native speakers. They can just compare language with their native language and learn to read and write any language. So, it is possible to learn any language without going into its social context.

However, to learn a language really well, understanding the culture and lifestyle of those people is a must. Firstly, there are dialects, nuances and idioms of a language, which can only be learnt if the culture and lifestyle of the native speakers is known. For instance, the Eskimos have 24 different words for snow like - 'aput' means snow on the ground, 'gana' means drifting snow. Snow has a greater impact on their culture than ours and so on their language. So definitely learning about their culture and lifestyle would help understand the value of these meanings.

Moreover, the main aim of learning a foreign language is to be able to communicate with the native speakers, and having no insight into their culture and lifestyle can lead to misunderstandings. For instance, if a person is conducting business meetings in another market in their native tongue, he should also know what products or services would be needed by them. Finally, learning about the country, its history, traditions, government and geography allows the learner to enrich the learning process and use this newly acquired language more confidently.

To sum up, although learning a foreign language is possible, no language can be learnt effectively without any understanding of the culture and life style of those people.

Plan followed:
Intro: Agree
Para 1 – Exceptions
Para 2 – language by visiting the place
Para 3 – language by visiting the place
Conclusion:

71. *Some languages are increasingly spoken in different countries, while the usage of others is rapidly declining. Is this a positive or a negative development?*

In today's global village there is more interaction among people of different parts of the globe than ever before. Therefore, some languages are being spoken more, and the use of a few languages is declining. While there are a few negatives of this imminent death of certain languages, I believe the positives are much more.

Admittedly, the decline in use of some languages is also something to be concerned about. It is a well-known fact that language and culture are interrelated. If languages die out, then culture also dies out. Moreover, we all enjoy life on this planet because of its diversity. If diversity decreases, then boredom sets in and the earth becomes a dull and boring place to live in.

However, the increasing use of some languages is easing communication among people. For example, English is now spoken in more than 86 countries of the world and French in around 33 countries. In fact, English has become the lingua franca in many parts of the world. Because of this people do not face difficulty when they travel from one country to the other. What is more, if people speak the same language then they also find it easy to do business with each other. Global trade is based on good communication. Businesses cannot flourish if for every small communication an interpreter is required.

Another positive effect of more people speaking a few languages is that it is helpful in getting jobs. Nowadays, multinational companies (MNC's) have opened in different parts of the world. The rich nations who own these MNC's provide jobs to millions of people worldwide. Naturally, a person who knows their language is better placed in these companies. The pay package is also better and chances to work abroad also go up. In a way the widespread use of a few languages also helps to decrease the gap between the rich and the poor.

To conclude, it could be said that, the increase in use of a few languages and the decline of others is more positive than negative. This situation is an inevitable sequel of globalization.

Plan followed:

Intro: It is both – a positive as well as a negative development
Para 1 – Disadvantages
Para 2 – Advantages of the increasing use of a few languages
Para 3 – More advantages
Conclusion: restate your opinion

72. *Because computers can translate all kinds of languages quickly and accurately, so learning foreign languages is a waste of time? Do you agree or disagree?*

It is believed that since there are machine translators now, which can translate one language to another, there is no need to learn foreign languages. While machine translation has its advantages, I completely disagree that learning foreign language is a waste of time.

Admittedly, machine translation has its advantages. Firstly, machine translators are quick and mostly available for free. We can easily look for information about any topic and even if it is available in a different language, it can be quickly translated and understood. The 'Google translate' tool is a very good example for this use. Even though there might be some sentence structure errors, we can mostly use such translators for personal use or internal use in offices. Secondly, machine translation can be done for almost any language which has been fed into the system. A human translator can only master two to three languages.

However, learning foreign languages has its own set of benefits. Firstly, human translators will still be needed because translating a language is a complex process, which involves the meaning, nuances, tone of the expression and many more such details. A human translator can gauge the underlying tone or emotion of the text, change the structure depending on the language and take care of the subtleties of the language. For instance, the meaning of one word can be changed in terms of the context it is used in. So, learning a foreign language is definitely not a waste of time.

Moreover, it has been proved by many researches that bilingualism and cognitive development go hand in hand. In other words, people who are bilingual or multilingual have better IQ than those who are monolingual. Finally, it is a well-known fact that language and culture are inextricably linked. Therefore, by learning other languages people become aware of other cultures and their outlook of life broadens.

To sum up, it can be reiterated that even though technology has revolutionized and eased our work, in areas like language translation, machines cannot surpass human ingenuity. Therefore learning foreign languages is worthwhile.

Plan followed:
Intro – Disagree.
Para 1 – advantages of machine translation
Para 2 – advantages of human translators
Para 3 – more advantages of learning foreign languages
Conclusion: reiterate opinion

73. *In some countries, fast food restaurants and supermarkets give money to schools to promote their products. Do you think this is a positive or negative development?*

In the highly competitive era of today, marketers such as restaurants and supermarkets have realized the marketing opportunity offered by schools and so are giving money to schools. While the administrators of schools can use that money to raise funds for school activities, this trend is definitely disadvantageous for school children.

Admittedly, the money such companies give for promoting their products inside the campus, helps financially-strapped schools to buy library books or improve sports facilities. Students benefit from the additional resources and facilities that schools can afford due to such funding. For example, schools can make smart classrooms and invest in multimedia resources for their students

However, the main reason why the funding provided by fast food outlets and supermarkets is negative is that adverts of fast foods and their availability within school premises develops children's taste for such foods. This can increase problems like obesity, which in turn is the root cause of many other health issues among children. As it is, children today have sedentary lifestyles, which makes it imperative that healthier food options should be made available to them. The welfare of students should be the top priority of schools and they should not fall in the bait of these companies for monetary benefits.

Secondly, such commercial intrusions within the academic environment can promote consumerism. For instance, if schools promote advertisements of any products like toys or computer games from supermarkets, children would think that they have the approval of teachers and school authorities to buy these products. Consequently, these vulnerable children pester their parents to buy those products, which can upset the family budget. This is a very vivid example of how commercialization of schools can promote materialism in children.

To sum up, despite the few benefits of monetary benefits provided to schools by fast food outlets and supermarkets, it is definitely a negative development as this may lead to unhealthy eating and a materialistic attitude in children.

Plan followed:

Intro: It is a negative development
Para 1: It promotes unhealthy eating and thus obesity
Para 2: It promotes consumerism
Para 3: View of the supporters of such practices
Conclusion: reiterate opinion

74. *Many people use distance-learning programs to study at home, but some people think that it cannot bring the benefit as much as attending college or university. To what extent do you agree or disagree?*

It is undeniable that the online learning has become very popular. While distance learning through technology has its advantages, I believe actually attending a college or university for tertiary education is more beneficial.

Admittedly, there are a few advantages of online learning. To begin with, students who for some reason cannot go to schools and colleges, benefit a lot from these online and distance-learning programs. For instance sites like Byju's and Classplus have helped thousands of students during the Corona pandemic to be in touch with studies. Secondly, the Internet is an ocean of knowledge. Students can get information about any topic on Earth from the Internet.

However, going to a university provides the opportunity of face-to-face interaction with the teachers. Classroom lectures are more educative and enlightening than mere reading of written courseware due to the direct interaction between the students and the teachers. If there are any doubts in the mind of the student, he can request that it be explained to him again. Students can also help each other through the exchange of ideas and information, after the class hours.

Secondly, students learn in a more disciplined atmosphere. This results in a more focused and systematic study. This leads to better preparation for the examinations and consequently better results. Students also gain by useful participation in other extra-curricular activities like sports, competitions, contests and the like. Another great advantage is that of campus placement opportunities. Many reputed companies approach the good universities with offers of campus placements for their students. They are thus saved from the uncertainty and hassles of a later job hunt.

To conclude, although distance education has its positives, a university education is certainly packed with much more benefits.

Plan followed:
Intro: going to a university scores over the distance-mode.
Para 1: Advantages of online mode
Para 2: Advantages of actually going to universities
Para 3: More advantages
Conclusion: reiterate opinion

In the past, lectures were used as a way of teaching large numbers of students, but now with the development of technology for education, many people think there is no justification for attending lectures. To what extent do you agree or disagree?

75. *Once children start school, teachers have more influence than parents on their intellectual and social development. To what extent do you agree or disagree?*

It is believed by some that once children get admission in school, teachers have more impact on them than even their parents. While parents have a role in the intellectual and social development of their school-going children, the role of teachers is definitely much more.

Admittedly, parents have a role in the cognitive and social development of children. To begin with, if parents keep an eye on what their children are doing at school by assisting them in their homework, children can perform better in academics. Parents who are themselves highly educated can add to the school learning of their children. Moreover, social development of children is also aided by parents as children observe and copy their parents behaviour.

However, children spend quality time with teachers. Although they spend more time with parents at home, this time is not as productive as the small amount of time spent with teachers. It is a bitter truth that parents are busy with their work most of the time and even if children are around, they hardly pay any attention to them. Teachers, on the other hand are in school for the students. All the time they are either teaching the students or guiding them in extra-curricular activities. They keep children focused on study and as a result have more intellectual impact on them.

What is more, teachers are role models for students. They are scholars in action. They not only influence intellectually but also socially. Students inadvertently follow their teachers' behaviour too. They observe how the teacher walks, talks and tackles difficult situations. At home they have parents to guide them socially, but it is seen that in nuclear families, parents hardly find time for this. Whatever social skills children learn are from TV or other activities they do at home. So definitely teachers have an edge over parents even as far as social skills are concerned.

To conclude, it can be said that once the schooling starts, teachers and parents both have influence but teachers influence children more.

Plan followed:

Intro: once children get admission in school, teachers have more impact on them than even their parents
Para 1: Parents role
Para 2: How teachers are more important than parents for social development
Para 3: How teachers are more important than parents for career counselling
Conclusion: reiterate opinion

76. Some students take one year off between finishing school and going to university, in order to travel or to work. Do you think advantages outweigh disadvantages?

A gap year is a year after high school when a student takes time to explore his or her interests, which usually entails some type of travelling or working. While there are a few downsides of a gap year, I personally believe that the benefits of 'gap year' outstrip them.

On the one hand, there are many benefits of taking a year off after finishing school. Firstly, during the gap year students can explore their interests and discover new passions. It is hard to decide on a major right out of high school. A gap year gives students time to introspect and they may find something they have never considered studying before. Secondly, they can work during the gap year and save money to finance their college education. This may help ease some burden off their parents' shoulders or reduce their college loans. It is also a great time to learn the importance of budgeting and saving.

Furthermore, a gap year is a great time to travel and explore the world. Students get to meet different people and experience different cultures. As a result their personality develops and they become more independent. Finally, gap year is a great opportunity to expand learning through volunteer activities and practical work experience. These skills are very attractive to college admission committees and future employers.

On the other hand, there are a few downsides of gap year and students should consider them before taking the decision to take the year off. Firstly, a year is a long time and a student may lose the momentum of studying and find it hard to start again. Secondly, if the gap year is not planned thoughtfully and constructively a student may lose focus and just sit around doing nothing for a year.

To sum up, although there might be a few drawbacks to a gap year, a well-planned gap year is a great time to explore college majors, travel and get some practical work experience.

Plan followed:
Intro: Discuss essay intro
Para 1: Advantages of gap year
Para 2: More advantages
Para 3: Disadvantages
Conclusion: Gap year has many advantages if planned well

77. *After completing high school and before going to college or university, some students take a year off either to work or travel. Discuss the advantages and disadvantages of both approaches. What do you think is better – travelling or working.*

Taking a gap year to travel or work is in vogue in some countries, resulting in a whole market being built around providing travel and work services to these youngsters. This essay intends to explore the pros and cons of working or travelling in this year and to find out which approach edges over the other.

On the one hand, there are several benefits and drawbacks of travelling in the gap year. Firstly, travelling broadens the mind giving young people skills they can use later on in life. For example, they learn how to be independent, manage their budget, improve their social skills, and enhance their geographical, cultural and general knowledge. The main disadvantage of travelling is that it requires a lot of funds. Some families are unable to fund their child's round-the-world trip.

On the other hand, if students choose to work, they get a taste of the working world and know what to expect when they complete their studies. This is especially helpful in cases where they are uncertain about their study choice. Work experience gives them time to introspect and decide on what they want to actually do in life. They also earn enough to partly fund their higher education. or working before embarking on further studies. However, the negative side of working is that their earning may deter them from going back to study. Also, when young people are out of a study mind frame they might have difficulties getting back to study.

Having analysed the pros and cons of both approaches, it is clear that both have their own set of pros and cons. A well-planned gap year may provide the opportunity of working while travelling. For example, they may work in local farms or local hotels. This may be a win-win situation for them because they may get the opportunity of mingling with the local people and getting know-how of their culture.

To sum up, a gap year is a good idea for the youngsters of today and the choice to travel or work is a matter of personal choice as there are advantages and disadvantages of both. If planned well, the advantages outweigh the disadvantages.

Plan followed:
Intro
Para 1: Advantages and disadvantages of travelling
Para 2: Advantages and disadvantages of working
Para 3: Own view
Conclusion:

78. *Students today can access information online, so libraries are not necessary. To what extent do you agree or disagree?*

Libraries are the repositories of never ending knowledge known as books. Some people opine that we can do away with traditional libraries because technology has given us the facility of virtual or online libraries. I believe that even though technology has reduced the need to go to the libraries, traditional libraries can never become redundant.

Admittedly, the new technologies have brought revolutionary changes in the field of Library and Information Science. The traditional libraries containing a large number of printed documents are in the process of being transformed to paperless libraries containing a large number of digitized documents. This has led to the creation of virtual libraries i.e. libraries without walls through which the user has access to information at anytime, anywhere in the world by using the modern tools of communications, such as computers and Internet.

However, the traditional libraries will always hold their place because of many reasons. Firstly, a person goes to a library not only to search and get information from books, but also to sit and study there. The ambience and the peaceful and scholarly atmosphere of the library helps one to concentrate more on one's work and study. Thus, libraries will never become unneeded. They will always be there to indicate the presence of a well-read and educated society.

Another important point is that it is very difficult to always read books from the computer monitor. Traditional books can be issued from the library and read in the comfort of one's bed. Virtual libraries can be accessed only by those who are computer literate. The access to virtual libraries can be affected by power cuts and network failures. Moreover, in a traditional library people are guided by the librarians if they need any help in searching for the book.

To conclude, it can be said that advancement should be welcome in every field but the importance of the libraries for their fundamental role cannot be put aside. Every library should have its digital segment also so that more and more people can access them.

Plan followed:
Intro: Disagree
Para 1: How technology has brought about virtual libraries
Para 2: Advantages of libraries
Para 3: Advantages of traditional books vs high tech media
Conclusion: Every library should have its digital segment also, but libraries should be there.

79. *The main purpose of public libraries is to provide books and they should not waste their limited resources and space on providing expensive hi-tech media such as computer software, videos and DVDs. To what extent do you agree or disagree with this statement?*

It is believed by some that libraries should only provide books and not other hi-tech media such as computer software, videos and DVDs. While such hi-tech media can distract students, I strongly believe that it should be there in libraries in addition to books.

Admittedly, the traditional book may lose its appeal as because of technology, books are now being converted into digital forms as e-books. Such electronic books are putting in danger the importance of the traditional libraries, which house only traditional books. Moreover, instead of using this hi-tech media positively students may use it for chatting and surfing objectionable sites.

However, there is a lot of advantages of adding hi-tech media in addition to physical books in the libraries. To begin with, libraries have to keep in stock many copies of a single book. E-books occupy less space and so their availability in addition to books seems very practical because of the shortage of space in most libraries. Secondly, a person goes to a library not only to search and get information from books but also to sit and study there. Some books, which are out of print or not available in that particular area can be accessed as e-books.

My final argument would be that with the help of computers the records of the books in the library could be maintained very efficiently. For example, most modern libraries can be maintained by just one or two librarians, whereas earlier they needed a lot of manpower. Therefore, computers and the Internet should be available in libraries.

To conclude, it can be said that advancement should be welcome in every field. Equipping libraries with high-tech media will add more crowns of success to the importance of libraries.

Plan followed:

Intro: such hi-tech media should be there in libraries
Para 1: Disadvantages of CDs and DVDs.
Para 2: Advantages of adding this media
Para 3: More advantages
Conclusion: Equipping libraries with high-tech media will add more crowns of success to the importance of libraries.

80. *Some people think that the government should establish free libraries in each town. Others believe that it is a waste of money since people can access the Internet at home to obtain information. Discuss both sides and give your own opinion.*

Some individuals opine that free libraries should be there in towns, whereas others think that it is futile to have free libraries as all the information can be accessed from the computer and the Internet. In this essay I shall analyse both perspectives. I am personally in favour of the former view.

On the one hand, there are many reasons why some people assert that it is very essential to have traditional libraries, which are free. To begin with, knowledgeable librarians can be of practical help when it comes to offering professional advice about where to find information on particular topics. Secondly, the reliability of information on the Internet is not guaranteed, as anyone can post anything on the internet. In addition, computers in libraries offer free Internet connection and other electronic resources, which all people may not have in their homes.

On the other hand, there are many reasons given by those who say that free libraries are not needed in today's era of technology. Firstly, online resources can be obtained from all over the world 24 hours a day, seven days a week, while a library's publications cannot provide up-to-the-minute information. People can read newspapers, magazines, journals and encyclopedias, no matter when or where. Furthermore, the Internet offers a complete multimedia experience such as texts, video, audio, and graphics, all at once, but such advantages often cannot be expected from town libraries.

I believe that it is imperative to have free libraries because libraries have many other roles apart from storing books. For example, libraries are places, which provide the ambience to sit and study. Such places are needed to increase the reading habits among the youth of today. Also, today children already spend a lot of time in front of screens and e-books can cause more eye strain, fatigue and headache. Finally, the elderly, who are not so tech-savvy, may not be able to access information online.

To sum up, free libraries are important and governments cannot do away with libraries just because of the online resources available today.

Plan followed:
Intro:
Para 1: Importance of Internet for getting information
Para 2: Importance of traditional libraries
Para 3: own view importance of traditional libraries.
Conclusion:

Written by: Deepa Singh Makkar

81. *Some children find some subjects such as mathematics and philosophy too difficult to learn, so some people argue that those subjects should be optional rather than compulsory. To what extent do you agree or disagree?*

It is believed by some that the study of mathematics and philosophy should be left on the choice of students and not made compulsory. While maths should be compulsory in schools even if students find it difficult, I believe philosophy can be made optional.

There are many reasons why mathematics should be a mandatory part of school curricula. Firstly, maths is the basis of all other subjects. Children need to be taught numeracy from early childhood. Secondly, the knowledge of maths makes children smarter as it teaches them to think critically. If maths is not taught, then the phobia some children have of maths will be even more pronounced when they are older.

Moreover, if maths is studied in school, then it opens doors to many interesting subjects and careers. Many good universities and colleges in Canada and USA, require the knowledge of maths till Senior Secondary level. Many high paid jobs require analytical thinking which only those children have who have a good mathematics base. Therefore, maths should be compulsory in schools. The onus is on the teachers to make it interesting for the students.

On the other hand, philosophy can be made optional because of many reasons. Firstly, school children are too immature to learn about the complexities of human relationships. They can learn such social skills from parents and teachers in an informal way by just observing them. Secondly, philosophy, as a subject, would be too boring and would only add to the burden of the students. As it is, today's children are over-burdened with tough academic subjects to make them competent enough to be a part of the global village of today. So, only those who are really interested to study philosophy should be given the option of studying it.

To conclude, it can be reiterated that maths should undoubtedly be compulsory but philosophy should be optional as maths is needed to survive today in this era of technology, whereas philosophy can be left for college or university studies.

Plan followed:
Intro: Maths should be compulsory but philosophy can be optional
Para 1: Importance of maths
Para 2: More importance
Para 3: why philosophy should be optional
Conclusion: reiterate opinion

82. *Teachers think that international student exchange would be beneficial for all teenage school students. Do you think its advantages outweigh its disadvantages?*

Student exchange schemes have become very popular in the last few years and more and more educational institutes are offering students the opportunity to study abroad as a part of their course in the home country. While I believe that there are certain drawbacks of such programs, their benefits are far more.

The main benefit of international exchange programs is that students build acceptance and understanding for a different culture. Besides this, students also get a chance to practice the foreign language with its native speakers. In the long run, students who go for such exchange programmes are able to get better employment opportunities. Employers are always on the lookout for employees with a foreign country exposure.

Another benefit is the awareness and adoption of different approaches to learning. This can help students not only in academics but also in their personal life. Above all, the most noticeable change in returned exchange students in their enhanced self-confidence and self-esteem. They become mature, as they get to confront challenges outside a familiar comfort zone. They develop life-long friendships and also build a deeper appreciation for their family.

On the other hand, the most obvious disadvantage of a student exchange program is the cultural shock that any student has to go through. Especially, if the student is not acquainted with the language of the foreign country, it would be difficult to stay there. Next, the student has to adjust or compromise with the habits of the homestay family. If there are big cultural differences, it can lead to misunderstandings and make it all the more challenging for the students.

To sum up, there might be some problems staying in a foreign country for students, but it is an opportunity that can change the students' life for the better.

Plan followed:
Intro: Advantages more than disadvantages
Para 1: Benefit
Para 2: Another benefit
Para 3: Disadvantages
Conclusion:

Written by: Indroop Singh

Similar essay: As part of education, students should spend a period of time studying and living in a different country to learn language and culture. To what extent do you agree or disagree?

83. *Students at schools and universities learn far more from lessons with teachers than from other sources (such as the Internet and television). To what extent do you agree or disagree?*

It is irrefutable that students can learn a lot nowadays from Internet and television and these have become an indispensable part of education. While the Internet and television are very good sources of knowledge, I firmly believe that teachers play a more significant role in the classroom.

Admittedly, the Internet is an ocean of knowledge. Students can get information about any topic on Earth from the Internet. The television also has a lot of educative programmes, and students, who for some reason cannot go to schools and colleges, benefit a lot from these programs. For instance sites like Byju's and Classplus have helped thousands of students during the Corona pandemic to be in touch with studies.

However, teachers can stimulate interest and can keep students focused on study, whereas a student studying by himself through Internet and TV, may get bored and stop studying. Secondly, teachers can provide a faster and simpler way to present information to the students. They can come down to the level of a student and so are definitely better than computers. In addition, teachers are role models for students. They not only teach academic subjects, but also many social skills.

Furthermore, there are many practical subjects, which students can learn better from the teacher. For example, experiments of physics and chemistry, are best learnt by the teacher guiding the student at every step. What is more, teachers give assignments and regularly check them. All this cannot be done by the Internet and TV. Also, there is no authenticity of information on the Internet. Therefore, students need the guidance of the teachers at all stages of learning.

To conclude, it can be said, that no doubt TV and the Internet are very educative these days but students definitely learn more from the teacher. I believe that no amount of technology can ever undermine the importance of the teacher.

Plan followed:

Intro: no amount of technology can ever undermine the importance of the teacher.
Para 1: Advantages of the internet and TV
Para 2: Advantages of teachers
Para 3: advantages of teachers
Conclusion: Teachers are always better
(Similar essay - The computers are widely used in education and some people think that teachers do not play an important role in the classroom. To what extent do you agree?)
(Similar) School teachers used to be the only source of information. However, some people argue that teachers are not as important as before as the increasing variety of information resources. Do you agree or disagree?
Some people think computer and Internet are important in children's study, but others think students can learn effectively in schools and with teachers. Discuss both sides and give your own opinion.

84. *Computers are increasingly used in education. In which areas do you think are computers more important and in which areas are teachers more important?*

It is irrefutable that computers have become an indispensable part of education. In this essay I will discuss the areas in which computers edge over teachers, and also those areas where teachers have more value than computers.

On the one hand, there are certain areas in which computers supersede teachers. Firstly, computers simplify the topics through the audio and visual aids. Also, they can teach students for 24 hours a day. Computers also enable students to study from any teacher around the world. Furthermore, being human beings, teachers have a limited knowledge whereas computers offer students a complete and thorough understanding of the subject which has been fed into it. Finally, computers are more important in those areas in which repetition is needed. For example, in elementary maths and elementary language learning, a computer can be programmed to provide answers to an endless number of simple questions.

Nevertheless, the role of teachers cannot be refuted. To begin with, they are the actual scholars in action. Although computers can be accessed for 24 hours a day, the 8 hours spent with a teacher is the quality time. A computer can efficiently check the answers but the corrections can only be made by a teacher. Moreover, only a teacher can lend a practical hand to a student. For example, only a doctor can teach his students on how to perform a surgery. It cannot be taught by a computer in any way. Finally, teachers help a student develop good communication skills and other social skills. The basic characters of a good human being are also inculcated by a teacher.

To summarise, both computers and teachers are specialists in their own areas of education. They should be looked on as two angels supplementing each other for the betterment of our children.

Plan followed:

Intro: both are required for the holistic development of a person. Here, I am going to discuss the roles of both.
Para 1: Role of computers
Para 2: Role of teachers
Conclusion:

85. *Some people think typical teaching of a teacher and students in the class will not exist by the year 2050. Do you agree or disagree?*

Technology is progressing at an exponential pace, and this makes it very difficult to predict what the schools and the teacher-taught relation of 2050 will be like. I agree that the trend of education in the future would be very progressive and technology driven.

There are many ways in which education in the future would be different. Firstly, because of technology learning will be able to happen anytime and anywhere and the classroom will be a place for putting the knowledge to practical use. The teachers would record content for the students to learn at their own pace and students would come to the classroom already possessing basic knowledge. In other words, the classroom will not be a place for learning new information but rather for applying the knowledge learnt to solve problems.

Secondly, teachers will become facilitators of knowledge and no longer the experts, because of the rapid and constant changes to information that can be found. For example, it is said that half of what engineering students learn in their first year is obsolete or revised by the time they graduate. The teacher will still guide students through learning, but it will be impossible for teachers to have all the knowledge.

Finally, students will also be able to make choices in how they learn the content. Learning will be based on individual interest and need. It will be student-centric, and not teacher-oriented. Education will also be more holistic and real-world oriented. For example, a lesson on Indian freedom struggle would not only be about learning history and geography but also learning about the importance of rights and appreciation of liberties the society enjoys today.

To sum up, I believe there will be vast changes in education in the next 30 years and not only would it be more technology driven but also more holistic and student oriented

---

Plan followed:

Intro: agree
Para 1: How education would be different
Para 2: Teachers will become facilitators of knowledge and no longer the only experts
Para 3: Student-centric education
Conclusion: reiterate opinion

86. *Some people think that universities should provide graduates with the knowledge and skills needed in the workplace in the future. Others think the true function of a university is to provide access to knowledge for its own sake. What do you think are the main functions of a university?*

It is believed by some that university education is only for securing high-paid and respectable jobs, whereas others believe that it serves a lot many purposes. While preparing students for the job market is one major function of university, its other functions are as important.

Admittedly, the main reason why students opt for university education is to raise their chances of getting a good job. Universities provide specialised education in fields such as medical, engineering, commerce etc. They provide library facilities, which support the curriculum. They provide laboratory facilities for science and technology related subjects. They send students to factories and industries so that they get practical experience. This job-oriented training helps them to understand the working conditions and also gives them an idea about competition in the market. They also create job opportunities for the students by arranging campus interviews.

However, universities also perform other functions, which help the students in their personal life. They organise co-curricular activities such as cultural programmes, sports, debates, fairs etc. Students gain many qualities such as self-confidence and positive attitude, which help them in their future life. Moreover, some people just go to university for gaining knowledge just out of interest for the subject. For example, a doctor may want to learn French language just for interest in the language.

Furthermore, a university is a place to know more about the world because there are students from across the globe in a university. For many, who may never travel abroad, this may be a chance of a lifetime for them to broaden their horizons and know more about the different cultures of the world. For example, in LPU (Lovely Professional University), there are 200 students from Malaysia, Korea and other parts of the world.

To conclude, universities do not simply prepare a person for employment, but also have many other functions.

Plan followed:
Intro: I shall discuss the various functions of a university.
Para 1: Universities provide professional knowledge and jobs
Para 2: Other functions
Para 3: a university is a place to know more about the world
Conclusion:

87. In some countries, students must pay their own college or university fees while in others government pays. Do the advantages of using government money for college and university fees outweigh the disadvantages?

It is true that the government bears the cost of tertiary education in some countries. Although this is advantageous for some underprivileged students, I believe the drawbacks certainly outweigh the benefits.

The main advantage of the government paying for college and university is that this creates equal opportunity for everyone and reduces the disparity between the poor and the rich. The poor are unable to afford college education because of lack of family support and concerns about debts in the future. With government paid university education, everyone can go to college and acquire a college degree without crushing debt on their shoulder. The career opportunities that come with a university education can get them out of the endless cycle of poverty.

However, the drawbacks of public funded university education are far too many. One of the main drawbacks is that the quality of education goes down. When more people go to college, the campuses get overcrowded, making the classes larger and reducing teacher attention to students. Also, the value of education comes down. Universities become full of non-serious students, just whiling away their time and the number of dropouts also increases. If students know that their parent's hard-earned money is going into their higher education or if they have monstrous student debts, they would not relax and study seriously.

Another drawback of government paying the fee is the lost opportunity cost. In other words, tertiary education is very expensive and if the government pays college fees for everyone, it is going to be left with little resources to spend on other important sectors like healthcare and infrastructure. The government can offer loans or scholarships for poor students, but completely funding higher education would come at cost of development in other areas.

In conclusion, I would like to reiterate that though government paid college education benefits the poor, the disadvantages are far too many to be ignored.

Plan followed:
Intro: Disadvantages of government paying for tertiary education are more
Para 1: Advantages of government paying the fees
Para 2: Disadvantages of government paying the fees
Para 3: Disadvantages of government paying the fees
Conclusion:

Written by: Deepa Makkar

Similar essay - Some people believe that everyone has right to university education. Therefore, government should make university education free for everyone, no matter what their financial background is. To what extent do you agree or disagree?

88. *Higher education can be funded in several ways including the following three: 1. All costs are paid by the government. 2. All costs are paid by the student. 3. All costs are paid by the student using loans from the government that must be repaid after graduation. Discuss the benefits of each option. Which is the best one?*

The rising cost of higher education is a significant issue facing governments around the world. Three ways are there to fund higher education and each has its own merits. This essay shall discuss the benefits of each method and identify the best one.

To begin with, if the government pays for higher education it would contribute to a prosperous and civilized society. It is true that human resource is of great importance to every nation. Investing in higher education, therefore, helps establish high-quality labour force with great expertise in the future. Moreover, it gives students from all walks of life the equal chance to further their education.

If the student has to cover the full fees of his tuition then naturally he would be more serious in his study. The onus of getting the full value for money spent on higher education would be on the student and this would result in better graduates, which would benefit the nation as a whole.

The third option in which all costs are paid by the student using loans from the government that must be repaid after graduation is the best one in my opinion because even the have-nots would get equal opportunity to get higher education and as the students would know they have to repay the loan after they have finished education, the universities would not be flooded with non-serious students. Such a method is being followed in Australia and is benefiting the society and the individual both.

To conclude, it can be seen that each of the above methods has its own pros but the third method in which all costs are paid by the student using loans from the government that must be repaid after graduation is the best.

Plan followed:

Intro: This essay shall discuss the benefits of each method and identify the best one.
Para 1: benefits if govt. funds higher education
Para 2: benefits if students pay for their higher education
Para 3: benefits of the third approach
Conclusion: Third approach is best

Similar essay - The government should pay the university fee for all those who want to study at the university. Do you agree or disagree?)

Similar essay - Students should pay their full university fees themselves as they benefit from having university studies and not the society as a whole. To what extent do you agree or disagree?

89. *Government spends much money for education. More money should be spent on free-time activities. To what extent do you agree or disagree?*

It is true that spending on education is top priority for many governments across the world, and in doing so they ignore the recreational activities, which are as important. While spending on education is essential, allocating some funds to recreational activities is as important.

Undoubtedly, spending on education is very important. Firstly, the basic knowledge of academic subjects such as maths, life sciences, social sciences and languages makes children well-informed citizens of tomorrow. Secondly, the competition today is very stiff, and students have to excel in academics to secure a seat in a good university or college. It is also a well-known fact that academic subjects taught at school enable students to be competent in the future work place.

However, spending on free-time activities is equally important. Such activities benefit students academically. They learn character-building lessons that they can apply to their study habits and to their lives. Activities such as athletics, music, theatre, and organizations teach students how to discipline themselves through drills, practices, or rehearsals. In addition, extracurricular activities in the arts teach students analytical skills and creative problem-solving skills since they have to think creatively to successfully perform music, act in a play, or produce a work of art.

Furthermore, life is stressful and free time activities act as stress-busters. They break the monotony of hectic day-to-day life. They also build community spirit among people as during free time people meet each other and socialize. It is the responsibility of the governments to provide stadiums, playgrounds, gyms and community centres where people can do free-time activities.

To sum up, I would like to reiterate my opinion that apart from education, spending on recreational activities is a must. These activities are as important as education for the overall development of any society.

Plan followed:
Intro: Agree
Para 1: Importance of education
Para 2: Importance of free-time activities
Para 3: Importance of free time activities
Conclusion:

90. *It is neither possible nor useful for a country to provide university education to a high proportion of young people. To what extent do you agree or disagree?*

It is believed that providing tertiary education to a vast majority of youngsters would be neither achievable nor advantageous. I also believe that providing university education to a high number of youth is quite unrealistic and can be rather counterproductive.

The main reason why I think pushing for greater university level coverage is not possible is the exorbitant university fees. Most individuals from middle class or poor backgrounds do not have required fees to afford university education on their own. The option of taking loans to fund education is also unviable, considering the increasing lack of job assuredness on completing education. Similarly, government funded education is not realistic because it would take away funds from other critical areas like healthcare and infrastructure. Furthermore, universities would not be able to handle the increased enrolments and the quality of education would certainly suffer.

In addition, having a high proportion of youth with college education can create its own set of problems. Firstly, it would further increase the mismatch between the jobs people want and the jobs available. For example, after completing tertiary education, people would consider themselves overqualified for jobs like truck driving, plumbing, carpentry etcetera or in other words, jobs where there is an actual shortage of workers today. By contrast, it would add to the competition for white collar jobs and further decrease the already low prospects of acquiring such jobs. Secondly, I believe that the importance of university education is highly overrated and this is clearly visible from the fact that a substantial number of youth are working in professions, not aligned with their college education.

To sum up, I reiterate my view that it would neither be feasible nor profitable for the government to ensure that a majority of young people have higher education.

Plan followed:
Intro: Agree
Para 1: Why not possible
Para 2: Why it would not be practical
Conclusion: Reiterate opinion

91. *The best way to remove poverty in developing countries is to provide 6 years of free education to all children so that they can read, write and use numbers. Do you agree or disagree?*

Education plays a key role in alleviating poverty. That is why, providing six years of free education to children seems to be a good solution to reduce poverty. While I believe that providing 6 years of free education to all children is a good way to eliminate poverty, it is definitely not the best way.

There are many reasons why 6 years of free education is a good way to lessen poverty. Admittedly, the basic skills of reading and writing, throws open many doors. Building a skilled workforce can lift many households out of poverty. Statistics show that if all children of low-income countries left school with basic reading and writing skills, it could eradicate 12% of the world poverty. It has been seen that the direct cost of sending a child to school, as well as the indirect cost of losing a source of labour, deters the poor from sending their children to school. Therefore, providing 6 years of free education seems a viable solution to eradicate poverty.

However, delivering six years free access to education alone is not enough, and so it cannot be considered as the best way to lessen poverty. All children need the chance to complete not only primary school, but also secondary school. For instance, in a survey in El Salvador it was seen that 5% of working adults had only primary education, compared with 47 % who had secondary education. This data clearly shows that only 6 years of primary education will not land all people into jobs.

Furthermore, if students step into the job market immediately after primary education, they will remain at the same level of earning for years and years, even if they start earning early. What is more, primary education is complete at the tender age of ten and this is far too early to think about getting to work. In contrast those who step into the job market on the basis of their academic qualifications may be late in starting their jobs, but once they do so, they are better placed than those with only primary qualifications.

To sum up, six years of free education can go a long way in eradicating poverty, but I reiterate that six years education is not the best solution, as it is not enough, and also steps need to be taken to ensure the quality of this education.

Plan followed:
Intro: Disagree
Para 1: Why 6 years free education can help to decrease poverty
Para 2: Why six years is not enough
Para 3: Other steps, which are needed
Conclusion

92. *Students from poor background such as rural areas often find it difficult to access university education, so people think universities should make it especially easy for them to study at. To what extent do you agree or disagree?*

It is undeniable that students from rural areas find it problematic to get tertiary education. Therefore, it is believed by some that universities should take a step forward and make it easy for them to get enrolled. I strongly agree with this proposition. In the following paragraphs I intend to discuss why this needs to be done and suggest ways how universities can help.

The main reason why universities should help the disadvantaged sections of the society is that this would help to bridge the gap between the rich and the poor. It is a well-known fact that higher education raises the level of people both socially and economically. The students of rural backgrounds may not be able to compete with their urban counterparts for entrance to universities. Competition is very stiff nowadays and cut-off rates for engineering, medical and commerce courses is very high.

Universities can help poor students from rural areas by giving fee waivers. It is a well-known fact that university education is very expensive and is out of the reach of many. Many students from poor backgrounds do not get tertiary education for want of money and so join some job after secondary school. This is very detrimental for their future because they remain at the same level of earning for their whole lives and so cannot progress in life. Even their future generations remain underprivileged.

Secondly, universities can introduce a rural quota which can ensure that some rural students do get into universities. Moreover, interest-free loans, which have to be returned after the completion of education, can be provided to the students. Many leading universities are already doing all that for the needy students. Universities can also provide online and distance education courses at very nominal fees to such students.

To sum up, universities should help the poor and rural students because it will reduce inequality among the people and raise the level of the nation as a whole.

Plan followed:
Intro: Agree
Para 1: Why should universities do so
Para 2: How universities can help
Para 3 : How universities can help
Conclusion:

93. *Memorization of information by frequent repetition, namely rote learning, plays a role in many education systems. To what extent do the advantages outweigh the disadvantages?*

One of the most common methods of learning in many education systems is rote learning, or learning by frequent repetition. While I believe that there are certain advantages of rote learning, its drawbacks certainly outweigh them.

The main advantage of rote learning is that it helps students to quickly recall facts. This helps the students in exams, where time is limited and depending upon concepts and understanding may make it difficult for the student to complete the exam. In addition, rote learning is the only way to learn certain facts. For example, there is no logic to irregular verbs in English and the only way to remember them is frequent repetition.

Despite these advantages, I hold the opinion that rote learning is actually harmful in the long run. Firstly, the knowledge acquired by rote is not retained for long. If a person does not repeat information learnt by rote for a few days, the whole thing may be forgotten. Secondly, information learned by rote, cannot be applied in a wide variety of new problems or concepts. For example, if students learn something by rote in math, they cannot apply it in other subjects like physics. In meaningful learning, the transferability of knowledge is high.

Another drawback of rote learning is that it does not lead to development of social skills. Students who learn through understanding of concepts are confident to discuss ideas and exchange information with others. This discussion not only increases their knowledge but also develops skills like persuasion, ability to resolve disagreements and accept different thinking. Last but least, it may result in the wrong impression or misunderstanding of a concept.

To sum up, although there are situations in which rote learning may come in handy, its drawbacks are far too many for students to rely on it.

Plan followed:
Intro: Disadvantages are more
Para1: Advantages of rote learning
Para 2: Disadvantages of rote learning
Para 3: More disadvantages
Conclusion:
Written by: Indroop Singh

94. *Nowadays education quality is very low. Some people think we should encourage our students to evaluate and criticize their teachers. Others believe that it will result in a loss of respect and discipline in the classroom. Discuss both sides and give your opinion.*

Some individuals hold the opinion that students should be allowed to assess their teachers, whereas others assert that it will lead to indiscipline in the classrooms and teachers would lose their respect. In this essay, I shall analyse both perspectives. I believe that there is a lot to gain for both teachers and students, if regular evaluations are made a part of education.

On the one hand, those who say that students should be made to rate their teachers, give their reasons as follows. To begin with, feedback makes education and teaching more student centric. In other words, students' constructive suggestions give teachers a better idea of what students' needs are, and they can then adjust their teaching to meet them. In addition, the process of writing evaluations helps the students think independently. Students should be encouraged to learn by even challenging their teachers' thinking.

On the other hand, there are many reasons why some people assert that if students assess their teachers, it would lead to chaos in the classroom. First of all, students are very young and, compared with their teachers, are less knowledgeable both in theory and practice on a subject. Therefore, they are unable to evaluate their teachers' performance in a sound way. Secondly, student assessment would lead to poor discipline in the classroom. If every student is allowed to comment on the teacher's performance, there would be chaos in the classroom.

I believe that student evaluations of teachers would be beneficial to both teachers and students. In the case of students, it helps them feel more engaged in their education. Students who feel their opinion matters are far more likely to take more interest in the educational process. Teachers are also less likely to become complacent in their work if they are evaluated regularly. Finally, receiving positive feedback can make the job more rewarding for them.

To sum up, it is definitely worthwhile for students to rate their teachers, as it would benefit both the students and the teachers.

Plan followed:
Intro: - Discuss essay template
Para 1: First view
Para 2: Second view
Para 3: Own view
Conclusion: Evaluation of teachers by students has more pros than cons
Written by: Deepa Singh

95. Some people say that schools should reward students who show the best academic results, while others believe that it is more important to reward students who show improvements. Discuss both views and give your own opinion.

People are divided on the issue of rewarding students for academic achievements. Some support the idea of rewarding pupils who are the toppers, whereas others opine that it is better to reward those who show major improvements. This essay intends to delve into both perspectives. I, however, believe in encouraging both categories of students with rewards.

Those who say that the toppers should be rewarded, give their reasons as follows. They say that the students with the best academic performance should be recognised, because rewarding them will motivate all other students to study hard and achieve the best results. Exams are like a competition, and the winners deserve to be recognized.

On the other hand, there are many reasons why some people assert that the students who have shown marked improvement in their grades should be rewarded. The mediocre students, despite spending lots of time and effort, are still incapable of competing with those having higher IQ. Therefore, it is imperative to acknowledge their effort also. The policy of rewarding them would encourage a wide range of students who persevere and make improvements in their results.

I believe that encouraging all achievers is a must. The achievement of the toppers is visible to all, and should be remunerated with reward. But, the onus is on the teachers to identify the students who show the maximum improvements and encourage them also by bringing them into the limelight. For example, if a student gets 40% marks in first semester exams, but manages to reach 60-70% in the second semester, then he should be given due recognition for his hard work. This would be a better motivation for a wider group of students.

To conclude, it is necessary to reward all achievers – the toppers, as well as the ones showing good progress in their study.

Plan followed:
Intro: Discuss essay intro
Para 1: benefits of rewarding toppers
Para 2: benefits of rewarding those who show progress
Para 3: Own view
Conclusion:

96. Some people believe that studying literature is important for individual character building while others think it is a waste of time. Discuss both points of view and provide your own opinion.

Some individuals hold the opinion that studying literature is significant for developing a person's personality, whereas others think that it is futile to study literature. In this essay I shall analyse both perspectives. I am personally in favour of the former view.

Those who say that studying literature, such as poetry and prose, is useless give their reasons as follows. Firstly, they say that studying the practical skills such as business and technical education is what is needed in today's era. Moreover, today there is cut-throat competition, and so students should not waste time on the study of literature. They should focus on subjects, which would help them earn a better livelihood today.

On the other hand, there are many reasons why some people assert that it is very essential to study literature. Firstly, literature has cultural value. Cultures are built on stories and these stories form the literature. For example, a book 'Pinjar" by Amrita Pritam, can help us understand what women faced when India was going through the freedom struggle. The second advantage of the study of literature is that it expands people's horizons. Through literature, people get to walk in the shoes of a character whose life is different than their own. Such reading allows them to understand things through a fictional world.

I believe that the study of literature is very necessary. Apart from the above-mentioned benefits, literature expands our vocabulary. The larger our vocabulary is, the easier it would be to understand other subjects also. The best way to become exposed to new words is to read. For example, any novel we read will include plenty of words we have perhaps never seen or heard before. When we see those words in context, we learn their meanings passively and do not have to work hard on learning them. We probably do not even realize we are building our vocabulary.

To sum up, the study of literature is very essential even in the practical world of today. We need to study literature to understand the world and its people better and also to develop our vocabulary.

Plan followed:
Introduction:
Para 1: Reasons of those against the study of literature
Para 2: Reasons for the study of literature
Para 3: Own view
Conclusion:

97. *Some people think it is important for children to take lessons outside classroom, for example, by visiting places such as local companies or public buildings. To what extent do you agree or disagree?*

Many individuals believe in providing more innovative learning experiences to children by taking them to local commercial establishments or public buildings where they are exposed to a great deal of practical knowledge. I agree with their perspective. This essay shall discuss, how such practices have an edge over mere classroom learning.

The major advantage of field-based learning is that it provides a more holistic and well-rounded education experience. Students are energized by the excitement and anticipation of leaving the school environment. Such outings make learning creative and students get a break from the monotonous classroom learning. It especially helps students who struggle with traditional learning. Studies show that integrating field trips in a school's academic curriculum increases test scores.

Furthermore, field trips provide students practical, hands-on experience. Students can access tools and environments that are not available in school. When students leave the classroom, they see the connection between the real-world and what is taught in school. These connections reinforce to students that what they're learning is useful beyond their time in the classroom.

Finally, field trip offers students and teachers an opportunity to get to know each other more. Relationships between teachers and students are often transformed by field trips. Some students who are quiet and overlooked in class can really come alive on field trips. Students who have a personal connection with teachers are more motivated and connected to what they are being taught.

To conclude, most children benefit greatly from such educational tours. Therefore, school authorities should arrange field trips to local businesses or public buildings in order to make education more creative and interesting.

Plan followed:
Intro: Agree
Para 1: First reason
Para 2: Second reason
Para 3: Third reason
Conclusion:
By Deepa Singh (25th May 2021)

98. *Some people believe that teaching children at home is best for a child's development, while others think that it is important for children to go to school. Discuss the advantages of both methods and give your own opinion.*

Some people believe that home-schooling is better than traditional schooling methods, whereas others believe that nothing can be better for children than actually going to school. This essay intends to explore the benefits of both approaches. Personally, I side with the latter view.

On the one hand, there are many reasons why some people favour home-schooling. Firstly, when home-schooled, the child has the undivided attention of the teacher and the lesson plans can be tailored according to the ability of the child. For example, parents can incorporate subjects that might not be included in the local school's curriculum, such as foreign language. Secondly, when a child is home-schooled, there is the guarantee of his safety. Bullying, fights and other school violence become a non-issue when the child is educated from home.

On the other hand, those who oppose home-schooling give their reasons as follows. To begin with, keeping the children out of a traditional school environment greatly inhibits their access to their peers. Learning to make friends and exist within a group are important life lessons that children could miss out on through home-schooling. Home-schooled children may be less inclined to share, may demand personal attention, or become socially awkward and anxious. Additionally, cultural and other opportunities can be provided, while home-schooling the child, these are not the same as the child would experience in a group of his or her peers.

I believe that the benefits of traditional schooling certainly makes it a better option than home-schooling. Primarily, children learn valuable social skills such as teamwork, cooperation, conflict resolution and diplomacy etcetera. Furthermore, home-schooled children are generally not provided with competitive opportunities. For instance, traditional schooling events such as team sports and spelling bees encourage the children to do their very best. These things give children something to strive for, and to uncover natural aptitudes that might go untapped in home-schooled environments.

To sum up, even though home-schooling has its merits, nothing can be better than sending the child to a traditional school.

Plan followed:
Intro: Discuss essay intro
Para 1: One view
Para 2: Other view
Para 3: Own view
Conclusion

99. *Some people think it is not necessary for adults to receive education in class. Self-study is a good way for them to study more effectively. To what extent do you agree or disagree?*

When adults choose to study, they have two options in front of them. One is to do self-study through various resources such as the Internet or libraries and the other is by enrolling in regular classes. While I agree that self-study is more convenient for adults, a more effective approach would be to do major part of the study on one's own and top it up with a few days in the classroom.

With the help of the Internet self-study can be a very useful way to learn anything nowadays. There are thousands of resources available on the Internet that can help one to traverse the ins and outs of any subject. Many sites also offer video tutorials. By utilizing the vast amounts of teaching resources as well as authentic materials, such as official online sites of some universities, one can really develop one's skills independently. Besides the Internet one can purchase textbooks or borrow books from libraries that can help in learning about any subject.

Furthermore, self-study is considered better because many adults find it difficult to return to a classroom setting after spending years in the workplace. Many adult students also struggle to find the time to pursue education alongside their obligations at work and at home. In addition, self-study requires very little finances and one can also look after family commitments.

On the other hand, there are some disadvantages of self-study. To begin with, it is difficult to remain focused on study and one can get bored or distracted very soon. The teachers in the classroom setting can keep one focused on study. Secondly, while doing self-study, there are chances that one can study incorrectly. Nonetheless, for adults self-education is much more convenient as the classroom may not be in an approachable location or the timing may not suit them.

On balance it can be concluded that, as there are many barriers to adult education such as time, money and family commitments, I agree to quite some extent that self-study is a good way for them. However, I would also like to say that the ideal approach would be to have a blend of self-study and classroom learning.

Plan followed:

Intro: I do agree that self-study is more convenient for adults; however, the most effective approach would be to do major part of the study on one's own and top it up with a few days in the classroom
Para1: how self-study is good
Para 2: More advantages of self-study
Para 2: disadvantages of self-study
Conclusion: reiterate opinion

100. *Some people believe that courses of performing arts (e.g. dance, music, drama etc.), should be funded by government. Others believe that these should be funded through other ways (e.g. businesses or student's family). Discuss both views and give your opinion.*

Some opine that government should provide financial support to talented students who intend to pursue a career in performing arts, whereas other people believe that taxpayers' money should not be wasted for this purpose, and students should look for private sponsorship from other sources. This essay intends to examine both perspectives. I, however, side with the former view.

The major reason why some people favour state funding for students of performing arts is that these courses do not have any surety of a stable career. So, the private companies and even the student's family do not wish to fund these courses. Consequently, students choose other streams. These performing arts are very important for the preservation and spread of our culture and tradition, and so to keep these performing arts alive, state funding is very essential.

On the other hand, those who are opposed to state funding contend that since it is mostly students themselves who benefit from art education, they should seek aid from other sources such as corporate funding and their own parents. For instance, like any other professionals, musicians, dancers and actors also earn large sums of money from stage shows and other public performances. They also believe that since enormous amounts of money is required to fund art education, it would become an unnecessary liability for government, as it has more important priorities to deal with.

Looking at the convincing arguments put forth by the proponents and opponents of government funding for arts courses, I believe that a middle approach could be the solution. For instance, the government could provide interest-free loans for those wishing to pursue such courses. With this approach only the serious candidates would pursue these courses. Repaying these loans would also not be difficult for the serious candidates as they would have more chances of doing well in these fields later on in life also.

To sum up, funding of performing arts courses, should be done by government, as these courses keep our culture and tradition alive, but these should be through loans which have to be repaid later. Funding of such courses should not be on businesses or families of students.

Plan followed:

Intro:

Para 1: Why government funding
Para 2: Why private funding
Para 3: Own view

Conclusion

101. *In many countries, more and more people are competing for a place to study in universities. Why does this happen? Do you think this is a positive or negative development?*

More high school students than ever are competing for seats for their tertiary education. This essay shall analyze the reasons for this phenomenon. While there are a few negatives of this situation, I believe it is on the whole a positive development.

There are many reasons why the entrance to the universities is becoming tougher. Firstly, the number of students graduating from high school is rising steadily each year. For example, in 1997 there were 2.6 million high school graduates in USA, but today, the number has grown to 3.3 million. So, more students are seeking to attend four-year colleges. Another major reason is the marketing efforts made by the universities. Colleges want to attract talented students, and they often go to great lengths to do it. This, coupled with the ease of application process through the Internet, enables more students to apply.

This is a positive development because students plan well in advance for getting into the university of their choice. They focus on doing well in school to get good grades. Secondly, more students going for higher education can never be a negative development. The universities also make efforts to better their standard so as to lure the top cream of students. More and more universities are coming up which are hiring the best faculty. For instance, in my small hometown, Lovely Professional University opened about a decade ago, and today it has about 30,000 students from across the globe.

On the negative side, this competition leads to stress among students and some can even resort to suicide. It is also true that it is hard for students to get into colleges because they only want to get into colleges that are hard to get into. As word spreads about the competition for college admission, students respond by applying to even more colleges to increase their chances of acceptance. In doing so, they end up contributing to the very problem they are trying to solve for themselves.

To sum up, there are many reasons for the increasing competition for university entrance, and despite a few disadvantages, it is advantageous for students in the long run.

Plan followed:
Intro:
Para 1: Reasons
Para 2: Positives
Para 3: Negatives
Conclusion: reiterate opinion

102. *Some people think that schools should teach students according to their academic abilities, while others believe that it is better to have students with different abilities study together. Discuss both views and give your own opinion.*

It is a matter of intense debate whether children should be segregated according to their intelligence level in schools. Some people feel that there should be separate teaching for intelligent students and weak students. However, others believe that it would be better to teach all children together. This essay intends to analyse both perspectives. I, however, side with the latter view.

Those who favour teaching intelligent students and weak students in separate sections, say that the intelligent and weak students can be taught at their pace and the sessions can be made more interesting for them. In a mixed group, many times weak students cannot cope up with the pace of studies and so come under high pressure. Furthermore, it has been seen that sometimes the more intelligent students show disruptive behaviour. They can grasp things very soon and then can be disturbing elements in the class. So, teaching them separately would be better.

On the other hand, the main reason for teaching students of all abilities together is that otherwise the weak students would develop an inferiority complex if they were separated. On the contrary, when students study in a mixed group, a sense of competition develops, and weak students are motivated to study. The intelligent students can help weak students in studies and the bond can be strengthened. This way, even weak students would not feel belittled.

In my opinion, children should not be separated, as only academic abilities are not enough to judge the intelligence of the students. A student who is not good at studies, may have some other qualities, which he may pass on to the other students. I would rather suggest what I had in my school, and that is extra coaching to weak students. It serves the purpose best as teachers save their time and energy and yet maintain the effectiveness.

To sum up, although there are merits of both approaches to teach students of different abilities, it would be better to teach them in a mixed class.

Plan followed:
Intro: Discuss essay intro
Para 1: Benefits of teaching intelligent and weak students separately.
Para 2: Advantages of teaching together.
Para 3: Own opinion
Conclusion: Children of all abilities should be taught together.

103. *It is generally believed that education is of vital importance to the development of individuals and the wellbeing of societies. What should education consist of to fulfil both these functions?*

It is indubitable that education is of great significance to the progress of people and societies. This essay intends to analyze what education must consist of so that it can uplift the societies as well as benefit individuals.

For the development of individuals, education should impart professional knowledge, thereby enabling them to become self-sufficient in adulthood and ensure a comfortable life for themselves and their families. Besides this, education should make individuals wise and informed. In other words, a well-educated person should not just be a wage-earning robot, who is only concerned about his work, but also a person who is concerned about and deeply thinks about what is happening around him or her. Finally, it must lead to the holistic development of the individual. In effect, besides imparting academic knowledge it should help in the physical, social and cognitive development of the individual.

For the development of society, education should teach moral values. There is less violence and less crime in society if people have a strong sense of what is right and wrong. For example, countries like Japan with strong focus on morals and ethics have less corruption. Moreover, these values make people adaptive to society. Because of such values, citizens become more open minded and live in harmony with each other. Last but not least, environmental education is the need of the hour. All schools should have mandatory lessons on saving the environment. Only if people are educated and aware about the importance of protecting the environment, they would take steps to protect it.

In conclusion, I would like to reiterate that a well-rounded education should not be limited to only development of the individual but also the development of society as a whole.

Plan followed:
Intro: (vital – crucial) (irrefutable)
Para 1: Academic education – jobs – vocational education
Para 2: Physical education – healthy individuals – healthy society
Para 3: Moral education
Para 4: Environmental education
Conclusion

104. *Some people think the main purpose of schools is to turn the children into good citizens and workers, rather than to benefit them as individuals. To what extent do you agree or disagree with this opinion?*

It is believed by some that the primary aim of schools is to turn children into good inhabitants and personnel rather than benefit them personally. While I agree that the purpose of education should be to make children productive members of society, I also believe that education should help children grow as individuals.

On the one hand, learning academic subjects is the main aim for what students go to schools. Definitely, the job market requires professional knowledge the most. Preparing children for employment will ensure their livelihood. If youngsters are taught subjects aimed at the job market, they will be recruited by companies or become entrepreneurs. Such citizens pay taxes and help the governments run the country. In this way they become productive members of the society.

On the other hand, schooling can help to shape the personality of children. For example, teachers are able to mould children by identifying their hidden strengths, which may later make them into what they want to be. For example, a child may want to be a singer or painter, then schools and teachers can help him, even against the wishes of parents at times. Finally, subjects taught in schools, such as moral science and physical education are meant to make the children physically and mentally strong. This makes them good and law-abiding human beings.

To conclude, the main function of schools is to make students good and responsible workers and also to make them good human beings at the same time. It would not be right if schools focus only on making students productive citizens and not put efforts for their personal growth.

Plan followed:
Intro: Balanced view
Para 1: why schools should make children productive citizens
Para 2: Why schools should also focus on the personal growth
Conclusion: Reiterate opinion.

105. *In some countries, university students live away from home and in another city while studying. Do you think the disadvantages outweigh the advantages of living in another city?*

In some parts of the world, students live away from their family or in another city while studying in universities. While there are certain disadvantages of this trend, I believe its advantages certainly outweigh them.

There are several benefits of staying near the universities. The first advantage is increased personal space and less restrictions. There is no doubt that while living with parents, students have to take permissions for decisions. In other words, students enjoy living alone because of the freedom to enjoy leisure activities. Secondly, it enables students to learn how to cope with things independently. Before enrolling in college, students mainly rely on their parents for everything, but when living alone they have to manage all the tasks like cooking, laundry and cleaning on their own.

Finally, in most situations students have to share an apartment or a dorm with other students for economic reasons. This develops useful social skills among children like how to adjust and cooperate with others, how to calmly handle disagreements and conflicts and how to share responsibilities. Such social skills are not only useful in college life but also later on while working as an employee in a company.

However, there are also a few drawbacks of living away from home. The main disadvantage is the added financial costs of housing rent and food. While living with parents, such expenses are non-existent. So, students are forced to pick up a part-time job while studying and this may leave them very less time for social activities or study after classes. Another issue is safety, as unlike their hometown, children might not know many people in the new city. They might make friends or acquaintances with people with questionable intentions.

To sum up, although there are a few drawbacks of living away from parents in a different city, I believe living away to be more beneficial.

Plan followed:

Intro: Advantages of living near the university are more
Para 1: Advantages of staying near the university
Para2: More advantages
Para 3: disadvantages of staying away from home
Conclusion: Staying near the university has more advantages

106. Money offered for postgraduate research is limited; as a consequence, some people argue that financial support from the government should only be provided for scientific research rather than research for less useful subjects. Do you agree or disagree? (Similar to 425)

Scientific research is very important for the economic and social development of any country. While I agree that government should focus on scientific research because of its limited funds, I also believe that some funds should be allocated to other subjects, such as economics, history, literature etcetera.

There are many reasons why science subjects should be publicly funded. To begin with, scientific innovations have the power to change our lives for good. Take, for instance, the invention of the vaccine for covid19. This wonder vaccine is helping to save the lives of millions of people. The computer is also the result of scientific research. This invention has changed the way people work and store information. Today, it is impossible to imagine a world without computers. Other inventions like electricity, motor vehicles and home appliances have also revolutionized our lives. Finally, there are some other areas of science, like atomic energy which need a lot of research because these areas are pivotal to a country's security.

However, I do not think that all of the government money should go towards scientific research at postgraduate level. Other subjects, for example, arts, also deserve the attention and support of the public and the government. Philosophy and literature prompt students to reflect on the significance of life and develop a positive attitude towards the world. History and geography help to broaden the horizon of students and make them wise and open-minded. Historical research also teaches people about mistakes they must not repeat. The truth is that there are still a lot of things which can be learnt from previous generations. Therefore, government should not ignore the status of other subjects in our education system.

To conclude, not only scientific research but research in other fields also provides great value. Therefore, the argument that only scientific research should receive government funding does not hold water.

Plan followed:
Intro: Disagree
Para 1: Importance of spending on scientific research
Para 2: Importance of other research
Conclusion:

107. *It has been observed that in many countries not enough students are choosing to study science subjects at university. What do you think are the causes of the problem? What are the effects on society?*

It has been seen that very few students select science streams for their tertiary education. This essay intends to delve into the reasons for this trend, and also discuss the adverse effects of this development on our societies.

There are many reasons for the young people's lack of interest in science subjects. The first reason is that in most schools the sciences curriculum is outdated and irrelevant, with little emphasis on practical education. As a result, children find science boring and do not pursue it further on leaving school. Secondly, learning science requires hard work and considerable time and many youth are not interested in devoting so much of their time and effort into it. Moreover, despite putting in more hours and effort, science graduates earn substantially less than graduates in other fields like IT, business management, economics etcetera.

In addition, it is not fashionable to pick up science as students who choose to study science are perceived as boring and nerdy. Students fear that if they choose science, they will have no social life in college and they would be social pariahs. Finally, science as a subject is dependent upon basics and foundational knowledge. However, due to the lack of well qualified primary and high school teachers, students fail to develop these rudimentary concepts and as such are not confident to pursue science as a career.

The shortage of scientists can be very detrimental for societies. To begin with, it impacts the society as employers are unable to find people with the skill they need to innovate and grow. As a result, many companies are also forced to hire people from other countries, and this negatively impacts the economy of the country. Last but not least, societies are dominated by ideas and products from science and technology, but if there is a shortage of science graduates, it may impact the development and progress of society.

To sum up, there are many reasons for students not taking up science subjects at university and this phenomenon is definitely detrimental for society.

Plan followed:
Intro:
Para 1: reasons for not opting to study science
Para 2: More reasons
Para 3: Effects on societies
Conclusion:

108. *In developing countries, rural children have less access to education. Some people say that the problem can be solved by providing schools and teachers. Others say that computers and internet should be provided. Discuss both sides and give your opinion.*

Education and technology are instruments for accelerating development in the developing countries. The issue of debate is whether new technology should be provided in developing countries, or education should be offered. I believe that a combination of education and technology has to be given.

Those in favour of providing free education say that these countries need schools and teachers before anything else. A good educational system should focus on laying the best foundation of knowledge and skills that are laid during the first years of education. It is very imperative that swift steps be taken to bridge this knowledge gap without which the economic and social disparity will widen even more rapidly. What these countries need is good education and training that can match today's times.

Supporters of technology say that if these poor countries were provided access to technology they would catch up with the rich and this would definitely bridge the gap between the rich and the poor. They also opine that it would be almost impossible for these countries to setup efficient educational systems without the availability of multimedia and information technology. Cultural development will also benefit as knowledge bases of art, culture and history can be easily created, made widely accessible and easily updated.

I believe that a combination of schools and technology are needed in the developing countries. Schools and teachers would not be able to provide quality education without technology. Good teachers may not like to go to those areas to teach, but with the help of technology their lectures could be made available to those children. However, schools and teachers would still be needed because children would not be able to assimilate that information on their own.

To conclude, the best possible thing to do would be to provide both education and technology simultaneously. Education without technology and technology without education would be futile.

Plan followed:
Intro: I believe that a combination of education and technology has to be given.
Para 1: Views of supporters of providing free education
Para 2: Views of supporters of providing technology
Para 3: Own view
Conclusion: Both together would be much better

109. *Unemployment is getting increasingly serious in many countries. Some people think students only need to get primary education, while others think secondary education is necessary. Discuss both views and opine.*

Joblessness is an issue of concern in many countries. Some people argue that if students receive 'only' primary education, the problem of unemployment could be lessened. However, others believe secondary education is necessary. Both views will be discussed in the following paragraphs. I personally am in favour of the latter view.

Those who say that only primary education should be there, feel that education has little influence on finding a job. To begin with, the competition for jobs is increasingly tough, since there are more and more job seekers. Therefore, the earlier one goes to find a position, the better for a person. Furthermore, they think people can acquire the technique through work instead of school. In other words, higher education does not provide practical technique for factories. It is unnecessary for people to receive more education than primary courses.

On the other hand, there are reasons why some people believe that only primary education is insufficient to get a good employment. Firstly, secondary education definitely enhances the chances for work. For instance, in a survey in El Salvador it was seen that 5% of working adults had only primary education, compared with 47 % who had secondary education. Moreover, receiving secondary education widens one's horizons. Some students may even set up their own business, creating a new approach to unemployment.

I believe that students should get at least secondary education before stepping into work. If students step into the job market immediately after primary education, they will remain at the same level of earning for years and years, even if they start earning early. What is more, primary education is complete at the tender age of ten and this is far too early to think about getting to work. In contrast those who step into the job market on the basis of their academic qualifications may be late in starting their jobs, but once they do so, they are better placed than those with 'only primary qualifications.

To summarise, although 'only' primary education is sufficient for a few kinds of work, I firmly believe that the value of secondary education cannot be challenged.

Plan followed:
Intro: Secondary education is a must
Para 1: Views of those who say only primary education is good enough
Para 2: Benefits of secondary education
Para 3: Own view
Conclusion: reiterate opinion

110. *Some people think that the government should decide which subjects, students should study at the university, while others think that students should be allowed to apply for the subject they prefer. Discuss the two views and give your opinion.*

It is believed by some that the government should choose the disciplines that students have to study at university, whereas others opine that the choice of subjects should be given to the students. This essay intends to analyse both perspectives. I am personally in favour of the latter view.

On the one hand, there are many reasons why some people say that the government should decide the subjects for the students. Firstly, if the government chooses the subjects it would naturally be taking into account the job sector. There would be less unemployment, as the government knows which sector has job vacancies, and would suggest only those subjects. Therefore, it would be more efficient for students to find jobs after graduating from the university. Secondly, it would help those students who find it difficult to decide what career to pursue.

On the other hand, those who say that the choice of subjects should be left on the students, give their reasons as follows. If students choose their major, then they do well in it because it would be of their interest. Moreover, there would be fewer dropouts of universities, which is common if students are forced to study what they do not like. This also instils a sense of responsibility in the students when they make a decision about their subject because they know that their whole future rests on that decision.

I believe that the subjects should not be forced on students and the choice of what to study should be left on them. However, career counselling centres should be set up by the government, which should be compulsory for the students to attend. These centres should check the aptitude of each student and advise subjects accordingly. If students are enlightened about the long-term benefits of each subject, they would make better choices of their career path.

To conclude, I believe that there are merits of both situations, but on the whole, it would be better to leave the choice to students to select their subjects as there would be less dropouts and they would excel in their field.

Plan followed:
Intro: discuss essay intro
Para 1: Advantages if the government chooses the subjects
Para 2: Advantages if students choose the subject
Para 3: Own view – students should choose subjects
Conclusion:

111. *Some people say that the best way for children to learn to read is by using online materials. Others say that printed materials should be used. Discuss both views and give your opinion.*

Some individuals hold the opinion that online materials are better for teaching the skill of reading to children, whereas others opine that printed materials should be used. This essay intends to discuss both perspectives. I believe that traditional books are better in early years of life, but after that online materials may be used.

The main reason why some people are in favour of the traditional, printed, reading materials is that reading is a good workout for the brain. Just like muscles, the brain benefits from a good workout, and reading is more demanding than watching TV or listening to the radio. Secondly, it is not good to expose children to the computer screen so early in life. So, traditional printed material is better than online material.

On the other hand, those who say that online reading materials are better to teach children the skill of reading, give their reasons as follows. Firstly, today's children are exposed to technology and they find it boring to read from books and other printed materials. In such cases, online materials prove to be very helpful. Studies have shown that, new multimedia such as electronic books and stories stimulate students' interest and help them be prolific readers.

I believe that reading habits should be instilled in children right from preschool years. At that stage printed materials are better, because they do not strain their eyes. Moreover, it is difficult for parents to keep a check on the material their children access online. Parents should also set an example. If a parent regularly picks up a book, the child will do the same. Parents should read out to children. They will get excited in stories and begin to read on their own.

To conclude, it is important to teach children how to read and in my opinion during early years (when it is the time to teach reading), printed materials prove better than online materials.

Plan followed:
Intro: Discuss essay
Para 1: Benefits of traditional reading materials
Para 2: Benefits of online reading materials
Para 3: Own view
Conclusion:

112. *Schools should stop using books for teaching children as they find them boring, and use films, TV and computer instead. To what extent do you agree or disagree with this?*

It is believed that the use of books should be replaced by computer and TV in schools, as students find books uninteresting. I definitely agree with this perspective. I believe that films, TV and computer are better educational tools, and are more engaging for the students.

There are many reasons why multimedia tools have an edge over the traditional book. To begin with, the absorption of written material is insufficient and uninteresting in today's scenario. Children need something, which can stimulate their interest and keep them engaged. The computer can stimulate and educate students better than books or speech alone ever could. Electronic search mechanisms can help students find passages instantly, which would be hard to find in a book, unless they remembered precisely where to look. Further, through such media there could be immediate exchange of ideas with other students across the globe, which could be very exciting for the students.

Furthermore, such a practice of using these computers and TV's in classrooms would ensure that students all over are receiving the same education in the same way, and this could prove very useful especially when there is lack of good teachers, such as in remote areas. For example, in remote areas, the children are taught by local teachers, who have themselves not received a very good education. So, those children can never shine and compete with children of big cities, even if they have the ability in them. This situation can be fought with, by the introduction of computer, TV and films in schools. Very few good teachers could cater to a wider network of schools in remote areas with the help of these tools. Finally, it would be good for the environment because paper would be used less.

To sum up, I reiterate my opinion by saying that it is the need of the day to familiarize students with multimedia gadgets in schools right from school days and definitely these AV aids have an edge over the printed book as far as piquing the interest of today's students is concerned.

Plan followed:
Intro: Agree
Para 1: Advantage of computers and TV over books
Para 2: More advantages of computers and TV over books
Conclusion: Reiterate opinion

113. *Some children can learn efficiently by watching TV. Therefore, they should be encouraged to watch TV both at home and at school. To what extent do you agree or disagree?*

It is believed by some that television is a very efficient teacher, so children should be motivated to watch TV both at home and at school. While TV is a good educational tool, too much exposure to it both at home and school is not advisable.

Admittedly, TV can be a powerful means of delivering information and a nice part of learning process. Being an audio-visual medium more effective result can be achieved. What is seen is retained longer in the minds of children. There are some things which can be very easily taught by visual illustrations. Even boring subjects like history can be made interesting with the help of TV.

However, if TV is to be used as an educational tool then very strict monitoring would be needed as to what children watch on TV. All those talk shows and soap operas we can see every day are a complete waste of time and can even have negative effects by distracting children from their studies. Moreover, the most of so called educational programmes like National Geographic cannot replace books and academic lectures because they tend to entertain people and do not have an aim to give deep and concentrated knowledge. It is highly unlikely that TV channel directors would abandon their profits and change talk shows to lectures and video lessons.

Furthermore, if children watch TV in school also then their interaction with the teacher would be limited. Teachers teach a lot of things apart from academics. They can come down to the level of the student and can also stimulate children to learn. What is more, children would read less when they learn everything from TV. Reading is an active activity as compared to TV which is a passive activity. So, it would be detrimental to the holistic development of children.

To conclude, although TV is a very good educational medium, it should be used within limits and whatever children learn from TV should also be carefully monitored by parents and teachers.

Plan followed:
Intro: disagree
Para 1: How TV can be beneficial
Para 2: Disadvantages of watching too much TV at home
Para 3: Disadvantages of watching too much TV at school
Conclusion: although TV is a very good educational medium, it should be used within limits and whatever children learn from TV should also be carefully monitored by parents and teachers

114. *Everyone should stay in school until they reach the age of 18. To what extent do you agree or disagree?*

In many countries, school attendance is mandatory for all children up to a specific age. In India this is 14 years, and in the UK and many other countries it is 16, although the UK government now has plans to raise the school leaving age to 18. While there may be a few disadvantages of extending the school leaving age to 18, I agree that children should be in school till the age of 18.

The most important reason for raising the school leaving age to 18 is that the age of 14-18 is the most impressionable age of a child's life. During this period of adolescence, the children undergo physical and hormonal changes, because of which they are under a lot of pressure. Therefore, lengthening compulsory schooling helps protect childhood. Providing them with space to grow for as long as possible can make them better prepared for adult life.

Secondly, more education provides the opportunity to acquire more skills and therefore more options. It has been seen many times that those with more education find it easier to find work, and that they are more likely to find that work satisfying. What is more, raising the school-leaving age is a crucial investment in society's future. Doing so increases the economic potential of the future workforce, and so will bring increased tax revenues in the long term.

Admittedly, extending the period of compulsory education requires a huge investment in teachers, books and new school buildings, which would be very expensive. Also, many families need their children to make an economic contribution to the family income, and working early can help these families to survive. Finally, just being in school does not guarantee that a student is learning. Unwilling students become disruptive and damage the education of others in their class.

To sum up, even though compulsory schooling till 18 has some drawbacks, these are nothing as compared to the vast benefits this approach would bring and the cost needed to implement would be negligible if compared to the huge economic potential of the future workforce.

Plan followed:
Intro: Agree
Para 1: advantage of this approach
Para 2: other advantages
Para 3: Opponents view
Conclusion: restate opinion

115. *Some teachers say students should be organised into groups to study. Others argue that students should be made to study alone. Tell the benefits of each study method. Which one do you think is more effective?*

Nowadays, many educationists are advocating the group study approach to make students successful learners. However, some students prefer to study alone at their own pace. Both approaches have their own advantages, and students should be encouraged to study by both methods.

There are a number of advantages of studying in a group. Firstly, it provides learners the opportunity to share their ideas among group members, so that they can broaden their knowledge in much less time than they would be able to do while studying alone. Secondly, when students study in groups, they develop social skills, like making a contribution, agreeing or disagreeing with someone and asking a person to give examples of their point. Finally, studying in groups in class prepares students for the future work life, in which they will have to work in groups.

On the other hand, there are some reasons why students should be made to study alone. To begin with, when students study alone then they have no distractions, and they can concentrate on study in a much better way. This is especially helpful in subjects like mathematics and physics. Studying alone also increases the confidence and ability to solve problems on one's own. Students become more competitive which is a necessary virtue in the competitive era of today.

I believe that teachers should mix and match both these methods depending on the subject and the situation. For boring subjects like history and philosophy, students should be organised into groups, but for subjects that need concentration, individual study should be encouraged. Both methods have their own importance and should complement each other rather than being treated as rivals.

To sum up, there can be no clear-cut demarcation in deciding whether to organise children into groups to study, or to make them study individually. Teachers should employ both methods to make learning more effective.

Plan followed:
Intro: -
Para 1: Benefits of group study
Para 2: Benefits of studying alone
Para 3: Own opinion
Conclusion:

116. *Some people think students should learn more practical courses like computer, but others think they should learn more about theoretical courses like geography and mathematics. Discuss both views and give your opinion.*

It is believed by some that students should focus on practical courses, whereas others hold the view that theoretical courses should be studied. This essay will analyze both perspectives. I believe that a combination of both practical and theoretical methods is necessary for holistic learning.

On the one hand, there are many reasons why some people say that students should do theoretical courses. Firstly, theoretical knowledge is the base of doing anything practically. Theoretical knowledge explains the 'why' factor at the back of any situation and technique of working. To be practically successful students need to have a strong and solid theoretical foundation. For example, medical theories help us combat diseases, economic theories explain inflation and unemployment, and gravity theory explains the presence of planets. Even marketing, which was once thought to be purely practical, is based on statistical data, which require the knowledge of mathematics.

On the other hand, those who advocate practical courses give their reasons as follows. To begin with, these days practical courses have more job opportunities. Practical knowledge and application skills are essential to survive in this competitive world of today. It is important to understand how things actually work. Sometimes, there are some intricate lessons, which are not easy to understand if done only theoretically, so practically demonstrating the things will be helpful for proper understanding. That's why practical training is beneficial to both the trainer and the learner.

In my opinion, both practical and theoretical subjects go hand in hand and, and each has its own significance. Theory and practical are interrelated. Especially in the professional education scenario, practical knowledge helps in the deep understanding of the concepts along with the origin and the importance of the facts learned through theoretical knowledge. Theory is the basis of all practical knowledge. For example, a person becomes a doctor in five and a half years, which has four and a half theory plus one year practical. So, for the overall development of the students, a mix of all subjects should be there.

To sum up, it can be said that both theoretical and practical subjects have their own importance. Both should be incorporated simultaneously in the school and university curricula.

Plan followed:
Intro: I shall discuss both issues.
Para 1: Advantages of studying theoretical subjects
Para 2: Advantages of studying practical subjects
Para 3: Own opinion – both go hand in hand
Conclusion: Both should be incorporated in the school and university curricula

117. *Pressure on the school and university students is increasing and students are pushed to hard work when they are young. Why is it so? Do you think it is a positive or negative development?*

It is irrefutable that the burden on school and university students is burgeoning and they have to work very hard at a young age. Many factors are responsible for this excessive stress on students. While there are a few negatives of this development, the positives are much more.

Pressure on students is increasing because of many reasons. Firstly, today we belong to a highly competitive era. Students need to get good scores to get into a good college. To add to it, higher education is very costly and students need to do part time work to fund their education. What is more, sometimes parents push children to adopt those subjects in which the child has no aptitude. This also creates tension on the mind of the students.

This is a positive development because the habit of working hard right from early years makes them realise the dignity of labour and they are better placed in life later on. Secondly, they do not indulge in any violence and crime and drugs. This is because they do not have time for such activities. Finally, if they work hard in early years they will develop a sound career and will have a happy and contented later life.

It is a negative development because it leads to stress and strain. Sometimes, students cannot strike a balance between work and leisure, which may result in boredom. Secondly, when students face failures or cannot cope with the pressures, they can have suicidal tendencies. Students also face stress if they are forced to choose a course against their wishes.

To sum up, I believe that being pushed to hard work is a positive development. However, parents and teachers need to do proper counselling and guide them properly. Aptitude of the student needs to be given consideration. Alternate career choices should be explained to both parents and children.

Plan followed:
Intro: situation has both positive and negative effects
Para 1: Why is the pressure increasing
Para 2: How it is a positive development
Para 3: How it is a negative development
Conclusion: reiterate opinion

118. *Schools offer a wide range of courses such as physical education, music, economics, philosophy, math, English, geography, physics and history. Among all these subjects, which one do you think is the most important and which one is the least important?*

Deciding which subject is the most important and which is the least important is a daunting task. Each and every subject has its own importance which cannot be underestimated but if I have to choose one I would choose physical education as the most important one and philosophy as the least important one.

Physical education is the most important for all students at school level. These classes improve students' health, now and in the future. They burn calories, and this helps them to maintain a healthy weight. The classes' regular exercise develops good habits for the present and the future. People who exercise as children are more likely to continue exercising when they're adults. This reduces the risk of heart disease, diabetes, and other serious illnesses.

Physical education also improves students' mental health. It can be difficult to sit in class all day. Students can exercise and then relax after their physical activity. This helps them to feel happier and more comfortable at school. When they have good mental health, they can do well in other subjects also. Finally, physical education classes may give the opportunity to communicate with their classmates. The students also learn how to work in teams. Teamwork is an important skill that they will use when playing sports or even at their jobs in the future.

As for the least important course, I have to say that I think philosophy is not so important after all. School children are too immature to learn about the complexities of human relationships. They can learn such social skills from parents and teachers in an informal way by just observing them. Philosophy, as a subject, would be too boring and would only add to the burden of the students. This is a subject which can be there at the higher level for those who want to study it. That is why, perhaps, in our Indian school curricula philosophy has no place.

To conclude, it can be said that, although all subjects are important, I believe that physical education is the most important and philosophy is the least important.

Plan followed:
Intro: Physical education is the most important and philosophy is the least important
Para 1: advantages of physical education – improve physical health
Para 2: advantages of physical education – improve mental health
Para 3: Why philosophy is least important
Conclusion: Reiterate

119. *Universities should accept equal numbers of male and female students in every subject. To what extent do you agree or disagree?*

It is believed by some that universities should fix equal number of seats for both genders in all subjects. In my opinion, men and women should have the same educational opportunities, but fixing a quota for the seats would not be practical.

Firstly, it would be unrealistic to have the same number of men and women in all courses. Many courses are more popular with one gender than the other, and it would not be practical to aim for equal proportions. For example, nursing course is more popular among female applicants, whereas mechanical and civil engineering are more common among the male applicants. This would lead to many seats remaining vacant and many deserving candidates would not get the course of their choice.

Secondly, universities should select the best candidates for each course according to their qualifications. In this way, both men and women would have the same opportunities, and applicants would know that they will get in a good university if they achieve good grades at school. Quota systems are not fair. A deserving male student may be left out, but a female with lower grades may get admission in the same course. Such a step would not solve discrimination against women, and may add to discrimination against men.

Finally, it could be argued that such a step could lead to unwilling students in a few courses. What sort of graduates would the society have of students who have studied half-heartedly just because of the fact that they could not get into the subject of their choice. What is more, the numbers of drop-outs would also increase and many would not complete their higher education.

In conclusion, the selection of university students should be based on merit, and it would be both impractical and unfair to change to a selection procedure based on gender.

Plan followed:
Intro: Disagree
Para 1: it would not be practical to have the same number of men and women in all courses.
Para 2: universities should select the best candidates for each course according to their qualifications
Para 3: such a step could lead to unwilling students in a few courses.
Conclusion: reiterate opinion

120. *Full time university students spend most of the time studying. They should be doing other activities too. To what extent do you agree or disagree.*

It is believed by some that students who are enrolled full time at the university should participate in a range of extra-curricular activities besides studying. While academic study is important, extracurricular activities are as important.

Firstly, participating in extracurricular activities benefits students academically. One of these reasons is that students learn character-building lessons, which they can apply to their study habits and to their lives. Activities such as athletics, music, and theatre teach students how to discipline themselves through drills, practices, or rehearsals. What is more, by participating and persevering in any of these activities, the students gain a sense of self-respect, self-esteem, and self-confidence.

Through extracurricular activities, students learn life skills such as time management that benefit them a lot. These activities take time out of the students' schedules, therefore the students must plan their time wisely and efficiently to complete the assigned tasks. In addition to organizational skills, extracurricular activities in the arts teach students analytical skills and creative problem-solving skills, since they have to think creatively to successfully perform music, act in a play, or produce a work of art.

Furthermore, education is not solely learned by reading the textbook, for students can learn an incredible amount from their peers through extracurricular activities. Students learn how to compromise and work in a group. Extracurricular activities also allow students to meet and interact with peers that may not be within their close group of friends. In addition, extracurricular activities help to enhance these social skills and teach lessons not learned in a classroom. Finally, it is well known that nowadays, even recruiters look for social skills in addition to academic qualifications while looking for employees.

To sum up, I would like to reiterate my opinion that students at university should not just be engrossed in their books, but also do many other activities because these help students to receive better grades by teaching them character building lessons, teaching them lifelong skills, and helping students develop social skills.

Plan followed:
Intro: Agree
Para 1: participating in extracurricular activities benefit students academically
Para 2:
Para 3:
Conclusion: Reiterate opinion

121. *Many people who leave school hold a negative attitude towards learning. Why does this happen? How to solve the problem?*

It is a harsh reality of today that many students are not satisfied with their education at school and have a negative attitude when they leave or drop out of school. In this essay, I shall discuss some reasons for this phenomenon, and suggest some solutions to mitigate the problem.

The first and foremost reason is that students see examples of their seniors around them, who are still struggling to find jobs, and even those who have found jobs are being underpaid and exploited. So, they presume that even after graduating from school they may not get a suitable job. They cannot see any benefit of studying and getting some degree. So, their negative attitude to learning is well justified.

Another reason for the students' negative attitude towards learning, is that their course of study is forced upon them by their parents, and their aptitude is not taken into consideration. For example, if a student wants to make his career in the field of music, but is forced to study commerce, he can never feel positive about his studies. Finally, the teacher-taught relation is very strained these days. Education has become a business and the student is the customer. To earn more, teachers deliberately do not teach well in school, so that students join them for private tuition after school hours.

There could be many ways to address this situation. To begin with, education should be made more job relevant. For example, having more vocational courses can definitely bridge the employability gap. In addition, while selecting courses, parents should take the aptitude of their children into consideration and not force their choice on them. This would not only make children more passionate about their studies but also help them in securing jobs that they enjoy. Finally, the pay scale of the teachers should be so lucrative, that the best people want to enter this profession.

To conclude, there is no doubt that most students hold a negative attitude towards learning, but the problem can be addressed in many ways.

Plan followed:
Intro:
Para1: Not sure of getting a suitable job
Para 2: Their aptitude was not taken into consideration. Teacher-taught relation is very strained
Para 3: Solutions
Conclusion:

122. *The subjects and lesson contents are decided by the authorities such as the government. Some people argue that teachers should make the choice. Do you agree or disagree?*

In almost all parts of the world, there is a national curriculum decided by the government, which is followed in all schools. Some people, however, feel that teachers should decide the school curriculum. I disagree with the statement. While teachers should have some say in the national curriculum, I believe that the final decision should be of the administrators.

The main advantage of the government deciding the subjects and lesson contents is that a national curriculum standardizes what is taught across the country. Later on, while applying to different universities and colleges it would give equal opportunity to all. It would also give the opportunity to the authorities to compare and rate the schools. This would also make it easier for the authorities to provide quality education in the whole country.

Secondly, a national curriculum is decided after a lot of research. The government knows better what subjects and skills are needed in the society. It should be the one to decide what all choices to be given to the students as to their main subjects and optional subjects and how much syllabus should be covered per school year. Its goal is to ensure vocational and economic success for the individual and the nation. It is also less expensive to implement across the country. The teacher's job is only to deliver good teaching.

There are reasons why teachers should be given some say in deciding the school syllabus. Firstly, only the teachers can look into individual aptitudes and interests. Sometimes the authorities do not realise how much can be taught in a year. Only the teachers can do that well. However, leaving the whole choice of subjects and lesson contents on the teachers would bring a lot of confusion and inconsistency. Students would be taught different things in different schools, and therefore many students would not receive a well-rounded education.

To sum up, it can be said that a national curriculum should be there, and it should not be left on the teachers to decide the subjects and lesson contents.

Plan followed:

Intro: Disagree

Para1: Why national core curriculum should be there

Para 2: second view

Para 3: Reasons in favour of teacher, with refutation.

Conclusion:

123. *Nowadays sending children to boarding school (either in other countries or in one's own country) is becoming increasingly popular. Why is it? Is it a positive or a negative development?*

Nowadays, boarding schools are becoming very popular. This essay shall probe into the causes of this phenomenon. I believe that boarding schools have equal advantages and disadvantages, so it depends on the need of the parents to decide whether to send their child to one.

People send their children to boarding schools for a number of reasons. Firstly, some parents who work overseas or travel frequently choose boarding school, because they know they will be inconsistent in parenting or in providing for the needs of their children. Secondly, some parents choose boarding school for their children as a way for them to experience more of the world, as children from diverse areas study there. Still other parents put their children and teens in boarding school if they are having trouble disciplining their children or keeping them out of trouble.

There are many advantages of boarding schools. After all, these schools are not just about studies - they also give a child time and exposure to a lot of other things like sports and art. The after-study hours are also well-planned and it is made sure that holistic development of children takes place. Also, children in such schools are more likely to have stronger bonds with their friends, since they spend a lot of time together.

On the other hand, there are drawbacks such as homesickness. Some children cannot adjust separation from their family and become withdrawn. As a result, many parents, who place their children in boarding schools, fail to develop a close bond with their children. Moreover, children in residential schools may face bullying from other children studying there and so may suffer psychologically.

To sum up, it can be said that we cannot say whether the trend is positive or negative. It depends on an analysis of the child's needs and the circumstances of the family. Also, it is generally advisable not to send a very young child to boarding school.

Plan followed:
Intro: This essay shall probe into the causes of this phenomenon and also discuss whether this trend is good or bad.
Para1: Reasons
Para 2: The positives
Para 3: The negatives
Conclusion: It depends on an analysis of the child's needs and the circumstances of the family.

124. *Some people think secondary school students should study international news as one of their subjects. Other people say this is a waste of valuable school time. Discuss both views and give your opinion.*

It is believed by some that international news should be added as a subject in secondary schools, whereas others are opposed to it. In this essay I shall discuss both views. I personally am in favour of the latter view.

Those in favour of having international news as a subject, give their reasons as follows. Firstly, from the news of any part of the world, students would become aware of the social, political and environmental problems faced by other countries. This could motivate them to do something for their own country, if they are lagging behind or even help the other nations by volunteering to help. For instance, when Tsunami struck Japan voluntary workers from all parts of the world reached out to help. Moreover, the significance of opening international news subject is that students can have a general view of the world, which could help them decide their career.

On the other hand, there are many reasons why some people oppose adding international news as a subject. To begin with, secondary school students face stiff competition nowadays, so it would be unfair to add the burden of another subject. Moreover, 'international news' would have an ever-changing syllabus and so would be practically impossible to introduce as a subject. Finally, in the pluralistic society of today, some news may hurt the sentiments of any particular sect of people and could give rise to conflicts.

In my opinion, international news should not be introduced as a subject. However, steps should be taken by secondary schools to keep students abreast of what is happening in the world by having a short (5 minute) session in the morning assembly in which every day a student could speak the headlines. This would keep students up-to-date without having the tension of memorizing things.

To conclude, it could be said that international news should not be a subject, but students should be made aware of the international scenario in other informal ways.

Plan followed:
Intro: Discuss essay intro
Para1: advantages of studying international news
Para 2: disadvantages of international news as a subject
Para 3: Own view – international news should not be a subject but a 5-minute news break in morning assembly can be there which would keep students abreast of the latest happenings of the world
Conclusion: Subject of international news should not be there

125. *In schools and universities, girls tend to choose arts subjects, while boys choose science subjects. What is the reason? Should the trend be changed?*

It is generally seen that in secondary and tertiary educational institutes, girls opt for arts subjects whereas boys take up science subjects. This essay intends to look into the reasons for this phenomenon. I agree that this situation needs to be addressed and more women should choose science fields.

There are many reasons why girls choose arts and boys choose science subjects. Firstly, right from early childhood, traditional society ingrains into girls that they are meant to become good housewives and mothers. So, instead of science subjects, they are encouraged to study arts subjects such as home sciences and social studies which would later on help them in running the home. On top of that, even teachers at schools do not dispel this stereotypical thinking and motivate girls to pursue arts instead.

Another factor that discourages girls from pursuing science is that science jobs require a lot of hard work especially at the early stage of the career. Women are not able to spend long hours for work due to family issues or small children at home. Finally, women are not as aggressive or competitive as men and careers in science are more challenging. For example, at the academic level, science professors are at constant pressure of publishing papers to have a successful career.

I believe that this trend should be changed as this would be beneficial for society and women. Firstly, having women in technology spurs innovation and creativity as women can bring in a different perspective and solve problems differently than men. So, countries will do better if there are more women in the industries that drive science and technology. Secondly, this would change traditional thinking, improve the social status of women and thus lead to women empowerment.

To sum up, there are many reasons for the gender biased choice of subjects in schools and universities, but this needs to be changed for the betterment of women and society.

Plan followed:
Intro:
Para 1: Why girls choose arts and boys choose science subjects
Para 2: More reasons
Para 3: this trend should be changed.
Conclusion:

126. *Some people think that students benefit from going to private secondary schools. Others, however, feel that private secondary schools can have a negative effect on society as a whole. Discuss both these views and give your own opinion.*

It is believed by some that studying in private secondary schools is better for students, whereas others think that these schools are detrimental for the society. In this essay I shall analyse both perspectives. I am personally in favour of the latter view.

On the one hand, those who say that studying in private secondary schools is beneficial for students, give their reasons as follows. Firstly, most private schools offer smaller classroom size, and so the child can receive more individual attention from teachers. Secondly, private secondary schools offer better academic and extracurricular programs. As a result, there are lower dropout rates. Finally, there is less on-campus violence in private schools as compared to government schools.

On the other hand, there are many reasons why some people assert that these private schools do more harm than good. To begin with, there is less diversity in private schools as compared to public or government schools. Only children from the higher socio-economic background get into such schools. As a result, children will meet fewer peers from diverse backgrounds. Another negative of private secondary schools is that these do not conform strictly to educational regulations. For instance, they may not follow the national core curriculum and add or delete subjects according to their will. So, parent have to do a lot of effort to select the right private school for their child.

I believe that private secondary schools create an imbalance in society. Only the children from affluent backgrounds can afford these schools. The disadvantaged children of poor backgrounds find it very difficult to study in these schools. So, they cannot compete with children who have studied in these schools when they apply for university education. So, such schools increase the gap between the rich and the poor.

Summing up, private secondary schools provide quality education and have a few advantages. However, their disadvantages to the society are far more.

Plan followed:

Intro: Discuss essay intro
Para 1: Why some people say these schools have more advantages
Para 2: Why some people say that the disadvantages of these schools are more
Para 3: Own view
Conclusion: Secondary schools are good, but their negatives cannot be ignored.

127. *More and more students choose to go to another country for their higher education. Do you think the benefits outweigh the problems associated with it?*

There is no doubt getting a higher education degree in another country is becoming more and more common nowadays. While overseas study has its drawbacks, the difficulties are far outweighed by the advantages.

The first advantage of studying overseas is that many employers consider overseas experience a positive and enriching attribute for any employee. They believe that a person who has qualified from a reputed college or university in a developed country is capable of working in a diverse work space, and has the ability to adapt to change. Thus, students with an overseas education have better employability. Secondly, students get a chance to learn about other cultures. This makes them more broad-minded and more accepting of people from different backgrounds.

In addition, students get a chance to practice and learn a foreign language. Learning a new language is always challenging but being able to practice with native speakers is the best way to become comfortable with it. Finally, being alone in a foreign country makes a student independent and self-reliant in terms of solving issues and making important decisions. Not only that, they learn how to manage most household chores themselves. For example in a foreign country, they have to manage all the tasks like cooking, laundry and cleaning on their own.

On the other hand, there are some challenges faced by students going abroad for higher education. The most difficult situation can be the culture shock a student has to face. The environment may be completely different, which may lead to homesickness and loneliness. Apart from this, overseas education is expensive and students face difficulties due to it. For example, some students take considerable educational loans for such opportunities and there is added stress of paying back such loans after completing education.

In conclusion, while any anxiety about going overseas for university study is certainly understandable, I believe that the benefits offered by the experience make it well worthwhile.

Plan followed:
Intro: while overseas study has its drawbacks, the difficulties are far outweighed by the advantages
Para1: Advantages
Para 2: More advantages
Para 3: Drawbacks
Conclusion: benefits offered by the experience make it well worthwhile

128. *Children find it difficult to concentrate on or pay attention to school. What are the reasons? How can we solve this problem?*

It is very common for children to have trouble staying focused in class. This essay intends to analyze the reasons for this situation and suggest some solutions to ameliorate the problem.

The main reason why children struggle with focus and concentration in school is sleep deprivation. Children who do not get the recommended 8-10 hours of sleep each night are exhausted during the day and do not have the energy to concentrate on schoolwork. In addition, many students lose focus because of long class hours and limited breaks in between classes. Because of this, children feel overwhelmed and their performance suffers as their brain does not get time to relax and revitalize itself.

Furthermore, a disorganized notebook or desk can be a cause of distractions for many students. Children may be spending more time searching for the tools and material needed to learn rather than paying attention to what is being taught in class. Noise and activity from other classmates can also distract them. Finally, a teacher's teaching style may be traditional, outdated and boring and thus may not be engaging enough for the students.

There are some solutions that can help with children's focus issues and increase their attention span. First of all, parents need to make sure that their children stick to a nightly routine and sleep on time. A good sleep gives a child's mind a chance to absorb everything from the day and recharge for tomorrow. Secondly, children focus better if they are given brief breaks for physical activity in between classes. For example, including some outdoor play times, or providing a quick stretching or jumping jacks break in the classroom, can all help children stay focused. Last but not least, if teachers are enthusiastic and make lessons fun and interesting, students are more likely to stay engaged.

To sum up, the concentration issues children have in school are caused by a number of different reasons, but this situation can be dealt with by the combined efforts of parents and teachers.

Plan followed:
Intro:
Para 1: Reasons for lack of attention
Para 2: Reasons for lack of attention
Para 3: Solutions
Conclusion:

129. *In many countries, sport and exercise classes are replaced with academic subjects. Why is it so? What are the effects on the children in their lives?*

It is irrefutable that academic subjects are crucial in today's era of cut-throat competition. Although there are reasons why more and more schools are axing sports and physical exercise classes for academics, I believe that this trend has a detrimental effect on children.

There are many reasons why educational institutes are replacing sports and exercise classes with academic classes. Firstly, the competition today is very stiff, and students have to excel in academics to secure a seat in a good university or college. So, parents also force schools to focus more on academic subjects so that their children have a good future. The second reason why schools are focusing more on academic subjects is that they are under pressure to show better academic results to get more government funding and more student enrolment.

However, the increased focus on academics and the neglect of sports and physical education has severe consequences for children. The major adverse effect is on the physical and mental health of children. Children who do not engage in physical activity are physically unfit and are more prone to diseases like obesity and diabetes later on in life. Moreover, due to excessive academic pressure and lack of participation in sports, children are stressed and their academic performance also suffers.

Finally, a major benefit of sports is that students learn skills like teamwork, co-operation, discipline, sportsman spirit, punctuality etc. These skills have become the need of the hour, with the ever-growing competition in every field. By replacing sports and physical education classes with academics, schools are depriving children from developing such skills. This in turn reduces the children's ability to work and coordinate well with others during adulthood.

In conclusion, although it is important for a child to succeed academically, the chances of success are increased with a balanced approach that includes sports and physical education.

Plan followed:
Intro:
Para 1: reasons for schools replacing sports with academics
Para 2: negative consequences of replacing sports with academics
Para 3: negative consequences of replacing sports with academics
Conclusion: Reiterate opinion

130. *We have three important parts of education: reading, writing and math. Some people think every child will benefit from a fourth skill added to the list: computer skills. Do you agree or disagree?*

Some people propose that computer skills should be regarded as an additional part of education. While I do agree that computer skills are indispensable in today's times, I do not agree that these should be added as a subject.

Undoubtedly, computers play an important role in our life. They have become an indispensable part of our lives. In workplaces and even in the homes, they have made their presence felt. Computers, topped with the internet have brought many new opportunities in the lives of people. That is perhaps why some people opine that computer skills should be added in the school curricula.

However, important as computer skills may be in today's world, I do not think it necessarily means computer skills should be taught to every child in the school. Most school children today are under heavy academic pressure and so, adding computer skills to their curriculum surely means an extra burden to them. Besides, it has to be noted that today's computer technologies are ever-changing. Software is frequently updated. This means that the computer skills students learn today will probably become obsolete in a few months.

Finally, the development of technologies has made most of today's computers user-friendly. Therefore, even a person who is totally computer illiterate can learn the minimum basics in a few hours and the rest is all practice. For example, many young children can proficiently use an I-pad to read or write. So, to those children who can already operate a computer well, it is obvious that there is no need to teach them a skill they are already good at.

To conclude, while it has to be admitted that computer skills are crucial today, the nature of computer technologies (ever-changing, user-friendly) has made computer skills an unnecessary skill for school children to learn. For this reason, I disagree with the opinion that computer skills should be added to the school curriculum.

Plan followed:

Intro:
Para 1: Advantages of computer skills
Para 2: It would add to pressure on students
Para 3: Computer technologies are ever changing
Para 4: Children are born into homes where technology is being used, so they already know
Conclusion:

131. *Some people think that schools should concentrate on academic classes, because they are helpful for future career, and they think music and sports classes are not useful. To what extent do you agree or disagree?*

It is believed by some that educational institutes should focus only on academic classes and ignore music and sports classes as they do not aid in career building. I believe that while academic subjects are important, music and sports are as necessary. So, there should be all these subjects at school level for the holistic development of children.

Undoubtedly, academic subjects are very important. Firstly, the basic knowledge of academic subjects such as maths, life sciences, social sciences and languages makes children well-informed citizens of tomorrow. Secondly, the competition today is very stiff, and students have to excel in academics to secure a seat in a good university or college. It is also a well-known fact that academic subjects taught at school enable students to be competent in the future work place.

However, there are many advantages of non-academic subjects. To begin with, non-academic subjects break the monotony of tough academic studies. Participating in sports keeps children physically fit. We all know that a healthy mind resides in a healthy body. Subjects such as music also have proved to be helpful in improving the IQ of children. Therefore, the importance of these subjects cannot be undermined.

Moreover, a mix of academic and non-academic subjects in schools is needed for the holistic development of children. In traditional curriculum there is a wide variety of subjects. There are academic and non-academic subjects. In this way a young person is formed with a rounded education. Non-academic subjects include sports, cooking, and music. I believe this is the best form of education. A young person should learn things other than academic subjects.

To sum up, I reiterate my opinion by saying that non-academic subjects are as important as academic subjects in today's syllabuses.

Plan followed:

Intro: non-academic subjects are also very important for the holistic development of the children
Para 1: advantage of studying academic subjects – holistic development of children
Para 2: advantages of non-academic subjects – good for health and for breaking monotony
Para 3: advantages of mix of non-academic subjects and academic subjects
Conclusion: non-academic subjects are important inclusions in today's syllabuses

132. *Some people believe that reading stories from a book is better than watching TV or playing computer games for children. To what extent do you agree or disagree?*

It is believed by some that reading stories from books is a better leisure activity than watching TV and playing computer games. Although watching TV and playing computer games benefit children in many ways, I also agree that reading books offers more advantages.

Admittedly, there are many advantages to watching TV and playing PC games. The biggest advantage of playing electronic games is that they improve and quicken decision making. In many such games, players have to keep track of a large pool of information and make split-second decisions and this in turn enhances decision making in real life as well. Besides this, electronic games also improve hand-eye coordination. Similarly, watching TV can help to learn about other cultures and help relieve stress of studies.

However, reading is more effective because it provides active learning, while playing video games and watching TV are passive. In other words, reading books enhances children's imagination. For example, children make different images in their mind when they read some articles or sentences and then use their imagination to put the story together. By contrast, the TV audience just passively accepts information from the TV screen.

Furthermore, reading stories also helps children master language development, as by reading stories, children learn pronunciation and vocabulary. Although children also develop language and vocabulary through TV, the language used in movies and TV shows is much more basic. Finally, TV and video games actually reduce focus and concentration as there are constantly changing camera angles, short scenes and breaks. Books, on the other hand, increase focus as they engage and hold on to the reader's concentration.

In conclusion, it can be reiterated that reading stories in books is better, and more time should be allotted to reading than to watching TV and playing on computers.

Plan followed:
Intro: Agree
Para 1: Advantages of reading
Para 2: More advantages
Para 3: Advantages of computer games and TV with reasons why they are not better than reading
Conclusion:

133. *Environmental problems are too big for individual countries and individual persons to address. In other words, we have reached the stage where the only way to protect the environment is at an international level. Do you agree or disagree with this opinion?*

Environmental degradation has become an issue of grave concern. While I believe that big steps to save the environment are needed to be taken at the global level, I disagree that no steps can be taken at the national and individual level.

There are many reasons why steps need to be taken at the international level to save the environment. Firstly, pollution caused by one country can affect many others. For instance, the whole Pacific Ocean has now been polluted with mercury due to release of industrial wastewater into the Pacific Ocean by Japan's industries. Similarly, the ozone hole is the biggest over the Antarctica, nowhere near the industrialized nations of US or Europe, which were the main polluters in the 20th century. Therefore, global intervention is needed to ameliorate these issues.

However, it would be wrong to say that nothing can be done at the individual country's level. To begin with, countries have to make rules and laws at national level to be followed by people. In addition, countries can take the lead and take steps, which show the way for other countries to follow. To exemplify, many countries are now copying the Israel's desalination water model. Here a single country's efforts have resulted in a global solution to fresh-water concerns.

Similarly, small measures taken at the individual level will take mammoth dimensions when mounted up. For example, if 9 billion people of the world plant a tree each, say no to plastics and start using public transport more, it would have gigantic results. People can take simple steps like recycling things such as newspapers, plastics and glass. They could also walk for short distances instead of using their vehicles and for long distances they could use the public transport. Thus, individual participation is actually critical to the success of global and national level environmental efforts.

Summing up, to protect the environment, steps need to be taken at all levels – individual, national and international.

Plan followed:
Intro: Disagree
Para 1: Why international level efforts are needed
Para 2: Steps at national level
Para 3: Steps at individual level
Conclusion: Reiterate opinion
***Similar essay**: Individuals can do nothing to improve the environment. Only governments and large companies can make a difference. To what extent do you agree or disagree with this opinion?*
***Similar essay:** The responsibility to prevent global environmental damage is on politicians rather than individual. Do you agree or disagree?*

134. *Some people think climate change has a negative impact on business, while others think that it provides more business options. Discuss both views and give your own opinion. (6th July, 2022)*

It is believed by some that climate change is detrimental for companies, whereas others believe that climate change offers many business opportunities and so is good for companies. In this essay, I will discuss both perspectives, but I agree with the former side.

On the one hand, those who believe climate change negatively impacts companies give the following reasons. Firstly, climate change poses a physical risk to many companies. For example, extreme weather events like hurricanes, snowstorms, and floods force many companies to close operations for days. Many sectors like agriculture that heavily depend on climate and natural resources also suffer a lot because of extreme environmental conditions. Secondly, climate change has resulted in stricter greenhouse gas emission regulations and thus companies are forced to spend a lot of money to cut down their emissions and pay huge fines if they fail to do.

On the other hand, there are many reasons why some people believe that climate change is beneficial for businesses. The most important reason is that climate change spurs innovation, inspiring new products and services which are environment-friendly. For example, global carmakers are transitioning to electric vehicles, energy companies are shifting towards renewable energy. Climate crisis has led to the growth of many companies that make green products. Many businesses have found success by catering to consumers who make environmentally-conscious choices when they shop. From large multinationals to local start-ups, all companies are capitalizing on the green revolution. Companies are also able to reduce their operational costs by being more energy-efficient.

I believe climate change is damaging to businesses. In addition to the increasing operational costs like significantly higher air condition expenses, businesses also face competition from new start-ups that offer cleaner products. Another climate-related risk to companies is the legal repercussions for emitting greenhouse gases. For example, recently fossil fuel companies have faced many legal cases for damaging the environment. This also damages a company's reputation and in extreme cases can lead to consumers boycotting them.

In conclusion, I believe that climate change has many adverse business outcomes like higher operational costs, legal challenges, and reputation damage.

Plan followed
Intro: Discuss essay
Para 1: One view
Para 2: Other view
Para 3: Own view
Conclusion

135. *Scientists have been warning for many years about protecting the environment and that people must limit the use of energy in their daily lives. Despite warnings, many people do not do so. What are the reasons for this and how can people be encouraged to protect the environment?*

It has been known for a long time that human beings need to limit everyday energy use and that environment needs to be protected. However, it is also a fact that very few people actually take steps to improve the situation. There are several reasons behind this, but if proper measures are taken this situation can be rectified.

There are many factors responsible for the indifference towards the environment among people. To begin with, people are accustomed to the luxuries of life and it is very hard to switch back to a simpler life. For example, it is certainly impossible to go back to washing clothes by hand or to live without air conditioners or cars today. In other words, people are not willing to make the changes because they prioritize their comforts over the environment.

Another reason is that people consider that their individual action would not make a big difference. In other words, people think that environmental issues are too big to be resolved at the individual level and the only way to address these issues is at the government level. Finally, some people are also of the opinion that environmentalists are exaggerating the consequences of climate change and global warming. They trust science to find them the solutions to these issues.

Despite all these reasons, I still believe that many people can be encouraged to take steps. Firstly, the government can implement strict rules and regulations, which would ensure energy efficiency in homes or use of renewable energy in homes. For example, many local governments pass large new residential building plans only if the plan incorporates solar rooftop panels. The second measure that governments from around the world can do, is penalizing wastage or excessive use of energy by very high rates. Nothing would prompt a bigger reaction than a hit at people's pockets.

In conclusion, there are many reasons for people not taking steps to safeguard the environment and to cut down their energy use. However, I still believe that a lot of people can still be motivated to mend their ways.

Plan followed:
Intro: Problem solution intro
Para 1: Reasons
Para 2: Reasons
Para 3: Solutions
Conclusion
Similar essay: Many people think it is important to protect the environment, but they make no effort on it themselves. Why is it so and what can be done about it?

136. *Some think that these environmental problems are too big for individuals to be solved, while others think that governments cannot solve these environmental problems unless individuals take some action. Discuss both views and give your opinion.*

Some people hold the opinion that individuals on their own cannot do much to protect the environment, while it is believed by others that even governments can make a difference only with the active support of people. This essay shall discuss both views. I believe that while there are some environmental areas in which government intervention is paramount, I also believe that in some areas individuals must lead the way.

There are many reasons why some people say that people cannot do anything for the environment. The first reason is the lack of professional knowledge needed to cope with serious environmental issues like soil erosion and salinity, which require a significant amount of investigation and research. Secondly, when an environmental emergency or accident happens such as an oil spill near the border line, only government action or international coordination is required.

On the other hand, those who say that even governments cannot do anything unless individuals cooperate, give their reasons as follows. Firstly, if government enacts laws for the betterment of the environment, and individuals do not cooperate, then there would be no results. For example, in India, there is a strict ban on the use of single use plastics, but people are still using them. So, the involvement of people is imperative for any government action to be useful.

I believe that individual actions, small as they may be, can prove very effective. For example, people can avoid driving the car, and take public transport, walk, or bicycle instead. This will reduce the use of fossil fuels and cut pollution. So, individual action can never be overstated. However, there are steps which can only be taken by the government. For example, protection of wildlife and forests, implementing strict punishment for violators of environmental laws and signing international treaties regarding environment. In these aspects the governments must show the way and individuals should support the government.

In conclusion, when it comes to environmental problems, individual actions are indispensable in the problem-solving process. But the most pressing and complicated problems go far beyond an individual's capability and so require the effort of the government.

Plan followed:
Intro: This essay shall discuss both views
Para 1: View one
Para 2: View two
Para 3: Own view
Conclusion:

137. *Environmental problems such as pollution and climatic variations are increasing nowadays. The governments have taken some measures at a global level. But they got only few solutions. Why is it so? How can this problem be solved?* (20/2/22 CBT)

Saving the environment has become the top priority across the world. However, the measures taken have not been enough to address the issue. This essay intends to look into why the measures have always fallen short of the mark, and suggest some solutions to mitigate the problem.

Many reasons can be attributed for the failure of governments in finding solutions. The first and foremost reason is the difficulty in balancing the economic development and environmental protection. It is irrefutable that steps taken for the protection of the environment have some sort of adverse effect on the economy, albeit little. For instance, although solar power is renewable and non-polluting it is still considerably costlier than thermal power. This is a major reason why the world hasn't already shifted towards solar power completely.

Secondly, there is the problem of consensus when it comes to global issues. For some countries environmental issues are not so high on the priority list and for others it is critical. For example the island nations of Pacific have been the biggest champions of environmental treaties because their very survival is at stake with global warming and consequently sea level rise. On the other hand, there are some countries like the Arctic countries, which might be benefited from global warming as it may lead to an increase in the growing season.

Solutions to environmental issues are not straightforward first because of the very magnitude of the problem and also for the reasons cited above. It requires a change in outlook towards environmental issues. Just as pollution is not bound by political boundaries, in the same way our solutions cannot be in silos. The world truly needs to come together as one to tackle this issue. Countries have to make compromises, for instance rich countries have to help developing countries with technology and financial aid. Developing countries also must balance their growth, keeping the environment in mind.

To sum up, it can be seen clearly, why the steps taken so far have failed to save the environment. However, the time has come to do some soul-searching and take proactive steps for the environment.

Plan followed:
Intro:
Para 1: First reason of failure
Para 2: Second reason of failure
Para 3: Solutions
Conclusion

138. *Some people say that industrial growth is necessary to solve poverty, but some other people argue that industrial growth is leading to poverty and it should be stopped. Discuss both views and give your opinion.*

The persistent problem of poverty in the developing world has put a question mark on the relation between economic growth and poverty. Some individuals are of the opinion that when economy develops because of industrial growth, poverty comes down. Others believe that industrial growth leads to poverty. This essay intends to analyse both perspectives. I personally agree with the former view.

The main reason given by those who say that industrial progress lessens poverty, is that rapid growth in manufacturing sector creates a lot of new jobs, which eventually increases the earning of people. It benefits nearly all citizens of a country, even if not equally, and therefore poverty comes down. For example, even in rural areas, when the country grows through agricultural exports, it benefits both poor farmers and the even poorer labourers they employ.

Secondly, history is witness, that industrialisation leads to improvement in the standard of people. Western countries began discovering the positive relation between economic growth and poverty reduction around 1820 and as a result the living standards in Europe and the United States improved manifold in the next years. Economic growth thus eliminated mass poverty in what is today considered the developed world. Even a short-term view confirms that the recent acceleration of growth in many developing countries has reduced poverty.

Those who claim that economic progress leads to poverty, assert that industrialisation leads to inequality between the rich and the poor. They opine that a handful of rich are getting richer while the poor are being driven to the wall. However, results have proved that such inequality is only short-lived and everyone has benefited in the long run. It is because of the high initial inequality that it appears as if economic growth is leading to poverty.

Summing up, industrial progress definitely reduces poverty. Sometimes, there is unequal distribution of wealth in the initial stages of economic development. Nonetheless, everyone benefits eventually.

Plan followed:
Intro: when economy develops, poverty comes down
Para 1: View 1
Para 2: View 1
Para 3: View 2
Conclusion: economic progress definitely reduces poverty

139. *Some people say that economic development is necessary to reduce the poverty in the world. Others say that economic growth should be stopped immediately to stop damaging the environment. Discuss both sides and give your opinion.*

It is believed by some that development in economy is essential in addressing poverty, whereas others say that it should be stopped as it is causing irreversible damage to the environment. This essay intends to analyze both perspectives. While economic development does cause environmental damage, stopping it is not the way out, as it is essential to remove poverty. The answer lies in finding ways of sustainable economic growth.

The main reason why some people say that economic progress mitigates poverty, is that by the development of economy people can improve their quality of life. For example, in developed countries even the poorest of the poor have the basic amenities of life such as food, clothing and shelter. All the citizens enjoy high level of social welfare and they enjoy free medical care and free education. Even in countries like India and China, because of the increase in GDP, the quality of life of people has improved.

On the other hand, those who say that economic progress should be stopped, because it harms the environment, give their argument that in the name of progress industries are being set up, which require some kind of energy to manufacture, operate and maintain. Most of the energy that is used is polluting the environment. Effluents from large factories are being dumped indiscriminately and landfill sites are filling up with non-biodegradable wastes.

I believe that with economic development, the damage to the environment is inevitable. Therefore, methods have to be looked into by which progress can be achieved without damaging the environment. So, the answer lies in the green technologies, which increasingly use renewable resources of energy. We should also remember the three "Rs" - reduce, reuse and recycle. In this way we can achieve an ecologically sustainable development.

Summing up, there is no doubt that with economic development, poverty is lessened. At the same time, it is also definite that development is leading to pollution. However, instead of stopping development we can work upon environmentally friendly development.

Plan followed:

Intro: Discuss essay intro
Para 1: How poverty is reduced by economic development
Para 2: Pollution due to economic development
Para 3: own view
Conclusion

Similar essay: Pollution and other environmental problems are resulting from a country's developing and becoming richer. Some think this cannot be avoided. To what extent do you agree or disagree?

140. *Some people think governments should focus on reducing environmental pollution and housing problems to help people prevent illness and disease. To what extent do you agree or disagree?*

Some people are of the opinion that governments should focus on the environment and housing to avoid illness and disease. While I agree that reducing pollution and addressing housing issues can prevent certain diseases, I also believe that governments need to spend on awareness and on healthcare for other diseases.

Admittedly, the environmental problems and housing conditions are two main sources for illness and disease. For instance, in many parts of my country, India, people live in slums and do not have access to potable water and proper sanitation facilities. Because of this, many people in these areas suffer from diseases such as dengue, malaria, diarrhoea and so on. These diseases can be prevented if governments provide basic housing, with access to clean drinking water and toilets. Similarly, many lung ailments like asthma are caused due to air pollution and controlling pollution can reduce their incidence.

However, simply focusing on the environment and housing cannot prevent all diseases. Governments also ought to allocate budget for other preventable diseases such as polio and TB, whooping cough, measles, mumps and so on, which need immunization. Moreover, there are diseases such as cancers, which can be prevented by screening tests. Such tests can diagnose the diseases much before the actual symptoms appear and in such early stages, these cancers are totally curable and relatively inexpensive to treat as well.

Furthermore, today, a lot of people suffer from lifestyle diseases like diabetes and obesity. The only solution to these illnesses is lifestyle modification or in other words, a change in diet and more time for exercise. So, governments need to focus on creating awareness about the benefits of a nutritious diet and the harmful effects of fast foods. Similarly, governments need to encourage people to adopt more physical activity in their daily routines by building healthcare centres and gyms.

In conclusion, I reiterate that simply giving priority to environmental pollution and housing will not prevent all diseases. Government should allocate funds to screening tests, vaccination and awareness of the people also to prevent disease.

Plan followed:
Intro: Disagree
Para 1: Advantages of addressing environmental problems and housing
Para 2: Other areas to focus
Para 3: More other areas
Conclusion:

141. *The best way to solve the world's environmental problem is to increase the price of fuel. To what extent do you agree or disagree with this statement?*

It is believed by some that the most effective solution of addressing the issue of deteriorating environment is increasing fuel prices. While I believe that raising the price of fuels such as petrol and diesel may help in curbing this issue to some extent, it is not the best solution to solve the environmental problems of the world.

Admittedly, it is true that increasing fuel prices will cause some car owners to use public transportation systems or rideshare services, drive less, and walk more. This means fewer vehicles on the road and that will cause a drop in the carbon emissions that are very bad for our environment and health. Industries might also turn to eco-friendly options if possible.

However, this solution is certainly not without its flaws. Firstly, a great number of vehicles in a country are owned by the affluent. For them, the cost of fuel is very low compared with life's other necessities and so an increase in fuel prices may not change their nature towards car usage. Instead a better solution could be to improve road conditions and build a faster and more efficient public transport system, so that people are motivated to use it. For example, not only the poor but also the rich prefer the Delhi metro over cars.

Another effective way to reduce transportation-related air pollution emissions is to use clean vehicle and fuel technologies. These include fuel-efficient vehicles that use less oil, cleaner fuels that produce fewer emissions, and electric cars and trucks. In fact, all the major car companies like Honda, Toyota, Ford are ramping up electric car production. So instead of raising fuel prices and invoking hard feelings among people, the government can give incentives to people to buy these environment-friendly vehicles.

Summing up, higher fuel prices may put a small dent in air pollution but other measures like building a better public transport system and cleaner environment-friendly vehicles are better solutions to our environmental problems.

Plan followed:

Intro: Disagree with some concession
Para 1: Benefits of increasing fuel prices
Para 2: Why other methods are better and flaws of this method
Para 3: Other effective methods
Conclusion: Reiterate opinion

Written by: Indroop Singh (Exam question 10/4/2021 9am)

142. *The natural resources such as oil, forests and fresh water are being consumed at an alarming rate. What problems does it cause? How can we solve these problems?*

It is true that the rate of consumption of natural resources like oil, water and forests is exceedingly high. There are many adverse effects of this problem, but if timely steps are taken, this problem can be addressed.

The main issue because of the fast pace of exploitation of fossil fuels like oil is the increase in pollution. Pollution has many harmful effects on health. Apart from health issues like cancers, asthma, skin problems and lung diseases, pollution also reduces work efficiency. Moreover, the areas where the oil is taken out are facing many environmental issues like destruction of forests and noise pollution. Many earthquakes are also caused due to drilling of oil.

In addition, the increasing use of freshwater and deforestation has many detrimental effects. To begin with, the fast use of freshwater is leading to water scarcity. Some areas do not even have enough water for drinking. Deforestation has led to destruction of animal habitats. As animal homes are being destroyed, there has been an increase in human animal conflicts. Moreover, the destruction of trees is causing environmental problems like droughts as forests are rain magnets.

Although there are many issues caused by the overconsumption of these natural resources, I believe that governments can implement measures and tackle it. First, the use of oil can be reduced by promoting renewable sources like solar energy and wind energy. This can be done by levying taxes on oil and coal. Secondly, recycling of water and rainwater harvesting can be promoted to tackle problems like water scarcity. For example, a few years back there was a water crisis in Chennai. However, after strict implementation of rainwater harvesting in home designs, Chennai has now started exporting water to other cities. Lastly, there should be strict fines and punishment for people involved in deforestation.

In conclusion, although there are many negative consequences of the increasing use of natural resources, I believe this problem can be tackled by implementing some strong measures and policies.

Plan followed:
Intro:
Para 1: Oil – effects of overconsumption
Para 2: Fresh water and forests – effects of overconsumption
Para 3: Solutions
Conclusion

Written by: Indroop Singh

143. *Some people believe that taxing companies which cause pollution, is the best way to reduce industrial pollution, whereas others suggest that the government should deal with this on its own. Discuss both the views and give your opinion.*

Some individuals are of the opinion that businesses and individuals should pay for the pollution they cause, whereas others say that governments should find other ways to handle this pollution. In the following paragraphs, I will discuss both perspectives. I, personally side with the latter view.

There are many reasons why some people opine that companies should be levied a carbon tax for the pollution they cause. Firstly, it would motivate them to switch to cleaner energies. These include solar energy, wind energy and hydro powered energy. Secondly, this tax would raise substantial revenue as it would increase the cost of fuel. This money could be used by the governments for other useful purposes, or to cut other taxes.

On the other hand, those opposed to a carbon tax, give their reasons as follows. First of all, it may not be possible to pinpoint the extent to which each company has to pay for pollution. Such businesses will find loopholes to avoid heavy bills. Secondly, the big companies may be unwilling to accept the responsibility of paying the additional bill of pollution and may pass on this tax completely to the consumers by increasing the cost of their products.

I believe that a carbon tax would not be practical as many industries may shift to non-tax nations. In addition, with the increase in cost of fuels, the common people would suffer, as everyone uses some carbon in their lives. Finally, it has been seen that in countries which have imposed the tax, there has been no significant fall in pollution levels. In fact, it has had an opposite effect as the companies paying the tax, stop feeling guilty about creating pollution. Instead of taxing, it would be better to give incentives to these companies to switch to greener energies.

Summing up, pollution is a serious issue and the government should not leave it to the companies to pay its bill. It can however, make it mandatory for the companies to use solar and wind energy, so that pollution is minimized.

Plan followed:
Intro:
Para 1: One view
Para 2: Other view
Para 3: Own view
Conclusion:
Similar essay
Some people argue that companies and private individuals, rather than governments, should pay the bill of pollution. To what extent do you agree or disagree?

144. *Development in technology causes environmental problems. Some people believe the solution for these problems is that everyone should accept a simpler way of life, while others say that technology can solve these problems. Discuss both views and give your own opinion.*

It is irrefutable that progress in technology leads to environmental problems. Some individuals are of the opinion that if people live a simple life and do not use the things that technology has brought them then these problems can be solved, whereas others opine that only technology can solve these problems. In the following paragraphs, I intend to discuss both viewpoints. I, however, side with the latter view.

The main reason why some people say that if humans lead a simple way of life, only then they can save the environment, is that it is the luxuries people use, which damage the environment. If people do not use air conditioners, automobiles and other such things that technology has brought us, then naturally there would be less pollution and natural resources like fossil fuels would be saved and all this would save the environment.

On the other hand, there are reasons why people say that technology alone could save the environment. Firstly, there are a lot of advances going on in technology, which are helping the environment a lot. For instance, in Africa, desalination plants have been set up to get clean drinking water from sea water – an almost inexhaustible resource. Furthermore, Japan is working to build a working space solar power system by 2030. It could meet the entire world's electricity requirements indefinitely without nuclear or GHG emissions. If successful, the impact on the world would be monumental.

I believe that the people of today's fast paced life, simply cannot take a U-turn to the age of the bullock cart. We have to look upto the technology to save the environment. For example, air conditioners are no longer a luxury; they have become a necessity because of global warming, but these air conditioners can be made in such a way that they use less energy and provide more cooling. The 5-star AC's of today are the eco-friendly technological creations.

Summing up, technology alone can solve the world's environmental problems. We are finally entering an era where engineering and technology are making the world a better place. It would be highly impractical to ask people to adopt a simpler way of life.

Plan followed:

Intro: Discuss essay intro
Para 1: Why some people opine that we should adopt simpler ways of life
Para 2: Why some people say technology alone can help
Para 3: Some examples of how technology is helping us
Conclusion:

145. *Most countries do not recycle their waste like paper, glass, and aluminum cans. Why does this happen and what steps can be taken to encourage recycling?*

Many countries consider recycling to be a waste of money and resources, and question environmentalists who think recycling is better for the environment. This essay intends to look into the reasons why countries do not recycle and also suggest ways to encourage them to recycle.

There are many reasons why most countries do not recycle. Firstly, the cost involved in recycling is much more than alternatives like landfill and incineration. Recycling is much more expensive because the material must be hauled and sorted before it can be used to create new products. Also, most countries lack the technology and equipment needed to process the recycling waste. So, the simplest and cheapest option is usually to bury garbage in a landfill. Secondly, in many countries the consumer demand for recycled products is low and countries are not able to make profits by selling products made from recycled material like newspapers and glass bottles.

Furthermore, in many cases recycling is worse for the environment than alternatives like a properly run landfill. For example, plastic recycling process involves washing the materials, producing wastewater full of contaminants, and heating up the plastic to produce pellets which releases chemical additives and emissions into the air. Similarly, reusable metal straws and canvas bags require a lot of energy and materials to manufacture, and unless people use them many times, they end up having more environmental consequences.

There are many ways to encourage countries to recycle. To begin with, demand for recycled products needs to be increased by creating awareness about the greener products and encouraging consumers to buy these products. Also, research needs to be done to create a sustainable, affordable and environmentally friendly recycling system. Countries will start recycling if it starts making economic and environmental sense. Finally, many developed countries which successfully recycle must come forward and share their recycling technology and strategies with developing countries.

To sum up, countries do not recycle for various reasons, but effective steps can be taken to encourage them to recycle.

Plan followed:
Intro:
Para 1: Why countries do not recycle
Para 2: More reasons
Para 3: Solutions
Conclusion:

146. *Some people think that the amount of noise people make has to be controlled strictly. Others, however, say that people should be free to make as much noise as they wish. Discuss both views and give your own opinion.*

Noise pollution is a matter of great concern nowadays. Knowingly or unknowingly, every one of us contributes to noise pollution, because most of our day-to-day activities generate some noise. Some people are of the opinion that there should be some restriction on the level of noise from human activities. Others do not believe in such regulations. This essay intends to discuss both perspectives. I, however, side with the former view.

The most important argument given by those in favour of noise control is that loud noise may adversely affect people in many ways. Noise above a certain level can cause hearing loss. Occupational noise exposure is the most common cause of Noise-Induced Hearing Loss (NIHL). For example, repeated exposure to noise pollution at a construction site can cause NIHL to construction workers, an effect that cannot be reversed.

Furthermore, there are the emotional or psychological effects such as irritability, anxiety and stress. Lack of concentration and mental fatigue are significant health effects of noise. It has been observed that the performance of school children is poor in comprehension tasks when schools are situated in busy areas of a city and suffer from noise pollution disturbance. Therefore, it is imperative that some check should be there on noise production.

On the other hand, those who oppose such laws against noise generation, give their reasons as follows. They assert that some amount of noise is inevitable. The sources may be domestic, natural, commercial or industrial. People believe that making noise at times is their basic right to express their emotions. They want to cheer and shout for their favourite team and dance to the beat of loud music when happy. They take any regulation on noise, as infringement of their basic rights.

To sum up, suitable action has to be taken to attenuate the noise levels and control noise pollution. It is high time we all realize that noise pollution is a slow poison.

Plan followed:

Intro: Discuss essay intro
Para 1: Why it should be controlled
Para 2: Why it should be controlled
Para 3: Why some people say it should not be controlled
Conclusion:

147. *The level of noise around us is constantly increasing, and is affecting the quality of our lives. What causes this noise? What should be done about it?*

All displeasing sound is known as "Noise pollution." It has harmful effects on the physiological and psychological health of human beings. This essay shall discuss the causes and possible solutions to reduce noise problems.

There are many causes of noise pollution. One of the major sources of noise pollution is the traffic noise. The number of vehicles on the road is increasing day by day and the sound produced by them is chiefly responsible for the noise pollution. To add to it, industrial noise also leads to noise pollution. Machinery and motors used in the industries create a lot of noise.

Furthermore, the construction of buildings, highways and city streets also cause a lot of noise and hence leads to noise pollution. People living beside railway stations also have to put up with a lot of noise from engines, horns and whistles. Other causes are the loudspeakers usually used in marriages, social and religious functions. The noise is just jarring and harmful for the ears. It can cause sleep disruption. It can also cause deafness.

Many steps can be taken to control noise pollution. Firstly, roadside plantations are one of the great solutions to help in reducing noise pollution. Changing the design and operation of machines like sound proof cabins and sound-absorbing materials can also greatly help in reducing noise pollution. To block unwanted noise from outside soundproof doors and windows can be installed. The major cause of noise pollution in public areas is the loudspeaker. For the welfare of the people it should be banned at any cost. There should be strict laws imposed against those who use loudspeakers in crowded areas and public places. .

To conclude, there are various sources of noise pollution, but many steps can be taken to mitigate it.

Plan followed:
Intro: Problem solution essay intro.
Para 1: Causes
Para 2: More causes
Para 3: Solutions
Conclusion:

148. *In some cities, the government has tried to reduce traffic. For instance, they imposed a congestion tax during rush hours. Do you think this development is positive or negative?*

With the increasing number of vehicles on the roads, the traffic problems have also increased. In certain cities, these traffic-related problems, like congestion, have been addressed by implementing taxes and other traffic rules strictly. While there are a few drawbacks of implementing a congestion tax, the benefits are much more.

On the one hand, the main drawback of the congestion tax is that in many places the public transport system is not enough to accommodate the population of that area. So, people have to use their vehicles as a compulsion. Secondly, there are already very high charges for buying a private vehicle, starting from getting it registered, paying road taxes and then further maintenance, when needed. Therefore, such taxes are not the answer to the congestion issues.

On the other hand, the first major advantage of imposing traffic rules and taxes is that more and more people are discouraged from using their private vehicles. It has been noticed in cities where the road taxes are high, most of the people prefer using the public transport, thus leading to less congestion on the roads. For example, in London, when the congestion tax was implemented, it reduced the traffic in the central parts of the city by around 15%. People start looking at other options of transport, like car-pooling, walking short distances and using the public transport more often. The added advantage is the reduced pollution, which has also become the need of the hour.

Moreover, the government can use the money collected from such taxes and use it for improving the public transport infrastructure. Government can invest in building new transport systems, like the metros and the subways, building more freeways, widening the existing roads, etc. For instance, in New Delhi, many people now prefer to travel by Metro rather than their private vehicles because of the comfort and the quality. The government has constantly maintained and improved the quality of this system over the years and more and more routes have been added. This has been a major factor in reducing the use of private vehicles.

To sum up, the pros of implementing more road and traffic related taxes are definitely more than the cons. These benefit both the individuals and the nation.

Plan followed:
Intro: Pros more than cons
Para 1: Advantages of such taxes
Para 2: More advantages
Para 3: The other view with refutation
Conclusion:

149. *Some people say that instead of preventing climate change we should find a way to live with it. Do you agree or disagree?*

It is believed that rather than stopping damage to the environment people should find a method to adapt to the climate change. While finding ways of adaptation are needed, I disagree that we should not take steps to stop further harm to the environment.

The main reason why steps are needed to find ways to alleviate the problem of global warming is that the rate at which the climate is warming and changing, is alarming. If this rate is not controlled soon, we may be looking at the doom of our planet. If we do not take measures soon to stop further changes in our environment and the global climate, there might be drastic changes in our ecosystem, leading to the extinction of many plants and animal species, including the human beings.

Secondly, the ways adopted to live with the climate change, may further hasten the process of global warming and things may be complicated beyond repair. For example, using more air-conditioners to fight the longer summers may cause even more pollution and global warming, and the rise in temperature may go up exponentially. This may lead to even more extreme climatic changes than ever before. Only over the last decade, we have had the highest and the lowest ever recorded temperatures, the worst ever floods and many other natural disasters which are the direct result of the climate change.

Unarguably, prevention and adaptation have to go side by side. People have to adapt to these changes in the climate, which have already taken place, as these are irreversible. New building material is required to deal with these changes in the temperatures. For example, insulated materials can be used to make buildings in places where the temperatures have risen in the recent years. People need to see that the methods they are using to adapt are environment friendly. People also need to change their lifestyle so that they can prevent further damage as much as possible.

To sum up, it can be reiterated that the rate at with the change in the climate is occurring needs to be controlled, but at the same time we have to adapt to these changes also.

Plan followed:
Intro: disagree
Para 1: First reason
Para 2: Second reason
Para 3: Why adapting is also needed
Conclusion

150. *Nowadays in many countries household waste e.g. food packaging is increasing day by day. What are the causes for that? How can this problem be solved?*

The statistics about the household waste being produced today are alarming. Roughly 50 tonnes of household waste is being produced every second, and this number is projected to double by 2030. This essay intends to analyze the reasons of this phenomenon and suggest steps to mitigate the problem.

To begin with, modern lifestyle has contributed greatly to the increasing amount of waste and garbage we produce every day. In other words, we have turned into a materialistic and mass-consumption society, where we use more and throw away more than ever before. Once new things are acquired, we dispose-off these "unwanted" things to second hand shops, or just in the trash cans.

Secondly, the markets today are flooded with cheap, single-use-only things that are more in demand than high priced quality items. Our houses and closets seem to be overflowing with goods that are more in quantity and less in value. Then, there is too much packaging done by the companies in a bid to make their things more attractive. Mostly this packaging is made from non-biodegradable products, such as plastic.

The solution lies in changing our attitude. We should get old things repaired and try to use them as long as possible. We should not buy things with excessive packaging. This will deter companies from doing too much packaging. We can also bring our own personal shopping bags instead of using plastic bags provided by stores and shops. Besides, the government can enforce stricter laws on companies to use biodegradable packaging. Furthermore, plastics, metal, glass can be recycled. Companies can also contribute by developing new raw material, which is recyclable and will ultimately lead to less garbage.

To sum up, there are many reasons for the increase in household waste being generated. However, some simple steps can be taken to ameliorate the problem. If we do not take steps to tackle this problem on a war footing, our Earth will become uninhabitable very soon.

Plan followed:
Intro: Problem solution essay intro
Para 1: First reason
Para 2: Second reason
Para 3: Solutions
Conclusion:

151. *Fossil fuels (coal, oil, natural gas) are the main sources in many countries, but in some countries the use of alternative sources of energy (wind energy and solar energy) are encouraged. To what extent do you think it is a positive or negative development?*

It is irrefutable that most of the countries depend on fossil fuels for energy generation, but it is also true that many countries are shifting towards renewable sources like wind, solar and tidal energy. Although there are a few drawbacks of renewable energy, I believe the lowering dependence on fossil fuels is a positive development.

Firstly, alternative sources are renewable, while the conventional sources like coal and oil are non-renewable. Fossils take millions of years to make and countries are using them at an alarming rate. This means that if people continue using them at the same rate, there will be nothing left for our future generations. The second advantage is that these non-conventional sources do not pollute the environment. It is well known that fossil fuels are a major contributor to greenhouse gases and consequently global warming.

In addition, renewable energy sources reduce dependence on foreign energy imports as they can be produced locally. Thus, these sources can not only increase energy independence but also save valuable foreign exchange. Finally, these sources require less maintenance because they have fewer movable parts as compared to conventional energy sources.

On the other hand, there are also a few drawbacks of renewable energy. The main drawback is the high upfront cost, which is considerably higher than conventional energy sources. Another major issue with them is that they are not as reliable as fossil fuel-based energy generation as they depend upon wind speed and hours of sunshine, which varies from day to day and season to season.

Summing up, despite the problems associated with renewable energy, I consider the shift towards it to be beneficial on the whole.

Plan followed:
Intro: Positive with some concession
Para 1: First advantage of alternative sources – renewable
Para 2: Second advantage of alternative sources – non polluting
Para 3: Some drawbacks of alternative sources
Conclusion: Reiterate opinion

Written by: Indroop Singh (Example essay Positive and negative development)

152. *Nuclear energy is a better choice for meeting increasing demand. Do you support the use of nuclear technology for constructive purposes? Use your own knowledge and experience and support your arguments with examples and relevant evidence.*

Many people believe that nuclear energy can be the answer to our energy problems. Although there are many advantages of nuclear energy, I cannot support its use even for peaceful purposes.

The main advantage of nuclear energy is that it is environment friendly. In other words, no harmful gases like carbon dioxide and sulphur dioxide are released in this process. If the world continues to rely on thermal energy and oil and gas, the earth would become unliveable because of global warming. Another benefit of nuclear energy is that it can produce huge amounts of energy. Other sources like solar energy and thermal energy cannot compete with it in the amount of energy produced.

However, despite the benefits mentioned-above, I am against the use of nuclear energy for the following reasons. First and foremost, nuclear waste is radioactive and this can cause permanent health damage to people who work in nuclear power plants. Till now, no method has been found to safely dispose of nuclear waste. The second reason is that if there are accidents in nuclear power plants, it can have disastrous consequences for the people and the environment of nearby areas. For example, the survivors of Chernobyl nuclear disaster and the descendants are still suffering from many ailments and diseases and the area is still unsafe for human habitation. Finally, if the nuclear technology falls in the hands of terrorists or irresponsible countries, it can be used for making bombs, which will be the end of the world.

In conclusion, I would like to reiterate that while nuclear technology has many benefits over other energy sources, I still believe that its use should be avoided.

Plan followed:
Intro: Disagree
Para 1: Advantages of nuclear power
Para 2: Disadvantages of nuclear power
Conclusion:
Written by: Indroop (9/3/22)

153. *International community must act immediately to ensure all nations reduce their consumption of fossil fuels e.g. gas and oil. Do you agree or disagree?*

A lot of people believe that urgent action needs to be taken on the global level to cut down the consumption of fossil fuels. I strongly agree that the international community like the United Nations must take immediate actions to ensure that all countries lessen the use of such resources.

The main reason for the international community to intervene and see to it that all nations curtail their use of fossil fuels is that no individual nation would take this initiative on its own. Any country, which takes the step to reduce the use of fossil fuels, would have to invest in the alternative resources, which would raise the price of their goods and their economy would suffer. If there is pressure from the international community then all countries would have to comply with it.

The second major reason is that it might be too late to save the planet if urgent action is not taken globally. Many international organisation have predicted the end of earth by as early as 2100 if steps are not taken on a war footing. The increase in unchecked pollution levels and rise in temperatures would make the earth uninhabitable. Moreover, the rise in sea-levels due to global warming would lead to submergence of many low-lying islands. These consequences can already be seen in many parts of the earth and if we wait more the situation might get completely out of hand.

Finally, an urgent action needs to be taken for reducing the use of conventional sources like coal and oil because these are non-renewable. They take millions of years to make and are being used at an alarming rate. This means that if international action is not taken immediately, these resources will be gone forever, and there will be nothing left for the future generations. On the other hand, energy from the wind, the sun and the sea are an everlasting source of power and they are environmentally friendly as well.

In conclusion, it is vital for international organizations to implement strict regulations on consumption of oil and gas worldwide, and all nations must take part in reducing the usage of fossil fuels.

Plan followed:
Intro: Agree
Para 1: Reason 1 – no nation would take any step on its own
Para 2: Reason 2 - Why urgent actions are needed
Para 3: Reason 3 – More reasons for urgent actions
Conclusion:

Written by Indroop Singh 1/6/2020

154. *Some people think that the government should strictly control the supply of fresh water, as the resources are limited, while others think we can use as much water as we want. Discuss both sides and give your opinion.*

(One method: Completely with one side)

It is believed by some that there should be strict regulations on the use of fresh water, while others hold the opinion that individuals should have complete freedom on water use. I strongly support a strictly controlled water supply as it is the need of the hour.

There are two main reasons why some people believe that government should strictly control the usage of water. The main reason is that fresh water is scarce and already many countries are facing a severe water shortage. Controlling supply of fresh water is the only way to ensure that there is adequate water for everyone and there is water left for our future generations. Another result of controlling fresh water supply would be that it would coerce people to use it more wisely and reduce its wastage.

On the other hand, those who believe that there should be no restrictions on water, give the following reasons. Firstly, they believe that rather than benefitting everyone, strict control would have negative consequences. For example, the rich might try to bribe officials to get illegal water connections installed. Secondly, people might be forced to procure water from unregulated contaminated sources, which may lead to diseases and other problems.

I am strongly in favour of government controlling and regulating water supply as water is a basic necessity. Human beings cannot survive without water and water is also one of the most important resources in agriculture and industries as well. Therefore, it is the government's responsibility to provide fresh water to everyone. This in turn can be ensured if government keeps a tight control on water usage.

In conclusion, I believe that a strong level of control on water supply is no more an option but a necessity.

Plan followed:

Intro: Discuss essay with own view matching either view
Para 1: One side view
Para 2: Other side view
Para 3: Own view
Conclusion

Written by Indroop Makkar

155. *Some people think that the government should strictly control the supply of fresh water, as the resources are limited, while others think we can use as much water as we want. Discuss both sides and give your opinion.*

(Another method: Have a different view not matching the two views)

It is believed by some that there should be strict regulations on the use of fresh water, while others hold the opinion that individuals should have complete freedom on water use. I do not believe tight regulation is practical or possible, but there should be some level of control on water supply and use.

There are two main reasons why some people believe that government should strictly control the usage of water. The main reason is that fresh water is scarce and already many countries are facing a severe water shortage. Controlling supply of fresh water is the only way to ensure that there is adequate water for everyone and there is water left for our future generations. Another result of controlling fresh water supply would be that it would coerce people to use it more wisely and reduce it wastage.

On the other hand, those who believe that there should be no restrictions on water, give the following reasons. Firstly, they believe that rather than benefitting everyone, strict control would have negative consequences. For example, the rich might try to bribe officials to get illegal water connections installed. Secondly, people might be forced to procure water from unregulated contaminated sources, which may lead to diseases and other problems.

I believe that there should be some level of government control on water use, but I also recognize that keeping a tight control on water is impossible as it is present everywhere. Some level of control would definitely be beneficial as it would create more awareness about the severity of increasing water scarcity. It might also encourage people to take positive initiatives to save water. For example, rationing of water in some Indian cities have led to people installing rainwater harvesting systems at home.

In conclusion, I believe that a strong level of control on water supply is not possible, but there should be some check on wastage of water.

Plan followed:
Intro: Discuss essay with own view different from either view
Para 1: one side
Para 2: other side
Para 3: Own view
Conclusion
Written by: Indroop Singh

156. *Some people think the main benefit of international cooperation is in protection of the environment, while others think that the main benefit is in the world business. Discuss both views and give your opinion.*

It is believed by some that the main benefit of global cooperation has been in protection of the environment, but others hold the view that the main benefit has been in international trade. In this essay, I intend to delve into both views. I personally side with the latter view.

On the one hand, people who believe that global cooperation contributes mainly to environmental protection give their reasons as follows. Firstly, governments from around the world have collectively pledged to slow global warming in various international agreements. For example, through the Kyoto Protocol and the Paris Agreement, countries agreed to reduce greenhouse gas emissions. Secondly, developed countries have been helping poor and developing countries switch to renewable and sustainable energy sources by sharing technical knowledge, funds, and resources. Without international help, developing countries will not be able to prevent and adapt to climate change.

On the other hand, there are many reasons given by people that say that international cooperation is mainly boosting trade and business. To begin with, international cooperation has opened doors for international trade, and companies are not limited to business within their national borders. Because of this, organizations are growing faster, innovating, and improving their revenue and productivity. For example, companies like Nike, McDonalds, Toyota have all expanded internationally. Moreover, businesses and economies of developed countries have been boosted because of multinational companies moving many of their operations to these countries.

In my opinion, although a lot has been done in both areas, a lot more needs to be done in the field of environment. The steps already taken are not enough and the governments need to tackle this issue on a war footing. When countries step forward to do something for the environment, the issue of CDR (common but differentiated responsibility) comes in, and there are differences among the developed and developing countries. The developed world, which is mainly responsible for damaging the environment, should take more responsibility in saving the environment.

Summing up, although international co-operation has benefited the world business as well as the environment, the benefit to the business has been much more than to the environment.

Plan followed:
Intro: Discuss essay intro
Para 1: What has been done internationally for environment
Para 2: What has been done internationally for business
Para 3: own view – a lot more needs to be done for the environment
Conclusion: More has been done for trade than environment

157. *The increased world demand for oil and gas has made it necessary for locating these sources in remote and untouched natural areas. Do you think the advantages outweigh the disadvantages of damaging these natural areas?*

There is a race for seeking oil and gas resources in remote and previously untouched areas such as Alaska and Antarctica. While there are a few advantages of remote drilling for oil, the disadvantages are far more.

Admittedly, oil drilling in these remote areas has a few advantages. The first benefit of oil drilling is that the process of drilling itself and development of land after the extraction helps in creating jobs for locals. Secondly, it leads to the development of the areas as it would increase the connectivity of these areas with the rest of the country.

However, the major downside to extracting oil and gas deposits found in remote and untouched locations is the environmental impact. Such activities endanger the unique and exotic flora and fauna of these regions as they lead to destruction of their natural habitats. For example, the Exxon Valdez spill that took place in Alaska killed thousands of marine animals and birds like sea otters, seals, bald eagles, killer whales etcetera.

In addition, this also impacts the economy of these areas because it harms their principal industries like commercial fishing and tourism. Such activities destroy the pristine nature of such regions and thereby reduce their appeal among tourists. Similarly, oil exploration interferes with fishing and thereby might take away local people's livelihood. Finally, extraction of fossil fuels in these remote areas is more expensive because of the costs associated with transportation of these fuels. A lot of infrastructure is required, with pipelines and shipping routes stretching thousands of kilometres.

To sum up, although there are a few advantages of oil and gas exploration in remote places, the disadvantages are far more.

Plan followed:
Intro: cons of tapping these resources outweigh the pros
Para 1: pros
Para 2: cons
Para 3: cons
Conclusion:

158. *On vehicle-free days, private cars, trucks and motorcycles are banned in the city centre, while public transport is permitted such as bicycles, buses and taxis. Do the benefits of vehicle-free day outweigh the disadvantages?*

In some cities, there are special days called vehicle-free days on which private vehicles are not allowed and only public transportation like buses, trains etcetera is allowed. Although there are a few drawbacks of such days, I believe the advantages are far more.

Admittedly, there is a downside to banning private vehicles in the city centers. The main disadvantage is inconvenience, especially people who live far from bus stops or railway stations would face significantly higher travelling time. Apart from this, if the government does not increase the availability of buses and trains, it would lead to delays and excessive crowding. Thus, the governments must make preparations before implementing such plans.

However, there are several benefits of vehicle free days. Firstly, such days bring down the pollution level as vehicular pollution accounts for a significant proportion of pollution in most cities. The second is reduction in traffic congestion, which in turn has two benefits, fall in noise levels and reduction in road accidents. Most noise stems from traffic and the negative consequences of loud noise go far beyond just irritation. Similarly, research has shown that traffic accidents on such days are significantly lower than normal days due to less number of cars on roads.

Such car free interventions are also helpful from a health perspective as they lead to an increase in physical activity. Many people are forced to walk to nearby markets for buying essentials instead of driving. In addition, this increases social interaction because people are more likely to meet friends on the streets and roads while walking. Finally, such days promote use of public transportation and many people have had their hesitations about buses and local trains disappear after being left with no alternative option.

In conclusion, despite the few drawbacks of vehicle free days, I consider them to be beneficial for the environment and the society overall.

Plan followed:
Intro: Advantages are more
Para 1: Disadvantages
Para 2: Advantages
Para 3: More advantages
Conclusion:

159. *Nowadays, people always throw the old things away when they buy new things. Some people claim that the broken things should be repaired and used again. What factors cause this phenomenon? What effects does the phenomenon lead to?*

Modern culture is a consumerist one. It is also known as 'disposable culture' or 'use and throw' culture. In this essay I shall deal with the causes and effects of this phenomenon.

The most important reasons leading to the use-and-throw trend are the consumerist society of today and the increase in the buying capacity of people. They are flooded with choices and want to buy the latest models of things and the latest fashion of clothes. So, the old things have to be discarded. Secondly, people do not have the time to get old things repaired. In order to buy more and more things, people have become workaholics and therefore they do not find time to get things repaired. Finally, the manufacturing companies are compromising quality when they are doing mass production of things. So, the things stop functioning very soon and have to be thrown..

The most serious effect of this use-and-throw culture is on the environment. The landfill sites are filling up with non-biodegradable wastes. Destroying used plastic is becoming a major problem everywhere. Even the recycling of plastic needs a lot of electricity. Conventional methods of generating electricity add to pollution. Disposing off a lot of waste materials also adds to pollution. The amount of energy used in manufacturing and disposal of consumer goods is leading to a brink of energy crises.

Another effect is that these discarded things are being dumped in the oceans and are being consumed by marine life which may ultimately end up on our plates. This waste is also acting as a sponge for oil spills in the oceans which makes it even more difficult to clean the oceans. There is also the question of e-waste. The technological gadgets people use and throw, add lead, cadmium and mercury to soil and water. This makes it clear how disastrous the consequences of this use-and-throw culture are.

To summarise, there are many causes and effects of this use-and-throw culture and steps must be taken on a war footing by the individual and government if we want to save our environment for our coming generations.

Plan followed:
Intro:
Para 1: Causes
Para 2: Effects – on environment
Para 3: More effects
Conclusion –

Similar essay: Nowadays, we are living in a throw-away society. What are its causes and what are its problems?

160. *Many people say that we have developed into a "throw-away" culture, because we are filling up our environment with so many plastic bags and rubbish that we cannot fully dispose of. To what extent do you agree with this opinion and what measures can you recommend for reducing this problem?*

Environmentalists today are campaigning for "reduce, recycle and reuse" in a bid to save the world, but we as a nation, have adopted "replace" as our mantra. This and many other factors are leading to a throwaway society. In this essay, I shall discuss some steps that can be taken to solve this problem.

There are many reasons leading to too much waste in land-fill sites. To begin with, modern lifestyle has contributed greatly to the increasing amount of waste and garbage produced every day. In other words, we have turned into a materialistic and mass-consumption society where we use more and throw away more than ever before. Once new things are acquired, we dispose-off these unwanted things to second hand shops or just in the trash cans.

Secondly, the markets today are flooded with cheap, single-use-only things that are more in demand than high priced quality items. Our houses and closets seem to be overflowing with goods that are more in quantity and less in value. Then, there is too much packaging done by the companies in a bid to make their things more attractive. All this is leading to a use and throw culture.

The solution lies in changing our attitude. We should get old things repaired and try to use them as long as possible. We should not buy things with excessive packaging. This will deter companies from doing too much packaging. We can also bring our own personal shopping bags instead of using plastic bags provided by stores and shops. Besides, the government can enforce stricter laws on companies to use biodegradable packaging. Furthermore, plastics, waste metal, glass can be recycled. Companies can also contribute by developing new raw material which is recyclable and will ultimately lead to less garbage.

To sum up, individuals, business and the government can share the responsibility to reduce the amount of waste material and to save the earth. If we do not take steps to tackle this problem on a war footing, our Earth will become uninhabitable.

Plan followed:
Intro:
Para 1: Reasons
Para 2: More reasons
Para 3: Solutions
Conclusion –

161. *The best way for the government to solve the problem of traffic congestion in cities, is to provide free public transport 24 hours a day, 7 days a week. To what extent do you agree or disagree with this statement?(3/3/22 – India)*

Some people opine that the most effective solution to urban traffic congestion is to provide free public transport round-the-clock. I believe that while free public transport could help in solving the traffic problem to some extent, it definitely is not the best solution, and other methods are better.

Admittedly, free public transportation would reduce traffic congestion as some people would definitely switch to public transportation if such a step is taken. Rising inflation and increasing fuel prices have drastically increased the living expenses especially in big cities and thus free public transportation would be a welcome step. It would not only increase money in people's pockets but also provide them with a cleaner environment.

Despite the benefits of free public transportation, I believe that other ways are better suited to address the traffic problems. The most effective would be to make public transportation more comfortable and frequent. In many cities, even though there is free public transportation, most people prefer their own vehicles for travelling. It is not cost that is a motivating factor for drivers to take public transport, it is convenience. Thus, rather than making public transportation free, governments should focus on making it more frequent and comfortable.

Another method that can be more effective is to improve parking facilities. A lot of traffic congestion is cities is due to the fact that people are forced to park on the roads due to lack of proper parking facilities. Thus, having proper parking would reduce people parking on road. Another innovative solution recently adopted by many local authorities has been different work timings for different industries and offices. This would mean that less people are travelling together at the same time and thus less traffic.

To sum up, although I believe that the number of private vehicle commuters would definitely come down with the introduction of free public transportation, making public transportation frequent, improving parking facilities and having different work timings for different offices would prove more effective in addressing it.

Plan followed:
Intro: Disagree
Para 1: Why public transport could be good
Para 2: Better methods to reduce traffic congestion
Para 3: Better methods
Conclusion: reiterate opinion
Written by Indroop Singh 1/6/2020
Similar:

162. *Some people believe that the government should spend money to provide faster public transport. Others think that there are other important priorities for public transport such as cost and environment. Discuss both views and give your opinion.*

Some individuals hold the opinion that while investing on public transport, the government should focus on the speed, whereas others believe that the cost and the environment should be given more weightage. I shall discuss both perspectives in the following paragraphs. I side with the former view.

There are many reasons why some people say that the government should spend on faster public transport. Firstly, it will give people more time for themselves and their families. There would also be less physical and mental exhaustion and they will be able to strike a balance between work and family time. Secondly, they would avoid using their personal vehicles, which would reduce congestion on roads, especially during peak hours.

On the other hand, those who favour investment on cheaper and eco-friendly public transport, give their reasons as follows. Firstly, more people would be able to afford such transport. Moreover, investment on buses and trains powered by renewable energy would be very good for the environment as there would be no emission of harmful greenhouse gases in the environment. This would ultimately benefit the health of the people.

I believe that investment on faster public transportation would be more worthwhile, as time is the most important factor for most people. Most people consider that time saved is money saved. So, they would be ready to spend more on a faster mode of public transport. For example, in New Delhi, ever since the metro rail has come into operation, many people have started commuting by it and do not use their own vehicles. It would automatically benefit the environment as there would be fewer cars on the roads.

To sum up, if a choice has to be made between the spending on the speed, or on the cost and eco-friendliness of public transport, then it would be more worthwhile to spend on making public transport faster. People would not mind the cost and the environmental benefits would automatically ensue.

Plan followed:

Intro: Discuss essay intro
Para 1: One view
Para 2: Other view
Para 3: Own view
Conclusion:

Written by: Indroop Singh

163. *Nowadays, some countries are spending a lot of money to make it easier to use bicycle. Why is this so? Is it the best solution to transport problem?*

It is true that many countries, such as the Netherlands, Denmark, Sweden, Japan, Switzerland have started investing in the bicycle industry. This essay intends to analyse the reasons of this phenomenon. I believe that although it is a good solution to the traffic problem, it is not the best solution.

The main reason is that these countries realize that cycling is a clean alternative to motorbikes and cars, and so investing in facilities for cycling will help reduce congestion and pollution. Secondly, cycling is cheaper and healthier than other forms of transport. Bicyclist commuters are generally healthier than those who drive motor vehicles to work. They also remain unaffected by OPEC decisions about crude oil production or the price per barrel.

Another very important reason for investing in this industry, is the potential of this industry to provide jobs. Every cycle lane which is made, and every cyclist who is created, contributes to job growth. In Europe alone, more than 6 lac people are employed in the cycling industry - more jobs than in mining and quarrying, the steel industry, and even any other automobile industry. There are more than a billion bicycles in the world, twice as many as automobiles. In recent years, bike production has climbed to over 100 million per year (compared to 50 million cars).

As far as the best solution to transport problem is concerned, cycling comes second to public transport. First, these need to be balanced by the rider in order to remain upright. Not everyone can ride one. Second, there is reduced protection in crashes, in comparison to motor vehicles. Another disadvantage is that there is longer travel time (except in densely populated areas). Cycling is also vulnerable to weather conditions. Finally, a basic level of fitness is required for cycling moderate to long distances. Public transport, on the other hand, caters to all segments of society.

To summarise, there are many motives for countries to invest in making cycling easier, which have been explained in the above paragraphs. However, cycling is not the best solution to transport problem. Investing in public transport takes the lead in this arena.

Plan followed:
Intro:
Para 1: Reasons
Para 2: More reasons
Para 3: Why investment in cycling is not the best option. *Conclusion::*

164. People are encouraged to get rid of things in order to get the newest fashion and the latest technology. Do the disadvantages of a throwaway society outweigh the economic advantages?

It is irrefutable that more and more people prefer buying new things rather than getting their old products repaired. While this craze for novelty or the latest products and fashion has some advantages, its drawbacks certainly outweigh them.

Admittedly, there are some benefits of consumerism. Firstly, consumerism leads to mass production, and mass manufacturing leads to mass employment. This is undoubtedly beneficial for the overall economy of the country. Secondly, consumerism leads to innovation. In other words, manufacturers are under constant pressure to innovate as people are consistently looking for the newer product or service.

However, despite the advantages, I consider consumerism to be a very detrimental trend. The main drawback is that consumerism leads to environmental degradation. The increasing demand for goods leads to increase in use of natural resources and energy consumption and this further leads to increase in pollution and waste. Another major disadvantage is the increase in the debt levels. A large number of people today are taking short loans for buying luxuries or things they can live without.

In addition, consumerism is changing society's value system with people shifting towards materialism and competition over integrity. People want to buy things they do not need so that they can stay above others. Finally, consumerism also has a negative effect on relationships as it forces people to work harder and spend less time with loved ones. In the long run, the love for materialistic things can never compete with satisfaction people achieve from relationships. Thus, most people despite being richer and having more luxuries are less happy than before.

To sum up, although consumerism does have economic benefits, I consider it to be a degeneration of our society.

Plan followed:
Intro:
Para 1: Positives of consumerism
Para 2: Cons of consumerism
Para 3: More cons of consumerism
Conclusion:

165. *An increase in production of consumer goods results in damage of the natural environment. What are the causes and possible solutions?(24/4/2021- India)*

Today we live in an era of continuously increasing consumer demand. This rate of consumption is increasing at an alarming rate. This essay shall deal with the causes of increase in production of goods and how it affects the environment and suggest some ways forward.

The first and foremost reason for the increase in production of consumer goods is the burgeoning population of today. More people lead to more demand. Secondly, because of globalization people are flooded with choices. When they see a new product they want that too. What is more, the buying capacity of people has gone up because of developing economies. Finally, the manufacturing industries are producing cheaper consumer goods by compromising with quality. Mostly these things have to be discarded after some time of use.

The most serious effect of this phenomenon is on the environment. Our landfill sites are filling up with non-biodegradable waste. It is also leading to pollution. Destroying used plastic is becoming a major problem everywhere. Even the recycling of plastic needs a lot of electricity. Conventional methods of generating electricity add to pollution. Disposing off a lot of waste materials such as heavy metals like lead and mercury and poisonous gases also adds to pollution. The amount of energy used in manufacturing and disposal of consumer goods is also leading to a brink of energy crises.

The solutions are not easy. People have to be made aware of the disastrous consequences of consumerism. People should buy only what is absolutely necessary. As far as possible, biodegradable materials should be used as raw materials and excessive packaging should be avoided. Industries should be encouraged to use alternative sources of energy during production. Quality should not be compromised with. This would definitely help in reducing the use-and-throw culture. Finally, waste disposal methods should be very good. Strict action should be taken against those industries, which dump their effluents indiscriminately.

Summing up, consumerism is rampant nowadays and it is having a detrimental effect on our environment but steps can be taken to minimize the bad effects of excessive consumerism.

Plan followed:

Intro: This essay shall deal with the causes of increase in production of goods and how it affects the environment and suggest some ways forward.

Para 1: Causes of increased production of consumer goods

Para 2: How it damages the environment

Para 3: Solutions

Conclusion:

166. *Nowadays, people live in the society where consumer goods are cheaper to buy. Do you think its advantages outweigh disadvantages?*

Globalization has ushered in an era of consumerism and people are flooded with cheap consumer products. While I believe that the lowering costs of consumer goods has its advantages, its drawbacks are certainly more.

The main advantage of cheap consumer goods is they can be afforded by the majority and this in turn means more production and employment. This is definitely beneficial for the overall economy of the country. In addition, it is bettering the quality of life of the poor and decreasing the difference in the lifestyles of the rich and poor. For example, today, even the poorest of the poor own consumer goods like televisions, mobile phones and computers.

Despite the advantages, I still consider the lowering of consumer goods prices to be harmful overall. Firstly, cheap consumer goods means there is a compromise with the quality and thus the life-cycle of today's consumer products is a lot shorter than before. Ultimately, the consumers suffer and they spend more because they end up buying the same product more often. Also, by making repair comparatively uneconomical, in a way, these cheap products are also leading to closure of small repair shops.

In addition, to offer cheap consumer goods without sacrificing profit margins, companies are resorting to automation and this results in further job losses. Last but not least, cheap consumer goods are leading to environmental degradation as they consume more natural resources and more energy. This further leads to increasing waste as evident from the overflowing landfill sites in urban areas and pollution.

To conclude, cheap consumer goods do have their advantages but these advantages come at a heavy price to the consumer and the environment.

Plan followed:
Intro: I believe that the disadvantages far outweigh the advantages
Para 1: Advantages
Para 2: Disadvantages
Para 3: Disadvantage to environment
Conclusion:

167. *It has been suggested that everyone in the world wants to own a car, a TV and a fridge. Do you think the disadvantages of such a development outweigh the advantages?*

It is irrefutable that more and more people are running after materialistic things like cars, television and refrigerators. While there are a few benefits of this materialism, I believe the drawbacks are much more.

Admittedly, there are certain advantages of the increasing demand of consumer goods. The main advantage is that the increasing demand means increasing production and employment. Thus, the increasing demand directly boosts the economy. Another advantage is that the quality of life of people is getting better. The luxuries of yesterday like cars, refrigerators and air conditioners have become the necessities of today. There is no doubt that people are living a more comfortable life than ever before.

However, this trend has several drawbacks. Firstly, the rising demand and use of such products is leading to environmental degradation. In fact, today a major source of air pollution in the cities is the exhaust fumes from cars. Similarly, more consumer goods means more use of natural resources and more waste. Waste is also increasing as companies are using lower quality materials like plastic to maintain profit margins.

Secondly, materialism also has a negative effect on relationships as it forces people to work harder and spend less time with loved ones. In the long run, the love for materialistic things can never compete with satisfaction people achieve from relationships. Thus, most people despite being richer and having more luxuries are less happier than before. Finally, materialism is leading to crime as more and more people are resorting to unethical means like stealing to get such things. People today value owning such things much more over integrity and honesty. Thus, society's value systems are being corrupted by this trend.

To sum up, there is no doubt that the increasing demand for materialistic things has some advantages, but the drawbacks certainly outweigh them.

Plan followed:
Intro: the disadvantages definitely outweigh the advantages
Para 1: Advantages of materialism
Para 2: Disadvantages of materialism
Para 3: Disadvantages of materialism
Conclusion:

168. *Some people feel that manufacturers and supermarkets have the responsibility to reduce the amount of packaging of goods. While others argue that customers should avoid buying goods with a lot of packaging. Discuss both views and give your opinion.*

It is a fact that the packaging done to attract customers is leading to environmental degradation. Some people say that the onus is on the supermarkets and manufacturers to cut off excess packaging, whereas others say that the customers should say no to products with excess packaging. I shall discuss both perspectives. I personally believe that a joint effort is needed by all.

The main reasons why some people say that the manufacturers and supermarkets should not do much packaging is that it would be a win-win situation for both – the manufacturer and the customer. For example, if the multinational company 'Colgate' gives up expensive packaging of its toothpastes, it could reduce its cost and pass on that profit margin to the customer, which would in turn increase its sales also.

On the other hand, those who say that customers should show greater interest towards items in simple packing, give the following reason. They say that companies would not take the risk of reducing packaging for fear of losing their market share. So, customers have to step forward. If customers start giving preference to materials with little or no packaging, then this would motivate producers to pack their products using the minimum packing and that too of biodegradable materials.

I believe that, both manufacturers and customers should take a step forward and save the environment. As it is, the excessive packaging only adds to the trash generated in the homes. Only the barest minimum packaging should be there to ensure the durability, safety and freshness of products. For instance, most instant foods have to be packed in several layers using aluminium foil and superior plastic, with the purpose of longer shelf life. In such cases, the packaging could be allowed. In all other cases packaging should be discouraged.

To summarise, manufacturers, supermarkets and customers have a collective role in reducing the amount of packaging of products.

Plan followed:
Intro: Manufacturers and consumers both should go against excessive packaging
Para 1: One view
Para 2: Second view
Para 3: Own view
Conclusion:

169. *More and more people want to buy famous brands of clothes, cars and other items. What are the reasons? Do you think it is a positive or negative development?*

It is irrefutable that branded products and services have become increasingly popular nowadays. This essay intends to discuss the reasons for this increasing brand consciousness. While there are some drawbacks of this trend, I consider it to be far more beneficial.

There are many reasons why people are going after brands. The first reason is that these are considered a status symbol. Brands speak about the person who is buying them. Secondly, advertising and the media have spread awareness about these brands like wildfire. Branded items are also shown to have better quality and thus people prefer them over other products. Moreover, these brands have come within the pocket of the ordinary person. With the growing economy, the purchasing power of people has gone up, which also makes them go for brands.

The increasing brand focus and consciousness has many advantages. The main advantage is that companies now emphasize on quality and customer service. Businesses know that to survive in today's competitive world, they need to have a good brand reputation, and hence people are offered better services. To cite an example, if a person buys a branded cell phone, but unfortunately it stops working for some reason, he gets a full replacement, provided it is within the warranty period. Companies are also benefited as it becomes easier to introduce new products into the market. They need to spend less on marketing, if they already have a good brand image. Another positive effect is that these brands have led to the emergence of another big industry, which is of imitations or copies. This secondary industry is catering to a far bigger population and is adding a lot to the economy.

On the downside, brands provide a feeling of inadequacy among those people who cannot afford them. Sometimes, people end up overspending on such items and this upsets the family budget. Some people may even resort to petty crime such as shoplifting, pickpocketing and chain snatching. Finally, people are becoming workaholics to buy such products, and are failing to draw a line between work and leisure and also between work and family, which is adding to their stress and strain.

To sum up, brand heedfulness can be attributed to many reasons. Despite the few drawbacks, I believe this rising lure of branded products to be a positive development overall.

Plan followed:
Intro:
Para 1: Reasons
Para 2: Why it is a positive development
Para 3: Why it is a negative development
Conclusion: *Written by: Indroop Singh*

170. *Some people say that the best way to improve road safety is to increase the minimum legal age for driving cars or riding motorbikes. To what extent do you agree or disagree?*

It is commonly believed that the ideal way to ensure road safety is to raise the minimum age for getting a driving licence. I believe that raising the legal age of driving would lead to more problems and other methods like banning the use of mobile phones and stricter punishments for traffic violators would turn out to be more effective.

I believe raising the minimum driving age would rather increase accidents. Today, most people are busy, and they do not have time to drive their children. Thus, teenagers and youngsters knowing driving is no more an option but a necessity. If driving is not allowed, it does not deter youngsters from driving but rather makes them drive illegally. For example, many teenagers are caught driving without a license in India as the legal driving age is on the higher side. Driving illegally means youngsters driving without knowing about traffic rules and driving fast to avoid police which leads to more accidents.

A more effective solution to reduce traffic accidents would be to ban mobile phone use while driving. Nowadays, the major reason for accidents is distracted driving, which means reading messages or taking calls while driving. Reckless and rash driving, which is associated with young age and lack of maturity, are certainly not the main reason for accidents. Thus, banning the use of mobile phones and inculcating a habit of undivided attention among people while driving would prove more effective.

Another solution that I think can prove more beneficial would be to have stringent fines and punishments for traffic violations and especially for repeat offences. In India particularly, many traffic accidents are caused by breaking of traffic rules, like jumping red lights or driving on the wrong side of the road to save time. Thus, a healthy culture of people following rules and regulations needs to be developed and this can be done by having harsher punishments like high fines, suspension of driving license and so on.

In conclusion, I think there are better alternatives to raising the legal age for driving as this could lead to more problems.

Plan followed:
Intro: Disagree
Para 1: It would lead to more accidents
Para 2: Other methods
Para 3: Other methods
Conclusion:
Written by: Indroop Singh (Exam question 7/11/2020, 9 am)

171. *The only way to improve the safety on our roads is to have stricter punishment for driving offenders. To what extent do you agree or disagree?*

It is believed that sterner punishment for violators of traffic rules is the only way to decrease accidents on roads. While I believe that traffic violators should be punished strictly, I disagree that stricter punishment for those violating the law is the only solution for ensuring road safety.

Admittedly, reckless driving, speeding and breach of traffic rules by careless drivers can cause accidents. Therefore, a more stringent punishment for drivers would be an effective measure to make roads safer. It would deter people from violating traffic rules such as jumping the red light and over-speeding. This would be a step towards road safety.

However, there are many other factors which cause road accidents, and it is equally essential to deal with them to improve road safety. To begin with, poor road condition is considered a major reason for road casualties. For example, narrow roads and sharp curves often force even law-abiding drivers to make mistakes. Therefore, drivers alone cannot be blamed for such mishaps and giving them stricter punishments in these cases is no solution.

Furthermore, poor climate conditions can be a major cause of accidents. For instance, poor visibility due to dense mist and rain, slippery roads on account of snowfall make driving difficult and cause serious accidents in many countries. Stricter punishment for drivers is a futile exercise in handling such problems. Modern technological innovations should be used to deal with such emergency situations.

In summary, while punishing drivers with heavier penalties would reduce accidents, there are certain situations where drivers are not responsible for accidents, and so other effective measures should also be taken.

Plan followed:
Intro: partial
Para 1: Driving offenders should be punished but that is not the only solution
Para 2: Poor road condition is considered a major reason for road casualties
Para 3: Poor climate condition can be a major cause of accidents
Conclusion: Hence apart from punishing drivers with heavier penalties other effective measures should also be taken

172. Some people believe governments should spend money on building train and subway lines to reduce traffic congestion. Others think that building more and wider roads are the better way to reduce traffic congestion. Discuss both views and give your opinion.

In order to mitigate the problem of traffic congestion, some individuals suggest that motorways should be made. Others, however, believe that trains and subway lines should be constructed. In this essay I will discuss both perspectives. I personally believe that a combination of both approaches is the ideal solution to ameliorate the problem of traffic congestion.

The main reason why some people are in favour of expanding the road network is that it could naturally reduce traffic jams. Obviously, more and more private vehicles would be accommodated, and commute time would reduce. This strategy would also be good from the economic perspective. The cost of road construction would be much lower than that of subway lines. The money thus saved can be used for other key sectors, such as healthcare and education.

On the other hand, those who are for the construction of mega rail systems, give their reasons as follows. To begin with, it is a more effective method to improve traffic condition. It has been seen that in countries where subway systems have been made up to standard, the number of private vehicles has come down. Trains can carry a much larger number of passengers than any other form of transport. Secondly, it saves time while commuting within the city. For instance, in New Delhi many people now prefer to travel by the metro as they can reach their destination in much less time than any other means of transport.

I personally believe that in places where the budget of the governments is constrained, a combination of both approaches is needed. For example, in India, the road networks are being expanded in almost all places, but subway lines are also being added slowly and steadily in many cities. In the foreseeable future, the expanded road networks are also going to prove inadequate, and so subway lines would remain the only solution.

To conclude, both methods discussed above can provide relief to traffic congestion. However, it is my opinion that the method to build trains and subways, would definitely prove better in the long run.

Plan followed:
Intro: Discuss essay
Para 1: Advantages of road network
Para 2: Advantages of subways and train network
Para 3: Own view
Conclusion:

173. *In some countries the number of people using bicycles as main transport mode is decreasing, even though it is so beneficial. Why is this so? How can people be encouraged to use more bicycles?*

It is indubitable that the bicycle is being used less and less as a preferred mode of transport, despite the fact that it is advantageous. This essay intends to analyze some reasons of this phenomenon and also suggest ways to motivate people to use more bicycles.

There are many reasons for not using the bicycles in today's world. The first reason is that life has become busy and everyone has so much to do and so little time. Other modes of transport are more time effective. Secondly, the roads are so full of heavy traffic that bicycles are not safe. Another reason for not using the bike is the unfavourable weather. The hot and humid summer months make it impossible for anyone to use the bike. Of course, no one wants to reach the office smelling of sweat. Last but not least, people want to show off their status, and riding a bike does not solve this purpose.

There are many ways to motivate people to use the bike. The onus is on the government to make cycling safer and more inviting. Investment needs to be done in a vast network of cycling paths. For example, in Denmark, there are 19000 km of cycle tracks, as a result of which many people ride bikes. These cycle tracks are clearly marked, have smooth surfaces, separate signs and lights for those on two wheels, and wide enough to allow side-by-side cycling and overtaking. Perhaps, that is why, there are more bicycles than the number of people in Denmark.

Furthermore, people could be made aware of the benefits of cycling. Bicycle is a cheap and green mode of transport. Media, such as the TV, could be used for this purpose. Our celebrities, who act as the role models for many, could be a lot of help. If they start using the bicycle, many youngsters would follow them and do the same. For example, a few months ago, Vidya Balan, India's famous film star, was seen on TV saying that whenever she has to gift something, she gifts a sapling. Since then, I have started giving a sapling to my friends on their birthdays.

To sum up, there are many reasons why people do not use the bicycle now, but some effective steps could be taken by the governments to promote the use of bicycles.

Plan followed:
Intro:
Para 1: Reasons
Para 2: ways to motivate people
Para 3: More ways
Conclusion:

174. *In some cities people are choosing cars instead of bicycles, while in other cities riding bikes is replacing cars. Why is this the case? Which development do you think is better?*

In some cities, people are switching to cars from bicycles as a popular means of transport, whereas in some other cities the bicycles are gaining more popularity than cars. There are many reasons why such trends are being observed. In my opinion, in the present scenario, the shift towards more eco-friendly modes, as bicycles is a better development.

There are many reasons why people prefer cars, to bicycles. Firstly, it is a sign of progress in developing cities and towns, where the buying capacity of people has increased. Moreover, people have moved their residences from crowded urban areas to the quieter suburbs, because of which cars have become a necessity. Finally, cars are more comfortable, faster, safer and more convenient than bikes. Cars are also better for the elderly, the handicapped and the sick people.

On the other hand, there are reasons why people are switching to bicycles. To begin with, people are becoming more aware of the damage being caused to the environment. So, they are switching to bicycles and reducing the use of cars. Governments in many parts of the world are also working towards promoting this trend. For example, in Denmark the government has provided 19000 km of bicycle tracks, which has encouraged many people to switch from cars to bicycles.

I believe adopting the use of bicycles and reducing the use of cars is better because of many reasons. Apart from the health benefits and benefits to the environment, the cycling industry has the potential of providing jobs. For example, in Europe alone, more than 6 lac people are employed in the cycling industry - more jobs than even in the automobile industry. More other countries have also started investing in a big way and have seen many positive effects. The overall economy of these countries has been boosted.

To sum up, I would reiterate my view that even though the car has some advantages over the bicycle, the use of bicycles is better, as it is not only a step towards saving the environment; it is also an economical way to remain fit and healthy.

Plan followed:
Intro: Problem solution essay intro
Para 1: Reasons of choosing cars over bicycles
Para 2: Reasons of choosing bicycles over cars
Para 3: More reason in favour of bicycles
Conclusion:

175. *In many cities and towns, the high volume of road traffic is a problem. What are the causes of that and what actions could be taken to solve the problem?*

In recent times there has been an unprecedented increase in the number of vehicles on the roads. This essay intends to analyze the reasons of this phenomenon, and also suggest some solutions to alleviate the situation.

There are many reasons why traffic has increased in towns and cities. One is that cars have become more affordable for the average consumer. For instance, Tata Motor's Nano car, is now called the poor man's car. Secondly, most of the people have to commute to work, and the public transport is not that frequent or reliable. Even the shopping malls and multiplex cinema houses have opened out of towns in the suburbs, which have made them even more inaccessible without the personal vehicle. Another obvious reason is that people have become more affluent, as women have also started working along with the men. This has also led to the need of two cars or more per household.

The solutions are not simple, because of the complexity of its causes. However, one option can be to improve the reliability of public transport to encourage people to take the bus or the train rather than get in the car. Bus passes or train passes could be issued to daily commuters, which would be very attractive for them. Steps could also be taken to discourage the people to use the personal car by increasing the toll tax, for example.

One more step, which has yielded results in many developed nations, is the HOV (High Occupancy Vehicle) lanes on motorways. This means that there are lanes reserved for those private vehicles, which are fully occupied. This has encouraged car-pooling. Another useful suggestion is to make bicycle tracks so that people are encouraged to cover short distances on bicycles. For example, Denmark has 19000 km of bicycle tracks, and that is why people prefer to ride bicycles.

To sum up, I feel that the problem of traffic is not easy to control. However, government rules and awareness among people can resolve this problem up to certain limit.

Plan followed:
Intro:
Para 1: Why traffic has increased in towns and cities
Para 2: More reasons
Para 3: suggestions
Para 4: Suggestions
Conclusion:

176. *The unlimited use of cars may cause many problems. What are those problems? In order to reduce the problems, should we discourage people to use cars?*

Nowadays, there are increasing number of cars on the road which are creating problems such as traffic jams, air pollution and longer commuting periods. In this essay I intend to discuss these problems. I strongly believe that this dependence on the car should be reduced by some proactive steps by the government.

There are many problems which are caused by the excessive number of cars on the roads. First, it leads to a lot of greenhouse gas emissions because of burning of petrol and diesel. Secondly, increased congestion leads to traffic jams and gridlocks, which wastes a lot of time. During peak hours the traffic moves at a snail's pace. All these problems definitely need to be addressed if people want to lead stress-free lives.

Many steps can be taken by the government to ameliorate the problems. One way to stimulate public transport use is to make private car use more expensive and inconvenient. The introduction of tolls along urban motorways has been successfully employed in many cities. Other such measures are high-priced permits for parking in urban areas and the restriction of parking to a limited number of cars. Faced with high costs or no place to park, commuters would perhaps be more willing to abandon their cars in favour of buses or trains.

The governments could also encourage public transport use. The construction of free car parks at suburban train stations has proven successful in quite a number of countries. This allows commuters to drive part of the way, but take public transport into the central, most congested, urban areas. Indeed, making public transport more comfortable and convenient should work to attract more commuters and decrease traffic congestion. Public transport that is convenient and comfortable retains its passengers, much like any business that satisfies its customers. The more commuters committed to taking public transport, the less congestion on city streets.

To sum up, the increasing number of cars is creating problems like pollution, accidents and traffic congestion but steps could be taken to minimize the problems.

Plan followed:

Intro:
Para 1: Reasons
Para 2: Solutions
Para 3: Solutions
Conclusion:

177. *Some people claim that there are more disadvantages of the car than its advantages. Do you agree or disagree?*

Someone has rightly said that – "The car has become an article of dress without which we feel uncertain, unclad, and incomplete". In my opinion, the merits of the car outstrip its demerits.

There are many advantages of car. The most important advantage is that it has given people freedom of movement. The ease of transportation, which a car brings, is more than any other form of transportation. For instance, a car takes people from destination to destination and no time is wasted waiting for the bus or train. Therefore, time and distance is not a barrier any more. What is more, families can go out together. This becomes especially helpful when there are elderly or the disabled and sick members in the family.

Furthermore, the automobile industry provides jobs to millions of workers. Filling stations, restaurants, and other businesses that serve automobile travellers are of major importance to a country's economy. In addition, many developing nations have begun making automobiles to boost their economy. That is why India has promoted many automobile-manufacturing industries such as Tata and Mahindra.

On the other hand, the disadvantages of the car cannot be overlooked. The increase in pollution, traffic jams and accidents are the natural sequel to the burgeoning population of cars. Moreover, people's overdependence on cars can lead to decrease in practices such as walking and cycling and this has led to a number of diseases such as obesity.

On balance, the advantages to people's lives and the economic impact created by the car definitely outweigh the disadvantages. However, we must know when and how-much to use the car so that we can minimize the cons to some extent.

Plan followed:
Intro: In my opinion, the advantages of the car outstrip its disadvantages.
Para 1: advantages of car
Para 2: the automobile industry provides jobs to millions of workers
Para 3: Disadvantages
Conclusion:

178. *The number of cars keeps increasing, so road systems should be expanded. Some people think the government should pay for it, while others think the car owners should pay for it. Discuss both views and give your opinion.*

In recent years there has been an unprecedented increase in the number of cars, which has led to the need for expanding the road systems. Some people opine that the government should pay for these motorways, while others contend that the car owners should pay. In this essay, I intend to discuss both viewpoints. I believe that the cost should be shared by the government and the users of the road systems.

Those who say that the government should bear the cost of road network expansion argue that people have already paid a lot of taxes and so now it is the onus of the government to provide them these services. Another reason is that these roads benefit the whole country and not just the car users. For example, when connectivity improves through efficient roads, then businesses and tourism flourish. This benefits the country and so it is unfair to charge extra from the car users.

On the other hand, there are many reasons why some people say that car owners should pay for the expanding road systems. Firstly, if this is not done then even those people who are not using the roads for their private vehicles would be paying for it through taxes. Secondly, people would also be encouraged to do carpooling so that the added expenses are shared. Finally, higher cost for car owners would encourage public transport use. This would definitely lead to less congestion on the roads.

I believe that, the government could make the roads and later recover some cost in the form of toll tax from the people using the roads. It would be unfair if government pays all the money out of the taxes. The government has so much else on its shoulders such as basic healthcare and education, which need a lot of funds. So, it would be advisable to put some part of the brunt of this extra expenditure on the car owners.

To conclude, expanding the road system is the need of the hour. The government should provide services such as good roads, but should recover most part of this money from those who use these roads.

Plan followed:

Intro: Some opine that the government should pay while others contend that the car owners should pay. I tend to agree with the latter
Para 1: Why government should pay
Para 2: Why car owners should pay
Para 3: Own view
Conclusion:

179. *In some countries, small town-centre shops are going out of business because people tend to drive to large out-of-town stores. As a result, people without cars have limited access to out-of-town stores, and it may result in an increase in the use of cars. Do you think the disadvantages of this change outweigh its advantages?*

In recent years, a mushroom growth of large shopping malls has been seen in the suburbs of the cities and towns. Many people are worried that this phenomenon may lead to the increase in use of cars and this would not be good for the environment. While there are a few disadvantages of having large shopping malls in the outskirts of cities, I believe that the advantages are far more.

There are many benefits of having shopping malls in the out-of-town sites. To begin with, such stores can sell goods at lower prices as the operating costs of these shopping complexes are much less. It is well known that the suburban land costs much less and therefore the rents and lower operating costs directly lead to lower prices. Secondly, the shopping centres in these areas would be definitely bigger because of more availability of land and so consumers will have more choices as more variety could be displayed.

Furthermore, it would help ease urban traffic and housing pressures in the city centre. The city centres are already too congested and opening big shopping centres here would worsen the situation. It is a fact that rapid urbanisation is taking place and more and more people are shifting from the villages to the cities. If these shopping centres are on the outskirts of cities, they would be nearer to the neighbouring villages and many of them would not then need to move to cities as some comforts of the cities would be nearer to their homes.

Admittedly, there are a few disadvantages of having these shopping centres outside the cities. Firstly, it would mean that the small stores within the cities would face challenges and may have to shut down altogether. Secondly, there would be some increase in the use of cars. However, on the whole the advantages would be much more.

To conclude, having shopping centres in the suburbs definitely has more advantages than disadvantages.

Plan followed:
Intro:
Para 1: benefits of having shopping malls in the out-of-town sites
Para 2: it would help ease urban traffic and housing pressures the city centre
Para 3: More benefits
Conclusion:

180. *Today, large shopping centres and shopping malls are more common than small shops. Is this a positive or a negative development?*

It is indubitable that supermarkets and malls have gained a lot of popularity and have driven many small shopkeepers out of business. While I agree that this trend is negative for the small shops and the environment, the positive effects are much more.

On the positive side, these mega stores and malls provide various things to people under one roof. For instance, people can buy grocery items, fruit, vegetables, stationery, clothes, shoes and many other things without having to go from one shop to the other. The second major advantage is that these stores provide things at a cheaper rate. This is because they buy things in bulk directly from the manufacturers. So, they get things at much less price than the small businessman. They pass on some of their profit margin to the customers. So, people are happy frequenting these stores.

Furthermore, shopping from these stores saves time. As these stores are usually in the outskirts of the city or town, people usually plan going there and have their list of things they need ready. They just move through the aisles with the shopping cart and pick up what all they need. No time is wasted waiting for the salesman to show them the things. Last but not least, these stores and malls have provided employment to many people. It has been seen that wherever these stores have opened, many people from the surroundings get work there in the different departments, such as unpacking, arranging, billing, maintaining stocks and so on.

On the other hand, it cannot be denied that these supermarkets and malls promote the use of cars, which leads to congestion on the roads and also adds to pollution. Secondly these stores have snatched away the livelihood of many small shopkeepers, who have been forced to shut down. In addition, these stores promote consumerism as people are attracted by the variety of things displayed beautifully and so tend to purchase things even if they do not need them.

To sum up, despite a few disadvantages of supermarkets and malls, the advantages are much more. That is perhaps why these have become popular among the people.

Written by: Kiranpreet Kaur

Plan followed:
Intro: Largely positive
Para 1: Positive
Para 2: Positive
Para 3: Negative
Conclusion: Reiterate

181. *Some people think that it is more important to plant trees in open areas of towns and cities than to build more housing. To what extent do you agree or disagree?*

It is believed that it is more meaningful to plant trees in the open urban areas, rather than build more houses. While housing is needed to meet the demands of the growing population, I strongly agree that trees should be planted in open areas as trees provide environmental, social and economic benefits.

Admittedly, housing is needed to meet the demands of the burgeoning population, but high-rise buildings should be made instead of spread out low rise houses and leave the open spaces for planting more and more trees. New housing can also be made in the countryside to convert villages into towns. In fact many people are opting to live there because of the fresh air and quiet atmosphere.

On the other hand, the main benefit of planting trees in cities is to the environment. Trees help purify the polluted air in the cities and towns. Research has proven that 100 trees can remove tonnes of carbon dioxide annually. Trees are also known to cut down everyday noise of cities, thus tackling noise pollution. To add to it, rainwater does not run off into drains if there are trees in urban areas. It is filtered into the ground, thus saving the city money that is spent on drains and artificial controls. Finally, trees provide shade to homes, roads, office areas and parking spaces, thus reducing the energy consumption. In parking lots also, trees help keep cars cooler, which leads to less pollution.

Planting trees in cities helps the city grow socially and economically as well. They provide an area where people can meet, socialize and also exercise. Children also get a close to nature place, where they can play. The commercial value of an urban property with trees is more than one without trees. Retail outlets and businesses located in areas with trees attract more customers.

To sum up, although houses are needed in cities to live in, trees are needed more to strengthen and improve the quality of the life in overcrowded cities. They play a vital role in combating climate change and provide numerous economic and social benefits.

Plan followed:
Intro: Agree
Para 1: Housing is needed but trees are more important
Para 2: Advantages of trees
Para 3: More advantages
Para 4: More Advantages
Conclusion

182. *The key to solving environmental problems is for the present generation to sacrifice their convenient life (or live a less comfortable life) for the sake of future generations. To what extent do you agree or disagree?(17/2/22 1pm)*

Some people think that for the benefit of future generations, and to solve the present environmental challenges, the current generation should live a less comfortable lifestyle. I completely agree with this statement, as it will be a great step for our planet and the future of mankind.

Firstly, it is a widely known fact that the biggest cause for environmental problems is increased human desires for luxurious lifestyles, which creates an undue pressure on our environment. If the present generation will not make a few changes in their everyday life, such as, using paper bags instead of polythene bags for carrying groceries, then the future generation will not be able to survive. However, these minor sacrifices will solve the environmental issues to a great extent.

Secondly, there is an impending crisis for future generations due to the depletion of natural resources which is happening at an alarming rate. The judicious usage of these resources by today's generation will ensure a positive outlook for future energy and environment needs for the upcoming generation. To illustrate, in most of the developed countries people have started adopting cycling as their preferred option to commute for work instead of going by cars. As a result, there is a steady decrease in carbon emissions and fuels like oil and gas will last much longer.

Finally, the reason why the sacrifices by people is the need of the hour is that other alternatives like stricter laws by governments have failed to make any impact in solving the environmental problems. The state efforts go in vain due to lack of funds, and manpower to implement the laws. Consequently, people's contribution has become the single most significant factor with the potential to mitigate the environmental challenges and provide a secure future.

To conclude, if the modern-day man makes certain cuts from his extravagant lifestyle, it can go a long way in dealing with the environmental crisis of today and secure a better future for the coming generations.

Plan followed:

Intro: paraphrase and give opinion
Para 1: Agree. Sacrifice is necessary for solving environmental problems
Para 2: Agree, sacrifice is necessary for future generations
Para 3: Agree, other alternatives are not effective. So, this is the key
Conclusion: Reiterate opinion.

183. *Living in close contact with nature is important for our physical and mental wellbeing. Why do people not keep adequate contact with nature these days? Suggest solution?*

These days people are becoming increasingly detached from nature and spending more and more time inside. Unfortunately, this behaviour has taken a toll on their health and happiness. This essay intends to analyze the causes of this situation and suggest some solutions to address this problem.

The main reason why people cannot keep adequate contact with nature is the kind of jobs they do these days. Years ago, life was simple, people mostly worked in farms and fields. Now people have high pressure jobs in factories and offices. Most jobs are in cities which are concrete jungles packed with people. People spend the majority of their time sitting in a stuffy cubicle in front of a computer. Basking in natural sunlight and fresh air has become a thing of the past.

The second reason people are spending more time inside is because of modern technologies like TVs, video games, computers, smartphones, etc. Instead of playing outside, people like to sit in front of a video game console and spend hours on it. Binge-watching a TV show on Netflix is so much more fun than going outside for a run or a walk. Most youngsters spend their free time on smartphones checking their social media. Today's generation is rightly called the indoor generation. Finally, due to the rising cost of houses people are living in flats and so do not have access to gardens or open spaces in their homes.

One solution to this problem is to bring nature inside the urban core, requiring office buildings to have windows that let in natural sunlight and fresh air. Workplaces filled with indoor plants have much better air quality. Also, sitting in a garden filled with plants and flowers during a lunch break can bring people closer to nature. In addition to this people should take extra effort to limit their inside time and instead engage in activities that bring them closer to nature like hiking, kayaking, fishing, gardening, etc. Also, children should be encouraged to play outside rather than be in front of a screen.

In conclusion, modern technology and urban jobs have alienated people from nature but there are numerous ways to feel closer to nature and reap its benefits.

Plan followed:
Intro: Problem solution essay
Para 1: Reason
Para 2: Reason
Para 3: Solutions
Conclusion:

(Exam question, 10/10/2020 Abu Dhabi)

184. *Some people believe that climate has the greatest effect on people's way of life. Others believe that the economy of the region has the greatest effect. Discuss both views and give your opinion. (7/1/23 India 9 am)*

It is believed by some that climate has the most significant impact on people's lives, while others argue that economy is the most significant factor. I believe that a good economy enables people to disregard the effects of climate and thus economy is the overriding factor.

On the one hand, the main reason given by those who believe that climate has the greatest impact is that climate determines the variability and availability of natural resources people depend on like food, water, and energy. For example, deserts are scarcely populated because of the hot climate which leads to water scarcity. Climate influences how people live and what jobs they do. People's lifestyle including what they eat, what clothes they wear, the type of houses they live in, all in some way or another depend upon the climate, the region experiences. Similarly, ice fishing is the most common profession in cold frozen countries, while agriculture is the most common profession in warm and humid climates.

On the other hand, those who believe that economy is the principal factor say that because economy frames the choices and decisions people make regarding work, leisure, consumption, and how much to save. For example, in rich and developed countries, people tend to spend more as the governments can provide social security in the form of pensions and free health care, while in poor countries people are more likely to save. Similarly, developed countries with good economies have a more educated workforce and thus their citizens secure better jobs, while people from poor developing countries are seen employed as labor.

In the past, I believe climate had the major impact on life, but today the impact of climate can be limited by a good economy. The biggest evidence for this can be seen in the oil-rich middle eastern countries, who have established modern cities in the middle of deserts with the help of their rich economies. Their people today have the same facilities and luxuries as available in other developed countries, despite the region's harsh climate.

In conclusion, I would like to reiterate that although both climate and economy impact people's way of life, the impact of economy is certainly more.

Plan followed:
Intro: Problem solution essay
Para 1: Reason
Para 2: Reason
Para 3: Solutions
Conclusion:
(21 August,2021 India, 9 Am)

185. *Some people think that cultural traditions may be destroyed when they are used as money making attractions aimed at tourists. Others believe it is the only way to save these traditions. Discuss both sides and give your opinion.*

It is believed by some people that cultural traditions may be destroyed if they are modified to attract tourists, whereas others hold the view that if we do not use them for tourism, these cultural attractions will die. This essay intends to discuss both perspectives. I, personally side with the latter view.

Those who say that cultural traditions should be modified to make them alluring for tourists, argue that to boost economy, every country should do its effort to attract tourists, even if it means changing some traditions to lure tourists. For example, there is a temple in south India where people can enter only after wearing a specific type of loincloth. My uncle was not allowed to go in because he did not want to wear that loincloth. Such rigid practices can deter many tourists and indirectly affect the economy.

On the other hand, the main reason why some people say that cultural traditions are damaged when used as revenue-earning attractions, is that when these traditions are altered then these lose their original features. Sometimes it makes cultural traditions disappear altogether. For example, in Jaisalmer in India the local arts and crafts are not completely produced in a local village with local stone. Instead, potters use materials of another territory to make goods glossy to attract tourists.

I believe that culture and tradition are deep rooted and minor superficial changes cannot harm them in any way. However, the changes should be made with caution to retain the inherent elements of culture. That is why a new concept of tourism, creative tourism has come up, which entails bringing in changes that would increase the number of tourists without damaging the basic culture and tradition of any place.

Summing up, to save cultural traditions there is a need to make some changes to make them captivate the tourist of today. If this is not done, then cultural traditions as well as tourists - both will be lost.

Plan followed:
Intro: Discuss essay intro
Para 1: One view
Para 2: Other view
Para 3: Own view
Conclusion: to save cultural traditions we need to make some changes to make them attract tourists

186. *When visiting other countries, some people take full advantage of opportunities to learn about culture and tradition of foreign countries. How can visitors learn about culture and tradition of other countries? Why do some people learn about culture and tradition of foreign countries while other people do not?*

Globalization has made it possible for people to travel around to visit other countries. While doing so, some people grab all chances of learning about foreign culture and traditions, whereas others do not. This essay shall analyze the reasons why people have different attitudes in this aspect and also discover the effective ways for people to learn about those culture and traditions.

The reason why some people do not learn about the culture and tradition is that they visit foreign countries just to relieve the monotony of their routine life. They only focus on visiting historical places and tourist attractions. They also do some activities which are unavailable in their own homeland. For instance, people go to Thailand just to do some paragliding and an 'Underwater Walk' in Coral Island at Pattaya. They do not have any enthusiasm to meet or intermingle with the local people to know about their culture and tradition.

However, other people are interested in learning the culture and traditions when they go in a foreign country. They want to absorb everything new and enrich their knowledge of the world. Anything different from their own life fascinates them and they love sharing their newly learnt culture and traditions to their kith and kin back home. It is not only a happy but a proud moment for them.

There are many ways in which culture and traditions of foreign countries can be learnt. Having some know-how of that country's language could help. Every possible opportunity should be grasped for starting a conversation with the locals of that place. There will be many in that country who would love to talk and mix up with you to learn about your culture and traditions. This culture exchange is a win-win situation for both the tourists and the locals. Of course, having an earnest desire to learn something new is definitely the primary motivating factor to learn about the foreign country's culture and tradition.

To sum up, through careful analyses of visitors motivation in their visits, we can understand why some people are interested in learning the foreign culture and tradition while others are not and there are many feasible ways of learning all that for those who are really interested.

Plan followed:
Intro:
Para 1: Why some people learn foreign traditions and culture
Para 2: Why some people do not learn foreign traditions and culture
Para 3: How people can learn foreign traditions and culture
Conclusion:

187. *Some people believe that air travel should be restricted because it causes serious pollution and uses up the world's fuel resources. To what extent do you agree or disagree?*

It is believed by some that air travel should be made less as it creates pollution and uses fuel. While it is true that air travel has a downside, I disagree that it should be decreased, as it would lead to many other problems. I believe other alternatives to save the fuels and environment should be considered.

Admittedly, there are a few disadvantages of too many flights. The main areas of concern are the decreasing level of fossil fuels and pollution caused by burning these fuels. The amount of carbon footprint left by a single flight is a huge contributor to global warming. The gases released cause erosion of the ozone layer which leads to many other health hazards besides global warming.

However, to simply discourage flights is not the answer. International tourism has become the backbone of many economies of the world. Many countries are earning from tourism. Many people are employed in this industry. Many businesses like hotels and leisure centres are dependent on tourists. So, if we discourage international tourism, it would create new and even worse problems. Many businesses would go broke and many people would be without jobs.

It is true that air travel consumes oil, but other modes of transportation are also causing pollution and using fuel. Discouraging private cars and encouraging people to use public transport could help save the environmental resources in a big way. Therefore, it would be a very unpractical decision to restrict air travel at the cost of people's mobility, or worse, at the cost of the development of the economy. Technology could also be used to produce more environmentally friendly and fuel efficient engines.

Summing up, instead of restricting air travel, we should develop more efficient engine that produces more energy output with less fuel and fewer major air pollutants. We should also focus on limiting private vehicles and encouraging public transport.

Plan followed:
Intro: Disagree
Para 1: Why we should not discourage flights
Para 2: More advantages of tourism
Para 3: Talk about other things causing pollution and using fuel
Conclusion: Reiterate opinion

Similar essay: Some people think the cheap air flight gives ordinary people more freedom. However, others think the cheap air flight should be banned because it pollutes the air and brings many other problems. Discuss both views and give your opinion.

188. *Air travel can only benefit the richest people in the world. Ordinary people can get no advantage with the development of air travel. To what extent do you agree or disagree?*

It is believed by some that air travel has advantages only for the wealthiest people and there are no benefits for the vast majority of the middle and lower class people. While air travel has a lot of benefits for those wealthy who actually travel, it also has innumerable benefits for those who depend on those tourists.

Admittedly, travelling by air benefits the rich. Firstly, they can travel to any corner of the world and learn about that place. They get first-hand experience of mingling with people of the host country and learn about their culture and lifestyle. Secondly, they get the opportunity of spreading their business worldwide and thus add to their wealth.

However, the ordinary man is also benefitted in various ways. To begin with, when rich tourists come to visit a place, they spend a lot in hotels, tourist places and also in the shopping centres from where they buy souvenirs. Many people are employed in the tourism industry. Even if they cannot travel themselves, their source of income is directly or indirectly dependent on these tourists who travel by air. For example, in India, during the tourist season, many guides, rickshaw and taxi drivers earn enough to last them a whole year.

Moreover, it is a well-known fact that, as tourists come, the governments spend on infrastructure such as stadiums roads and hotels. All these are used by the common man. In addition, the common man gets opportunity for culture exchange even without himself travelling by air. When other people come he learns about their culture and gives them the good points of his culture. Finally, nowadays, most of the airline companies are offering economy class tickets which are affordable by the common man.

Summing up, air travel benefits all people and not just the most affluent. It has direct benefits for those who travel, but indirect benefits for those who do not themselves travel.

Plan followed:
Intro: Disagree
Para 1: given statement is not justified in today's scenario.
Para 2: ordinary man is benefitted in various ways
Para 3: More advantages for the common man
Conclusion: air travel benefits all people and not just the most affluent.

189. *International travel makes people prejudiced rather than broad-minded. What are its causes and what measures can be taken to solve this problem?*

It is irrefutable that international tourism has taken mammoth dimensions. Unfortunately, sometimes, international tourism creates tension rather than understanding between people from different cultures. In this essay I intend to delve into the causes of this situation and suggest some ways to alleviate the problem.

The most important reason why some are opposed to international tourism is that tourists may unknowingly show disrespect for local culture. For instance, we generally cover our heads in a religious place. A tourist may not do so or take his shoes inside a temple. This may offend the local people. Sometimes, youngsters may be attracted towards the western culture, which the tourists bring with them and many may find this as a threat to the local culture.

Moreover, the tourist dollar may not be helping the local people. We all know that tourists stay in five-star hotels and enjoy the best facilities. They may be taking two showers a day, whereas the local people may not have enough water to drink. This has been the case in Shimla, which is a very popular hill station in Himachal Pradesh, India. On top of that, when tourists buy souvenirs from local artisans, they bargain a lot. The poor artisans, who look up to tourists for their livelihood, end up earning the bare minimum. Finally, tourism creates pollution, which helps nobody. We are all suffering the consequences of global warming.

The solutions are not simple. Tourism cannot be discouraged. It is the backbone of many economies of the world. First of all, the tour operators should take the onus of guiding the tourists about the main things of local culture. Secondly, the tourists should stay with locals as paying guests. This would be a win-win situation for both. Local people would earn and the tourist would taste the local culture. Finally, ecotourism should be promoted. For example, if an elephant ride is possible, the tourist should avoid using car. After all, a good tourist is one – who takes away nothing, but photographs, and leaves behind nothing, but footprints.

Summing up, international tourism does have a downside to it, but many steps can be taken to lessen the negative effects.

Plan followed:

Intro: This essay shall discuss why International tourism makes people prejudiced and suggest solutions
Para 1: Reasons
Para 2: More reasons
Para 3: solutions
Conclusion:
Similar essay: Tourism is an excellent way to develop a country, but it can also cause harm. How can countries ensure that tourism benefits the development?
Similar: Most countries believe that international tourism has harmful effects. Why do they think so? How to change their views?

190. *People have to spend more and more time to travel from their homes for jobs and study. What are the reasons? How can we solve this problem?*

It is indubitable that commuting time for study or work has increased in the past few years. This essay intends to analyze some causes behind this situation and also suggest possible ways to alleviate this problem.

The most obvious reason is that roads are very congested, as the number of vehicles has increased to unprecedented levels in the past decade or so. Everyone seems to own a car nowadays and so the traffic during peak hours moves at a snail's pace. What used to take 20 minutes earlier, takes about 50 minutes now. Second reason for this is the suburbanization of cities. People are moving to the suburbs in search of quieter, cheaper and more open houses, as a consequence of which travel time to work or study has gone up.

The solutions are not easy, but joint efforts by the government and the people can help to lessen the gravity of the situation. At the government level, steps could be taken to improve the public transport. This could be done by increasing the comfort and frequency of public transport and decreasing the fare. That way more people would be motivated to use the public transport. People should be motivated to do car-pooling by having HOV (High occupancy vehicle) lanes. Only those cars, which are fully occupied, are allowed to move on such lanes, because of which the traffic on these lanes moves faster. Such a system is being used very successfully in many parts of the USA.

At the individual level, people should voluntarily opt for public transport even if that involves being bound by the time of the bus or train. Wherever office and lecture timings are flexible, people can choose to work or attend lectures in those hours when commuting can be done at off-peak hours. Car-pooling should be done by conscious effort. For example, my friend works in an office, which is in a city, which is 20 km from her home. Other people in her neighbourhood also commute to the same city. She approached them for car-pooling, and now every day, one person takes his car. Instead of five cars on the road every day, now there is one and each one is doing some extra saving too.

To sum up, it is undeniable that commuting time has increased, but many steps can be taken to ameliorate the situation.

Plan followed:
Intro:
Para 1: Reasons
Para 2: solutions
Para 3: Solutions
Conclusion:

191. *It is now possible for scientists and tourists to travel to remote natural environments such as the South Pole. Do you think the advantages outweigh the disadvantages?*

Remote tourism, or the name given to visiting undiscovered habitats, is becoming very fascinating for both scientists and tourists. While the exploration of such areas has its positives, I believe the associated drawbacks are far more severe.

Admittedly, the idea of more people travelling to remote locations is seen as favourable for a number of reasons. To begin with, it leads to the development of infrastructure like roads, electrical grid systems and telecommunications in these areas. It also creates new jobs and results in economic growth of these areas. Furthermore, geologists can tap these previously inaccessible sites as resources of fossil fuels. This is increasingly significant to the human kind, as the majority of the current fossil fuel sources have been overexploited and there can be a global energy scarcity in the near future.

However, I believe that the disadvantages of increasing tourism and geological research in these areas are certainly more. Firstly, this heavily disturbs the flora and fauna of the remotely located places. As tourism and scientific research increases, wildlife could abandon their normal habitats and this negatively impacts their breeding and the balance of the surrounding ecosystems. Tourists and research scientists may also unknowingly bring seeds and spores of plants from other areas. If these species are invasive, the local vegetation may even die out completely.

Secondly, the increasing influx of people can pollute these pristine lands and in turn have a profound impact on the earth's global climate. For example, the melting of ice and glaciers in the Arctic and Antarctica can lead to rise in the sea level and thus increase the risk of submergence of low-lying islands. Finally, development in these areas can affect their scenery and aesthetic nature, thereby destroying the quality that makes them a tourist attraction site in the first place.

In conclusion, although there are some advantages of travelling to secluded places, the drawbacks to the environment and ecosystem are far more.

Plan followed:

Intro:
Para 1: Advantages of remote tourism
Para2: Disadvantages
Para 3: More disadvantages
Conclusion

192. *More and more children from wealthy countries are doing unpaid work in poor countries, such as teaching, building houses etcetera. Why are they doing this? Who gets more benefit, the community or the young people?*

In the last few years, volunteer tourism has become very popular among the youth from the developed countries. They travel to the developing and underdeveloped nations to contribute towards the development of the infrastructure or to educate and aware people. There are many reasons, which have led to this tendency, and in my opinion, both the youth and the communities they are serving, benefit from it equally.

There are several factors, which have led to the popularity of the volunteer work in the underprivileged sections of some nations. The main reason is the spread of awareness and information by the digital and other forms of media, which connects us to the events all over the world. There is news about natural calamities and other emergency situations from all over the world, which makes the youth, want to help the needy and lend a helping hand to the local authorities. Also, in most developed countries, it is a part of the education to sensitize the students towards the importance of sharing and helping others, as this helps them to become better citizens.

This development has benefits for both the youth volunteers and the people they are serving. For the youth, volunteer work adds to their work experience, and gives them an opportunity to put to work the skills they have learned at school and college. These days even the employers look for employees who have a volunteer work experience. So, the youth can get better jobs if they have a good background of some social work. To add to it, they get more exposure because of the travel to other countries and coming in contact with people from different cultures and social strata. It broadens their horizons.

The communities these youth volunteers work in are definitely benefitted, as their standards of living are improved, with the development of the homes and other infrastructure. In times of calamities and other natural disasters, the volunteer workers help rebuild their homes and other facilities. The education provided to them helps them to gain knowledge and makes their future brighter. It improves their chances of getting a better job, which in turn improves their quality of life.

To conclude, it can be said that the volunteer work done by the youth is a positive trend, which is advantageous for them, as well as the communities they work with.

Plan followed:
Intro:
Para 1: Reasons
Para 2: Benefits to young volunteers
Para 3: Benefits to communities
Conclusion:

193. *It has become easier and more affordable for people to travel to other countries. Do you think it is a positive or a negative development? Give your opinion and relevant examples from your experience.*

It is irrefutable that international tourism has taken mammoth dimensions because of the ease of travel and cheap tickets offered by various airline companies. While there are a few disadvantages of the increasing international tourism, the advantages are far more.

Admittedly, there are some problems associated with international tourism. Firstly, there is the increasing crime rate. Some locals see tourists as easy prey because they carry visible items of wealth, such as cameras and jewellery which can be disposed quickly for a profit. Another major problem is that there is greater danger of spreading infectious, contagious diseases around the world. The COVID 19 pandemic saw this flaring up because of people travelling from one place to the other. Perhaps the most serious disadvantage is to the environment. As the number of flights goes up, more fuel is used and more harmful greenhouse gases are liberated in the atmosphere.

However, international tourism can have many benefits for individuals. The most important benefit is that tourism provides regular employment for many local people who can find work in restaurants or hotels, or with tourist agencies as guides or drivers. The second benefit is that tourists spend money in the country and this allows local businesses such as restaurants, bars and taxi companies to flourish. In turn, other businesses, food suppliers or petrol stations, for instance, may be established in order to provide services to support the companies, which cater to tourists. In other words, the whole economy of the region develops.

A third benefit is that in order for tourists to be able to visit remote areas, roads, airports and hotels have to be built and local people also benefit by being able to use these new facilities. A final advantage of tourism is that visitors from outside bring fresh ideas and different ways of doing things to the local community. Consequently, local people may learn from tourists. Likewise, visitors learn about the local people and culture, and return home with a deeper understanding of the host country.

Summing up, international tourism has both advantages and disadvantages. However, the advantages outweigh the disadvantages.

Plan followed:
Intro: This situation has both pros and cons
Para 1: Benefits of international tourism
Para 2: More advantages of tourism
Para 3: Disadvantages of tourism
Conclusion: Advantages of tourism outweigh the disadvantages

194. *Some people believe that tourists should accept social and environmental responsibility while others believe that tourists should not accept any responsibility at all. Discuss both views and give your opinion.*

The negative social and environmental impacts of tourism have led many to suggest that tourists should accept accountability for this. However, others say that the social and environmental impacts of tourism should be the responsibility of the local authorities and not the tourists. I will discuss both views in this essay. I personally side with the former view.

The main reason why some people say that tourists should be responsible for the social and environmental impact of tourism is that many tourist destinations are endangered now because of the litter and pollution spread by the tourists. Secondly, there is over-consumption of resources such as water and fuel by tourists, which may lead to injustice with the locals. Also, the 5-star hotels in which tourists stay do not add anything to the local economy. So, tourists should accept social and environmental responsibility.

On the other hand, those who say that tourists should not worry about the culture and environment of the places they visit say that if the local authorities manage things well, there would be no negative impact at all. For example, if there are dustbins at frequent intervals, tourists would not litter the place at all. If there are enough guides to tell people about the local culture, then tourists would not do anything which is antisocial. If the government provides security personnel and surveillance cameras, then the tourists would not have to take that onus at all.

I believe that for tourism to sustain, tourists have to be held accountable for the social and environmental impacts they cause. Otherwise, tourism can kill tourism. Tourists should inquire about the culture and traditions of the places they visit, so that they plan their clothing accordingly. To help the local economy, tourists could stay with the local people as paying guests and not waste much water in places where water is scarce.

To sum up, responsible tourism is everyone's responsibility. The wellbeing of the destination is not only the responsibility of the tourism sector - it is also the responsibility of the tourist. That is why it has rightly been said that – 'A good tourist is one who leaves behind nothing, but footprints; and takes away nothing, but photographs.

Plan followed:

Intro: Discuss essay
Para 1: one view -
Para 2: Other view
Para 3: Own view
Conclusion

Similar essay

Some people think that we need to be "responsible tourists" who care about the culture and environment of the place they visit. However, some people think that it is impossible to be "responsible tourists". Discuss both views and give your opinion.

195. *Some people think visitors to other countries should imitate local customs and behaviours. Other people disagree; they think the host country should welcome cultural differences. Discuss the two views and give your opinion.*

It is believed by some that tourists should do and behave as the people of the host country, whereas others say that the host country should accept visitors as they are. I will discuss both views in this essay. I personally side with the latter view.

On the one hand, there are many reasons why some people say that visitors should respect and follow host country's customs. Firstly, it decreases chances of misunderstanding and embarrassment. For e.g. in the UK it is offensive to ask about pay to anyone, which is common in India. Secondly, a nation's customs and traditions are fascinating and offer a deep insight into that country. So, if immigrants copy the customs of host country, they learn more about them and that too in an interesting way.

On the other hand, those who say that the host country should embrace visitors as they are, give their reasons as follows. To begin with, everyone should accept the new customs and traditions brought by visitors. Secondly, there should be no binding on the visitors to adopt the customs and traditions of the hosts. For example, if the visitors are pure vegetarians, they should not be forced to eat non-vegetarian food just because the host country's people eat that.

I feel that a visitor to another country should respect the customs of that country but should not be obliged to copy them. Respecting those customs is necessary because a visitor is like a guest in someone else's home. The host country should accept the tourists as they are, because they get to know about other culture and traditions without going anywhere and without spending a single penny.

Summing up, mutual understanding between both the visitor and the host is necessary to maintain harmony. So, the host country should accept tourists as they are, and visitors should respect the customs of the host country without having to imitate them.

Plan followed:
Intro: Discuss essay intro
Para 1: One view
Para 2: Other view
Para 3: Own view
Conclusion:

196. Some people think that people moving to a new country should accept new culture in the foreign country rather than living as a separate minority group with different lifestyle. Do you agree or disagree?

It is believed by some that immigrants should follow the local customs and traditions, instead of sticking to their own customs. While the host country's customs and traditions should be given due importance, I disagree that immigrants should totally forget their roots.

On the one hand, there are many benefits of respecting and following host countries' customs. Firstly, it decreases chances of misunderstanding and embarrassment. For e.g. in the UK it is offensive to ask about pay to anyone, which is common in India. Secondly, a nation's customs and traditions are fascinating and offer a deep insight into that country. So, if immigrants copy the customs of host country, they learn more about them and that too in an interesting way.

On the other hand, there are many advantages of sticking to one's own customs and making a minority group. This keeps a person connected to his roots, and also gives a chance to spread the good points of their own culture. For example, the Indian style of greeting others with folded hands is now being accepted worldwide, especially during the covid times. Secondly, if he retains his old customs and lives with his own community as a separate minority, he will not suffer from homesickness. Maintaining a minority group with others of the same country also gives a feeling of security in an alien place.

On balance, I feel that someone who is moving to another country should respect the customs, culture, traditions etc. of that country, but should not change himself altogether. Respecting the host country's culture is necessary, but it should not be obligatory for him to follow those customs and change himself totally. As time passes and he gets to know the hosts better then he can decide if he wants to adopt any custom or stick to his own.

Summing up, it is a matter of personal choice. Mutual understanding between both the visitor and the host is necessary to maintain harmony. A cosmopolitan society in which everyone is tolerant of each other's customs and traditions is the need of the day. After all, today, we are part of a small global village and not a big planet Earth.

Plan followed:
Intro: It is necessary to look into pros and cons of both situations before forming an opinion.
Para 1: benefits of adopting host countries customs
Para 2: advantages of making a minority group
Para 3: Own view
Conclusion: Personal choice. Mutual understanding between both the visitor and the host is necessary to maintain harmony

197. *Some people think foreign visitors should be charged more than local people when they visit the cultural and historical attractions in a country. To what extent do you agree or disagree? (one sided)*

It is believed by some that ticket prices for cultural and historical sites should be more for international tourists than local tourists. I also strongly believe that charging foreigners more than locals for entry to cultural and historical attractions is justified.

The main reason why charging foreigners more than locals for visiting historical and cultural sites is acceptable is that local people have already contributed to the upkeep and maintenance of such sites in the form of taxes. In other words, the foreign tourists are not being charged more, but rather locals are getting a discounted price as they have already paid some part of the entrance fee in the form of taxes. So, it is actually fair to set a higher entry ticket for foreign tourists.

The second reason is that the cost of running such sites is sizeable. Already, governments around the world are finding it challenging to organise funds for all these expenses. If international tourists are also charged the same prices as local people, it would be nearly impossible to manage these expenses. Also, I find it significantly better than alternatives like privatization of such sites, which comes with its own set of problems.

In addition, if the cultural attraction is a temple or a place of worship, which locals visit daily, it would be unfair to charge them heftily. This is especially true in poor and developing countries like India, where a substantial population is below the poverty line. Finally, governments spend a considerable amount to provide facilities like language translators and special signpost to make museums more appealing to foreigners. This also makes it reasonable to charge them more than locals.

In conclusion, I would like to reiterate that charging overseas visitors more than the locals when they visit historical and cultural sites is justifiable.

Plan followed:
Intro: Disagree
Para 1: Reason 1
Para 2: Reason 2
Para 3: Reason 3 and 4
Conclusion: Reiterate opinion

198. *Some people think foreign visitors should be charged more than local people when they visit the cultural and historical attractions in a country. To what extent do you agree or disagree? (one sided but with concession)*

It is believed by some that ticket prices for cultural and historical sites should be more for international tourists than local tourists. While I agree that charging international tourists more than locals is justified, I also believe that the difference in charges should not be considerable.

The main reason why charging foreigners more than locals for visiting historical and cultural sites is acceptable is that local people have already contributed to the upkeep and maintenance of such sites in the form of taxes. In other words, the foreign tourists are not being charged more, but rather locals are getting a discounted price as they have already paid some part of the entrance fee in the form of taxes. So, it is actually fair to set a higher entry ticket for foreign tourists.

The second reason is that the cost of running such sites is sizeable. Already, governments around the world are finding it challenging to organise funds for all these expenses. If international tourists are also charged the same prices as local people, it would be nearly impossible to manage these expenses. In addition, if the cultural attraction is a temple or a place of worship, which locals visit daily, it would be unfair to charge them heftily.

However, I also believe that the difference between ticket prices for locals and foreigners should not be too excessive. It would create a negative image about the country and the tourists might be put off. As a result, they might dissuade their friends and family from visiting the particular country and might not return, preferring other countries for future vacations.

In conclusion, I would like to reiterate that although charging overseas visitors more than the locals when they visit historical and cultural sites is justifiable, the difference should not be sizable.

Plan followed:
Intro: Agree
Para 1: Reason 1
Para 2: Reason 2
Para 3: Concession
Conclusion: Reiterate opinion

199. *The traditional lifestyle of local people in developing countries is attracting and increasing the number of tourists to the countries, which has the effect of preventing local people changing to modern ways. To what extent do you agree or disagree?*

Recent years have witnessed a marked interest in international tourism, and the traditional lifestyles of people in the developing countries are acting as magnets to the tourists. I firmly believe that this is deterring the local people to change their customs and traditions and adopt modern ways of life.

The main reason why local people retain their traditional lifestyle is that when visitors praise their culture, it gives them pride and makes them believe that their culture is glorious. This realization removes any possibility in the people's mind that their lifestyle is in any way inferior to that of advanced nations, and plays an important role in retaining their lifestyle in general. For example, when tribal people of Rajasthan, India are appreciated for their clothing style and their dances, such as the 'Snake Charmer's Dance', they put even more effort to practice those art forms and present them to the tourists.

Secondly, the poverty of the tribal people is alleviated when the tourists visit them for what they are. They come to realise and accept the fact that their bread and butter will be lost if they change to modern lifestyles and therefore they stick to their culture and traditions. An interesting example where people are retaining to their old ways of life even in the developed country such as the USA can be seen in the Amish village Philadelphia. It is a very popular tourist destination and people go there to see how those people are living without what are considered the basic necessities of modern life.

The final reason for people retaining their traditional lifestyle is that the facilities developed for tourists benefits them eventually and they know very well that if the inflow of tourists stops then government will not invest in those areas and they will be the losers in the long run. Benefits can include upgraded infrastructure, health and transport improvements, new sport and recreational facilities, restaurants, and public spaces as well as an influx of better-quality commodities and food.

To summarise, I side with the view that tourism is motivating people to retain their culture and tradition and not be lured into following the modern ways of life.

Plan followed:
Intro: Agree
Para 1: presence of visitors gives people a kind of confidence and pride in their traditions
Para 2: Culture sells
Para 3: facilities developed for tourists benefits them eventually
Conclusion: Reiterate opinion

200. *Some people think that it is necessary to travel abroad to learn about other countries, while other people think that it is not necessary to travel abroad because all the information can be seen on TV and the Internet. Discuss both views and give your opinion.*

Some individuals hold the opinion that travelling abroad is required to learn about other countries, whereas others assert that technology has given us armchair tourism, through which we can see all the information on television and the internet. This essay intends to analyse both perspectives. I am personally in favour of the former view.

Those who believe in actually touring foreign places, give their main reason that images on computers can never replace real places. No matter how real and vivid computer images are, they are only images and can never be likened to the historical objects and natural wonders that we see in real or even might be allowed to touch with our fingertips. The difference can be compared to seeing the picture of a mango rather than actually eating it.

On the other hand, those in favour of armchair tourism also have valid arguments. Firstly, not all people can afford the expenses. Secondly some people may have limitations because of age or failing health. Armchair tourism is a boon for those people. Another argument, which goes in favour of armchair tourism, is that people are very busy and have no time. They have become workaholics in the rat race of money and material wealth. Finally, extremes of climate also make certain places inaccessible to some people.

I believe that visiting other countries is a rewarding experience in many respects. Firstly, when people make the trip to a foreign country then they visit the places of interest there and also get some exercise, which does a lot of good to their health. They generally go with family and friends and enjoy a lot. They also learn about the culture and tradition of the place. All this broadens their horizons, which can never be done by the passive activity of seeing something on the computer screen. At the same time, they also get a chance to spread the good points of their own culture.

In conclusion, armchair tourism is there today but international travel will still be needed. I believe that the experience of actually going to a foreign country can never be compared to just seeing those places, sitting at home.

Plan followed:
Intro: Discuss essay
Para 1: One view
Para 2: More points of that view
Para 3: Other view
Conclusion: armchair tourism is there today but international travel will still be needed.

201. *Today, people can use the internet to learn about the culture and lifestyle of the people of other countries. So, there is no need to travel to other countries to learn their culture. Do you agree or disagree?*

There is no doubt that nowadays people can find a lot of information online about the culture and lifestyle of foreigners. While I agree that the internet can be useful to some extent to learn about another culture, it cannot match what a person can learn by actually visiting a country.

The main reason why I believe that travelling to a country is a must to learn about its culture, is that learning about a culture from the internet is just not the same. Experiencing a culture in reality is totally different. People expose themselves to foreigners and lifestyles that are usually totally different to what they find back home. They visit museums, meet new people and try out completely different cuisines. There are also some nuances in every culture, which can never be expressed in words or shown in a video. So, real culture is much more than what the internet can show.

Moreover, although the differences between two countries might not be that different, every new country people visit teaches them to appreciate new cultures. Travelling abroad makes people more broad-minded and more accepting of new things. Reading about a culture in a book or watching a video on the country can never bring about that appreciation. Besides this, travelling is just not about learning culture, it makes us patient, it makes us try new things, it teaches us how to make friends out of strangers, it is so much more.

Admittedly, the internet can be an alternative if a person is curious to learn about another culture but cannot afford visiting the country. In the same way, it can be an effective solution for people who cannot travel due to physical ailments. A person can certainly get an idea about a foreign culture by watching their movies on the internet or by reading online travel blogs.

To conclude, although the internet is a vast source of knowledge including information about other country's culture and traditions, it can never be the same as learning about a culture by actually experiencing it.

Plan followed:
Intro: Disagree with some concession for the view
Para 1: Reasons for disagree
Para 2: More reasons
Para 3: Some concessions
Conclusion

Written by: Indroop Singh

202. In many countries, mainly tourists, but not local people, visit museums and historical sites. Why does this happen, and what can be done to attract more local people to visit these places?

Museums and other historical sites seem to be less attractive to local people than to tourists. This essay intends to delve into some reasons why this is occurring, and put forward some solutions to arouse the interest of local people in visiting these places.

The first reason is due to the fact that the local people take these places for granted, and think that they will see them sooner or later. However, that time seldom comes. On the other hand, tourists who come there are on a holiday, and their main motive is visiting these historic places and museums. For instance, recently, I visited Hyderabad as a tourist and went to see Ramoji Film City, which is the biggest Film City in the whole world, but my relatives who are staying in Hyderabad have never been there once.

Secondly, nothing new is added to these places over the years and so local people who have been there once, do not wish to frequent these places again and again. These places do not intrigue the locals so they do not feel motivated to visit regularly. Furthermore, museums and historical sites are not cheap to visit. In fact, to get admission to these places, visitors are often required to buy expensive tickets.

In order to spur up more interest of local people in coming to museums, a number of ways can be employed. School trips could be organized for children to enjoy these places with their friends. Passes for entry to these museums and historical sites could be arranged for local people so that it does not cut a hole in their pocket every time they visit them. A day could be fixed every month when the entry to the museum is made free. For example, on every first Tuesday of the month, the entry to the Houston Museum of Natural Science is free, so there is a great rush of local people on that day.

To conclude, many reasons can be given as to why local people lose their enthusiasm for museums and places of historical importance, but many steps can be taken to motivate locals to visit these places.

Plan followed:

Intro
Para 1: First reason
Para 2: More reasons
Para 3: Solutions
Conclusion

203. *Nowadays it is easy to apply for and be given a credit card. However, some people experience problems when they are not able to pay their debts back. In your opinion, do the advantages of credit cards outweigh the disadvantages?*

Some people believe that credit card debts can cause a lot of problems to the consumer and so their use should be avoided. Although credit cards present some challenges when not used responsibly, I believe the benefits certainly outweigh them.

Credit cards offer many advantages and thus have become very popular with consumers. Firstly, credit cards are far more secure and convenient than cash as it is more easy to conceal and carry them than large amounts of cash. If they get lost or stolen, people can get them cancelled to avoid fraudulent purchases. Credit card companies monitor spending and notify customers if they notice any suspicious activity. Credit cards have also made it very convenient to shop online, pay utility bills, book travel, reserve hotels etc.

Secondly, credit cards give immediate access to funds and provide financial security. They are helpful when people do not have enough funds to pay upfront for any unexpected expenses like medical bills, car repairs etc. Finally, most credit cards allow members to earn rewards and points on everyday purchases. These membership perks quickly add up and can be used for cash, gift cards, air travel, merchandise etc. Some retail stores give customers heavy discounts for shopping with store credit cards.

On the other hand, a major downside of using credit cards is the heavy burden of credit cards debt. People tend to overspend when they make purchases on a credit card, instead of using cash. They are not able to make their full payments on time, which coupled with high interest rates makes their credit debt grow. These debts hurt their credit scores and their ability to get approved for future loans.

Summing up, although credit cards may lead to debt issues, I still believe people gain a lot more than they lose.

Plan followed:
Intro: Advantages or disadvantages lie in the hands of the holder
Para 1: Advantages
Para 2: More advantages
Para 3: Disadvantages
Conclusion:

204. *More and more people do online shopping. Why is this the situation? What is the effect of online shopping on shops and communities?*

Today, with the Internet so readily accessible to us, more and more people are turning to online shopping for all their needs. This essay will look into the reasons why people are switching to online shopping instead of traditional shopping, and also discuss its effects on shops and societies.

There are several reasons why people are opting for online shopping. The first is the ability to shop at any time of the day or night. In today's 24/7 society, people are working odd hours and so it may not be possible for them to visit the regular shops to purchase things. The second advantage of shopping online is that goods are often cheaper as the seller does not have the costs of running a shop. Online shopping can also be a lot more comfortable than real world shopping, as people do not have to go out in bad weather sometimes.

Another huge advantage of shopping online is that people can compare the products on different online sites and can also read reviews that have been written by other people who have purchased the item they are considering. They are able to find out about the item from a genuine user, not just the salesperson. Finally, they are able to find and buy products from all over the world, and not just in their local area.

There are many negative effects of the trend of online shopping on people and societies. Firstly, people have to wait for the items they purchased to be shipped and delivered. Secondly, they cannot feel or see the item they want to buy. Another disadvantage of shopping online is that a person's credit card number could be hacked and misused. Societies also become more aloof as people do not come out for shopping. The sales of the local shopkeeper can go down as more and more people shop online.

In summary, there are many reasons of shopping online such as convenience and cost saving, and there are both positive and negative effects on local shops and societies. However, despite the negatives, I believe that online shopping is here to stay and prosper.

Plan followed:

Intro: Discuss essay intro
Para 1: advantages and positives
Para 2: more advantages and positives
Para 3: Negative effects on people and societies
Para 4: More negative effects on people and societies
Conclusion:

205. *Some people think that personal happiness is directly related to economic success. Others argue that happiness depends on different factors. Discuss both views and give your own opinion.*

It is believed by some that economic success is an essential element to happiness, but others opine that factors like a stable family life, secure source of income and good health are more important in achieving happiness. This essay intends to analyze both perspectives. I believe that while economic success has a role in happiness, other factors are more important.

The main reason given by those who say that money is needed to achieve happiness is because one needs sufficient money to live in a spacious apartment, to have a private car, fashionable clothes and latest household electrical appliances, which are all indispensable for happy life. A person who has to struggle for even the basic necessities of life cannot be happy.

On the other hand, those who say that happiness depends on other factors, give their reasons as follows. Firstly, cordial relations among family members are needed to be happy. A person who has the barest minimum, but a very understanding life partner and obedient children can be very happy. Good health is another factor needed for happiness. A multimillionaire suffering from cancer can never be happy. Another big factor is a stable source of income. One can never be happy if one is not sure whether his business will pick up or if his job is secure. So, happiness is in things other than economic success.

I believe that money is important, but only as far as the basic necessities of life are not fulfilled. After that other factors play a more important role. Money can buy medicines, but not health. With money one can buy a bed, but not sleep. Happiness is also in contentment. Those who are contented with what they have, are happy. There is no upper limit to economic success. So, contentment is the key to a happy life. A person should know where to draw the line between work and personal life to be happy.

To conclude, economic success is important, but other factors have more weightage as far as the pursuit to happiness is concerned. Ultimately it is contentment which leads to happiness.

Plan followed:
Intro: Discuss essay intro
Para 1: One view
Para 2: Other view
Para 3: Own view
Conclusion:

206. *Some people believe they should keep all the money they have earned and should not pay tax to the state. Do you agree or disagree?*

A few people are opposed to paying taxes to the government as they believe it is their hard-earned money. I believe that paying taxes is not only really important but also a citizen's duty.

The main reason why people should pay taxes is that tax money is used for the development and the running of the country. Not paying taxes can drastically affect a country's revenue generation. For example, the government provides basic amenities, various services to citizens and also uses this money for government administration and projects like running of jails and defence systems. It is not wrong to say that "taxes run a country."

Secondly, paying taxes is a way of saving for retirement. Those who pay taxes during their work life are given pensions after they retire. In some countries the pensions provided by the government are directly proportional to the taxes they have paid. So, it motivates them to pay taxes. Also, taxes increase civic engagement. When people pay taxes, it makes them feel part of the political system. They ask questions from the government and cast their vote.

Finally, citizens can contribute towards social welfare by paying taxes. Taxes are the best form of wealth redistribution and governments spend a considerable amount of the taxes collected to give back to the poor. For example, Indian government gives subsidies on food grains to ensure the poor do not die of hunger. Thus, paying taxes is not only people's legal duty but also their humanitarian duty. Also, if there is no income retribution through taxes, there would be increased wealth inequality, and this would impact social harmony.

Summing up, I reiterate my opinion by saying that it is the duty of every citizen to pay tax and the duty of every government to use it appropriately in public interest.

Plan followed:
Intro: Disagree
Para 1: Advantages of taxes
Para 2: More advantages
Para 3: More advantages
Conclusion: Reiterate opinion

207. *Some people think that paying taxes is enough to contribute to the society. Others argue that being a citizen involves more responsibilities. Discuss both views and give your opinion?*

A good citizen is a blessing to society. Some people opine that paying taxes is enough contribution towards the society whereas others believe that a good citizen has a lot more responsibilities than just paying taxes. In the following paragraphs I intend to discuss both views. I personally go with the latter view.

There are many reasons why some people say that if a person pays taxes, it is sufficient contribution to the society. Firstly, paying all the taxes and in a timely manner is one of the major responsibilities of a citizen. If one pays taxes, then the government can use the money for constructive purposes, like building and maintaining roads, schools, fire protection, defence services etc. The different types of taxes to be paid by citizens are income tax, excise tax, property tax, sales tax etc. All taxes paid by people make their lives better.

On the other hand, those who say that just paying taxes is not enough give their reasons as follows. They say that there are many other obligations, which a good citizen must fulfil. To begin with, voting in elections is very important. When citizens fail to vote or have political opinions, they allow vested interests to have their way. Secondly, they must obey law and order. If all citizens are law abiding, then the whole nation would be a paradise on Earth.

It is also the responsibility of a good citizen to provide public service to the government. This means volunteering for various agencies and charities. Finally, it is a citizen's duty to scrutinize the government's actions and take a stand when something wrong happens. When citizens get too complacent, they will not notice when their freedom is being cut down.

To sum up, a good citizen should pay taxes, exercise his voting rights, be law abiding, do voluntary work to help the government and take a stand if anything goes wrong. Just paying taxes is not sufficient contribution to the society.

Plan followed:
Intro: a good citizen has a lot more responsibilities than just paying taxes
Para 1: One view
Para 2: Other view
Para 3: Other view
Conclusion: Reiterate opinion

208. *Some people say that it is the responsibility of individual to save money for their own care after they retire. To what extent do you agree or disagree?*

It is believed by some that the individual should save money for his post-retirement life, and not fritter away everything to enjoy the present. I also believe that one must be frugal and save for the future. In this essay I will discuss why it is important to save for the future.

My first argument is that the span of life is getting longer, but the period of earning is comparatively limited. Nobody knows how long he would live, but the age of retirement is generally fixed. Therefore, during a person's earning span, he has to make sure that he puts aside enough money that will enable him to lead a comfortable life in his later years, when he will be able to work no more.

Secondly, the requirements in old age are sometimes more than a person's needs during the period of his youth. Deteriorating health translates into higher medical bills and hospital charges. Being weak and infirm, one needs to spend more on commuting. He will need to hire assistants to help in the house.

Finally, the elderly may incur extra expenditure on leisure activities. People generally travel more after retirement to meet their relatives and friends who may be settled and staying far away from them. Thus, there are so many needs that would surface in the future. Some may be quite unexpected and traumatic like accidents in the family, which may entail high expenditure. There would be the usual expenses on house maintenance and repair, and the payment of personal and property taxes.

To sum up, I reiterate my opinion that a person should plan wisely for his future. If he has saved enough, he can sit back and enjoy peace and comfort in his later years and even witness the smile of joy on the faces of his children.

Plan followed:
Intro: Agree
Para 1: How saving money is important for one's own needs in future
Para 2: How saving money is important for one's family in future
Para 3: More time for leisure in old age so more money needed
Conclusion: Reiterate opinion

209. *As well as making money, businesses should also have social responsibilities. Do you agree or disagree?*

It is believed by some that apart from making money, corporate houses should also be responsible for the societies they operate in. While the corporate sector should focus on creating personal wealth, it should also shoulder social responsibilities. This would be beneficial to the society and also for the companies themselves to sustain in the long run.

Admittedly, it is an inescapable responsibility of every business enterprise to create more money for itself and its employees. Only when businesses achieve profitability can the employees remain loyal to the organisations that they work for. Meanwhile, companies can themselves remain competitive in the long run. In the initial stages, great amount of investments are needed for employee training, buying equipment, advertising, marketing, research and development. Therefore, economic stimulus is the driving force for employers and employees to work hard.

However, social responsibility is also very essential for businesses. In times of natural disasters, business houses are supposed to make generous donations and set an example. All businesses should also abide by the law and never make profit by unethical means. If any business becomes prosperous by honest hard work, it can provide a number of job opportunities, which can greatly reduce the pressure of social unemployment.

Furthermore, taking social responsibility would help these large business houses themselves. For example, when any business house donates for charity, the media spreads a word about their efforts and they get advertisement for free. In my hometown, many parks and roundabouts are maintained by the textile, sugar and starch mill in my hometown. These business houses do not need to spend extra for their adverts. Providing scholarships to poor, meritorious students is another way these enterprises can take social responsibility.

To sum up, it can be reiterated that businesses need to make money and also look into their social obligations. This would be a win-win situation for the society and the enterprises themselves.

Plan followed:
Intro: Agree
Para 1: Why businesses should make money
Para 2: Why and how they should have social responsibilities
Para 3: Doing for society would help themselves also
Conclusion: reiterate opinion

210. *In recent times economic growth has made some people richer in both developed and developing countries. While studies show that people in developing countries are happier now than before, people in developed countries are no happier than they were before. Why do you think this is and what lessons can be learned from it?*

The growth in global economy means different things to different people. To the developing world, recent growth is seen as positive. To the already developed countries, this growth brings with it increased global competitiveness, and is thus seen as negative. The reasons for the unhappiness of people in the developed countries and the lesson we get from this will be discussed in this essay.

The main reason why people in developing countries are happier is that it means better opportunities for personal and professional growth. Now they have high incomes to lead luxurious lives. They can now buy the latest gadgets, travel to the most exotic places on earth and own luxury apartments and cars. Their children now get world-class education and healthcare. So, for people in the developing world growth in the economy is a positive development.

On the other hand, people in the developed world already led comfortable lives. The recent growth in the global economy hasn't really done anything to further improve their standard of living, and now they face stiff competition from their counterparts in the developing countries. More and more jobs now get outsourced to the developing world, where the cost of labour is low, and so people in the developed world are now losing their jobs. Therefore, they are not all that happy with this sudden spurt in global economy.

The lesson we learn is that the growth of economy in developing world should not hamper the economy of the people of the developed countries. Jobs and opportunities for the people of the developing countries should be generated within their countries and not in the developed countries. Governments of developed countries should not lay-off their people to give low paid jobs to others.

To sum up, the facts given above should explain why researchers feel that people in the developing countries are happier with the growth in global economy than the people in the developed world.

Plan followed:
Intro:
Para 1: Why developing countries are happier
Para 2: Why developed countries are less happy
Para 3: lessons we learn
Conclusion:

211. *Some people believe that the best way to produce a happier society is to ensure that there are only small differences between the richest and the poorest members. To what extent do you agree or disagree?*

Some individuals are of the opinion that the most effective way to bring about a satisfied society would be to narrow the wealth inequality. I believe that increasing wealth inequality is the main reason for dissatisfaction in society and governments must take steps to reduce it.

The main reason why I think wealth inequality makes people unhappy is that it makes them feel that people are rich because of unfair means. In effect, the rising wealth gap leads to the feeling that those at the top are there because of their connections and not because of their hard work. Therefore, if governments come up with policies for wealth redistribution like higher taxes for the wealthy and subsidies for the poor, it reduces this feeling of unfairness and thereby increases happiness.

Secondly, unhappiness is created when those at the bottom are struggling for even the basic necessities and those at the top are spending millions on luxuries. In other words, happiness can be created when everyone can enjoy a decent life with basic necessities like clean drinking water, electricity, housing, healthcare and education. The only way governments can ensure this is through equal distribution of wealth.

Finally, if the wealth gap is considerably large, it creates the feeling for the people that reaching the top levels is nearly impossible. In other words, not only the poor but also the middle class become less hopeful regarding upward mobility. This leads to feelings of jealousy and a negative attitude towards those at the top. For example, there are more thefts and house burglaries in rich localities near poor neighbourhoods. So, wealth redistribution would reduce crime and lead to more peace and harmony in the society.

To sum up, there is no doubt that rising economic inequality can be pernicious and damaging for society and governments must take measures to address it.

Plan followed:
Intro:
Para 1: Why decreasing the financial gap is not the best way
Para 2: Other way to get happy society – facilities for the poor
Para 3: Other way to get happy society – educational opportunities for the poor
Para 4: Other way to get happy society – pollution-free environment
Conclusion:

212. *Some people believe the range of technology available to individuals today is increasing the gap between poor people and rich people. Others think it is having an opposite effect. Discuss both views and give your opinion?*

Some individuals opine that technology increases wealth inequality, whereas others believe that technology has brought the rich and the poor closer. This essay will discuss both views. I believe, although wealth inequality has increased in the last few years, technology is not the reason. Technology has actually reduced the gap between the rich and the poor.

There are many reasons why some people think that technology increases the gap between the rich and the poor. To begin with, new technologies favour the rich as they can afford them and use these technologies to further earn more money. Furthermore, technologies in the form of machines are being used by rich corporations to either replace labour or force them to work for cheap. Thus, while the profits of the rich are increasing, the poor are losing jobs and becoming poorer.

On the other hand, those who believe that technology is actually beneficial, cite the following reasons. Firstly, technology has created huge opportunities for the poor where none existed previously. For example, some technologies such as communications or networking give poor people a chance to earn a better living and also increase their education opportunities. What is more, technology has been the answer to many problems faced by the poor like water purification without electricity, cheap transportation and so on. Last but not least, technology has increased transparency in governance, bringing down corruption and thus helped the poor immensely.

I believe that technology is not the reason for the increase in the gap between the rich and poor. The real reason for the increasing gap is actually the lack of regulation on new technologies, which allows their benefits to be hoarded by the rich. For example, no price control on even life-saving medicine, which makes these medicines unaffordable for all but the super-rich. The same medicines after price checks and regulations can not only save lives but also save the poor from falling into poverty. Thus, technology when regulated properly decreases the rich-poor gap rather than increasing it.

Summing up, technology can actually lessen the gap between the rich and the poor. It is not the technology to blame for the gap; it is the access to technology, which is to blame.

Plan followed:
Intro: Discuss essay intro
Para 1: Why some people say technology increases the gap
Para 2: Other view
Para 3: Own view
Conclusion: *Written by: Indroop Singh*

213. *The gap between the rich and the poor is becoming wider, the rich are getting richer, the poor even more poor. What problems can the situation cause and suggest solutions.*

It is indubitable that the gap between the affluent and the needy has widened. This essay intends to analyse the problems caused by this phenomenon and suggest ways to mitigate the problems.

The most significant problem is that a vicious cycle emerges from which the poor find it difficult to come out. In order to make both ends meet, both parents have to work for supplementary income and the children are left in the house, unattended. Their future becomes blurred, as they do not get quality education. This deprivation of the children is very high in ultra-poor families.

Furthermore, poverty and conditions resulting from poverty, such as lack of education leads people to lawlessness and violence (e.g. robbery, theft, kidnapping, rape, murder, gang war, and drug addiction). Their pent-up desires for the finer things in life find a common outlet in the commission of crimes. The underdeveloped economies of Asia and even America are full of high crime rates due to poverty. Even countries such as Iraq, Iran, Afghanistan, Indonesia, and Philippines face poverty-related evolution of these events.

The solutions are not simple, but government effort could improve this situation. To begin with, luxuries should be taxed heavily. A balanced taxation should be there and penalties against tax fraud and evasion should be more severe. Free or highly subsidized education should be provided to the needy. The problem of youth unemployment should be dealt with by creating job opportunities. Self-employment should be encouraged by promoting small-scale industry. At the global level, international organizations, such as United Nations and World Bank, should provide support to developing countries in both technical and financial fields enabling them to improve infrastructure and strengthen industries.

Summing up, the increasing gap between the rich and the poor should not be ignored as it causes political and social instability in the country and effective steps should be taken to close this gap.

Plan followed:
Intro:
Para 1: The most significant problem
Para 2: lawlessness and violence
Para 3: Solutions
Conclusion:

214. *Some people think that government should not give international aid if they have disadvantaged people like unemployed and homeless in their own country. To what extent do you agree or disagree?*

Some people believe that the governments should not give aid to poor countries if there are underprivileged people within their own country. I believe that the developing and developed countries should always step forward to help the impoverished countries.

The main reason why countries should give aid is that international aid not only helps the recipient country, but also the donor country. In other words, as poor countries develop through aid, it fosters international trade. This creates higher demand for products made in the rich countries, which improves the economy of rich countries by creating jobs. So, homelessness and unemployment of donor country is also addressed.

Secondly, international aid is not only given to reduce poverty, but also to improve the country's own security. By giving aid, the economic condition of the poor countries improves and so the conditions that promote terrorism, such as poverty, unemployment and corruption are removed. So, this aid promotes peace and stability in the whole world.

Finally, giving aid adds to the power and influence of the rich countries. Today, the status in the world is not based on military strength, but on relationships with other countries. This aid is accompanied by development of people-to-people contacts between the two countries and raises the image of that country in the eyes of the people of the recipient country. For example, recently, the United Nations HR commission's chairman had to be elected, and an Indian was elected because of the soft power that India has.

To sum up, I reiterate my opinion saying that all countries should help by giving foreign aid even if there are problems of unemployment and homelessness within them.

Plan followed:
Intro: Disagree
Para 1: First reason for giving aid
Para 2: Second reason
Para 3: Third reason
Conclusion

215. *Rich countries often give financial aid to poor countries, but it does not solve the poverty, so rich countries should give other types of help to the poor countries rather than the financial aid. To what extent do you agree or disagree?*

It is believed that the rich countries should not give monetary aid to developing and under-developed countries as it does not combat poverty. I believe that the developed countries should give some other types of help to the poor countries and not direct financial aid.

My first argument against financial aid is that this aid may not actually reach those for whom it is meant. It may go into corrupt pockets. Secondly, it would make those people lazy, as they would be getting aid without doing any work. Thirdly, the aid may be used for wrong purposes. For example, the aid may be given for development projects but it may be used to promote terrorism.

The best way to help poor countries would be to open good educational institutes, good health centres and create job opportunities for people of the poor countries. If people of the poor countries start earning well their standard would definitely become better and the whole country would become richer. It has been wisely said by someone, 'Give a man fish to eat, and you feed him for a day. Teach a man how to fish, and you feed him for a lifetime'.

If rich countries open factories and multinational companies in poor countries it would be a win-win situation for both, as the poor would get employment and the rich would have to pay much less to these workers than they would have to pay their counterparts in their own country. Direct financial aid would not bring such a situation.

Summing up, financial aid is not the best way to help poor countries. From my own perspective, the developed countries ought to assist the impoverished countries through other approaches.

Plan followed:
Intro: Agree
Para 1: negative effects of financial help
Para 2: advantages of helping in other ways
Para 3: More ways of helping
Conclusion:

216. *Some people think that charity organizations should only offer help to people of their own country, but others believe that these organizations should give aid to people in great need wherever they live. Discuss both views and give your opinion.*

Some people hold the opinion that support should be provided to people in their own country, whereas others say that the needy should be helped irrespective of their country. In this essay I intend to discuss both viewpoints. I personally believe that help should be given to the needy irrespective of their geographical location.

There are many reasons why some people are in favour of charities helping the needy in their own country. Firstly, these organisations remain directly in touch with the needy. They can see how the money or the other resources provided by them are being used. It has been well said that charity begins at home. What is more, domestic charities target problems specific to their home country. For instance, the Help Age India is an Indian charity providing help for the aged in India.

On the other hand, those who wish that the needy should be helped in any corner of the world, give their reasons as follows. Firstly, this aid would also help their own country. In other words, as poor countries develop through aid, it fosters international trade. This creates higher demand for products made in the rich countries, which improves the economy of rich countries by creating jobs.

In my opinion, help should be given globally. By giving aid, the economic condition of the poor countries improves and so the conditions that promote terrorism, such as poverty, unemployment and corruption are removed. So, this aid promotes peace and stability in the whole world. Finally, giving aid adds to the power and influence of the rich countries. Today, the status in the world is not based on military strength, but on relationships with other countries.

Summing up, the purpose of charity organizations is to help people in need, and it does not matter where this help goes. If people of the home country need help, then it would certainly be advisable to help those around you first.

Plan followed:
Intro: Discuss essay intro
Para 1: Advantages of helping your home country
Para 2: Advantages of helping the needy irrespective of country
Para 3: Own opinion
Conclusion:

Similar essay: Some people prefer to provide help and support directly to those in the local community who need it. Others, however, prefer to give money to national and international charitable organisations. Discuss both views and give your opinion.

217. *Some people believe that success in life depends on hard work and determination, while others believe that other factors like money and personal appearance are important. Discuss both views and give your opinion.*

It is believed by some that success can be achieved by hard work and determination, whereas others say that money and good looks can lead to success. This essay will discuss both these views. I personally believe that more often success comes from hard work and perseverance and only on some odd occasion money and looks can play a role.

The main reason why some people say that determination and hard work is an important prerequisite for success, is that determination gives people an impetus of setting up goals, which lead to success. For example, Marie Curie (Madame Curie) determined to finish her husband's lifetime unfinished work after his death and eventually discovered radium. Similarly, hard work is also very important as without hard work determination is of no value. It has been well said that 'Genius is one percent inspiration and ninety-nine percent, perspiration'. Take the example of businessmen. Only those succeed who have determination and who put in a lot of sweat and toil in their business.

Those who advocate that money and good looks are needed for success, believe that good looks increase the confidence of a person and a confident person has more chances to succeed in his life. With good looks a person can succeed in the acting and modelling fields. They also opine that money is needed to become an entrepreneur and those who have the capital to invest have more chances to succeed. For example, a person with lots of bank balance may sustain through any ups and downs in business and finally succeed, but any person without any financial backing may break down if his business goes through a bad phase.

To sum up, I believe that success depends on how firmly people hold on to their determination and how much effort they put into their work. A powerful background of money as well as attractive looks can help a certain number of persons to succeed, but too much reliance on these is unpractical.

Plan followed:
Intro: Discuss essay intro
Para 1: Role of determination and hard work
Para 2: Importance of money and looks
Conclusion: With own view

218. *Whether or not someone achieves aim in their life is mostly a question of luck. Do you agree or disagree?*

Some people believe that success in life depends primarily on luck. While I believe that luck can make a person successful and rich, it is certainly not the most important factor.

There is no doubt that luck matters in some ways. Firstly, luck helps people get opportunities. For example, people who win the womb-lottery and are born in rich families, certainly get more opportunities than people born in poor families. Secondly, today success is mainly defined by wealth and there are a lot of ways in which luck can help people to become wealthy. To illustrate, they can win a lottery or win money through shares in the stock market.

However, I believe that hard work and talent are much more important than luck. The main reason is that luck can get people opportunities but to have sustained success in life people need to work hard. For example, because of nepotism, an actor's son may get a movie role, but if he is not talented and hardworking, he would not get future opportunities. Similarly, a person might be lucky to be born rich but unless he studies hard, he would not be able to get into a good university, and without good education, it is nearly impossible to be successful in life today.

Moreover, there is so much competition in the world today that luck alone is not enough. If people are not hard working, they cannot grow. They would be stuck at the same position. Finally, I think success is also about a person's mental satisfaction and the satisfaction that people achieve from hard work can never be achieved by winning a lottery or getting lucky.

In conclusion, I would like to repeat that luck can help us be successful in some ways, but hard work and talent matter much more.

Plan followed:
Intro: luck help with success but hard work and talent help more
Para 1: how luck helps
Para 2: how hard work and talent helps
Para 3: how hard work and talent helps
Conclusion: reiterate

219. *Some people say the most important thing about being rich is that it gives you the opportunity to give back or help the poor. To what extent do you agree or disagree with this statement?*

It is believed by some that the best thing about being affluent is having a chance to help the needy. While one benefit of being rich is that they can help the impoverished, there are many other advantages of being rich, which are perhaps more important.

Admittedly, the richer a person is, the more taxes he pays and that tax money is used by the government to provide for the impoverished. The tax collected by the government could be used for providing education and job training. The rich can also become entrepreneurs and create jobs for many who are unemployed. In all these aspects, it can be said that the rich can contribute a lot in helping the poor.

However, the comfortable lives led by the rich holds much more value than just the ability to do something for the have-nots. The wealthy do not have to yearn for the basic necessities of life and can also enjoy all the luxuries like cars, air conditioners and other household gadgets without having to worry for their running costs. They can also provide the best education to their children, and can also get the best health care for themselves and their families.

Furthermore, the rich enjoy a status in society that only money can bring. People look upon them for their guidance and support in times of need. Finally, wealth provides security in adverse circumstances. For example, in Covid 19 pandemic, the rich could sail through comfortably sitting at home, whereas the poor had to struggle for their daily bread and butter.

To sum up, if one is rich, he is in a better situation to help others who need money and all the things which money can provide. However, other things such as a luxurious lifestyle, status in society and security in adverse circumstances are more important than the ability to help the poor.

Plan followed:
Intro: Disagree
Para 1: Concession
Para 2: Other things more important than helping the poor
Para 3: Other things more important than helping the poor
Conclusion:

220. *Some people believe famous people's support towards International aid organizations draws the attentions to problems, whereas others think celebrities make the problems less important. Discuss both sides and give your opinion.*

Some individuals are of the opinion that if celebrities provide assistance to global charity organisations, people become more attentive towards these issues, whereas others believe that celebs can lessen the severity of the situation. This essay intends to delve into both perspectives. I believe that when celebs are associated with any organisation, people also put in their contribution.

The main reason why some people say that celebs draw attention towards problems by aiding international charity groups is that these charities can get publicity through celebrities. Famous singers, movie stars and sports professionals endorse the activities or campaigns of international charity organisations, which attracts more people to participate. Stars enhance the reputation and credibility of the charities. Secondly, when celebrities are called upon for helping NPOs (Non-Profit Organisations) or Charities, they themselves become aware of these problems, and come forward in donating for such causes.

On the other hand, those who say that these celebs dilute the severity of the problems, give their reasons as follows. Firstly, in some instances, celebrities take part in charity work just to improve their image. For example, if some stars are doing publicity for the anti-drug organization, but they themselves have their own history of drug use or crime, then obviously the public would look at that charity with suspicion. Secondly, sometimes, when the famous people are seen working for some charity then people start thinking that enough is already being done, and that their help is not needed. This can be detrimental in the long run.

I believe that celebs coming forward to help, is a very good thing and motivates others also to step forward to help. All famous people should do their utmost to fulfil their social obligations and do some public service activities for those charity organizations. This can be an effective way to serve those in need. The international charities should also be judicious enough to select which celeb they would like to be associated with.

To summarise, international aid organizations can attract more citizens' attention on problems if celebrities give the right support and set up good images

Plan followed:
Intro:
Para 1: One view
Para 2: Other view
Para 3: Own view
Conclusion:

221. *Some people think we need to give aid to all poor countries. Others, however, argue that we should not give international aid to countries with corruption in their system. Discuss both views and provide your own opinion.*

Some people hold the opinion that aid should be given to all the impoverished countries, whereas others say that help should not be provided to those countries which have corruption in their administration. In this essay I intend to discuss both perspectives. I believe all poor countries should be provided aid but to ensure that it reaches the poor people, it should be in non-monetary form.

There are many reasons why some people say that all poor countries should be supported by aid. Firstly, international aid is not only given to reduce poverty, but also to improve the donor country's own security. By giving aid, the economic condition of the poor countries improves and so the conditions that promote terrorism, such as poverty, unemployment and corruption are removed. So, this aid promotes peace and stability in the whole world.

On the other hand, those who say that countries with corruption should not be helped give their main reason that all the aid given will not reach the people for whom the aid is meant for. It may go into corrupt pockets. Secondly, it would make those people lazy, as they would be getting paid without doing any work. Thirdly, the aid may be used for wrong purposes. For example, the aid may be given for development projects but it may be used to promote terrorism.

I believe that the best way to help poor countries would be to provide non-monetary aid, as it would reach the people it is meant for. For example, good educational institutes, good health centres and job opportunities can be created for people of poor countries. Furthermore, it would leave no scope for the corrupt politicians to siphon the funds away and ensure that the people in need are actually benefited.

To sum up, international aid should be given to all poor countries, but if there is corruption it should not be in the form of monetary funds.

Plan followed:
Intro: Discuss essay intro
Para 1: One side view
Para 2: Other side view
Para 3: Own view
Conclusion:

222. *Some people think that giving aid to the poor countries has more negative impacts than positive ones. To what extent do you agree or disagree?*

It is believed by some that helping the poor nations has more detrimental effects than benefits. I believe that while there are a few negatives of helping the impoverished nations, the advantages are far more.

Admittedly, a major negative effect is that poor countries could become over dependent and stop making efforts of their own. This would halt the long term progress of the poor countries. Secondly, the aid given by rich countries could go into corrupt hands and not reach those for whom it was meant for. Then, the aid may not be that useful. For example, the people's need may be clothes and food but the aid may be in the form of making a bridge or something like that which people may not need. Finally, the rich countries may have their own selfish motives behind giving aid. For instance, they may provide employment but they may be underpaying and exploiting the poor.

However, the advantages of the rich countries helping the poor are manifold. To begin with, nowadays we belong to a global village and all countries are so interconnected that all problems that arise because of poverty – crime, terrorism and diseases will directly or indirectly affect the rich countries. It is a well-known fact that terrorists can infiltrate the rich countries and cause violence and crime there. Moreover, if poor countries suffer diseases then these diseases can spread to the neighbouring rich countries. So, it can be said that it is a necessity for the rich to save the poor in order to save themselves. It has been well said by John F Kennedy that "if a free society cannot help the many who are poor, it cannot save the few who are rich".

Furthermore, there are many problems which the world is facing today, such as global warming, which can be solved by joint efforts of all countries. Such joint efforts can only be possible if the gap between the rich and poor is narrowed. This can only be achieved if the haves help the have-nots. Finally, the rich countries also have a moral duty to help the poor. They should help them on humanitarian grounds.

To conclude, I reiterate by saying that the rich must help the poor. However, it must be well researched first as to what sort of help is most needed. Help can be provided in the form of food, medicine and education.

Plan followed:

Intro: disagree - There are negative effects, no doubt, but positive effects are certainly more
Para 1: negative effects of help
Para 2: advantages of helping.
Para 3: More advantages
Conclusion:

223. *Individuals and countries cannot help everyone who needs help in the world, so they should only be concerned about their own communities and countries. To what extent do you agree or disagree?*

It is believed by some that governments and individuals should only help their own citizens as it is impossible to help everyone. While I agree that governments ought to prioritise their own people, I also believe that they should help countries which are too poor to help themselves.

The main reason why governments should focus on their own citizens first is that if there is a perception that the government is helping other nations at the cost of its citizens, it would create resentment among the citizens. In other words, people might lose faith and protest against their elected government officials if they feel their hard earned tax money is being spent on helping other countries rather than leading to better facilities and services for them. Another reason is that a government's ability to help other nations depends upon the taxes and finances it collects, which ultimately depend upon prosperity of its own society. If its own society is poor, its capacity to help people in other countries would also be limited.

However, I also feel countries and especially rich countries should not turn their back on the underprivileged countries. First, it is the right thing to do from a humanitarian standpoint. Countries which have enough, have a moral duty to help those who fail to even meet their basic needs. Secondly, it would be mutually beneficial for rich to help the poor. Issues such as diseases, extreme weather events, international migration, organised crime and terrorism have transnational causes. No country can solve these problems 'by itself'. They need multinational cooperation. The recent Corona pandemic has emphasised the importance of international cooperation even more. Thus, it would be beneficial for not only the poor countries, but also the rich countries to help the poor.

In conclusion, I would like to reiterate that although countries should put their own citizens first, I also believe that they should try to help the deprived nations.

Plan followed:
Intro: Disagree.
Para 1: Why own country should be helped first
Para 2: Why other countries should be helped
Conclusion:
Written by: Indroop Singh

224. A lot of charities and organisations have to publicize their activities by setting up a number of days to name the special day like National Children's day and National non-smoking day. Why do they do so? What are the effects?

These days many NGO's and NPO's need to advertise their efforts by naming days like 'Mother's Day' and 'No Smoking Day'. In this essay I shall discuss the causes and effects of this phenomenon.

The main reason why these NPOs publicise their work is to raise funds for their working. When they publicize their activities, they get people's attention and so people contribute wholeheartedly. Sometimes, in times of calamities, they need a lot of funds and manual help. They need voluntary workers. For example, recently in Ladakh, a cloudburst caused havoc. Many people lost their lives and there was a lot of damage of property. The Rotary Club and Jaycee Club of my hometown sent many volunteers to help. The government alone cannot be at all places. Because of such organisations, people get timely help and a lot of burden is eased from the government's shoulders.

Furthermore, when these organisations name special days, it brings people together. With more activities opened and more days named, more and more people focus their attention and put their time and energy and realise the importance of doing for others. As a consequence, community spirit increases in society. As it is nowadays, people are getting self-centred and alienated from each other. So, such days are the need of the day.

Such days also, keep our youth in touch with our culture and traditions. With the exposure to global culture, youth today are forgetting their traditions. Establishing some days may help the young people understand the importance of such events. Such days also increase awareness of offering help selflessly. Hence, some virtuous habits may pass from one generation to the other. Finally, such days deter people from bad habits. For e.g., on National No Smoking Day people are made aware about the harmful effects of smoking.

To summarise, charities and NPOs publicize their activities because they need funds, and they name certain days so that people come together and celebrate and realize the importance of their culture and tradition

---

Plan followed:
Intro: In this essay I shall discuss the causes and effects of this phenomenon.
Para 1: The main reason why these NPOs do so is to raise funds for their working
Para 2: Secondly, it brings people together
Para 3: Such days keep our youth in touch with our culture and traditions. Such days deter people from bad habits *Conclusion:*

225. *Some people think that economic progress is the only way to measure a country's success, while others think that there are other factors, which can be used to measure a country's success. What are these factors? And among them, which one is more important than others?*

It is irrefutable that economic progress is one yardstick of determining a country's success, but there is a range of other non-economic factors such as healthcare, standard of education and availability of human rights which can be used to judge the well-being of a nation. I believe that the standard of education is the most important factor.

One of the main factors besides economic progress which determines a country's development is the standard of education. The standard of education is important because a society to truly progress needs inquisitive minds. In other words, the education should focus on innovation and curiosity. Moreover, I think there should be good teaching and institutions right from primary level to the tertiary level.

Another factor which is important is healthcare. A healthy workforce is not only more productive and efficient but also more creative and innovative. Healthcare should be complete with focus on wellness and prevention to the cure. Besides healthcare, I think that the availability of basic human rights is fundamental to a progressive society. Fundamental human rights are essential for people to achieve their true potential and for a society to develop. For example, a society where people are not able to express themselves freely can certainly not develop and progress.

I believe that out of all the factors listed above, the standard of education is the most important. Education in a way determines other factors like economic progress and healthcare and even availability of rights. An educated society would mean an efficient and creative workforce and thus a good economy. Similarly, education is critical to a good healthcare system, in the sense that doctors and nurses need to be educated first before they can treat others. Last but not least, an educated society is more liberal and democratic and thus more accepting of everyone's rights.

In conclusion, I would like to reiterate that although many factors can be used to measure a country's progress, I consider that level of education is the most significant.

Plan followed:

Intro: This essay shall delve into all such factors and also pick out the most significant one.
Para 1: One main factor besides economic progress is education
Para 2: Other factors – healthcare and availability of human rights
Para 3: The most important factor - education
Conclusion: Reiterate

Written by: Indroop Singh

226. *If children behave badly their parents should take responsibility and also be punished? Do you agree or disagree?*

It is believed by some that if children break the law, their parents should be held responsible and punished. While I certainly agree that parents are responsible for their children's actions, I do not agree that they should be punished.

The main reason why parents are responsible for their children's actions is that children's behaviour to a large extent is dependent upon their upbringing, which in turn depends upon their parents. Young children imitate their parents and later on these behaviours become their habits. So, if parents are abusive and disrespectful, their children are also likely to behave in such a way. In addition, it is the onus of the parents to keep an eye on them so that they do not exceed their limits and commit grave crimes.

However, at the same time, I do not agree that parents should pay the price for the actions of their children. Firstly, although children's behaviour depends upon their upbringing, it is certainly not the only factor. In fact, children's behaviour also depends upon external influences like media and peer pressure. So, it would be unfair to blame only the parents and punish them. Secondly, punishing parents would mean children stop taking responsibility for their actions. They would go in adulthood never having taken accountability for their actions. In adult life also, they would try to blame others for their actions.

Finally, although parents are responsible for teaching moral values to the children, children still commit crimes even if they are taught that is wrong. For example, many children are caught shoplifting even if parents have taught them that stealing is wrong. This has nothing to do with parents, but only the child committing the offence. In a way, punishing parents would also remove the feeling of guilt among children and they are more likely to commit crimes because they would think they can get away with it.

In conclusion, although I believe that parents are responsible for children's actions, I cannot support the idea of punishing them.

Plan followed:
Intro: parents have responsibility but should not be punished
Para 1: Why parents have responsibility
Para 2: Why parents should not be punished
Para 3: More reasons why parents should not be punished
Conclusion: Reiterate
Similar Essay
If a five year old commits a crime (any kind), should his/her parents accept responsibility and how should they be punished. What is the age of a child when parents no longer have the responsibility of a child's behaviour?
Written by: Indroop Singh

227. *In recent years, the number of crimes committed by teenagers in major cities throughout the world is increasing. Give reasons and suggest some solutions.*

It is a very shocking situation that the number of youngsters involved in crime is increasing day by day. In this essay, I intend to discuss the reasons for this phenomenon and suggest some solutions to address the issue.

A number of factors are responsible for juvenile delinquency. Media is one powerful influence. Many times, vulgarity and violence are shown on TV. Children are vulnerable and accept it as natural and try to copy what is shown. For example, in Virginia USA, a student killed 30 students just after watching a TV program. Another cause of crime among youth is the changing family structure. Nuclear families are the norm of the day. Earlier, there were joint families in which grandparents used to teach moral values to children. They kept an eye on the friend circle of their grandchildren. Nowadays, both parents are working and children are left unattended at home. They may fall into bad company and resort to drugs under peer pressure. For drugs they desperately need money, which turns them towards crime.

Furthermore, increasing poverty and competition are causing hopelessness and frustration among the youth. They are over ambitious and want to earn quick money. They have a lot of energy and if that energy is not harnessed in the right direction, they can go astray. Consumerist society is also a big factor to put them on the path of crime. When they see new things in the market, they want them by hook or by crook. Parents cannot satisfy all their whims and so they start doing petty crime, which turns to major crime very soon.

The solutions are not simple. The issue has to be dealt with on a war footing. Some censorship of TV channels is needed. Parents should ration the TV viewing hours of children. Parents should watch TV with children so that they know what their children are being exposed to. We should also encourage joint families. Parents should be good role models. Good family atmosphere should be provided to children. Friend circle of the children should be monitored. We should also educate children about the harms of consumerism. Schools should also provide good education. Finally, government should try and reduce unemployment and poverty, which are the root causes.

Summing up, crime among teens is a big problem and youth alone cannot be blamed for that. We should look into the causes and take relevant steps to fight this problem.

Plan followed:

Intro:
Para 1: Reasons
Para 2: More reasons
Para 3: Solutions
Conclusion:

228. *Young people who commit serious crimes should be punished in the same way as adults. Do you agree or disagree?*

The rising crime among teenagers and young has led to many people calling for change in laws to punish children in the same way as adults. I believe that trying juveniles in criminal court may actually result in bigger problems and so I am against this proposition.

There are many reasons why I cannot support punishing children in the same manner as adults. Firstly, although adolescents are old enough to understand the difference between right and wrong, they are too young to make the right choices. Studies have shown that adolescents are more likely to act on impulse and engage in risky behaviour. They are less likely to think before they act, or pause to consider the potential consequences of their actions.

Secondly, if tried in an adult court, they may even be sent to prison. Adult prisons are very harsh and these prisons expose these young children to hardened criminals. Juveniles tried and prosecuted in adult courts get influenced by adult prisoners and are more likely to reoffend. By contrast, juvenile detention facilities have programs to reform them and give them a chance of redemption. With appropriate treatment, teens who commit crimes can be made into responsible adults.

In addition, this is a critical age in the development of an individual. Sending children to prisons may affect their education and seal their fate in terms of rehabilitation back into the society. Adult criminals have the necessary skills to get employment after leaving prisons, but for young people it might be impossible because of their lack of education. Finally, Children are not permitted the same rights and responsibilities as adults (e.g. voting, drinking, smoking) because the society recognizes their inability to make adult decisions. So, the difference in terms of criminal law is also justified.

To sum up, juvenile delinquents should not be punished like adults and instead they should be given a chance to redeem themselves and make better choices.

Plan followed:
Intro: Disagree
Para 1: Reasons
Para 2: More reasons
Para 3: More reasons
Conclusion
Written by: Indroop Singh

229. *A recent newspaper article reported that a 14-year-old boy who seriously destroyed his school got the punishment to clean the streets, instead of being sent to prison. Do you think this is right, or do you think that such criminals should be sent to prison?*

It is generally seen that children who commit serious crimes like destroying school property are given lenient punishment such as cleaning streets. I believe that such punishments are justified because of various reasons and sending children to prisons would be wrong.

There are many reasons why children should not be punished like adults. Firstly, children do not have the same maturity level as adults. In other words, they are too young to understand the difference between right and wrong. They also cannot think about the long-term consequences of their actions. Rather than thinking first and then doing something, they act first and think later.

Secondly, these are the career building years and punishing them strictly by sending them to prisons can affect their education. In fact, it has been seen that if children are sent to prisons at a young age, they are unable to continue their education after completing their sentence. Thus, they are unable to join society as productive members and in many cases, such individuals commit crimes again and again as they have no skills of earning a good livelihood.

In addition, unlike adults, children are impressionable. Through an appropriate punishment, their behaviour can be changed. If they are sent to prisons, they would come in contact with hardened criminals and instead of correcting their behaviour, they might become attracted to a life of crime. Finally, I think crimes such damaging property are not as serious as harming other people because a financial compensation can make up for it. So, if the crime is limited to property damage, I think it would be better to give children another chance.

In conclusion, I would like to reiterate that children should not be sent to prisons for misdemeanours.

Plan followed:
Intro: Agree
Para 1: First reason for not punishing them as adults
Para 2: Second reason
Para 3: Third reason
Conclusion: Reiterate opinion

(Written by Indroop Makkar 26/10/2021)

230. *Studies show that many criminals have a low level of education. For this reason, people believe that the best way to reduce crime is to educate people in prison so they can get a job when they leave prison. Do you agree or disagree?*

It is generally observed that criminals are either illiterate or they have a low level of education. Therefore, it is thought that the most effective way to tackle crime is to provide education to criminals in prisons. While providing education in prisons can reduce crime to some extent, there are other better solutions to lessen crime.

Admittedly, providing education to criminals can certainly reduce crime. When criminals get some education, they would be able to get jobs after leaving prisons. Thus, they would be able to fulfil their basic needs and they will not be forced to resort to crime. Education would also increase the self-confidence of convicts and would make them more open minded and respectful.

However, I believe providing education in prisons would not be very successful in reducing crime. Firstly, the main reason why criminals commit crimes again and again is not the lack of education, but the inability to secure good jobs. This is because most people avoid hiring criminals and there is a need to change society's attitude towards criminals. Government could also facilitate this change through incentives like tax rebates to businesses and companies, which hire convicts.

Secondly, education in prisons may stop repeat offences, but it will not impact the first time crimes. Hence, rather than focusing on education in prisons, the government should focus on primary education, so that the overall illiteracy in society comes down and even first time crimes are reduced. Finally, the link between illiteracy and crime is overstated as some of the developed countries with high literacy rates have higher crime rates than developing and underdeveloped countries. So, focusing on education to address crime may not have the desired results.

In conclusion, although prison education would reduce crime to some extent, I believe that it is not the best method of reducing offences in the society.

Plan followed:
Intro: Disagree
Para 1: Why education in prisons is a good method
Para 2: Why it would not be successful
Para 3: Another reason why education in prisons would not be enough
Conclusion:

231. *Many people are afraid to leave their home because of crime. Some believe that more action can be taken to prevent crime, while others feel that little action can be done to stop crime. Discuss both sides and give your opinion.*

It is irrefutable that crime is burgeoning day by day in many countries. Many people are scared to go away from their home because of crime. Some people contend that a number of ways can be used to prevent crime, while other people argue that nothing can be done to prevent it. In this essay, I will discuss both perspectives. I believe that it is possible to tackle this serious issue by taking some action.

On the one hand, there are many reasons why some people say that nothing can be done to prevent crime. They say that despite having laws against crime, the incidences of crime are on the rise. Moreover, the rich and the influential can get away after doing crime by bribing the officials. People have become dejected and frustrated by all this. They see no improvement coming in the law and order situation. That is why they say that no steps can be taken to check crime.

On the other hand, those who say that if more steps are taken, crime can be averted, give their reasons as follows. Firstly, the authorities could increase the number of police on roads. A second possibility would be to make laws stricter and punishments more severe. Finally, people could use more effective alarm devices can be used in houses. Surveillance cameras can be used in homes with the help of which people can watch what is happening in their homes from anywhere. In this way one can feel secure about one's home.

I believe that crime can be forfended by taking several steps. For example, if more police were on the streets, whether on foot or on patrol cars, criminals would be less likely to commit crime and people would feel much safer. Moreover, if a criminal has to pay more money for doing something illegal or would have to face more time in prison, then this is likely to reduce the crime rate. It would be wrong to give up all hope of thwarting potential criminals from doing crime.

In conclusion, although crime is a major problem in most cities in the world, the situation can be addressed by adopting the methods mentioned above. It would definitely be wrong to say that nothing can be done to address this problem.

Plan followed:
Intro: I believe that it is possible to tackle this serious issue by taking some action.
Para 1: One view
Para 2: Other view
Para 3: Own view
Conclusion:

232. *Many people nowadays do not feel safe either when they are at home or go out. What are the reasons and what can be done to solve this problem?*

There is no doubt that an increasing number of people feel unsafe, not only when they go out somewhere, but also when they are at home. There are several factors which have led to this increasing fear, but many steps can be taken to address these problems.

The reasons why people are afraid of going out of their homes are very obvious. The crimes committed on the streets, are on a rise. The road mishaps have risen to a proportion, more than ever before and continue to increase every day. Some people are afraid to go out because of the fear of natural calamities and also, sometimes due to health related disorders, which might be caused due to the increase in pollution. The reports of bombings and terror attacks have become everyday news. As a result, people feel afraid of stepping out of their homes.

At the same time, people are also becoming increasingly scared within their homes. The main reason for this is the escalation in the crimes being committed at homes, like murders, robberies, etc. In a recent news article, it has been surveyed that there have been more crimes committed by domestic help at people's homes, than the crimes being committed on the streets. This has led to people feeling vulnerable, at home and when they are out on the streets.

There are certain steps, which can be taken, by the government and individuals, to make people more safe and protected. Firstly, if the youth of a country are provided vocational training and good job opportunities, they would not fall on the path of crime. Another important measure, which needs to be taken by the government, is to employ more security measures, like cameras, more police patrolling, and more security in public areas and even in homes. For instance, in Bengaluru, government has now made it compulsory for all showrooms and shops to install security cameras. Finally, stricter punishments for the offenders will act as a major deterrent for the criminals.

To sum up, people's fear and insecurity is justified, with the increasing reports of crime reported by the media. However, this situation can be mitigated by taking some measures, like tackling the unemployment problem, tightened security measures, stricter punishments and the use of advanced technology in households and commercial areas.

Plan followed:
Intro:
Para1: Why people are not safe when they are out of their homes
Para 2: Why they are not safe within their homes
Para 3: Solutions
Conclusion

233. *More and more measures to improve the security in large urban areas have been introduced in many countries because of the increased crime. Do the benefits of these measures outweigh the drawbacks?*

Crime and the fear of crime are very big concerns in big cities and so many security measures have been introduced to tackle crime. In this essay I intend to delve into the advantages and disadvantages of these methods. The advantages definitely outweigh the disadvantages.

On the one hand, the major benefit of surveillance cameras is that the police can catch criminals in the act, thus reducing crime. This has made the streets safer for ordinary people. A more important point is that criminals, particularly young offenders or petty criminals are deterred. They will not be tempted to carry out crimes, and thus society will be a lot safer. Cameras are also cost-effective and unobtrusive. Authorities do not need to spend large amounts of money on police.

Another security measure is the computerized data collection of individuals. This also helps the police force to operate more effectively. The data can be updated regularly and data retrieval is very easy and quick. These methods are also cost effective. Other methods like police patrolling on the roads has also been intensified. These methods bring a sense of security in the minds of people.

On the other hand, the biggest drawback is that people lose privacy. Many people feel that they should be free to travel or move around a shop, mall, street or country without being photographed or recorded. They feel that being watched constantly is like being in a jail, and that ordinary people are losing their freedom because of these devices. Even the computerized data collection of individuals can go in wrong hands.

Summing up, there are definite advantages to using such measures, but we need to balance the need for security with respect for the individual's privacy and freedom. If this is done then definitely the advantages outweigh the disadvantages.

Plan followed:
Intro: advantages definitely outweigh the disadvantages.
Para 1: Advantages of security cameras
Para 2: Advantages of computerized data collection of individuals
Para 3: Downside of such measures
Conclusion: Reiterate opinion

234. *Some people who have been in prison become good citizens later. Some people think that they are the best people to talk to school students about the danger of committing a crime. Do you agree or disagree?*

It is believed by some that reformed criminals who have served their sentence can become normal, productive members of society and are the best people to speak with school children and educate them against delinquency. While ex-convicts can educate school children against crime, they are not the best and other alternatives are better.

Admittedly, it is a good idea for ex-convicts to talk to students, as teenagers are more likely to accept advice from someone who can speak from experience. Reformed offenders can tell young people about the dangers of a criminal lifestyle and tough life in prisons. By listening to a wide range of real cases in person, the young generation will realize the consequences of irresponsible behaviour and discipline themselves strictly in the future.

However, I believe criminals are not always the best people to talk to students. To begin with, people have a fear towards criminals, especially those who have committed violent crimes and therefore face-to-face conversation between the school students and such ex-convicts may be not accepted by parents. Also, by inviting such people to schools to address the students, some vulnerable students might start thinking it glamorous to commit a crime.

So, other better alternatives should be taken into consideration. Policemen normally have a good impression among youngsters, and they can become the active voice in reducing juvenile delinquency. Senior police officials could be called to deliver lectures to students and show them videos of the harsh life in prisons to deter them from committing crime. Apart from them, parents can certainly be the first to help children learn the differences between right and wrong since they are the people who know their children the best in the world. Teachers also are good to guide children about what is right or wrong.

To sum up, I reiterate my opinion that ex-criminals are good, but not the best to guide children against immoral behaviour.

Plan followed:
Intro: Disagree
Para 1: How ex-criminals can help
Para 2: Why ex-prisoners are not the best.
Para 3: What other people can help
Conclusion:

235. *Prison is the common way in most countries to solve the problem of crime. However, a more effective solution is to provide people a better education. Agree or disagree.*

The traditional solution is to punish the criminals by putting them in prison. However, some hold the view that education and job training can be better long-term solutions to lower crime. In my opinion, although education and skill training can certainly be more effective to tackle crime, it does not mean that prisons are not needed.

There are a number of reasons why I consider education and skill training to be more effective. Firstly, many people commit crimes because they are unable to fulfil their basic needs. The time spent in the education system increases labour market prospects and makes crime relatively less profitable. In other words, a stable and well-paid job would mean that individuals not only have a lot less to gain but also a lot more to lose by committing crimes.

Secondly, keeping teenagers in school during a key period of criminal activity can prevent the exposure of individuals to crime and ensure that they never proceed down the wrong track. This kind of incapacitation is better than prison because there is less opportunity to learn about criminal techniques than in prisons, the universities of crime. Finally, the prisons are expensive to maintain and thus, education is much more cost effective.

However, prison is the only answer in case of repeat offenders or people who commit crimes even if they are wealthy and educated. Prisons are the only means to keep them away from society. Education can be more effective in preventing crime, but it cannot end crime. Prisons also act as a deterrent to crime by raising the cost of crime. Thus, they supplement education and reduce crime in their own way.

In conclusion, while I agree that educating people can be more effective in tackling crime, it is also irrefutable that prisons are also needed to curb crime.

Plan followed:
Intro: partially agree
Para 1: Why education and skill training is more effective
Para 2: Why prison is not the answer -
Para 3: Cases where prison is the answer
Conclusion:

236. Certain people believe that the only way to reduce crime is sentencing criminals for longer time periods, while others believe alternative methods should be used to lower crimes. Discuss both views and give your opinion.

There are many different opinions on the best way to reduce crime. Some people say that long term prison is the only way to curb crime, whereas others say that education, vocational training and rehabilitation are better. This essay intends to analyse both perspectives. I believe that long term imprisonment is the answer for heinous criminals, but on the whole, alternative methods are better to combat crime.

There are many arguments given by those who advocate longer terms in prison to combat crime. They say that there are criminals who are a risk to the society, such as murderers. They cannot be made to mix with society. There are also mentally insane people such as serial killers who should be kept away from the people. If such criminals are set free soon, they will reoffend and so should be in penitentiaries for longer terms.

On the other hand, there are many convincing arguments given by those who are against long-term imprisonment. Firstly, in traditional prisons, petty criminals learn a lot about crime, and so when they leave prison, they commit even more crime. In other words, prisons act as universities of crime. So petty offenders like shoplifters and pickpockets should be given some vocational training and education. It is a well-known fact that the basic causes of crime are poverty, illiteracy and unemployment. If some form of employment rehabilitates criminals, then they would certainly not re-offend.

I believe that alternative methods are better than the conventional prisons, because prisons are expensive to maintain. The government can spend that money on other important matters such as education and healthcare. This would ease some burden off the government's shoulders. The petty and minor criminals can also be employed in some community service projects after providing education and vocational training.

Summing up, we should hate the crime and not the criminal. To fight crime, the focus should be on fighting the causes of crime and on reforming the criminals. Education and job training help to rehabilitate the criminals. Longer terms in prison are not the answer to curb crime.

Plan followed:

Intro: Discuss essay intro
Para 1: One view
Para 2: Other view
Para 3: Own view
Conclusion:

237. Research suggests that majority of criminals who were sent to prison would commit crimes when set free. What do you think of this case? What to be done to solve this problem?

Crime is a big problem all over the world and there are many different opinions on the best way to reduce crime. The traditional solution is to punish the criminals by putting them in prison. It has been seen that when criminals are set free from prison, majority of them re-offend. In the following paragraphs, I shall put forth some causes of this phenomenon and suggest some solutions.

To begin with, in traditional prisons, people learn a lot about crime and so when they leave prison they tend to commit even more crime. In other words, prisons act as universities of crime. Secondly, after being set free some may even want to lead a good and peaceful life, but people of the community do not accept them and as a result they do not get any jobs. They are forced to re-offend because they have to fulfil their basic needs. Finally, some may commit crime again because they do not have the training or qualification to do any job.

Many steps can be taken to minimize the gravity of the situation. First of all, petty offenders like shoplifters and pickpockets should be given some vocational training and education. It is a well not fact that the basic causes of crime are poverty, illiteracy and unemployment. So, if we provide education and job training then we would be removing the causes of crime. If some form of employment rehabilitates criminals then they would certainly not re-offend.

Furthermore, community service such as maintaining parks and doing some construction work can be taken from criminals instead of just putting them into prisons. In this way, they feel they are part of the community and the community also starts accepting them.

Summing up, we should hate the crime and not the criminal. To fight crime we should focus on the causes of crime. Education and job training help to rehabilitate the criminals. So, the focus should be on reforming the criminals so that they do not re-offend.

Plan followed:

Intro: I shall suggest some causes of this phenomenon and suggest some solutions.
Para 1: Reasons for re-committing crime
Para 2: Solutions
Para 3: community service such as maintaining parks and doing some construction work can be taken from criminals instead of just putting them into prisons
Conclusion:

238. *Proper function of prisons is to punish criminals and life in prisons should be hard. Do you agree or disagree?*

Prisons are needed to punish criminals as well as deter potential criminals. While life in prison should definitely be difficult, proper function of prisons is not just limited to punishing criminals.

There are many reasons why it would be wrong to say that the proper function of prisons is to punish criminals. Normally, prisons have three basic functions. The first is to protect the society from offenders. There are some hardcore criminals and mentally sick people who should be behind the bars for the safety of the general public. Secondly, prisons punish offenders by keeping them away from their families. Thirdly, they rehabilitate or reform offenders. Prisons are correctional institutes where prisoners are reformed to become law-abiding citizens. Education and vocational training is given to inmates of the prison so that they are able to make a living after being set free and do not re-offend. Those prisoners who are mentally sick are given proper psychiatric treatment and are only set free when it is sure that the society is not at any risk from them. Therefore, it would be wrong to say that the proper function is only to punish offenders.

As far as the life in prisons is concerned, I believe that it should be very tough. By that it does not mean that inhuman, cruel or degrading treatment should be given to them. It simply means prisoners should be made to lead a very disciplined life and made to do some community work. This work could be any labour type work or any work depending on the capability of the inmates of the prison. If they have to be given vocational training, it should also be given seriously.

There would be many advantages of a tough life in prison. To begin with, it would act as a deterrent for prisoners to reoffend once they are set free. Another important effect would be that they would not have the time to learn crime from other serious offenders within the prison. It has generally been seen that prisons act as schools of crime for petty criminals. Another benefit that could ensue is that this prison labour could be turned into an industry and money could be generated for the maintenance of these prisons.

To conclude, I reiterate my opinion saying that prisons have other roles besides punishing criminals and the life within prisons should definitely be hard.

Plan followed:
Intro: I disagree
Para 1: Functions of prison
Para 2: Why life in prisons should be hard
Para 3: Benefits of hard prison life
Conclusion:

239. *Crime is a problem all over the world and there is nothing that can be done to prevent it. To what extent do you agree or disagree?*

It is true that crime is a very grave problem in many parts of the world and so some believe that it is impossible to address crime. I believe that although it might be challenging to control, it is certainly not impossible.

There are many reasons why I believe crime can be tackled. First, governments can try to address the causes of crime to reduce crime. Majority of criminals commit crime due to illiteracy, poverty or unemployment. Therefore, if the approach shifts from punishing the criminal to addressing why the person stepped onto the path of crime, crime can certainly be curbed. Harsh punishments can deter crime to some extent, but crime can only be prevented if the root causes are addressed.

Secondly, governments must employ the use of technology to tackle crime as it can address the problem of shortage of law and order personnel. For example, CCTV cameras not only deter criminals but also help police to catch criminals and bring them to justice. Similarly, criminal databases can not only help law and order personnel to share information about criminals with each other, but also better track movement of ex-offenders. This can certainly reduce recidivism to a great extent.

In addition, due to the global nature of crime, governments across the world must cooperate and work alongside each other to tackle crime. For example, investigation agencies from different countries must actively share data on criminals. Finally, governments alone cannot control crime without the active support of the people. In other words, people themselves need to be more aware and vigilant. For instance, people should report any strange behaviour or activity to the police and businesses should hire employees only after getting a background check done.

In conclusion, although crime is a major problem in most cities in the world, the situation can be ameliorated by adopting the methods mentioned above.

Plan followed:
Intro: I disagree that nothing can be done to prevent it. I believe that it is possible to tackle this serious issue in a number of ways.
Para 1: One approach
Para 2: Other approaches
Para 3: Other approaches
Conclusion:

240. *In some countries, some of the criminal cases in the law courts are shown on the television, so that the general public can watch them. Do the advantages outweigh the disadvantages?*

There are some countries such as the US, where court cases are televised, so that the public can view them. While there are a few drawbacks of telecasting criminal courts, the benefits are far more.

On the one hand, there are many arguments in favour of televising court proceedings. Firstly, this ensures that efficient and fair trials are there. Because of televising, many people will be able to access the court cases, and also will be able to criticize the judges for engaging in a trial insincerely. Secondly, it is the way to enhance trust towards the justice system by making the court transparent and open. It would allow people to know better of the judiciary system, and also give them knowledge of law related issues.

Furthermore, articles written by reporters about trials do not satisfy people's right to know. Right to know is a fundamental right, all people have. Journalists are allowed to write reports of the proceedings, but written judgments are full of jargon and complicated sentence constructions, which common people do not understand. What is more, televising trials would aware the potential criminals of the treatment they will receive when they commit crimes, and discourage them from doing it. Finally, some families of victims may not be able to go to the trial, but they can follow it on TV from a safe distance.

On the other hand, one of the arguments against televising criminal courts is that the presence of cameras could distort the very nature of the process. The jurors may be influenced by the media coverage. In particular, it has been argued that televising the events could act as a deterrent to victims and witnesses giving evidence. Witnesses will lose their anonymity, as everyone in the country will know their face. To add to it, showing trials on TV, could turn lawbreakers into celebrities. The procedures might turn into entertainment, like in the Judge Judy show.

To conclude, although televising the trial courts has both merits and demerits, the benefits definitely have an edge over the drawbacks.

Plan followed:
Intro:
Para 1: Advantages of televising
Para 2: More advantages
Para 3: Disadvantages
Conclusion: reiterate opinion

241. *Some people believe that if police force carries guns, it can encourage a higher level of violence. To what extent do you agree or disagree?(29 Jan 2022)*

It is believed by some people that an armed police force promotes a greater degree of violence. I believe that an armed police force discourages violence, and can protect the people and even themselves in fighting against criminals.

My first argument to support my opinion is that guns deter the potential criminals to a large extent. Police officers are responsible for taking care of all the citizens' safety and wearing guns largely make sure of this. For example, if someone has the intention to commit a crime, he would think twice about doing so if there is police carrying guns on patrol. Therefore, the level of violence decreases rather than goes up.

Secondly, criminals usually have guns and so police officers need them in order to control crime. Armed police officers are better able to protect themselves from dangers that directly threaten their life. They are able to chase criminals knowing that they are equipped to handle them. In other words, police officers are more likely to be proactive in their duties and be more prepared to jump into a violent situation, if they know they can protect themselves.

Finally, instead of taking guns away from the police, it is more important to make laws against the general public having guns. Countries with weak or ineffective gun laws need a police force that is not only armed, but is armed better than the criminals. In places where police are able to go without guns and also have crime in control is only because the general public are not allowed gun ownership. Therefore, police forces should carry guns.

To sum up, because criminals can easily come into possession of guns, therefore the police force needs to be armed. Armed police as such could never be a cause of increased violence.

Plan followed:

Intro: Disagree
Para 1: If police are armed, criminals are deterred from doing crime.
Para 2: Police need guns because criminals have guns.
Para 3: Instead of taking guns away from the police, people should not be allowed guns
Conclusion: reiterated

242. *Some people argue that public should be allowed to have guns. Others do not agree. Discuss both views and give your opinion.*

People are divided on the issue of gun ownership. There are some, who hold the opinion that gun ownership should be allowed, as it is in many countries such as the US, whereas others opine that people in general should not be permitted to keep them. This essay intends to analyse both views. I personally believe that gun ownership should not be allowed.

The major reason why some people say that the governments should not allow people to have guns is that there is a potential for accidents. In America, for example, a person can legally shoot people if he finds them robbing his house, but this can lead to innocent people dying. In addition, there are crimes where people act rashly or in anger, so guns that are intended for defense can be used aggressively. Another important argument against owning guns is that there can be intentional damage caused by guns. It is statistically evident that the number of gun-related crimes is higher in countries such as the US, where gun ownership is legal.

On the other hand, those in favour of gun ownership say that without the freedom to bear arms, there is no self-defense. Without self-defense, there would most likely be more break-ins, robberies and even deaths. In the UK it is illegal to have a gun, yet criminals can still get one. So, if anyone who had a gun used it harmfully, people would have no self-defense. They also argue that shooting is a sport, and so being prevented from owning their own firearm, is both unjust and a violation of their rights.

To sum up, although there are points to support gun ownership, they are weak in comparison with the rising tide of gun crime, a situation, which will only continue to worsen.

Plan followed:
Intro:
Para 1: Points against gun ownership
Para 2: Points for gun ownership
Conclusion: reiterate opinion

243. *Newspapers have influenced people's ideas and opinions. What are the reasons for this? Is this a positive or a negative situation?*

Newspaper is the oldest form of print media. In this essay I intend to analyze the reasons why newspapers affect people's ideas and viewpoints. While there are a few negative influences of the newspapers, the positives are much more.

The first reason why newspapers are very influential is their easy accessibility. In other words, newspapers are one of the cheapest and most widespread sources of information. Despite the fact that social media is gaining ground, news media still has more readership because there is a sizable population which is not comfortable with technology. Another reason is the newspaper's credibility. The newspaper's columnists are considered to be experts by the people. The final reason why I believe that news media have had an impact on people's perception and thinking is that when newspapers focus on a particular topic repeatedly, these create awareness.

Coming to the impact on the positive side, the media makes people more empathetic and alert. It updates people with both good and bad latest happenings, which is a helpful influence. For example, media's wide coverage of rapes and murders in surrounding areas creates sympathy as well as alertness in people. Furthermore, news media keeps a check on the government's autocratic tendencies. They aware people about both the positive and the negative consequences of governments intended measures. Many times, governments have retracted steps which have gained negative media scrutiny.

On the other hand, the main adverse effect of excessive media influence is that it sometimes leads to protests and even violence. Many times, due to excessive media reporting and over-exaggeration of negative consequences by news media, people begin to oppose government projects. This may slow down and, in some cases, even disrupt development. This has happened many times in India with protests leading to cancellation of projects like POSCO steel project in Orissa, Kundakulum nuclear power plants etcetera.

To conclude, the newspaper as one of the oldest media is powerful enough to influence one's attitudes and thought process because of many reasons. This influence is largely positive.

Plan followed:
Intro:
Para 1: Reasons
Para 2: Reasons
Para 3: Positive impact
Para 4: Negative impact
Conclusion:

244. *Although nowadays people are reading news through the Internet, newspapers still remain of value. Do you agree or disagree?*

There is no doubt that the Internet has changed the way people access information, but some people believe that newspapers still have their own importance. While I believe that the internet has impacted the readership of newspapers, I also agree that the newspapers still hold value.

The main reason why the printed newspaper is still important is that it does not require any technical equipment to read. It is cumbersome to read news on a laptop or a computer and in addition, it has adverse effects on people's eyes. Older people find it hard to use modern technologies and are more comfortable reading traditional printed newspapers. Moreover, the newspaper is still the cheapest source of information and many people in poor or developing countries cannot afford the internet and such gadgets.

Another big advantage of newspapers is that it can be one source of information. Instead of having to search out multiple web sites to find information, readers of a newspaper can instead have all of the day's information at one place. In addition, all the information available on the Internet may not be reliable, as there are a lot of fake news and articles posted online. Everyone who has access to this resource can post anything online and sometimes the information posted is not thoroughly vetted before it is published. By contrast, printable sources are always authenticated, and published after careful consideration of facts.

However, at the same time, I believe that the internet has dented the appeal of newspapers. Some people have definitely switched to the internet as their principal source of newspaper as they can get news in real time. In comparison, they have to wait for the next day to read the news in case of newspapers. Furthermore, people can watch a video while reading the news article on the internet and this makes the experience far better.

Summing up, although there has been a certain decline in the readership of newspapers due to the advent of the internet, they are still important.

Plan followed:
Intro: I agree
Para 1: main advantage of the printed newspaper Para 2: More advantages
Para 3: Advantages of the Internet but still newspaper is the king
Conclusion:

Similar essay: Some people think newspaper is the most effective way to get the latest information because it has more influence than other forms of media. Do you agree or disagree?

245. *Some people think that the news media nowadays have influenced people's lives in negative ways. To what extent do you agree or disagree?*

It is believed by some that media has a negative influence on people's lives. I believe that the media is doing a great service to mankind and whatever negative effect it has is negligible if compared to its benefits.

There are many positive effects of media. To begin with, the media provides information about events around the world almost instantly. Furthermore, media also shapes people's opinions. It is a link between the government and the people. People's conceptions of their elected officials spring from television images and newspaper stories. Most people will never meet prime ministers or presidents, but anyone who is regularly exposed to the media will know about them. When it is time to cast their vote, they make our decision based on the media coverage of candidates.

The media are also influential in the way they facilitate the spread of culture and lifestyle. Today, the popularity of Indian culture is an example of the media's enormous impact. What is more, the reality shows of today have given exposure and fame to the common man with talent today. Finally, the media also helps in providing justice to the common man. Who has not heard of the Jessica murder case and the case of Nithari killings? Were it not for the media, Jessica's parents would have never got justice.

On the other hand, the media too has its downside. The paparazzi can invade the privacy of famous people. Sometimes violence and vulgarity is shown and at times it can shape our opinion in negative ways. For that my counter argument is that once the person becomes famous then his private life becomes public and he has no right to crib about the paparazzi. People can choose what they want to see and technology has provided them the tools to block those channels, which they do not want their children to see. Finally, God has given people brains to judge what is right or wrong. The media is just doing its job by providing them with the latest information.

In conclusion, I would like to reiterate by saying that the influence of media on our lives is largely positive.

Plan followed:
Intro: Disagree
Para 1: Positive side of media
Para 2: More positives of media
Para 3: Opponents view with counter-argument
Conclusion: Reiterate opinion
News media is important in our society. Why is it so important? Do you think its influence is generally positive or negative?(Similar)

246. *Many people use social media every day to keep in touch with other people and for news events. Do the advantages outweigh the disadvantages?*

It is irrefutable that more and more people are using social media for staying connected with family and friends and for keeping up to date with the news. I believe that while there are certain drawbacks of this trend, the advantages are far more.

The main advantage of social media is that in this fast-paced era, it is only possible to stay connected with others through social media. An increasing number of people are working long hours and hence they frequently lose touch with each other. People can now reconnect with so many of their childhood friends, with whom they had lost contact over the years for various reasons.

Another benefit of social media is that it has made people more aware about global affairs. The traditional news media like the TV and newspapers mainly focus on domestic news, while social media covers both. For example, when people go through Facebook pages of their friends living abroad, they come to know about many international happenings. Moreover, today many people do not have the time to sit down in front of the TV or open a newspaper and read it, as they are always in a rush. Social media at least makes sure that people are aware about what's happening around them.

On the other hand, there are also some drawbacks of social media. The first drawback is that it has reduced face to face contact. People prefer chatting rather than visiting friends in person. As a result, they do not share the same kind of bond that they did earlier. Secondly, there is a lot of misinformation being spread on the internet. There is no way to verify what is true and what is false. For instance, because of fake news about northeast Indians being killed in Bangalore, a lot of people from that region left the city.

In conclusion, I would like to reiterate that despite the negatives of people preferring social media to keep in touch with each other and for reading news, its merits certainly warrant its use.

Plan followed:
Intro: Advantages are more
Para 1: Benefit
Para 2: Benefit
Para3: Drawback
Conclusion: Reiterate

Written by: Indroop Singh

247. *Nowadays, people get information through news and papers, but meanwhile are uncertain about the truth of these news. Should we believe the journalists? What qualities should a good journalist or correspondent have?*

News and newspapers are an indispensable part of our everyday life, because they keep us connected with the outside world. This essay will discuss whether or not we should believe the journalists, and also explain the characteristics of a good journalist.

We have to believe the journalists because they are our only source of information. However, we should take it all with a pinch of salt. Sometimes they may spread ill-founded news just to sell their papers. On the whole, they are doing great service to us. They are a link between the government and the people. They shape our opinions. They make us feel part of this global village by keeping us in touch with it, and at times they even provide justice. For example, in the Jessica murder case, it was because of the efforts of these journalists that a politician's son got punishment and Jessica's family got justice.

A good journalist should have many qualities. First of all, he should promote the truth, and not rumours of ill-founded news. Only authenticated news should be given. Secondly, he should be unbiased and not favour any group or political party. He should not hurt the sentiments of any particular community. This is very important in a pluralistic (multicultural and multi-religious) society like India. He should also have excellent communication skills.

Furthermore, a good journalist should be versatile – he has to cover varied fields such as sports, business, entertainment and politics. He should always be on his toes, because it can never be predicted when the sky is going to fall. Finally, he should be bold and brave because he has to handle tough situations. For instance, during the 26th November terrorist attack at Mumbai, it was these journalists who brought us the first-hand news.

Summing up, we have to believe the journalists because they bring us the latest news, and a good journalist should be a multifaceted personality.

Plan followed:

Intro: This essay shall discuss whether or not we should believe the journalists and also explain the characteristics of a good journalist

Para 1: Why we should believe the journalists

Para 2: Qualities of a good journalist

Para 3: More qualities

Conclusion:

248. *In some countries, celebrities complain about the way media publicize their private lives. Some people say that they should accept it as part of their fame. Do you agree or disagree?*

It is believed by some that celebrities have to accept the manner in which their private lives are made public by the media. Although media is responsible for keeping these celebs in the spotlight for their work, it has absolutely no right to their private life.

There are many reasons why the media should not march into the private lives of celebs. To commence with, celebrities are already under a lot of pressure to perform well, as they are public figures and are always in the public eye. Be it a politician, a sportsperson, a singer or an actor, all these professions require them to be at their best at all times. This stress of someone constantly following them affects the way they perform, which ultimately leads to a loss for the people.

Secondly, these celebs are role models for the people. When any negative side of their private life is exposed, their followers think it glamorous to do the same, which is definitely detrimental for the society as a whole. For example, if people come to know that the celeb they adore, smokes and drinks in private life, they think there is nothing wrong in doing so and also copy their idol. This is where responsible journalism is needed.

Finally, sensationalizing the news in order for the channel to get more TRP is unethical. Some ethics need to be followed by journalists, as they may adversely affect someone's personal and professional lives. Who does not remember the unfortunate incident when the world lost a very eminent public figure, Lady Diana? That accident happened because the paparazzi were chasing the car she was travelling in. Even though celebrities choose this life for name and fame and to be in the spotlight, it does not mean that the media and paparazzi have a right to stalk them at all times.

To sum up, it can be reiterated that responsible journalism means knowing its limits. Celebs too have their private lives and they have a right to privacy. The media has to be judicious in knowing what to report and how much to report, and should never misuse its power.

Plan followed:
Intro: Disagree
Para 1: It affects celebs performance
Para 2: It affects society
Para 3: Media should know its limits
Conclusion:

249. *Nowadays young people are admiring media and sports stars, even though they do not set a good example. Do you think this is a positive or a negative development? (UAE 5/11/22)*

It is commonly observed that the youth of today admire and follow celebrities like media and sports stars despite them not acting as good role models. I strongly believe that this is a negative development.

Media and sports stars have a lot of negative effects on the youth. Firstly, celebrities are often portrayed drinking or smoking in advertisements, TV shows and movies. Some stars post pictures of themselves partying and drinking on social media platforms. This normalizes and glamorizes behaviour like smoking, binge drinking and illicit drug use, making youth feel that it is appropriate to do the same. Experimenting with drugs and alcohol affects their health, behaviour and grades.

Secondly, some celebrities create impossible standards of beauty, as a result of which more and more young adults feel less confident and more dissatisfied with their looks. Teenagers are at a phase of their life where they undergo massive changes physically, mentally, and emotionally. As celebrities are becoming thinner and thinner, self-confidence of their fans is lost, and they suffer from body displeasure. This causes young fans to strive to be unhealthily thin and stop eating altogether, which may prove fatal at times.

Finally, sometimes celebrities ignore the public interest while endorsing latest fashions and products. Thus, in a way they promote trends which might be harmful for the youth and the society. For example, many celebrities promote sugary drinks or fast foods, even though they themselves do not consume them. Sometimes, they promote costly fashions and gadgets and teenagers force their parents to buy these products. Some teens or youth also resort to petty crimes like stealing just to acquire these products and consequently destroy their whole life.

In conclusion, I would like to reiterate that increasing influence of celebrities on youth has several adverse consequences for them as well as the society.

Plan followed:
Intro: I strongly believe that this is largely a negative development
Para 1: How celebs are setting some bad standards
Para 2: More ways in which celebs are negatively affecting their fans
Para 3: The youth are mad after celeb endorsed products.
Conclusion: Reiterate view

Written by: Indroop Singh (example essay of positive and negative development)

250. *Exposure to international media such as films, TV and magazines has a significant impact on local cultures. What do you think has been the impact? Do you think its advantages outweigh the disadvantages?*

The emergence of international media has really changed the face of the globe. It is true that exposure to international media has had a considerable impact on local cultures. In the following paragraphs I will discuss these impacts. While there are a few negatives, overall the impact has been largely positive.

On the one hand, internationalization of media can overpower national culture. People all over the world watch the dressing styles and eating habits of western countries and copy the same. All foreign brand outlets and food outlets are seen all over the world. This leads to dilution of the local cultures and loss of diversity.

On the other hand, today's communications and technologies allow a more open spread of culture around the world – people in far corners of the globe are able to be aware of and share each other's culture. A mixing of culture and has enabled people around the world to overcome national boundaries to embrace common causes. Thus, cultural globalisation in itself promotes diversity and a respect for other cultures.

Another positive effect that international media has had on India is that our media companies have improved dramatically under the stiff competition of global media and as a result they have found a place in the international market. For example, Bollywood studios release around 700 major films each year, three times the rate of the major Hollywood studios. Finally, if the local culture is strong, it can never be lost. For instance, the international media companies have to tailor their output so as to fit into the local cultural setting.

Summing up, the internationalization of media needs not necessarily undermine national culture. If the local culture is strong enough, it can withstand any foreign influence.

Plan followed:

Intro: In the following paragraphs I shall discuss these impacts. Overall, the impact has been largely positive

Para 1: Positive impact

Para 2: Opponents view with counter argument

Para 3: Another positive impact.

Conclusion:

251. *Recent advancements in technology have made the TV screen so live that people do not feel the need to go for any live performance (e.g. live shows or concerts). To what extent do you agree or disagree?*

It is believed by some that in the current age of live TV screening, there is little incentive to go out and see such events. Although the live plays and musicals have magic, and a strange mesmerising energy between the audience and the performers, I agree with the given statement.

Undoubtedly, the experience of live performance builds community. For instance, sitting in a theatre with hundreds of people who have the same interests is an unparalleled experience. Secondly, attending a live performance also provides the excitement of the actor-audience connection in real time. These will keep the theatre from fading away completely no matter how much technology takes over our lives.

However, the main factors in favour of TV are the high cost and the limited accessibility of actual live shows. Even if more people wanted to actually go and watch live shows, the seating capacity is limited. On top of that the tickets are very costly, especially if a person wants seats near the stage. Another thing, which goes in favour of TV is the lack of time in today's fast-paced world. People also have to stand in queues and drive distances to watch these shows. One 2-3 hour live show actually takes away a whole day at times.

Furthermore, people do not need to dress formally as live TV can be watched in the comfort of their sofa or bed and while doing some other household chores. The focus of the cameras is also on the main characters, because of which there is a better view of the actual show. Despite the fact that people want to experience live shows, such shows have become once or twice in a lifetime events and that too for those, who have the time and money to do so.

To conclude, I reiterate my view by saying that while actually going and attending a concert or drama is in itself a unique experience, the live TV screen of today has an edge over it all.

Plan followed:
Intro: Agree
Para 1: In favour of attending in person
Para 2: Disadvantage of actually attending
Para 3: More disadvantages
Para 5: More advantages
Conclusion: reiterate opinion.

252. *Most of our information comes from the Internet nowadays. Some people say that a large part of the information we get is incorrect. Do you agree or disagree?*

The internet has revolutionised the way people get information. It is believed by some that most of the information obtained from online sources is wrong. Although some information may be questionable, I believe that most information is correct.

Admittedly, some false, misleading or incorrect information does exist, but the person surfing the net has to learn how to look for the authentic websites. This takes a little time but ultimately people come to know about the websites imparting useful and correct information and then bookmark those sites and avoid going back to the fake sites.

There are many reasons why I believe that most of the information obtained through the Internet is correct. My first argument is that only if the information is correct, it can enjoy a lasting attraction to readers. With an expectation to have more readers, the author will be encouraged to post correct and authenticated articles which will in turn attract more and more visitors to the website. Otherwise, when the audience comes to know they are being cheated, then they will stop visiting the blog or website.

Secondly, as such a wide sea of information surrounds the people, they will definitely not believe in one report, but may search out all the related information to compare and form their own opinion. To add to it, the issue of cybercrime has also led to the websites being supervised which discourages people to post wrong and misleading information. Plagiarism is also considered an offence and so those posting any information know that they are being monitored.

To sum up, most of the information on the Internet is worth our trust. With the rise of people's awareness of its accuracy, more correct information will be there awaiting us in the future.

Plan followed:
Intro: Disagree
Para 1: some info may be wrong
Para 2: First argument in favour of internet
Para 3: Responsibility of the person accessing the internet
Conclusion: reiterate opinion

253. *Some people believe that the radio is the best way to get news, while others believe that TV is better for this purpose. Discuss both views and give your opinion.*

It is believed by some that the radio is the best of all the media for getting news, whereas others assert that the TV takes the lead in this respect. In this essay, I will discuss both views. I believe that both have their own importance as far as getting news is concerned, but TV certainly has an edge over the radio.

The main reason why some people say that radio is better than all other sources of news media is that the radio can be accessed while doing any other work. A person can put radio in his pocket and listen to the news or any other programs of his interest while jogging at a park, driving, commuting to and from work, having meals or even lying on the bed with lights off and resting. Furthermore, the news script is also different on the radio as compared to the TV. A radio newsreader has to describe the whole event through words without giving long pauses as in case of the TV. For example, if a cricket sports match is going on, a radio commentator will have to speak a lot more than what a TV commentator will have to speak.

On the other hand, those who opine that TV is a more effective way to get the news, give their reasons as follows. Firstly, it combines both sight and sound, which are the two major human senses for communication, and is therefore more influencing. For instance, if a person hears a news item about an accident, he may forget it soon, but if he has seen horrifying images of the same accident on TV news, he may not forget the impact on his mind for a long time to come. Secondly, with the advent of the latest technology, the TV has become as portable as the radio. The smart phones of today have apps such as 'Hotstar' and Zee5, which enable people to watch TV-on-the-go. Because of this reason mainly, the TV has gained an edge over the radio.

To conclude, both these media are not equivalent and interchangeable with each other, as they have unique characteristics. The television, however, is superior to the radio because of its visual impact.

Plan followed:
Intro: Opinion to be reached after comparing the two media.
Para 1: Advantages of radio
Para 2: Advantages of TV
Conclusion: TV is better

254. *All over the world, people watch foreign films much more than locally produced films. Why? Should the government provide financial support to local film industries?*

Foreign films are enjoyed more than the locally produced films. There are many reasons why this is happening, and I firmly believe that the domestic film industries should be supported by the government.

The main reason for the popularity of foreign films is that they use the most modern technology. For instance, the amazing visual effects and acoustics of the Hollywood movie Avatar won global audiences. What is more, a lot of money is put in to advertise these films. So it is not surprising that these films tend to do well overseas. In contrast, locally produced films are not publicised that much, and they often have familiar storylines that may not interest some people.

Another significant reason for watching foreign films is that people are curious to know about foreign lifestyles and culture. Watching foreign movies satiates their curiosity of knowing about them. Recently, I watched a Japanese movie, 'Okurobito' which means 'Departures' from which I learnt how the Japanese do the last rituals when a person dies. This movie fascinated me a lot and I came to know about Japanese traditions. Some people also watch Hollywood movies to learn English, which has become a global language and watching English movies is a good way to learn English.

I firmly believe that the government should invest in the local film industry. To begin with, films are the carriers of a country's culture. Supporting the local film industry will enable to spread its culture and this can make a country to be recognised in the world. Secondly, the unemployment rate in this country might substantially decrease, which will contribute to its economy. Recently, our Bollywood movies such as 'Dabang' and 'Jab Tak Hai Jaan' have done business worth crores and this has definitely boosted our economy.

Summing up, people watch foreign movies because of their better technology and to satisfy their curiosity of foreign culture. The government should definitely promote local film industry for spreading our culture and for boosting the economy.

Plan followed:
Intro:
Para 1: Reasons for the popularity of foreign films
Para 2: More reasons
Para 3: Why the government should support local film industry
Conclusion:

255. *The number of TV programs is growing day by day. Some people say that it is good as it gives people more choices, while others say it affects the quality of TV programs. Discuss both and give your opinion.*

It is believed by some that the fast growing number of television programs is good as it gives people a plethora of choices, whereas others believe that this is leading to a deterioration of the quality of TV programs. This essay intends to look into both perspectives. I am personally in favour of the latter view.

There are many reasons why some people are happy with the increasing number of TV programmes. Firstly, they have a lot of choices. For example, there are a number of daily soaps, reality shows, talk shows, sports and news programmes. People can watch whichever program they can relate to or whichever they are interested in. Secondly, some reality shows have given an opportunity to the common man with talent to come forward and show his talent to the world. For instance, in recent years, singing contest programs such as 'Sa-Re-Ga-Ma-Pa' and Indian Idol have uncovered many talented singers.

On the other hand, those who are against having too many TV programs, argue that most programs have no uniqueness and are similar to others in concept as well as content. These are a huge waste of resources and audience time. To exemplify, since the overwhelming success of Sony TV's 'Indian Idol' in 2005, a lot of such talent shows have cropped up. These programs have attracted a large number of viewers, but have also led to choice overload and boredom. At some point or the other, viewers need to decide what they have to watch and what they can ignore.

I believe that the vitality of the cultural industry comes from originality and creativity. Program producers must realize that people need a richer and varied choice. Having a lot of TV programs is good only if there is originality and people get value for the time they spend on these programs. So, less programs which are of very good quality should be there. However, these programs should be repeated frequently so that people can watch them according to their leisure.

To sum up, even though there are choices because of an abundance of TV programs, an excess of TV programs is definitely not good. We need fewer, quality programs, which make our leisure time worthwhile.

Plan followed:

Intro:

Para 1: Advantage of many programs

Para2: More advantage

Para 3: Disadvantage

Para 4: Another disadvantage

256. *In some countries, TV programmes are transmitted throughout the day and night. Some people think that 24-hour transmission has positive impacts, while others believe it is negative. Discuss both views and give your opinion.*

A variety of TV shows such as soaps, sitcoms, documentaries, adverts and news reports are transmitted round the clock. Some people claim that this is beneficial while others oppose it because of the negative influence. I will discuss both perspectives in the upcoming paragraphs. I personally side with the former view.

The main reason why some people are in favour of round-the-clock TV programmes is that it is keeping people abreast of what is happening around them. Moreover, with these repeat telecasts they can catch up with what they missed, at their own convenient time. Secondly, TV viewing is a passive activity which acts as a stress buster for people. For instance, when they return home after a hectic days work, watching their favourite TV soap or some sitcom relaxes them. Another big advantage is that TV acts as a platform for the publicity of new products, which is a win-win situation for both – the manufacturing companies and the audience as they have more choices of goods.

On the other hand, the telecast of TV programs throughout the day and night does not appeal to many people because of many reasons. To begin with, because of too many choices of TV programs all the time, people are not doing other physical activities, and so they are living unhealthy lives. Besides, to attract people there are many shows, which have violence and pornographic content, which is not appropriate for the mental health of people especially the young. Finally, the 24-hour transmission of foreign channels are luring the younger generation towards the global culture which is making them forget their own roots.

I believe that the telecast of TV programs is very helpful for people in the global village of today. The society is 24/7 and work hours have round-the-clock shifts, so entertainment should also be 24/7. The onus is on the people to have a check on their TV viewing and spare time for other activities. Parents can block channels, which they do not want their children to see. So, if all these things are looked into, the positives are much more.

In conclusion, non-stop TV transmission has both, pros and cons. However, the merits definitely outweigh the demerits as we belong to a 24/7 society and we need to know what is happening around us all the time.

Plan followed:
Intro: Discuss essay intro
Para 1: One view
Para 2: Other view
Para 3: Own view
Conclusion: Give opinion

257. More and more people are using the Internet to do their tasks rather than doing in person. (e.g. banking, shopping, hotel booking etc.). Do the advantages of this trend outweigh the disadvantages?

It is a fact that because of the internet daily tasks and business transactions can be performed without meeting other people, in person. While there are a few disadvantages of the online mode of doing things, the advantages are certainly more.

Admittedly, there are a few drawbacks of online transactions. Firstly, there is loss of direct human contact which results in people leading isolated lives. Moreover, the privacy of the individual can suffer as cyber-criminals can hack people's information and even steal people's money. Finally, internet and server problems may disable online payments.

However, e-transactions have a number of advantages. To begin with, it saves money as the cost of labour is cut down because these transactions are usually automatic. An e-commerce transaction also reduces the cost of middlemen and advertisement. Another big advantage of e-business is that there are no geographical boundaries. Anyone can order anything from anywhere and at any time.

Moreover, online businesses get benefits from the government as the government is trying to promote digitalisation. Also, e-business breaks down the time barriers that location based businesses encounter. A person can reach his customers and sell his product or service anytime since the internet is always available. Finally, people have more time to take part in social activities, pursue hobbies and interests and communicate with families, which are all indispensable parts of quality life.

To sum up, performing everyday tasks and business transactions by means of telecommunications benefits the individual and the society enormously. There is simply no going back.

Plan followed:
Intro: Advantages are more
Para 1: Disadvantages
Para 2: Advantages
Para 3: Advantages
Conclusion:

258. *More and more people are using computers and other electronic devices to access information. So, printing of books, magazines and newspapers should not be done. Do you agree or disagree with this?*

It is irrefutable that technology has become a part of many aspects of life, including the information available through e-books, e-magazines and online newspapers. However, I disagree with the view that there is no need to print books, magazines and newspapers because of these e-reading materials.

The first reason for continuing to print magazines and books is that there are still many people all over the world, who either do not have access to such technology, or who are not comfortable with the use of computers and other such electronic devices. This populace depends on printed information, rather than on the electronic form of that information. For example, newspapers are the most popular and affordable source of information among poor countries which still do not have reliable internet connection.

Another big advantage of printed sources is that it can be 'one' source of information. Instead of having to search out multiple web sites to find information, readers of a newspaper can instead have all of the day's information at one place. In addition, all the information available on the Internet may not be reliable, as there are a lot of fake news and articles posted online. Everyone who has access to this resource can post anything online and sometimes the information posted is not thoroughly fact checked. By contrast, printable sources are always authenticated, and published after careful consideration of facts.

Moreover, reading on screens has numerous health implications and can adversely affect people's brain and bodies. Most people already use computers in their jobs and reading online adds to screen time. This increased screen time often leads to headaches, blurred vision, eye strain, and long-term vision problems. Finally, the charm of holding a newspaper and the aroma of the printed books can never be replaced by reading something on the screen of a computer or a smartphone.

To summarize, it can be reiterated that the electronic information can never completely eradicate the need and the use of printed material, like books and periodicals. They will still remain an integral part of our education system, and for the news.

Plan followed:
Intro: Disagree
Para 1: Importance of traditional reading materials
Para 2: More importance
Para 3: Opponents' views with refutation
Conclusion Written by: Indroop Singh

259. *We can see more disasters and violence shown on TV. What are its causes and what effects will they exert on the individual and the society?*

It is irrefutable that television news is filled with violence and suffering. Crime and violent world events are among the most frequently covered topics on TV. In the following paragraphs I shall discuss the reasons and effects of this phenomenon.

The most important reason for this is obviously that television channels want to increase their TRP (television rating point). If any channel has high TRP, it gets more adverts and hence more revenue. Therefore the channels have to show such sensational news. Secondly, the news channels have to show what is happening around and disasters and violence have become very common in our surroundings. Finally, people demand that they should be well informed about all things, which are prevalent in society. So, media has to show all that to its viewers.

There are many harmful effects on the individuals and society. The most disturbing effect is on the children and youth. Media violence can stimulate fear in some children as it frightens them, making the effects long lasting. This can become traumatic in our children as they see it more and more. Children are starting to grow and are shaping their personality, values and beliefs. They can become aggressive or they can lose a sense of reality and fiction of what they are seeing.

Furthermore, young people imitate what they see and it is logical that they see glamour in what they do when they commit violence. Consequently, the society suffers as the streets are full of violence. Too much portrayal of these also leads to immunity among the people and they are not affected by the disasters any more. Disasters like Tsunami and earthquakes do not make people shed a tear any more.

Summing up, there are many reasons why media shows too much violence on TV and some steps should be taken to reduce this as it has a lot of detrimental effects on the individuals and society.

Plan followed:
Intro: I shall discuss the reasons of this phenomenon and suggest some ways forward.
Para 1: Reasons for this phenomenon
Para 2: harmful effects on the individuals and society
Para 3: More harmful effects
Conclusion:

260. *The government should control the amount of violence in films and on television in order to decrease the violent crimes in society. To what extent do you agree or disagree?*

It is irrefutable that the films and TV programmes today are filled with violence and as a result violence is increasing in our societies. I agree that by censoring such programmes and films some amount of violence can be decreased.

There are many reasons why the government should take steps towards reducing violence in the media. Firstly, media violence can stimulate fear in some children and affect their mental development and growth. Children are not able to differentiate between the virtual world and the real world. As a result, when children are often exposed to scenes of violence, they may view the world as a more dangerous place than it actually is.

Secondly, studies suggest a direct correlation between real and reel world violence. For example, many school shootings in the US have been associated with watching excessive violent content on the TV or playing violent video games. It is impossible to predict how portrayal of violence affects different people and thus it would be far easier to censor violence. In addition, many movies and TV soaps glamorize crime and the lives of criminals and this may lead to children and adolescents copying such behaviour blindly.

Finally, watching violence on the media leads to emotional distress, affecting people's mental health and making them more antisocial. As people watch more of such content on the media, they become less compassionate towards others and do not feel guilty when they hurt or cheat others. In other words, people are able to justify their wrong actions in their heads because they have seen much worse in the media.

Summing up, there are many adverse consequences of excessive portrayal of violence in movies and TV shows and so controlling it is certainly a step in the right direction.

Plan followed:
Intro: I agree
Para 1: First reason
Para 2: Second reason
Para 3: Final reason
Conclusion:
Similar essay: Media and newspaper show vulgar crimes on news, which cause fear and provoke culprits. Some people think that crime news on TV should not be broadcast. To what extent do you agree or disagree.

261. The detailed description about crime in newspapers and on television can affect the people and cause many social problems. Some people say that this should be restricted. Do you agree or disagree? (1/7/2021 India 1pm)

Many people complain about the excessive and detailed information about crimes on the Internet, newspapers and TV. This causes many problems in society and therefore I agree that there should be strict censorship of crime news.

There are several reasons why the news media should be restricted from sharing excessive details about crimes. Firstly, the details of crimes and especially how criminals evaded arrest or outsmarted the police glamorize crime and this may lead to children and adolescents copying such behaviour blindly. Moreover, the excessive violence and pornographic contents can also raise the adults' criminal tendencies.

Secondly, excessive criminal news can also instil fear in the society and as a result people become untrusting of others. Especially watching news with so much detail can have a long lasting impact on children's sensitive minds. In addition, the detailed report of a crime does not show enough respect to the victims and their family. For example, if any murder or robbery has taken place in someone's house, and then if it is shown in detail on TV, the whole privacy of those people is lost. In extreme cases, it may also put the life of the victims' and the witnesses' families in danger.

My last argument in favour of censorship of media is that sometimes this detailed description can also help the criminals. For instance, when terrorists attacked Hotel Taj in Mumbai, the media reported details of the commandos' position on TV. The terrorists hiding in the hotel also viewed this and changed their positions accordingly. Had there been some regulating authority the terrorists could have been caught much earlier.

Summing up, although it is the duty of the media to keep us informed, the details of crime should not be shown and for that censorship of criminal news is a must.

Plan followed:
Intro: Agree
Para 1: Drawbacks of detailed description
some people are likely to copy the criminal actions blindly
Para 2: More drawbacks
Not good for the victims' families
Detailed description may help the criminals
Conclusion: Reiterate opinion
Written By: Indroop Singh

262. *Many people regard films as less important forms of art than literature and painting. Do you agree or disagree?*

Some individuals regard art forms like writing and painting, as more significant than the movies. I believe that films are actually as important as or in some ways more important than other forms of art like literature and painting.

There are many reasons why I believe that films as a form of art are equally if not more important than books and paintings. Firstly, films are an amalgamation of various different art forms. These include both performing arts of dancing, acting, music etcetera and literature like script writing, poetry in the form of songs. So, in effect movies encapsulate multiple art forms and their importance should be more than paintings and literature, which represent just one art form. Secondly, movies have the unique ability to entertain and enlighten people at the same time. The increasing stress in people's lives means that people need art to unwind and relax, and movies can fulfil this function better than perhaps any other art form.

In addition, watching a movie leaves a much more lasting impression on people's minds than visiting a museum and looking at artifacts, pictures, paintings etcetera. Since films are an audio-visual form of art, they are perhaps a lot easier for people to understand and comprehend. For this reason, movies are also a popular method of spreading awareness and bringing about social change. Finally, movies and films reach a much wider audience than literature or painting does and this popularity itself makes them more valuable. For example, people might not be able to visit museums in other countries to see a painting, but they can easily watch foreign movies online.

To sum up, I would like to reiterate that considering movies and films as inferior to literature and paintings would be a mistake.

Plan followed:
Intro: Disagree
Para 1: First argument
Para 2: More arguments
Conclusion:

263. *In many countries, government spends a large amount of money on improving Internet access. Why is it happening? Do you think it is the most appropriate use of government money?*

Many governments realize that Internet access is an essential tool for sustainable economic growth and are investing a lot to make the Internet accessible for their citizens. There are many reasons why they are doing so, which will be discussed in this essay. While it is important to spend on internet access, I do not believe it is the most appropriate use of government's resources.

The main reason why some governments are spending on Internet access is that they realise that it is not expenditure but an investment, which eventually will come back to them in the form of corporate taxes. With increased and efficient Internet access, companies will be able to expand their businesses locally and internationally. Businesses can communicate better with their clients, study international markets, sell products online, and thus increase their profits.

Furthermore, governments know that Internet access promotes education which has a great impact on poverty eradication and overall development. The education people receive results in more healthy, independent and confident citizens that can contribute to the local and global economy in a more efficient way. Finally, better internet access provides opportunities to people living in remote areas or villages, creates jobs and allows people to do freelance work.

However, I believe that internet access should not be the government's primary focus. Firstly, in many countries a large majority of people are often unable to fully benefit from the information and communication provided by internet access. This is partly due to a language barrier in online communications and because many people are not comfortable using modern technologies. Secondly, many private companies are already investing in improving internet access, so governments should prioritize basic needs like healthcare, sanitation and access to drinking water etcetera, where the private companies are unwilling to spend due to lack of returns.

To conclude, there are many reasons why some governments are spending on providing Internet access to its people but it is not the most apt use of their resources.

Plan followed:
Intro: cause effect intro
Para 1: First reason
Para 2: Second reason
Para 3: Why it is a good thing
Conclusion:

264. *A tendency that the news reported in the media focuses on problems and emergencies rather than the positive developments is harmful to both the individual and the society. Do you agree or disagree with this statement?*

Some individuals opine that media's emphasis on sensational news is harmful for the people and the society. I believe that as long as the negative news reports are unbiased, the general public will not be harmed and there will be no detrimental effects on individuals and society. I also believe that equal focus should be there on the positive developments.

My first argument is that it is the duty of the media to keep the people abreast of what is happening all around. If negative things are happening, people should know all that because then they can be prepared if anything is likely to affect them. Secondly, if the media reports such news, then more and more people can volunteer to help. For example, two years ago when Tsunami hit Japan, the news was spread like wildfire through all sources of media and people from all over the world sent relief in whatever way they could.

Undoubtedly, it is the onus of the media to report positive developments also. The media is a link between the government and the people. Very few people get to meet any politician in real life. But we can reach our voice to the authorities through the media. Then, the media also helps to get justice at times. In the Nirbhaya rape case in December, 2012, it was through the efforts of the media that the culprits got a speedy punishment and Nirbhaya's family got justice. How can all these reportings be considered bad for the individuals and the society?

To sum up, it is imperative that media reports both positive and negative news without any bias and exaggeration. It is people's responsibility to take all the news with a pinch of salt and analyze it with their critical thinking skills. Therefore, reporting more news on problems and emergencies is definitely not bad for the societies and individuals.

Plan followed:
Intro: Disagree
Para 1: importance of reporting all news
Para 2: Media's responsibility
Conclusion:

265. *Some people think news has no connection to people's lives, so then it is a waste of time to read the news in the newspaper and watch television news programs. To what extent do you agree or disagree?*

It is believed by some that news has nothing to do with people's day to day lives and thus, it is pointless to spend time reading news or watching news channels. I believe that rather than a waste of time, there is actually a lot to gain by watching news on the TV and reading newspapers.

There are many reasons why people should keep themselves up to date with the news events. Firstly, news is the main source of information about the government policies, which directly impact people's lives. In other words, people can be better prepared to deal with change in laws, if they read news. For example, when traffic fines were increased, many people were caught unaware and had to pay huge fines. Moreover, as reading news makes people more knowledgeable, they are able to have more informed discussions with others.

Secondly, news is a source of inspiration. When people hear or read about others' misfortunes and how they overcame them, they learn to be resilient. Success stories motivate them to work hard and challenge their limits. Similarly by reading about adversity, they learn to appreciate what they have in life and it encourages them to help and support the less fortunate.

Thirdly, in this era of many truths, newspapers are the only thing that can help us differentiate the actual truth from the many rumours. By watching credible and objective news, people can learn how to distinguish fact from fiction, which in turn develops people's critical thinking abilities as well. Finally, newspapers not only enhance people's reading skills but also their writing, grammar, vocabulary and speaking skills.

To summarize, listening to the news or reading the paper daily is very important to be a part of the global village of today.

Plan followed:
Intro: Disagree
Paragraph 1: First reason
Paragraph 2: Second reason
Paragraph 3: Third and fourth reason
Conclusion: Reiterate opinion

Written by: Indroop Singh (Exam question 10/10/2020 9am slot)

266. Some people think that violent films and videogames have negative effects on people and should be banned. Others think that they are just relaxation sources. Discuss both sides and give opinion.

Some individuals argue that films and video games full of violence should be banned as they have detrimental effects on people, whereas others opine that they are just another form of entertainment. This essay intends to analyze both perspectives. I am against the idea of banning such movies and games as the correlation between violence and them is highly exaggerated.

On the one hand, the main reason why some people would like the government to ban violent games and movies is that they are likely to result in violence and aggressiveness in children and a decrease in compassion towards others. They cite the school shootings in the US as the proof of the link between this virtual violence and real world aggression. Moreover, these games and movies increase the threshold towards violent incidents in the society and people are less likely to be impacted by them.

On the other hand, those who view violent movies and video games as just relaxation sources, say that they can reduce stress by distracting adults from the pressures of everyday life. For example, college students attempting to juggle school, part-time work, finances and household chores, might find the role-playing and interaction in games a safe and enjoyable way to release pent-up frustrations. Violent video games are also recommended as therapeutic outlets to combat depression and anger.

I am against the idea of banning violent games and movies as humans have been engaging in violence since time immemorial, but movies and video games are recent inventions. So the link between them and violence is overstated and unsurprisingly there is no scientific evidence supporting that they actually lead to violent behaviour. Moreover, I do agree that they are a very good means to release the ever growing stress and frustration in life.

To sum up, I would like to reiterate that barning violent movies and games would not be appropriate as I do not agree that they have a correlation with real world violence.

Plan followed:
Intro:
Para 1: One view
Para 2: Other view
Para 3: Own view
Conclusion: should not be banned

267. Children are facing more pressures nowadays from academic, social and commercial perspectives. What are the causes of these pressures and what measures should be taken to reduce these pressures?

It is commonly said that today's children are pressurized and are facing harder and harder academic, social and commercial challenges. This essay intends to discuss the causes of these pressures and suggest some measures to alleviate the problem.

There are many academic pressures on children. Today's child is not competing with the child next door, or even of one's town or country. He is competing with the child of the global village. Parents want their children to excel in every field. They send their children to the best schools, where the school bag is often heavier than the child himself. Even after school hours there are private tuitions. Children do not have time to bloom and bring out their hidden talents.

There are also many social and commercial pressures. Socially, the children of today want to adopt the global culture, whereas their parents force them to confine themselves to the traditions. Then, they also face peer pressure, which can be either good or bad. This peer pressure coupled with the consumerist society of today can lead to a lot of stress and strain on children. They see the latest models of cell phones and other items with their peers and want to buy them. When they are unable to do so, they get stressed.

The solutions are not simple. Children have to be handled with great care. Parents should have a pro-active approach and give time to their children. The biggest onus is on the schools and teachers. They should strive to bring out the best in every child and competition and co-operation should both be taught simultaneously. The aim of competition should not be to win at all cost. Children have to be taught to win with modesty and lose with grace.

To summarise, there is no doubt that the children of today are facing so many pressures, but steps should be taken on a war footing to protect their innocent childhood. Otherwise, these pressures will stifle the physical and psychological growth of children.

Plan followed:
Intro:
Para 1: Academic pressures
Para 2: Social and commercial pressures
Para 3: solutions
Conclusion
***Similar essay**: Today's children are living under more pressure from the society than children in the past. To what extent do you agree or disagree with this opinion?*

268. *In many parts of the world, children are given more freedom than in the past. Is this a positive or a negative development?*

It is certainly true that in many countries children today have more freedom than the past. While there are certain drawbacks of this trend, I believe that on the whole this increased independence is beneficial for children.

There are many advantages of children enjoying more freedom. Firstly, the increased independence improves decision making. In other words, when children think independently, they are able to better consider the consequences of their actions and in the long run, this leads to better thought-out decisions. Such children are better prepared to face the rigours of adulthood. Secondly, more freedom also translates to better academic performance as it means that children explore more options, follow what they are passionate about and retain their interest in education.

The final benefit is that it improves the relationship between parents and children. In effect, because of increased freedom, children think that their parents trust them. This makes children more confident and reduces their rebellious tendencies. This improved relationship with parents also means that children are more comfortable sharing their problems with parents. Thus, parents are better able to help children with problems like bullying and academic pressures.

However, there can also be some drawbacks of excessive freedom. The main problem is that children are not mature enough to fully grasp the consequences of their actions. They can misuse this excessive freedom to make terrible choices that might ruin their future. For example, they might try out drugs or smoking under peer pressure. In addition, sometimes this unlimited freedom creates the feeling in children that they are not loved or their parents do not have interest in their lives.

To sum up, while there can be certain detriments of giving more freedom to children, I believe that overall, it is a positive development.

Plan followed:
Intro: Advantages are more than disadvantages
Para 1: Advantages
Para 2: More advantages
Para 3: Disadvantages
Conclusion: reiterate opinion

269. *Some people think that nowadays children have too much freedom. Do you agree or disagree?*

It is believed by some that these days children enjoy much more independence than children of the past. I strongly agree with this viewpoint. A number of arguments surround my opinion.

The main reason why children today are enjoying more freedom is that their parents realise that children today are capable of deciding things on their own. Today's children have the power of the Internet and the satellite TV in their hands. Today's young generation is the most well informed generation than ever in the history of mankind. Because of the IT boom, today's children grow up quicker than their parents did. They know what their parents and grandparents do not know. So, parents give their children the freedom to make decisions on their own. In the past, children were not exposed to so much information, and so meekly did what their parents told them to do.

Another important reason behind the freedom given to today's children is that parents do not have time to monitor their children's activities. In the fast paced world of today, both parents are working longer hours to meet the demands of the consumerist society of today. They are not working just to fulfil their basic necessities, but also to live a lifestyle of luxury and comfort. As a consequence, children are left unattended to enjoy their freedom. Earlier, only one parent worked and mothers were there to supervise their children. Workaholic culture was also not there and people worked limited hours.

Furthermore, the change in family structure from joint to nuclear families is responsible for the freedom showered on today's children. Earlier, grandparents were there to keep a watchful eye on their grandchildren, but today's children do not have such supervision on them, as a result of which they get a lot of freedom.

To sum up, it can be reiterated that the freedom enjoyed by today's children is, by and large, inevitable. The onus is on the parents to see to it that this excess freedom does not go against their children.

Plan followed:
Intro: Agree
Para 1: First reason
Para 2: Second reason
Para 3: Third reason
Conclusion: reiterate opinion

270. *Children are taught to push themselves to try and be better than their classmates, rather than work together for everyone's profit. Do you think the advantages outweigh its disadvantages?*

These days, competitiveness is encouraged more than cooperation. While it is important to teach competitiveness to children, I believe cooperation is as important a virtue to be instilled in children. Therefore, the disadvantages of teaching children how to compete at the expense of cooperation are more.

On the one hand, there are many reasons why competition is important for children's growth. When children are pushed to compete, their unlimited potential can be tapped. This also helps them to develop confidence. Pressure and competition is all around us nowadays. In achieving academic excellence as well as doing well in one's career, every person has to compete. There are many examples of people around us who have become successful in their lives by competing in sports events or music contests.

On the other hand, it is very important to cultivate cooperation abilities in children. Children who do not learn to cooperate are usually isolated, introverted and consequently they are socially inadequate. Cooperation is a contributing factor to the success of a community. Only with cooperation can children learn to live in harmony with each other.

I personally believe that children should be taught both, how to compete, as well as how to cooperate. It is more important to teach children the situations where they need to compete and where they need to cooperate. Both these virtues are needed in adult life. For instance, in solo sports and for sitting in an exam, children need to compete, whereas in team sports and in group-assignments children have to cooperate. Similarly, in adult life, no business house can rise to the pinnacles of success with the efforts of a single man. To compete with other businesses, members of one business house have to cooperate with each other. No single scientist can find the cure for cancers or AIDS. Scientists all over the world have to join hands to fight these deadly diseases.

To conclude, it can be reiterated that forcing children only to compete rather than cooperate has more disadvantages than advantages, as both competition and cooperation are equally important in our lives.

Plan followed:
Intro: Disadvantages are more
Para 1: Importance of competition
Para 2: Importance of cooperation
Para 3: Own view
Conclusion: Reiterate opinion

271. *Competitiveness is a positive quality for people in most societies. How does competitiveness affect individuals? Is it a positive or negative trend?*

It is a fact that many societies are progressing because of competitiveness. In the following paragraphs, I will discuss the effect of competitiveness on individuals. I believe that competitiveness is good, but over-competitiveness in which one uses unethical means to reach the top is bad.

At the individual level, competitiveness provides incentives for people to improve themselves. People set goals for themselves and try to achieve them by hard work and perseverance. These goals are based on others achievements. They try to break records and put their heart and soul to excel in all fields. This is what keeps them going. Then they become inspiration for others who also work hard for getting name and fame. If there were no competition, people would become lazy and there would be stagnation in their lives. This would result in dull individuals and lacklustre societies.

It is this competitiveness, which is the basis for the Olympics and other such international and national events. Individual competition translates to national and international level during such events. For example, when Abhinav Bindra won the first individual Olympic gold medal in shooting, he not only made a name for himself but also for the whole of India. Therefore, competitiveness leads to the progress of the individuals and societies as a whole.

On the other hand, it is important to realize that trying to be number one and trying to do a task well are two different things. One should not hold the delusion that one's advancement is accomplished by crushing others. Over-competitiveness, in which a person uses unethical means to win such as taking drugs before any sporting event to increase performance or hurting others to win, is bad.

Summing up, competitiveness is good and leads to the progress of individuals and societies but only as long as it remains a healthy competition. If unethical means are used or it leads to stress and others are hurt in the process, then it is bad.

Plan followed:

Intro: I shall discuss the effect of competitiveness on individuals. I believe that competitiveness is good, but over-competitiveness in which one uses unethical means to reach the top is bad
Para 1: At the individual level, competitiveness provides incentives for people to improve themselves
Para 2: Individual competition translates to national and international level during events such as Olympics etc.
Para 3: disadvantages
Conclusion:

272. *Team activities can teach more skills for life than those activities, which are played alone. To what extent do you agree or disagree?*

It is believed by some that group activities better prepare people for life than working alone. While I do believe that individual activities are important, team activities certainly hold more relevance.

On the one hand, there are many life skills people learn by activities on their own. The main advantage is that people learn how to be independent. They learn how to accomplish tasks on their own and make decisions without relying on others. This in turn makes them confident that they handle different situations on their own. Another benefit is that they learn that they are responsible for the outcome of their actions and so they are better able to assess themselves and make corrections.

However, skills learnt while working in a group certainly outweigh the benefits of working alone. Firstly, today social skills like communication, cooperation and listening to others are the need of the hour as non-social skill jobs are gradually getting replaced by automation. Computers cannot mimic human interactions and thus the need for such skills is definitely more today. In addition, due to globalisation, it is increasingly common for people to work with individuals from different backgrounds and cultures and thus working alone would not prepare people for this situation.

Secondly, working together also enables people to learn how to deal with conflicts. Disagreements are a part of both personal and professional life and people need to know to resolve them calmly and harmoniously. Finally, team work provides more learning opportunities as people get to work with others. For example, while working in a team, people get to know different perspectives and fresh ideas of doing things and they learn from their peers' mistakes and are able to avoid making them themselves in the future.

To conclude, I would reiterate that team activities and individual activities, both teach important skills of life, but the skills learnt by working with others have a lot more importance.

Plan followed:
Intro: Agree
Para 1: Some skills we learn thorough solo work
Para 2: Some skills learnt while doing team activities
Para 3: Some more skills learnt through team work
Conclusion: Team activities are definitely better teachers of life skills than solo activities

Written by: Indroop Singh

273. *In some countries, the parents expect children to spend a long time studying both in and after school and have less free time. Do you think it has positive or negative effects on children and the society?*

In today's competitive era parents have a lot of academic expectations from their children because of which children get no time for extracurricular activities. I believe long hours spent studying has adverse effects on children as well as the society.

Forced involvement in academics can have a lot of detrimental effects on children. Firstly, they have less time for sports and other extracurricular activities, which are very essential for them. This lack of physical activity affects their health and increases the risk of childhood obesity. Also, their mental health gets affected as they do not get enough time to recharge and relax. With a lot of memorizing and exercising of the academic knowledge, the children may feel depressed, which may even result in them losing interest in studies.

In addition, extracurricular activities teach students important personal and social skills such as self-esteem, goal setting, and leadership. They also learn about competition, cooperation and sportsman spirit. Extracurricular activities in the arts teach students analytical skills and creative problem-solving skills since they have to think creatively to successfully perform music, act in a play, or produce a work of art. So, focusing only on academics may deprive the children from developing such skills.

Finally, expecting children to spend most of their time studying is harmful for the future of the society too. Firstly, society cannot run healthily without people contributing to every walk of life. Not all jobs in society need just academic qualifications. Also, imagination, creativity and passion, the very factors that a society needs to progress, will be lacking if youngsters are good at academics only.

Summing up, spending a long time, studying is detrimental for the children as well as the society and the benefits of extracurricular activities cannot be underestimated.

Plan followed:
Intro:
Para 1: Disadvantages of studying all the time on children
Para 2: Advantages of extracurricular activities
Para 3: Disadvantages of studying all the time on societies
Conclusion:

274. Some people think that children should obey rules or do what their parents and teachers want them to do, but others think that children controlled too much cannot deal with problems well by themselves. Discuss both views and give your own opinion.

Some people hold the opinion that children should be controlled by their parents and teachers, whereas others are against this control. In this essay I will discuss both views. I personally believe that parents and teachers should know when and how much restriction to impose on children.

The main reason why some people say that children should be controlled is that rules of behaviour create responsible and respectful children who in turn mature into respectful adults. They know the value of respect for elders. They know the importance of relationships. They know about their cultural values as well. This forms a stable society, which is virtually free from vices such as prostitution and drug abuse. They face difficulties in a more mature and disciplined way. They are not lured by peer pressure and refrain from acting on impulse.

On the other hand, those who say that too strict rules should not be imposed give their reasons as follows. Firstly, they say that by doing so, children may become rebels. They may start doing just the opposite of what is told them to do. What is more, they may fall into bad company or resort to drugs because of frustration. Finally, imposing too strict rules destroys the individuality of children. They may withdraw into a shell. This may suppress their creativity and as a consequence, they may not be able to deal with problems well by themselves.

I believe that parents and teachers should learn where rules are needed and where it is necessary to give freedom to the children. Having absolutely no rules and letting children do whatever they wish to do would also be wrong. They are not mature enough to solve all problems and they have to be taught their limits. But, imposing too strict rules would stifle their personality and would be more detrimental for them.

To conclude, parents and teachers should impose rules on children, but they should know where to draw the line. They should be flexible and modify the rules according to the circumstances.

Plan followed:
Intro: Discuss essay intro
Para 1: One view
Para 2: Other view
Para 3: Own view
Conclusion:

275. *Some people say that parents should organise free time activities for their children. Others say children should be free to choose what they do in their free time. Discuss both sides and opine.*

It is believed by some that children's leisure activities should be decided and organized by the parents, whereas others opine that children should have the freedom to decide how they want to utilize that free time. This essay intends to delve into both perspectives. While I believe that parents should guide children, ultimately these activities should be decided by children.

The main reason why some people opine that planning free time activities should be in the hands of parents is that children are not mature enough to understand the value of time and may end up wasting their free time through unproductive extra-curricular activities. Parents can organize activities that will help their children's holistic development. For example, they can have them play outdoor games, learn music or dance, develop their creative skills like drawing and painting and so on.

On the other hand, those who say that children should have the liberty of deciding how they want to spend their leisure time, give their reasons as follows. Firstly, if children are always told what to do and follow a set of rules, it hinders their cognitive, emotional and creative development. Research has proven that the children, who perform unstructured free-time activities, are more creative, and become more successful when they grow up. Moreover, children, who are in-charge of choosing how they spend their free time, are more likely to have better concentration levels in their studies and later, in their professional lives.

I believe that children should have the independence to choose the activities for their free time, but parents should keep an eye on them. It may bring to light some hidden talent of the child, which may otherwise go unnoticed. For example, a child may be good at dance, and maybe parents notice him practicing steps after seeing some programme on TV. So, even if the free time planning is left on the children, the role played by the parents cannot be undermined.

To sum up, I would like to reiterate that children and youngsters should be given the independence to decide their free-time activities for the complete development of their mind, body and skills, but at the same time their parents' watchful eye should be there over them.

Plan followed:
Intro: Discuss essay intro
Para 1: One view
Para 2: Other view
Para 3: Own view
Conclusion:

276. Parents should encourage their children to spend less time studying, and more time doing sports/physical activities. Do you agree or disagree?(12/2/22 1pm)

Some people believe that sports are more important for children than academic education, and so more time should be devoted to sports. While I believe that parents should encourage their children to undertake more physical activities, I also believe that this should not come at the cost of their academics.

There are many advantages of physical activities and sports for children. To begin with, participating in sports and other physical activities has numerous health benefits. This includes reduced risk of childhood obesity, healthy bones, muscles and joints and increased cardiovascular fitness. They also help children relax, relieve stress and sleep better. Participation in sports recharges the batteries of children, and this in turn leads to improved academic achievement.

Another important benefit of physical activity, and sports in particular, is that children learn important virtues of life through them. It improves their personal skills like self-esteem, goal-setting, and leadership. They also learn about competition, cooperation and sportsman spirit. These personal and social skills are important later on in life and recruiting agencies look for such skills in job interviews.

However, academic education is also very important, so students must be pushed to achieve their best academically as well. They need to spend time on studies, so that they get into university and are placed in good jobs later in life. Devoting all time to sports and less to academics would also be detrimental for children. So, to allocate more time to sports, parents should cut down on time spent on mobile phones and video games rather than compromising with children's studies.

To conclude, I reiterate my opinion that academic studies and sports are equally important for children today. Parents need to cut down screen time to accommodate more physical activities into their children's schedules.

Plan followed:
Intro: Disagree
Para 1: Importance of sports
Para 2: More importance of sports
Para 3: Importance of academic education
Conclusion:

277. Today, many children spend a lot of time playing computer games and less time on sports. Why? Is it a positive or a negative development?

Today's children are different from the children of previous generations. They are more interested in playing video games and sitting hours on the play-stations than in playing outdoor games. This essay intends to analyze the reasons of this phenomenon. In my opinion, this is detrimental for the children.

The main reason why children spend more time on electronic games is that these electronic games are very addicting. It is very hard for children to stop playing. In comparison, while playing sports children naturally get tired after some time and stop. Parents also, prefer their children to play video games because they do not have to supervise them constantly. For sports, parents have to drive their children to parks and keep an eye on them.

There are several drawbacks of this addiction towards video games. The first disadvantage is that these games are isolating, as these are usually played alone. In contrast, outdoor games teach children to socialize and make friends. This manifests in isolation and anxiety, which sometimes leads to severe mental problems like depression. Secondly, this has effect on their physical health. This sedentary lifestyle is leading to many problems like obesity, diabetes and so on among children. A majority of children have to start wearing spectacles at an early age for the same reason.

Finally, playing video games continuously especially with violence is believed to lead to an increase in aggressive behaviour. Children find it hard to differentiate between the real world and the virtual world of games and children sometimes end up immersing themselves so much into this make-belief world that they ignore their parents and siblings. No doubt, this also has a negative impact on their education.

To sum up, there are many reasons why children of today prefer spending time on video games instead of sports and other outdoor activities, and it is indubitably a negative development.

Plan followed:
Intro:
Para 1: Reasons
Para 2: Disadvantages
Para 3: More disadvantages
Conclusion:

Written by: Indroop Singh (Exam question 17/9/2020)

278. *Studies suggest that children spend more time watching TV than they did in the past and spend less on doing active or creative things. Why do you think it is the case? What measures and methods can be used to tackle it?*

After coming home from school, children spend a lot of time in watching TV instead of playing outdoor games and pursuing other artistic hobbies like in the olden days. In the following paragraphs, I shall discuss the causes of this phenomenon and also suggest some ways to encourage children to do more productive things instead of watching too much TV.

The first and foremost cause of this is that due to the satellite TV, this medium is available all the time. So much so, that some channels are exclusively dedicated to children. This has made it very easy for the parents who use TVs as babysitters. Secondly, parents are busy to cope with the demands of the fast paced life of today and after coming home after a hectic days work do not have the energy to spend time with their children. In earlier times, there were very few programmes for children and because of slower life, even parents spent time with children.

Furthermore, earlier there were joint families and grandparents were there to look after children and encourage them to play in parks. Nowadays, there are nuclear families and children are left alone, which makes them spend time by watching TV. Finally, the cities have become concrete jungles and there is no place for children to play outdoor games. On top of that, the climate changes brought about by global warming make it difficult to pursue outdoor games.

The solutions are simple but the onus is largely on the parents. They should give quality time to their children and ration their TV viewing hours. Even the time to play video games should be set properly. Outdoor activities should be encouraged and neighbourhood societies should be formed where children can play outdoor games with each other. Parks should be maintained properly so that children have a safe place to play outdoors.

To summarise, television and video games, in moderation, can be a good thing. However, excess of everything is bad and therefore I believe parents should set viewing limits to ensure their children do not spend too much time watching TV and pursue other creative activities like they did in the earlier times.

Plan followed:
Intro: I shall discuss the causes of this phenomenon and also suggest some ways forward.
Para 1: First cause – satellite TV available all the time – parents busy – use TV as babysitter
Para 2: More causes – nuclear families – changing climate
Para 3: Solutions
Conclusion:

279. *Some people think watching TV is bad for children in every way. Others think TV has positive effects on children, as they develop to grow up. Discuss both views and give your own opinion.*

It is believed by some that watching TV develops children positively, whereas others think the opposite. This essay intends to discuss both viewpoints. In my personal opinion television viewing may actually enhance children's intellectual development, but only if it is done in limit and the programs children watch are selected wisely by parents.

There are many reasons why some people say that watching TV is beneficial for children. Firstly, watching the right kinds of shows increases children's knowledge and so they do better in academics. According to a research, young children who spent a few hours a week watching educational programs such as Sesame Street and Curious George had higher academic test scores 3 years later than those who did not watch educational programs. Secondly, children can be motivated to play sports by watching some sports on TV. Finally, children can learn about different cultures and lifestyles of the world through TV programs.

On the other hand, those who say that watching TV is detrimental for children, give their reasons as follows. To begin with, it impacts their health negatively. It reduces their physical activity and turns them into couch potatoes. Apart from causing obesity, too much screen time is also bad for their eyesight. It also impacts their social development as they do not get time to play and socialize. Finally, if the content they watch is not monitored, they may watch shows full of violence and vulgarity, which may be bad for them and affect their psyche.

I believe that watching TV is beneficial for children if done in limit. The effects also depend on the content and genre of the programs. Therefore, parents should set the TV time of the children and also select the programs for them. They should preferably watch TV with them, especially educational shows as these may seem boring to the children otherwise.

To sum up, I reiterate my view that TV is on the whole advantageous for children. However, the effects of television viewing depend on the program content, genre, and the time limit allocated to TV viewing.

Plan followed:
Intro:
Para 1: One view
Para 2: Other view
Para 3: Own view
Conclusion:
Written by: Kiranpreet Kaur (Exam question 1/2/2020)

280. *A report indicated that many children between 7 and 11 spend too much time watching television and/or playing video games. How does the problem affect the children, their families and society? What measures can be taken to control it?*

It is a fact that after coming home from school, children, especially those between 7 and 11, spend a lot of time in watching TV and playing video games. This essay will discuss the effects of this excessive TV viewing on children, their families and society, and also suggest some ways to address the issue.

There are many negative effects of spending too much time on TV by the 7-11 year olds. To begin with, the more time children spend on watching TV and playing video games, the less time they have for studying, exploring, playing and interacting with parents and friends. Children need interaction with the family and society for their holistic development. The societies also tend to be aloof as people do not know each other.

Moreover, excessive TV viewing can result in obesity as children are inactive and tend to eat junk food while watching TV. They are turning into couch potatoes. It is well known that 7-11 years is a crucial period of childhood when children develop the maximum, physically as well as mentally. Therefore, a sedentary lifestyle can be harmful for their physical fitness. Finally, there is a lot of violence on TV, which can have negative impact on children's psyche.

The solutions are simple but the onus is largely on the parents. They should give quality time to their children and ration their TV viewing hours. Even the time to play video games should be set properly. Outdoor activities should be encouraged and neighbourhood societies should be formed where children can play outdoor games with each other. Parks should be maintained properly so that children have a safe place to play outdoors.

To conclude, excess time spent on television and video games is bad and therefore I believe parents should set viewing limits to ensure their children do not spend too much time watching TV.

Plan followed:

Intro: I shall discuss the effects of this excessive TV viewing on the children, their families and society and also suggest some ways forward.

Para 1: How TV can affect the 7-11 year age group the most

Para 2: More negative effects

Para 3: Solutions

Conclusion:

281. *Many people believe that today there is a general increase in anti-social behaviour and lack of respect for others. What might have caused this situation? How to improve it?*

It is a fact that in the midst of vast progress in every field of life there is also a growth in the anti-social behaviour and people have become less respectful of each other. This essay intends to analyze some causes of this phenomenon and suggest some ways to ameliorate the situation.

The main reason behind the anti-social behaviour is that people have become too engrossed in making money. Most people have more than enough wealth, comfort and freedom, but their hearts desire even more. To satisfy their hearts greed they have become workaholics, and as a result have become selfish, isolated and indifferent. Secondly, even though people are connected to everybody through telephone lines and the Internet, the warmth of relationships has taken a back seat as face to face interaction has come down.

Another big cause of this phenomenon is the changing family structure. Earlier, people lived in joint families and the grandparents were there to supervise the children. Now there are nuclear families and children are left unattended in the hands of pervasive media like the TV and the Internet. No one monitors what they watch and they see the programs full of violence and crime, which makes them anti-social. The pressure of consumerist society and peers also breeds anti-social behaviour as young people resort to petty crime to get the things they desire.

There are many solutions to this problem. To begin with, people have to learn to strike a balance between work and family life. People should revert back to the old joint family system. This would be in the benefit of all. The children would learn moral values and the elderly would be well looked after. Negative effects of excessive consumerism should be taught to the people. Media can play a big role in highlighting the good points of the traditional and the western culture so that the people can adopt good social values. Neighbourhood associations should be set up to connect people to each other.

Summing up, anti-social behaviour and mutual lack of respect in today's times can be dealt with by taking simple measures, and individuals and governments should collectively take these steps.

Plan followed:
Intro:
Para 1: Causes
Para 2: More causes
Para 3: Solutions
Conclusion:

Nowadays some individuals behave in an anti-society way, such as committing a crime. In general, it is the society to blame. What causes the anti-social behaviours of individuals? Who should be responsible for dealing with it? (Similar)

282. Some people believe that young people know about international pop and movie stars but know very less about famous people from the history in their own country. Why is this? How can more interest be created in young people to gain more knowledge about their own famous people from history?

It is irrefutable that the youth of today know about global celebs but are ill informed about their own historical personalities. This essay shall analyse why this is happening, and also suggest some measures, to generate their interest in historical events and people.

The first and major reason for this is that the education system in most of the countries is test-based. Students are only taught to get good grades and as a result, they only focus on passing their exams, rather than gaining knowledge about any topic. On top of that, the youth today is more fascinated towards the celebrities because of the exposure and importance the media gives to them. Furthermore, most of the families have now started living in nuclear setups, where both the parents are working, and because of this the children's education about their roots and history has taken a back seat.

There are many methods that can be used by parents, schools and the media to develop the interest of youngsters in knowing about the famous people from history. The schools can organise educational trips to museums and famous historical places. The government should encourage children to visit museums by highly subsidizing tickets for the students. For example, the Shaheed Bhagat Singh Museum has become a great source of information about the freedom struggle and the sacrifices made by freedom fighters. Also, the Virasat-e-Khalsa museum has become very popular among the youth as they can learn a lot about Sikh history and culture.

Moreover, TV shows and movies can be made around famous historical personalities and their contributions. For instance, the recent Bollywood movie Bajirao Mastani, has been a super hit at the box office and has made a lot of people more aware about historical events and characters. TV channels like History channel has shows which run throughout the day, giving information about famous people and events from history.

To conclude, although there are many reasons why the youth of today know more about celebs than their own historical figures, several innovative and creative methods can be used to make the youth more interested and aware about the notable people from history.

Plan followed:

Intro:

Para 1: Reasons

Para 2: Steps, which can be taken

Para 3: More steps

Conclusion:

283. *In most of the societies, the role of mother and father differs. What are the causes of this difference? What will be the parental roles in future?*

It is true that in many nations, the part played by both parents in the upbringing of children is different. In this essay I will analyse the causes of these differences. The role of mother and father in the times to come will also be discussed.

There are many reasons for the differences in the parental roles. The principal reason is the orthodox thinking of people. They believe that role of mother is just to give birth to a child and look after child's schooling, eating and homework, whereas father's role is to fulfil the needs of the family. Another reason is that in these old-fashioned societies people do not have family planning, and so the birth rate is high so women are forced to sit at home and feed the children. Therefore, men are forced to work and earn money for fulfilling the requirements of the family.

However, in the future the scenario will change. Nowadays people are educated, literate, aware of things and are broadminded. Parents understand their responsibility and work equally for the holistic development of their children. In most families both mother and father will have to work, and so the household chores will also be done equally by both parents. So, in the future conditions will improve a lot. Parents will plan the things for the bright and shiny future of their children, and they will be united and the child will not be deprived of the father's love. Both will work so that they can do savings for the future for their child and presently in urban areas things have already begun to change.

To conclude, there are many reasons for the gender differences in parental roles, but the future is predicted to hold no such differences.

Plan followed:
Intro: So here I would like to discuss the reasons of these differences.
Para 1: Reasons
Para 2: the future scenario
Conclusion:

284. Some people say that playing computer games is bad for children, whereas others say that it has positive effects on the way children develop. Discuss both sides and give your opinion.

Some individuals hold the opinion that spending time on computer games is detrimental for children, whereas others assert that it is beneficial for children's development. I will discuss both views in this essay. I believe that computer games are good, but only if played in limit.

There are many reasons why some people say that playing electronic games is harmful for children. Firstly, overdependence on these games leads to social isolation, as these are usually played alone. Secondly, some games have violent characters, and seeing their violent acts leads to aggressive behaviour in children. Moreover, these games can confuse reality and fantasy. For example, when children play car-racing games then they may race their own vehicles in real life, which can lead to accidents. Finally, these games are addicting and once a child sits to play these games, time flies and everything else, such as studies and outdoor games are forgotten, which is indubitably bad.

On the other hand, those who say that playing computer games is advantageous for children, give their reasons as follows. To begin with, video games introduce children to computer technology. Secondly, some games provide practice in problem solving and logic, e.g. Age of Empires. Video games have proved to improve visual skills. They also improve motor and spatial skills. Children who play video games have better reflexes. What is more, these modern games make learning fun. The cost of failure is lower. For example, if the child gets the answer wrong or their character dies, he just starts the game over and tries again. Finally, some games have therapeutic applications.

I believe that on the whole computer games have more merits, but only if these are played for a controlled time. For example, the parents can allocate one hour of their children's free time on these games on weekdays and two hours at weekends. In this way the children can take benefit of the positives of these games and not suffer from the bad effects such as addiction and social isolation.

To summarise, on the whole these games are very good and certainly have more benefits, but only if these are played for a limited time.

Plan followed:
Intro: Discuss essay intro
Para 1: One view
Para 2: Other view
Para 3: Own view
Conclusion

285. *In some cultures, the old age is more valued, while in some cultures the youth is more valued. Discuss both views and give your own opinion.*

People of different cultures have varied attitudes toward age. They suggest that in Western societies old people are not respected, while in Asian societies elders are revered. Similarly, youth is either highly valued or ignored, depending on the culture. This essay intends to discuss both perspectives. I believe that each age has its importance and so should be equally treasured.

The main reason why old age is valued in some cultures is that age is often associated with wisdom. With age comes experience, and in many societies younger family members consult older ones for advice on relationships or problems. In some societies, not just older living family members but ancestors are revered and consulted. For instance, in the Far East, people respect grandparents, older leaders, and bosses.

On the other hand, the reason why the youth are valued in some cultures, is that a young and vibrant workforce is an asset. Most governments give priority to youth in terms of education so that they can move the society forward. A case in point is America, a country sponsoring university students by different forms such as scholarship and student loans. By doing this, young people can be well educated and equipped with proper knowledge and useful skills. Consequently, the young will be able to promote the development of the society.

I believe that age in itself is not a qualification for anything. If we look at western countries, we also find politicians in their sixties or seventies, and company executives in their sixties, despite strong business competition. In addition, as life expectancy increases, older people are becoming more important as consumers and voters. On the other hand, even in countries where elders previously were respected and obeyed blindly, people are realizing that old age does not always mean wisdom. The old way of running families, companies, or countries may not work today.

In conclusion, the old and the young are essential for any society, so they both should be valued. An ideal society should have a balance. We should appreciate both the vitality and potential of youth and the advice and experience of old age.

Plan followed:
Intro:
Para 1: One view
Para 2: The other view
Para 3: Personal opinion
Conclusion:

286. *In some parts of the world, it is becoming increasingly popular to try to find out about the history of your family. Why do people do this? Is this a negative or a positive development?(12/2/22 India 1 pm)*

The study of family history or genealogy has become very popular especially after the coming of the Internet. People are indulging in this study for various reasons. Although there are a few drawbacks of this development, I believe that it is largely a positive development.

The most popular reason for studying the family history is that people want to know their roots. Learning about their cultural background helps people develop a sense of identity and belonging. Another reason for studying family history is that it helps to predict risk for a range of health concerns and diseases, including heart disease, osteoporosis, type 2 diabetes, and some forms of cancer. Once a person's family medical history has been established, it is far easier for physicians to advise patients on how to keep healthy. Thus, people who know their family history are more aware of their identity and better prepared to deal with genetic diseases.

Along with the benefits mentioned above, knowing family history creates a resilience among people. Learning about stories of how their ancestors faced challenges and overcame them, makes people stronger. They learn that things do not always work out easily and despite challenges, they can still triumph and succeed.

On the other hand, there are some disadvantages of tracking family history. Firstly, genealogy begins as a curiosity, which becomes a hobby and then may become an obsession. That leads to people wasting too much time and money on it. One should not forget that it is the present, which influences the future more and not the past. Often knowledge of family history is disastrous, leading people to keep old enmities alive. It may also reveal unpleasant facts that one would regret knowing.

In conclusion, studying family history may come at the expense of some time and money but advantages like the feeling of belonging and knowledge about one's genetic health certainly outweigh them.

Plan followed:
Intro:
Para 1: Why people study family history / Advantages
Para 2: Other reasons/advantages
Para 3: disadvantages of tracking family history
Conclusion: it is good to know family history despite the
Written by: Indroop Singh Makkar (Exam question 31/10/2020, India, 1pm)

287. *The most important decision that young people have to follow is what career to choose. Do you agree or disagree?*

It is believed by some that the most pivotal decision that young people have to trail is what vocation to pick. I agree strongly with the given opinion. There are other critical issues of life which are very significant but career choice remains at number one.

The main argument which goes in favour of making career choice the most vital decision is that when the young persons have an idea of the career path they want to pursue, it can help them make the best decisions about their training and education. Many lines of work require specific degrees and certifications, which can take years to pursue. Understanding the requirements of their chosen path will allow them to plan to prepare themselves for the career they want.

Secondly, when the youngsters choose a career path, they position themselves to look far into the future at their ultimate objective. This can help them identify positions they want to hold and income levels they want to achieve. It can also help to guide them in building their personal and professional networks in the industry in which they are interested. Having long-term goals can help them stay focused on their ultimate career objectives, rather than moving aimlessly from job to job.

Finally, choosing a career path can help the youth make other important life decisions. Their choice of profession can dictate where they live and may affect if and when they marry and have a family. Choosing a life partner is another very important life decision, but it comes secondary to a career choice. Achieving a satisfactory work-life balance can be a challenge for many professionals, but career planning can help to minimize some of this stress.

To sum up, it can be reiterated that choice of career is certainly the most important decision for the young people and all other decisions depend on this one primary decision.

Plan followed:
Intro: Agree
Para 1: Main reason
Para 2: More reasons
Para 3: More reasons
Conclusion: Reiterate opinion

288. *Many people think young people should follow traditions. Others argue that young people should be free to be individuals. Discuss both views and give your opinion.*

It is believed by some that the youth should stick to traditions, whereas others say that they should have liberty to be what they want. In this essay I will look into both sides of the debate. I, personally side with the latter view.

On the one hand, there are many reasons why some individuals opine that the youth should follow traditions. Firstly, the young people of today need to be connected to their roots. They have been neglecting its own very rich culture and traditions in order to adapt to the western ideas. Another reason of people's opinion is that some traditions are very good and need to be preserved at all costs. For instance, touching the feet of the elderly as a token of respect and welcoming guests with folded hands.

On the other hand, those in favour of letting the youth have their own individuality, give their reasons as follows. To begin with, the youth of today do not just accept things without reasoning. It would be wrong to impose traditions on them, which are obsolete in the modern era. For example, the dowry system, in which the bride's parents gave her gold, money and household items, was acceptable earlier as women were not working. However, the youth of today condemn the dowry because they realize that it has led to many vices such as female feticide.

I believe that the young people are living in a modern world, which has a global culture, which is a blend of the good points of all cultures of the world. For example, the beautiful traditions of The West, such as celebration of Mother's Day and Father's Day are being celebrated in India today, and the good points of Indian culture like welcoming others with folded hands is being accepted by the western countries.

In conclusion, it can be said that the youth of today should be allowed all individuality. Traditions should not define them; they should define traditions. It has been rightly said that 'Traditions' should be guides and not jailors.

Plan followed:
Intro: This essay shall look into both sides of the debate
Para 1: one view
Para 2: Other view
Para 3: Own view
Conclusion:

289. *The best way to prepare for the future is to invest in young people. Do you agree or disagree?*

It is commonly believed that a nation can succeed in the future by spending on its youth. In my opinion, nothing can actually stop a nation from developing and succeeding if its youth are educated and healthy and thus there can be no better way than investing in these young resources to prepare for the future.

The first reason why I believe that investing in youth should be a priority for every country is that young people are the backbone of a country's economy. The success of the economy depends upon whether the country's working age population, or in others words the youth, is skilled, educated and healthy. If the youth are not skilled and educated, they would become a burden. Similarly, a country's success depends upon its worker's productivity and productivity in turn depends upon people's physical and mental health. Hence, countries must spend on their youth.

The second argument in support of my view is based on empirical evidence. About half a century ago, when most of Asia got independence, most of the countries like Korea, Indonesia, China and India had similar levels of development. However, today some of these countries like Korea and China are way ahead, while others like India and Indonesia are still facing many challenges. The main reason that experts attribute for this is the level of spending on health and education. Countries like Korea and China spent much more heavily on health and education than India and Indonesia.

Last but not least, a country to grow today needs innovation and new ideas. I believe that youth bring this to the table. Old people by nature are risk averse and are resistant to change, while youth are open to new ideas and change. If a country needs to really grow it must have young dynamic leaders with out-of-the-box thinking and ideas. Therefore, countries really need to spend resources and time on developing such young leaders.

To conclude, I would like to reiterate that importance of youth to the future success of a country cannot be overstated and thus investing in them is the most effective way for a country to secure its future.

Plan followed:
Intro: government should invest in young
Para 1: Why is it essential to invest on the youth.
Para 2: Second reason
Para 3: Third reason
Conclusion: investment on youth is better to secure the future

290. *Old generations often hold some traditional ideas on the correct way of life, thinking and behavior. However, some people think that it is not helpful for the young generations to prepare for modern life in the future. Do you agree or disagree?*

Generation gap has been a debated issue since the dawn of civilization. It is believed by some people that many ideas of the old generation are not suitable for today's life, and so would not help the youth to progress in life. While there are many viewpoints of the elderly which are of no use today, there are a few traditional ideas, which are evergreen and hold true even today.

Admittedly, there are many ideas of the elderly, which are beneficial for today's generation also. To begin with, the elderly had a very disciplined life. For instance, they believed in sticking to one job for life. They also believed in fixed-hours job. They had a stress-free work life. Moreover, they believed that marriage was for life. Divorces were rare. They had a stable family life. These values, if followed, are good for today's generation also.

However, in many ways the ideas of the elderly are obsolete in the times of modernity. Firstly, they want their children to follow the same profession. They do not give importance to aptitude. They live like a frog in the well. They forget that change is progress. Youngsters are more intellectually evolved. They want to explore the untrodden path to face the cutthroat competition of today.

Furthermore, the young differ in dress, food and habits. These things were not available to the elderly. The elderly had less opportunities to come in contact with the western world. The Earth was a big planet. Now it is a global village. The young speak a universal language, eat Italian pizza and Chinese food and wear a universal dress. The leisurely ways of the old are gone. The young have the speed of bikes, cars and planes. What can link them to the old bullock cart? The young today have to change to survive.

To sum up, there are some traditional ideas of the elderly that are evergreen and will hold true for times to come. But, in many ways, they are obsolete in today's time.

Plan followed:

Intro: Modern life has changed beyond recognition in many ways and so many ideas of the old generation are not suitable for today's life, but still there are some traditional ideas which are evergreen and hold true even today.

Para 1: Which ideas of the elderly hold true even today

Para 2: Which ideas of the elderly are obsolete today

Para 3: Why these ideas of the elderly are obsolete

Conclusion:

291. *Individual greed and selfishness has been the basis of the modern society. Some people think that we must return to the older and more traditional values of respect for the family and the local community in order to create a better world to live in. To what extent do you agree or disagree? (5/2/22)*

It is believed by some that we should go back to the old values in which the family and the local community was given respect, to lead a more pleasant life. I strongly agree that we must revert to the golden times when we valued traditions and respected the elderly and our neighbourhoods, so that we have a happier today and a happier tomorrow.

The main reason why we should go back to the past ways of life is that the modern lifestyle is making people selfish, isolated and indifferent. Today, people are connected to each other through telephone lines and the Internet but the warmth of relationships has taken a back seat. Most people have more than enough wealth, comfort and freedom but their hearts desire even more. To satisfy their hearts greed people have become workaholics and as a result have no time for family and friends. Each person is busy in his own quest for more. To add to it, the youngsters who are at ease with the new technology think that the elderly are good for nothing and that is why they do not respect them.

On the other hand, life in the past was slower and simpler. People loved and respected each other. Family members had a lot of face-to-face contact with each other. Older members of the family were well looked after and their advice was valued. Divorces were very rare as marriage was considered a sacred institution. Moreover, community get-togethers were often organized and people knew the farthest neighbours. Nowadays, the next-door neighbours are also not recognized. There were less worries and tensions in earlier times.

To conclude, living in this modern toxic world, we are all slowly being poisoned to death. Therefore, it is clear that the traditional value-based society is a better world to live in.

Plan followed:
Intro: Agree
Para 1: Where all we have fallen back in the modern world and why we need to go back to those traditions
Para 2: Good points of the old societies
Conclusion: Reiterate point.

292. *In some countries around the world men and women are having children late in life. What are the reasons for this development? What are the effects on society and family life?(29/1/22 & 26/2/22)*

In the modern society, young people have a tendency of postponing their parenthood until late 30's or even early 40's. This essay shall deal with the reasons for this phenomenon and the effects this has on the families and societies.

Many factors could be responsible for this trend. The most important reason is that in today's era of cutthroat competition, young people have to focus on their jobs and therefore have little time for their families. What is more, women of today have become more career oriented and do not wish to be held back by family responsibilities. Obviously under such circumstance, committing to a serious relationship or starting a family, which means tremendous responsibility and dedication, is not a preferable choice. The cost increase of raising a child is another barrier to late parenthood, and this is especially obvious in major cities around the world.

This change of lifestyle can have some negative effects on the society as a whole. Firstly, low birth-rates can result in an ageing population and a lack of labour force in the future. A greying society is a dependent society and is a burden on the shoulders of the government. Medical care services can be in high demand and medical cost can rise significantly.

The families too cannot escape the brunt of such a situation. The most disturbing effect is that chances of congenital anomalies rise significantly if a woman bears the first child after the age of 40. The families with mentally or physically challenged children can never be happy families. Another effect can be that the age gap between parents and children is too much and so chances of generation gap are strong.

Summing up, there are many reasons, which are responsible for people marrying late and having babies late in life and this definitely is detrimental for the societies and families. Therefore, young people should learn to give importance to both, a career and a family life.

Plan followed:
Intro: This essay shall deal with the reasons for this phenomenon and the effects this has on the families and societies.
Para 1: Reasons
Para 2: negative effects on society
Para 3: negative effects on families
Conclusion:

293. *Figures show that some countries have an ever-increasing proportion of the population who are aged 15 or younger. What do you think are the current and future effects of this trend for those countries?*

Demographic surveys of some nations have shown that the proportions of young people are rising rapidly. This essay shall delve into the immediate and long-term outcomes of this trend on those countries.

The most important current impact of such a trend would be on the national economy. For instance, goods and services would need to be imported, which would lead to an unstable economy. In addition to the effects on economy, there would be social implications also. The young population has lot of energy, which must be channelized in the right direction, or it would lead to crime and violence in society. The government will have to invest a lot on educational institutes, as more children need more schools and colleges. In addition more spending on health would also be needed.

If the government does careful management of such a situation, for instance, by providing good education and health facilities, then the future outcomes could be quite positive. The long-term result would be that the education and health infrastructure would be well developed. The society would be younger and more vibrant. The culture of those countries would be more fast-paced than the traditional culture.

However, in case the present time is not managed nicely, then the future effect would be different as there would be more people within the country needing employment. Then there might arise the problem of unemployment. Unemployment invariably leads to petty crime and violence.

Summing up, the long-term effects of having more young people, depend on how the situation is handled today. If handled well, the culture and lifestyle of these countries would be transformed as the population would be younger. Fresh opportunities and challenges would both be on the way. The trend would cause multiple possible effects and these countries should strengthen the education and health infrastructure to overcome its negative influence.

Plan followed:

Intro:
Para 1: Current effects on economy and society
Para 2: Future effects on society if today is handled well
Para 3: Future effects if careful management is not done today
Conclusion:

294. In some countries, more and more adults are living with their parents after graduating from college, university, or even after finding a job. Do the advantages of this outweigh the disadvantages?

The youth of today are finding it very difficult to find good employment and this has led to the increase in the number of young adults moving in with their parents. While there are certain drawbacks, I believe that the advantages of young graduates staying with parents as an adult are far more.

The first advantage of working adult children staying at home is that they contribute towards the household income and share the expenses. This not only reduces the burden on their parents but also helps them reduce their own expenses and save money. In effect, rather than struggling to pay rents, utility bills and other expenses, they can invest money or save money for a future home.

Secondly, there is a better bonding and stronger family ties in a family that stays together. Even though life has become hectic and there is not enough time to spend with family and friends, it is very comforting to know that there is someone at home to share problems. This helps them deal better with stressful situations in life and at work. Also, if children stay longer with their parents, they are more likely to support and take care of their parents in old age, due to the strong family bonds.

On the other hand, there are some disadvantages of children staying at home, which cannot be overlooked. Living with the parents after completing their education may make the children more dependent. They depend on someone to do the daily chores, like washing clothes, cooking food, cleaning dishes, and so on. They may never learn financial responsibility if they are dependent on their parents' hard-earned wages and do not contribute towards the household expenses.

To conclude, despite the few drawbacks of young adults sharing accommodation with their parents, I believe it is a positive trend on the whole.

Plan followed:
Intro: Advantages more than disadvantages
Para 1: Economic benefits
Para 2: Better family ties
Para 3: Disadvantages
Conclusion:

295. Nowadays, many families have both parents working. Some working parents believe, other family members like grandparents can take care of their children, while others think childcare centers provide the best care. Discuss both views and give your own opinion.

It is irrefutable that both parents are working nowadays, and as a result, children have to be raised by either child-care centres or grandparents. Some young parents believe that grandparents can take better care of their children, whereas others are in favour of child-care centres to look after their children while they are working. This essay intends to compare both options. I, however, believe that day-care centres are better than grandparents for the preschool years of children.

Most parents choose to leave their children with grandparents for many reasons. Firstly, grandparents would give more care than formal childcare centres. Looking after the grandchildren also keeps the grandparents energetic and vibrant. Grandparents bathe, feed and even read books to the child. This leads to a sort of symbiotic relation in which both grandparents and grandchildren are benefited. In other words, it is a win-win situation for both. Grandparents do not suffer from loneliness and depression, which is very common at that age and children are also well looked after.

On the other hand, those who prefer day-care centres, give their main reason that children become more social in these centres. A study found that grandparents may struggle to provide the educational and social experiences infants need. Children looked after by grandparents at the age of nine months were considered to be less sociable with other children at age three than those who had been in a child-care centre.

I believe that grandparents cannot be good child-care providers if they're in poor health and feel forced to provide childcare to their grandchildren. In such cases, the results can be nothing short of disastrous. Early childcare is a challenge, which may be simply too much for some grandparents to cope with, at this point in their lives. So, day-care centres are better as they are handled by professionals, who know the needs of children.

To sum up, although grandparental care is good in many ways for grandchildren, the advantages of day-care centres are more than those brought about by grandparents.

Plan followed:
Intro:
Para 1: Advantages of grandparents looking after grandchildren
Para 2: advantages of day care centres over disadvantages of grandparental care
Para 3: Disadvantages of grandparents
Conclusion: Day-care centres are better

296. *In recent years the family has changed as well as family roles. Why is this happening and is this situation positive or negative?*

Change is the law of nature and with the changing times the family's inner construction, along with the positions of its members have also changed. This essay intends to analyse the reasons of this trend. I believe that this situation has equal advantages as well as disadvantages.

The main factor contributing to this trend is the social change brought about by globalisation. The exposure to foreign cultures has changed people's mindset, and has also redefined the role of women in the family. Women are no longer limited to household chores, and are working shoulder to shoulder with men. The reins of the households are no longer in the hands of the man, the bread-earner, of the family.

The second major reason for this change in the fabric of the family is the economic condition. Since it is challenging to maintain a family with many members and to make ends meet, it is more feasible to keep the size of the family small. Thus, according to a recent study, the nuclear family has risen in popularity in the last one or two decades.

This modification in the family structure and family roles has brought about many benefits. Firstly, it has led to an egalitarian society, where gender differences are disappearing, and women can also fulfil their ambitions. The society has also benefited from a greater labour force.

On the other hand, the bonds between family members are being weakened. Since most parents have to spend time working, their children are left unattended or sent to childcare centers or boarding schools. The shrinkage in family size also results in more elders being sent to old-age home instead of staying with their children and grandchildren.

To sum up, due to the changes in culture and economy, the family structure and responsibilities among family members have been modified. While this trend positively contributes to gender equality and strengthens the labour force, it also has many adverse effects on family relationships.

Plan followed:
Intro:
Para 1: Reasons
Para 2: Reasons
Para 3: Advantages
Para 4: Disadvantages
Conclusion:

297. *Experts say if the old people spend time and get along with others and exercise every day, they will be healthier and happier. However, many elderly are suffering from loneliness and lack of fitness. Discuss the causes and solutions?*

It is indubitable that we are heading towards a greying society. The life spans have increased, but along with it the problems of elderly related to health and social isolation have also seen a surge. This essay intends to analyse the reasons of this phenomenon and also suggest ways to mitigate the problem.

The main reason of social isolation of the elderly is that they find it difficult to let go. The elderly often hold some traditional ideas on the correct way of life, thinking and behaviour, but their children and grandchildren do not want to be held back all the time because of their orthodox customs. So, this generation gap decreases the communication between the old members and young members in the same family, and as a result the old people feel isolated and lonely.

Secondly, the health of the aging population is a major concern. Human body is just a machine and like any machine needs lubrication from time to time to function well, the body machine also needs that oil in the form of exercise. The elderly who do not exercise daily, suffer from problems like hypertension and arthritis, which are further worsened because of the financial constraints of the elderly, who are no longer working and earning.

Simple steps can help to ameliorate the problem. One thing that has to be accepted gracefully is that the problems of ageing cannot be avoided. However, these problems can be delayed, and the quality of life can be improved. The elderly and the youngsters both need to make certain compromises. They both need to try and find common interest with each other. In addition, the elderly need to add exercise to their daily routine. Government should also focus on geriatric care, and provide special gyms and trainers for the elderly.

To conclude, the elderly themselves can alleviate the problems of the elderly, such as loneliness and failing health, to a large extent, but the government can also take some steps.

Plan followed:
Intro:
Para 1: 1st problem and solution
Para 2: 2nd problem and solution
Para 3: Solutions
Conclusion

298. *Nowadays some older people choose to live in the retirement communities with other people, rather than living with their adult children. Is it a positive or negative development?*

It is true that many aging parents are making the decision to live in a retirement home surrounded by agemates rather than staying with their children. I believe that this lifestyle choice is positive for both - the elderly and their adult children.

The most important benefit of elderly staying in a retirement community is that they have the company of fellow older adults, so they do not feel lonely or alienated. Seniors often feel isolated and neglected when they stay with their adult children as nowadays people have hectic lifestyles and are busy with their jobs, careers and children. In a retirement community it is easy for elders to find people who share their interests, and they can enjoy a lot of social activities together. Socially active seniors have better mental health, tend to live longer and also have a lower risk of dementia.

Secondly, living separately gives older people a feeling of independence. Seniors feel secure and their self-esteem is intact as they do not have to depend on their children. They also command more respect in the eyes of their children. Also, it is irrefutable that relationships become strong and meaningful when people are not under the same roof. Hence, if aged people are away from their children physically, both will be closer to each other emotionally.

Moreover, as people age, their health needs to be monitored regularly and these retirement homes have easy access to healthcare and medical facilities. Some seniors may need help with daily activities like bathing, eating, dressing etc. Living in such places ensures that seniors have staff that can take care of them and also gives their children the peace of mind that their parents are well taken care of. Finally, elderly can continue to prosper and prolong their good health through healthy eating options, yoga and exercise classes that such facilities offer.

To sum up, living in retirement homes is good for older people's mental and physical health, and strengthens their bond with their adult children.

Plan followed
Intro: It is a positive development
Para 1: Do not feel lonely and alienated
Para 2: Gives them a feeling of independence
Para 3: Better healthcare and medical facilites
Conclusion

299. *In some countries family and friends who care for the elderly do not find time to look after them. What are the reasons and solutions?*

It is a sad reality that in some parts of the world, close friends and even family members are facing difficulty in finding time to look after the older members. There are many reasons for this situation and steps are needed to ensure that people in their later stages of life are taken care of and loved.

Firstly, today most people have a busy and hectic schedule. Besides their caregiver duties, they also have to tend to their children, their jobs and other responsibilities. Secondly, the increasing life expectancy has meant that the working generations have to take care of the elderly for a longer time span than earlier. The longer life expectancy also means that in some families, young people have to take care of two old generations in place of one.

There are many steps that can be taken to address this situation. To begin with, whenever possible, people can take the work from home option, so that they can spend some extra time with the elder members. If this is not possible, they can hire caregivers for certain hours. Caregivers not only help with health and exercise needs of the elderly but also keep the old people lively by providing them someone to talk to.

In addition, the young members in the family can familiarize the elderly with technology, so that the elder members can stay connected with them, even when they are busy. Technology can also help reduce the dependence on the young. For example, if the old people have mobility issues, they can order things online instead of asking the young members to get them the items. Finally, the elderly need to be accommodating and must be willing to make certain changes, especially when it comes to their health.

To sum up, there are various causes why the young generation is facing time issues to look after their elderly family members, but with certain steps they can alleviate these problems.

Plan followed:
Intro
Para 1: Reasons
Para 2: Solutions
Para 3: Solutions
Conclusion

Written by: Indroop Singh

300. *Caring for children is an important thing of the society. It is suggested that all mothers and fathers should be required to take childcare training courses. To what extent do you agree or disagree?*

It is believed by some that all young first-time parents should receive formal training to care for their child. I strongly agree that all parents should get childcare training, even if they have to hire professional nannies for this purpose.

Childcare courses are important for many reasons. Firstly, traditional childcare skills, which are passed on from one generation to another, through oral and informal instruction, are not sufficient in today's era of nuclear families. So parents should undergo childcare training. It is also a misconceived idea that childcare is a simple process of feeding children, changing diapers and making them sleep regularly. Contemporary childcare is not limited to this. Childcare is a complex science that goes beyond nutrition. It involves the physical and emotional wellbeing of children. Therefore, with the changing times and changing family structure, childcare training courses should be the norm for all would be parents.

Secondly, childcare training teaches parents how to take a holistic approach to care for their children. Many people might wrongly think that childcare is all about love. Parents have to learn when to be firm, and when to give some room to children. For example, children eat a lot of candy, without knowledge that candy can cause obesity and tooth damage. Parents should not respond to children's needs for candy permanently.

Furthermore, quality childcare has many other far-reaching benefits. Current research has shown that the early years (ages 0-5) are the most sensitive for brain development. Over 90% of brain growth occurs during this period. Studies show that children who get good care, enter school with better math, language and social skills. Finally, parents, who have themselves done such course, can monitor the childcare being given by a professional nanny, better.

To summarise, successful childcare does not lie only in love but also in other skills. Therefore, all young parents should join childcare training courses.

Plan followed:

Intro: Parents' participation in care training is advisable.
Para 1: Childcare is much more than changing diapers and feeding children
Para 2: Childcare training teaches parents for a holistic approach of childcare.
Para 3: Far reaching benefits of quality childcare
Conclusion:

301. *When families have a meal together it is considered social activity. What are the advantages of a family meal? Do you think eating together is important to people in your country?*

It is irrefutable that eating together is a social activity. There are many advantages of families sitting together and sharing a meal. Eating together is definitely significant to people of my country, India.

The first and foremost advantage of eating together is that it creates a sense of belonging. Conversations during the meal provide opportunities for the family to bond and learn from one another. It is a chance to share information and news of the day, as well as give extra attention to your children and teens. Family meals foster warmth, security and love, as well as feelings of belonging. It can be a unifying experience for all.

Secondly, family mealtime is the perfect opportunity to teach appropriate table manners, etiquette, and social skills. Parents can be perfect role models in this and children learn by following them. What is more, meals prepared and eaten at home are usually more nutritious and healthy. They contain more fruits, vegetables, and dairy products along with additional nutrients such as fiber, calcium, vitamins A and C, and folate.

Furthermore, research shows that frequent family dinners (five or more a week), are associated with lower rates of smoking, drinking, and illegal drug use in pre-teens and teenagers when compared to families that eat together two or fewer times per week. To add to it, children do better in school when they eat more meals with their parents and family.

In my country most people do value shared mealtime. However, the fast-paced life and influence of the global culture is taking some away from this custom. Fortunately, some recent studies have shown that even in the developed countries people are realizing the importance of family meals and are downshifting. It is indeed time to bring the "family" back to the dinner table.

To conclude, eating together is definitely an important social activity. That is why it has been said that, 'The family that eats together stays together'.

Plan followed:
Intro: eating together is a social activity
Para 1: it creates a sense of belonging - a unifying experience for all
Para 2: Advantages of family meal
Para 3: More advantages
Para 4: Situation in my country
Conclusion:

302. *Some people say that parents have the most important role in a child's development. However, others argue that other things like television or friends have the most significant influence. Discuss both views and give your own opinion.*

Some individuals are of the opinion that parents have the most significant role in a child's development, whereas others opine that friends and other environmental factors such as TV have a more important role. This essay will discuss both perspectives. I believe that all the factors like parents, peers and TV, are inextricably linked and it is not possible to say which factor has more role.

There are reasons why some people hold the opinion that parents have the most critical role in a child's development. Firstly, parents have direct interaction with the children. They have their greatest effect on intellectual development and character traits of their children. They also play a very important role in the socializing process of the child. Right from the bedtime stories to the behavioural habits, parents play a very important role in making a child a responsible citizen. That is why it is believed by some that parents have the strongest role in a child's development.

On the other hand, those who say that friends and TV have more vital role on the development of children, give their reasons as follows. To begin with, children can relate better to their friends as they are of the same age group. They find comfort in these friendships when things get tough such as losing a pet or facing family problems. Television is also one of the most prevalent media influences in children's lives. How much impact TV has on children depends on how much they watch, what they watch and with whom they watch.

In my opinion, we cannot generalize as to what has more significance. In the early years family generally has more impact but in adolescence, peers and TV may impact more. It has also been seen that the power of the peer group becomes more important when the family relationships are not close or supportive. For example, if the parents work extra jobs and are largely unavailable, their children may turn to their peer group for emotional support.

To sum up, behaviour is affected by a complex interaction of many different factors such as parents, peers and environment. It is difficult to generalize which factor plays the most significant role.

Plan followed:
Intro: It is necessary to look at both arguments before forming an opinion.
Para 1: One view
Para 2: Other view
Para 3: Own view
Conclusion:

303. *Some scientists believe that studying the behaviour of 3-year-old children can tell which children would grow up to be criminals. To what extent in your opinion is crime a product of human nature or is it possible to stop children from growing up to be criminals?*

Some scientists are of the opinion that hereditary characteristics are responsible for the person's temperament and hence future career. While genes do play a role, I believe that the primary determinant is nurture – education and upbringing.

There are many reasons why I believe that nurture plays a more crucial role in children's development. It has been well researched that the way a child is nurtured is a key factor in shaping his or her personality and several behavioural characteristics. This is done by the family in the first few years of a child's development, and then later there are other influences like that of the society, teachers, and friends. Moreover, children imitate what they observe and if they have positive role models around them, it is highly unlikely that they will deviate from the right path.

Furthermore, children can rise above the gene pool and rise to great heights. Even if a child is born to criminal parents but brought up away from that environment and provided quality education, he will not grow up to be a criminal. To add to it, in many countries, teaching moral and social values is a part of their education system. This makes the children realize the importance of ethics starting at an early age, keeping them away from deviant and criminal behaviour.

Admittedly, there are many examples of children born in families of criminals, growing up to be criminals. However, there are several factors that this can be attributed to, like the lack of positive role models, negative conditioning of the child's mind during the developmental stages, physical and mental abuse in childhood, etc. Also, it is a fact that crime is a product of the circumstances of a person. Poverty, illiteracy and unemployment are the root causes of crime.

To sum up, the role of nature in determining the behaviour of a child cannot be ignored, but it is the way the child is nurtured that shapes the future behaviour and personality of a child, thus ascertaining that it is possible to prevent children from growing up to be criminals.

Plan followed:
Intro: Disagree
Para 1: Role of nurture
Para 2: More role of nurture.
Para 3: Role of genes
Conclusion:

304. *Some people say that every human being can create art (e.g. painting), others think only the people born with the ability can create art. Discuss both views and give your opinion.*

It is believed by some that artistic ability is inborn, whereas others say that such a talent can be acquired by training and hard work. This essay intends to analyze both perspectives. I personally believe that artistic knack is a combination of both, talent and training.

The main reason why some people hold the opinion that art is about natural ability is that some people are just innately good. They showcase such extraordinary talent at such a young age that leaves little doubt that they had such abilities since birth. History is full of examples of child prodigies like Mozart, who outdid others who had years of practice. In addition, they say that art is valued precisely because people feel that not everyone can make it.

On the other hand, those who say that anyone can produce art by practice and training give the following reasons. First, they say that had this not been the case, there would be no art schools, and art and fine art would not exist as subjects. Secondly, they cite the development of great artists over time. The only thing that separates most of these artist's earlier works from their latter works is practice and yet in most cases, the latter works are valued much more highly. People might not even consider some of these artists talented, if they looked at their initial works.

In my opinion, to reach the recognizable top, even those gifted with talent have to work hard and practice a lot. Even the most talented can lead a life of oblivion if they do not polish their art by continued practice. Conversely, anyone with a passion and determination can succeed in creating unique masterpieces of art. They might not be able to achieve the same level of success as someone who is extremely talented and hardworking, but they can still make a name for themselves.

To sum up, both talent and hard work have a role in creating art since both are inextricably linked. The nature versus nurture debate has no clear-cut answer and will never have.

Plan followed:
Into:
Para 1: Reason for one side
Para 2: Reason for other side
Para 3: My opinion
Conclusion

305. *Research indicates that the characteristics we are born with have much more influence on our personality and development than any experiences we may have in our life. Which do you consider to be the major influence?*

Nature versus nurture debate has been around for ages and has been supported well by both sides. Nature, referring to heredity, and nurture, referring to the environment, are two very reasonable explanations as to why we are the people we are today. I consider that both nature and nurture influence us in different ways and there is no way to show what has the bigger role.

Nature is believed to be what determines our personalities, looks, and other things because it is all genetically passed down. It has been seen that a new born does have a set of inherited traits. For instance, some of the great legends like Lata Mangeshkar, Asha Bhosle, Kishor Kumar became successful at a very early age even without much learning. Another example is that identical twins reared apart are far more similar in personality than randomly selected pairs of people. Each observation suggests that personality is inheritable to a certain extent.

On the other hand, with proper mentoring and practice, any person can achieve success in life. If a person has an environment in which everybody is in the same profession and are successful in it, there is a great chance that the person will land up in the same profession and will achieve heights, because in that environment he will get proper nurturing. If a person has true dedication then it can beat talent. Various singers, dancers, musicians, businessmen, entrepreneurs did work really hard for years, and because of that, they got recognition in the entire world.

The more we delve into the topic, the more the evidence reveals that the answer is "BOTH". There is a lot people inherit from their parents through genes, but there is also a lot people pick up by observing their parents. I believe it is impossible to determine what plays a bigger role. In some cases, people's environment and upbringing might be more responsible for who they turn out to be and, in some cases, it might be their natural inborn qualities, they inherited.

To conclude, I believe that it is impossible to compare the role of nature and nurture in the development of an individual as their influence varies from individual to individual.

Plan followed:
Intro:
Para 1: Nature
Para 2: Nurture
Para 3: Both
Conclusion

306. *Some are of the opinion that people are naturally born as good leaders while others feel that leadership skills can be learned. Discuss both views and give your own opinion.*

It is believed by some that people are born with certain characteristics that enable them to become great leaders, while others assert that leadership skills are learnable. In this essay, both views will be discussed. Personally, I believe that training and experience can make better leaders than any innate ability.

The main reason why some people believe that leadership qualities are inborn is that leadership is based on personality traits, which either a person possesses by birth or does not. For example, people who are naturally outgoing and extrovert get followers. Another great leadership trait is handling stress which all the leaders face at one time or another. People's genetic makeup influences their behaviour and those who are naturally balanced and composed handle stress more easily. According to them, leadership cannot be taught and people who do not possess these natural traits, fail at leadership.

On the other hand, some people think leadership skills are not in a person's DNA and can be learned through experience, education and training. Experiences and circumstances prepare people to deal with success and failure. Good communication skills and formal speaking are the essential traits of leaders and can be learnt through formal training and a well-rounded education. Creativity is another leadership skill that parents and good teachers can help children develop.

I believe that, while there are many skills that can be inborn, leadership is not one of them, and any person can be groomed to master skills for becoming a good leader. It is a fact that children of many good leaders have failed as leaders, but those with no such background have risen to great heights as leaders. The prime minister of India, Mr. Narendra Modi and the former President of India, Dr. A.P.J Abdul Kalam, have risen from humble beginnings and risen to great heights by acquiring such skills.

In conclusion, there is no doubt that becoming a good leader is challenging but this does not mean that only people with innate talent can become good leaders.

Plan followed:
Intro:
Para 1: One side view
Para 2: Other side view
Para 3: Own view
Conclusion

307. *Children who grow up in families, which are short of money are better prepared with the problems of adult life than children who are brought up by wealthy parents. To what extent do you agree or disagree?*

It is believed that children of poor families are better equipped in dealing with the challenges of adult life than children of rich upbringing. I believe that adversity is a good teacher of life and so children who have seen poverty in childhood are much better at facing adversities in adulthood.

The main reason is that children raised in poor families have more situations to solve a problem or make a decision as both parents are busy in earning for the family and are not always available to guide children or make decisions for them. So, these children become more confident in decision making in the future as well. They realize the value of money as they have to live with the barest minimum and as a result they find it less difficult later on in life when they face financial challenges.

Another reason is that most children from such families start working part time at an early age to help with household finances or to fulfil their needs. Thus, they better understand the value of money and this makes them more skilled at money management as well. In contrast, the children of wealthy families are born with a silver spoon in their mouth. They are completely ignorant of the value of money as everything is provided for them in their youth and expect the same situation in adulthood.

Furthermore, their situations force them to learn many essential life skills like cooking, plumbing etcetera as their parents are too busy to take care of these things and financial conditions might not permit them to hire a third person for such tasks. These skills make them more independent and confident than children of rich families. Finally, in poor families, it is generally the older siblings who take care of the younger children. Thus, these children are better prepared to raise their own children in the future.

To sum up, children who belong to families with weaker socio economic background tend to be better prepared in dealing with adult life challenges as compared to those who come from affluent families.

Plan followed:
Intro: Agree
Para 1: First reason
Para 2: Another reason
Para 3: third and fourth reasons
Conclusion:
Written by: Indroop Singh

308. *In many countries today there is insufficient respect to old people. What are the reasons? What problems might it bring to society?*

It is irrefutable that in some parts of the world, the respect and admiration for elderly has reduced in recent years. There are several factors responsible for the fall in respect for the elderly among the society and this can have many adverse effects for the society.

There are many reasons for lack of respect to the aged. The first reason is the increasing relevance of technology in the society. Elderly are not so comfortable with technology and so youth feel that elderly are incapable. In addition, earlier, senior citizens were one of the few sources of information but today there is so much information available on the internet. Children and youth feel that there is nothing special that they gain from the elderly. The second reason for the increasing disrespect is that due to increasing life expectancy, older people are living longer and thus competing with the young for jobs.

Furthermore, older people have certain set views and ideology about how people should live their lives and many among the new generation feel that these ideas and values are not suitable for today's time. When older people try to force these ideas on the young, it not only leads to conflicts but also leads to loss of respect for the elderly. Finally, the value systems of society have changed. Most cultures value youthfulness and in fact, getting old is looked down upon as a disease rather than as a natural process.

The major negative consequence of the falling respect for the elderly is that it leads to the feeling of helplessness and worthlessness among the elderly. This takes a toll on not only their mental health but also their physical health as the elderly stop taking care of themselves. Another major impact is that this lack of respect slowly develops into discrimination against them. For example, employers start preferring younger employees and the young get better service at shops and restaurants.

To sum up, the growing disrespect for the senior citizens can be attributed to various reasons and this has disastrous consequences for the elderly and the society as well.

Plan followed:
Intro: In this essay I intend to delve into the causes and effects of this trend.
Para 1: Reasons for lack of respect to the aged
Para 2: More reasons
Para 3: Effects
Conclusion

309. *Some people think parents should read or tell stories to children, while others think parents need not do that, as children can read books, watch TV or movies by themselves. Discuss both views and give your opinion.*

It is believed by some people that parents should read or tell stories to children, while others believe that children can come to know about stories themselves by reading books or by watching TV or movies. In this essay, I will discuss both views. I believe that self-reading and watching TV and movies is much less effective than a parent reading stories to children.

There are many reasons why some people believe that parents should read bedtime stories to children. To begin with, it encourages family bonding. In this day and age of hectic lives and busy schedules, reading together is a simple and enjoyable way for parents to take time out and focus on the family. Children also feel wanted and loved, when parents spend time with them. In addition, it builds listening skills, increases a child's attention span, and develops the ability to concentrate.

On the other hand, those who opine that children should themselves read stories from books or watch them on TV and in movies, give their reasons as follows. Firstly, they say that the parent's role should be limited to surrounding their children with books worth reading. When children read books on their own, they become much more independent with studies and this helps them academically as well later on. Secondly, TV programs and movies specially cater to children's stories in audio-visual format, which has a more lasting impact on children.

I believe that parents should read out stories to children. The main reason is that this can be started much before children can themselves read. When parents read out stories, children automatically start picking up books and reading them. Otherwise it is very difficult to motivate the children of today to read. Moreover, I consider letting children watch TV all the time as passive parenting, as parents lose control over what their children are picking up from the TV shows.

To sum up, it is always better for the parents as well as the children, if parents read aloud to their children. This would give them quality time together and loads of other benefits, which I have discussed above. Someone has rightly said that, "Stories are the currency of human contact."

Plan followed:
Introduction: Discuss essay
Para 1: One view
Para 2: Other view
Para 3: Own view
Conclusion:
Written by: Indroop Singh (Exam question 10/10/2020, 1pm, India)

310. *In some countries more people choose to live alone or by themselves in recent years. Why is this the case? Is it a positive or negative development for the society?*

As any country develops, people are faced with new challenges and set new goals for themselves. Many individuals have to leave their families and as a result this trend of living alone or in nuclear family units has increased. This essay intends to explore the reasons of this phenomenon in depth. Although there are a few advantages, I believe it is largely a negative development.

The first possible reason of this changing family structure is globalization. This situation has opened lots of opportunities for the people to travel to and work in other countries. Moving to foreign countries or even in far-off places in one's own country is not possible with the whole family. So this has led to the breaking of joint families into nuclear units. When children of such nuclear families grow older, they live individually to explore new avenues for themselves.

The second important reason is the growing generation gap. The elderly want to stick to their tradition and culture whereas the youngsters want to adopt the global culture. This leads to conflicts and so there is lack of harmony among the family members. The senior members of the family do not want to let go, but the youth want to be free birds and so living individually is the only option once they are able to earn for themselves.

The major negative effect is that living alone or in isolation can lead to depression. There are many ups and downs in life, when a person needs the loving and tender care of his nears and dears. In addition, children of nuclear families are often left unattended when both parents are working. They can become self-centred or can even go astray. The elderly also need the love and support of their children at this age. They are forced to live lives of isolation and depression. This has also led to the mushroom growth of old-age homes. On the positive side, this leads to faster progress, as family ties do not hold people back. Nuclear families are easy to maintain. Conflicts are also less and so love among the extended family members is maintained. Family get-togethers are celebrated with great enthusiasm.

To sum up, living alone has become common because of many reasons, which have been discussed above. In my opinion, the cons of this situation, overpower the pros.

Plan followed:
Intro:
Para 1: First reason
Para 2: Second reason
Para 3: positives and negatives of this situation.
Conclusion:

311. *In some countries, young people are not only richer, but also safer and healthier than ever before. However, they are less happy. What might be the main reasons for this? What can be done for this?*

In some countries young people are not as happy as before, although their living conditions have improved considerably. This essay intends to discuss the reasons for this, and suggest some solutions to alleviate the problem.

The first reason for the growing dissatisfaction and discontent is the multitude of choices available in the markets. The increasing choices mean that after taking a decision, most people feel that they could have made a better choice and thus instead of feeling happy, people regret most decisions. Perhaps, this is the reason why the young keep changing their profession constantly. Secondly, today the young are facing a lot more competition than the past. For example, it is becoming increasingly difficult for the youth to secure a good job or get into a good university. This increasing competition is making the youth stressed because they feel that despite their best efforts they might fail.

Another important reason for the discontent of youngsters is the consumerist society of today. Happiness is derived more from materialistic things rather than relationships. However, unfortunately the happiness derived from materialistic things is short lived as people have no emotional connection to these things. The final reason is that people's expectations are a lot higher than before. The young especially are very ambitious and when the reality does not match the expectation, it of course leads to discontent.

There are many steps that parents and young people themselves can take to feel happier. To begin with, the young should reduce the number of choices for non-important decisions. This would decrease the regret or the opportunity cost lost on making the wrong decision. The young should also set reasonable goals and expectations so that they do not constantly face failures. In addition, parents should help young people to develop a positive attitude towards life and the world. Traditional values, such as respecting the elderly, spending more time with family members, would help young people to become happier. Children loved by families are more likely to feel content.

To sum up, there are many reasons why the youngsters of today are not as happy as their counterparts of the past and this can only be changed with a fresh perspective towards life and goals among the youth.

Plan followed:
Intro:
Para 1: Reasons
Para 2: More reasons
Para 3: Solutions
Conclusion:

312. *It is expected that there will be a higher proportion of old people than young people in the future in some countries. Do you think it is a positive or negative development?*

It is undeniable that we are heading towards a greying society. Demographists predict that there would be fewer youth than the elderly in the near future. Although the population ageing should be seen as a success story, it brings social and economic challenges for the nations. So, it can be said that this situation is equally, positive as well as negative.

On the negative side, fewer youngsters would mean less people working, which will decrease the revenue received by the government from taxes. On top of that, pensions will have to be provided by the governments to the increasing number of the elderly for more years as the life span has also gone up considerably. Moreover, the retirement age may have to be extended and this may lead to youth unemployment. Young people have a lot of energy, which will have to be channelized in the right direction. If they are unemployed, they may resort to petty crime for fulfilling their needs. Finally, health care costs would be four to five times higher on the elderly because of their deteriorating health.

On the other hand, the ageing population can be beneficial in many ways. Firstly, arts and culture benefit from an older populace. It has been seen that the older generation are more actively involved in clubs, such as sports, drama, and other arts. Another major benefit is that older communities are more law abiding and are less inclined to commit crime. The Australian Institute of Criminology has projected that crime rates will drop by approximately 16% by 2050 because of increase in the aging population. There will also be money saved on prisons and policing costs in the future. Last but not least, the older people provide childcare, financial, practical and emotional assistance to family members including helping with the tasks of daily living.

In summary, aging is inescapable. A predominantly old-aged society can certainly have a negative impact as well as a positive impact on a country's advancement, and so it has to be planned well.

Plan followed:
Intro:
Para 1: Negative
Para 3: Positive
Conclusion:

313. Young people are often influenced in their behaviours and situations by others of the same age. This is called "peer pressure". Do the disadvantages outweigh the advantages?

Young people are influenced by peers because they want to fit in, be like peers they admire, do what others are doing, or have what others have. While there are certain advantages, I believe that the disadvantages of peer pressure are far more.

On the one hand, there are many disadvantages of peer pressure. Firstly, in order to conform, youngsters may engage in self-destructive behaviour like smoking, abusing drugs, drinking alcohol, shoplifting etc. They may blow good academic opportunities and make poor decisions that ruin their careers. Secondly, it can cause drastic change in teen behaviours and they can develop bad attitudes or unkind demeanour. This in turn increases conflicts with parents and may lead to even more rebellious behaviour among children.

Finally, peer pressure promotes herd mentality and youngsters are not able to think independently. It stifles their creativity, innovation and growth as they get comfortable copying each other and do not even try to think outside the box. In other words, they do not make conscious choices and simply do what everyone else is doing. For example, they may choose careers based on their friend's preferences, even if they are not passionate about them. In adulthood, this leads to lack of job satisfaction and depression.

On the other hand, peer pressure also has some benefits. The biggest advantage is that peers can set good examples for each other and can encourage each other to make choices that benefit them. For example, if a peer group values academic achievement, they can influence those around them to study harder and get ahead in school. Another benefit of peer pressure is that it can make children try out things that they are uncomfortable with and this can raise their self-confidence and make them more flexible.

To summarise, while there are certain positives of peer pressure, I think on the whole it is detrimental for children and teenagers.

Plan followed:
Intro: Peer pressure more negative
Para 1: How peer pressure can be negative
Para 2: How peer pressure can be negative
Para 3: How peer pressure can be positive
Conclusion: reiterate

314. *Society is based on rules and laws. If individuals were free to do whatever they wanted to do, it could not function. To what extent do you agree or disagree?*

It is believed by some that if the people of any society were given freedom to do whatever they want to, then there will be utter chaos and confusion. While rules and laws need to be amended with the changing times, I agree that such laws are absolutely essential for the proper functioning of any society.

To begin with, laws are made for the humans to function in an orderly manner. A civilized society exists only if the people respect each other's rights, lives and property. This can only be achieved if they are given a set of rules or orders to follow. Without these rules or laws, any society is deemed to fail. To add to it, it is human nature to pursue personal interests. If given absolute freedom to do whatever people want to do, there will be too many people who would certainly fall into bad habits and vices.

In addition to the above mentioned points, laws are made for the people to feel secure. The different types of laws, like corporate law, criminal law, civil law, constitutional law help the society on the whole, to feel safe and secure, and at the same time, deter those who have a tendency to harm others or commit frauds of any kind. For instance, if there were no traffic rules, there will be a huge number of casualties in road accidents, and there will be too much chaos and confusion on roads. Also, no one will be afraid of speeding or jumping a traffic light.

Admittedly, law cannot be absolute and needs to be amended with the changing world and the societal demands and values. A law written fifty years ago may not be applicable today. For example, till the first half of the 20th century, women in many countries did not have the right to vote. In today's world, we cannot even think of having such laws. Moreover, laws are there to make people realize their moral and social obligation, and to respect another person's rights and freedom.

In conclusion, I would reiterate that law is needed in any society to maintain order, ensure safety and to make people respect other members of the society. Also, in the absence of law, the wrongdoers will go unpunished, and it will lead to more chaos and crime in any society.

Plan followed:
Intro: agree.
Para 1: Rules are for orderly functioning of society
Para 2: Rules are for our safety
Para 3: Some rules are not befitting for today
Conclusion: the rules that we have are not too many but essential for the smooth functioning of any civil society

315. *History tells that people have often thought about creating an ideal society, but most of the time fail in making this happen. What is your opinion about an ideal society? How can we create an ideal society?*

If we look at history, it is clear that since time immemorial, people have always wanted to create an ideal society, but have been unsuccessful. In the following essay, I intend to discuss what makes an ideal society, and how it can be created.

In my opinion, there are three characteristics a society must possess in order to be considered ideal. Firstly, in an ideal society everyone should have access to basic necessities like clear drinking water, electricity, a good education and a quality healthcare. Basic necessity should also include a feeling of safety and security. Secondly, everyone should be treated equally irrespective of their race, religion, caste, background or physicality. People should not be judged or discriminated against on the basis of their appearance or their financial status. Finally, the environment should also be clean and free from pollution. This includes everything from the air people breathe, the water people drink and soil people grow their crops in.

An ideal society can be created in the following ways. For ensuring that basic necessities are met, there should be a government which works for the people, because only the government can protect and promote the economic and social well-being of all individuals. For equality, there should be balance and checks on the government institutions. There can be no equality if there is unchecked power and if violators of the law are not punished. Finally, a clean environment can only be ensured by limiting all activities that harm the environment and switching to alternatives that are non-polluting. For example, use of solar and wind energy in place of fossil fuels.

To sum up, I believe an ideal society meets the basic needs of everyone, has equality for everyone and has a clean environment although this may be difficult to achieve.

Plan followed:
Intro: In the following essay, I intend to discuss what makes an ideal society and how we can create one
Para 1: What makes an ideal society
Para 2: How we can create an ideal society
Conclusion:

316. *Some people think that in the modern society individuals are becoming more dependent on each other, while others say that individuals are becoming more independent of each other. Discuss both views and give your own opinion.*

It is believed by some individuals that in the contemporary society of today people are becoming more dependent on others, whereas others opine that people are less dependent on others. In this essay I intend to delve into both views. I personally believe that our dependence on others has grown, but it may not be that visible.

There are many reasons why some people think that the dependence of people on each other is increasing. Today, people depend on others for every household task, which earlier they did on their own. For instance, working couples rely on laundry services for washing and ironing clothes, on house maids for cooking and cleaning, on private tutors for teaching their children, on nannies for childcare and on home nurses for looking after their elderly.

On the other hand, those who say that inter-dependence has come down, give their reasons as follows. Firstly, because of technology, people can do a lot on their own without having to go anywhere or depend on office clerks. For example, people can do net banking sitting at home, and can do online shopping. They can entertain themselves alone by computer games and the Internet. They can book railway and air tickets online. They can eat ready to eat food available in the market. They are not dependent on somebody in their home to cook for them.

I believe that man is a social animal and will always be dependent on others. This dependence may be direct or indirect. When people are seemingly independent, they are still dependent on people behind the technology. For example, when they do net banking, they depend on all those software developers who have made it possible for them. When they eat ready to eat food, they depend on those who cook and pack that food.

Summing up, every person is part of a society and it is impossible for him or her to not depend on others. This dependence, however, may be visible or invisible.

Plan followed:

Intro: In this essay I intend to delve into both views and finally give my opinion.
Para 1: One view
Para 2: Other view
Para 3: Own opinion
Conclusion:

317. *In some countries the lifestyle of people is changing rapidly, and this affects family relationships. Do the advantages of this trend outweigh the disadvantages?*

It is irrefutable that in recent years, people's lifestyles have changed a lot, and this has influenced familial relationships in many ways. Although the changing lifestyles have brought families closer in some ways, I still believe that the disadvantages of this trend outweigh the advantages.

On the one hand, the main advantage of changing lifestyles especially people preferring to spend time indoors than outdoors is that it increases the time people spend with each other. For example, instead of playing sports outside, today people stay inside and watch TV with each other together at home. When people sit together, they talk more and thus it strengthens the bond between family members.

Despite the increased time spent with each other, I feel the disadvantages of these changing lifestyles are much more. Firstly, the boundaries between professional life and personal life have disappeared. People are always working, even when they are on vacations they are working. Thus, though people spend more time with each other, it is not quality time as they are focused on their work rather than on their family members. The growing addiction for internet also has the same effect. Family members might be sitting together at home, but they are mentally not present. They are engaged in talking with their friends.

Furthermore, the increasing preference for living alone is making people much more isolated. The lack of social connection with family members is leading to an increase in feelings of depression and loneliness. The connection through phones and internet can never match the feeling of security and calm that physical presence of a family member brings. Thus, because of these reasons I feel that changing lifestyles have harmed family relationships.

In conclusion, while there has been some increase in the time family members spend together due to changing lifestyle, overall the effect has been largely detrimental.

Plan followed:
Intro: Disadvantages are more
Para 1: Advantages
Para 2: Disadvantages
Para 3: Disadvantages
Conclusion: Reiterate opinion

Written by Indroop Singh

318. Throughout history, male leaders have always led us to violence and conflict. If female leaders govern a society, it will be more peaceful. To what extent do you agree or disagree with this opinion?

Some people believe if women were leaders of society instead of men, there would be less violence and societies would be more peaceful. I do not agree with this notion and I believe that policy of peace or war depends upon the situation a society faces rather than the gender of its leader.

There are many reasons why the belief that women leaders would lead to less violence, is wrong. Firstly, the main reason why people think that women leaders would lead to less violence is that women are soft-hearted, patient, compassionate and more pliable. However, I think that such women would not get a chance to lead a society in the first place. Only women who are strong-willed, objective and confident would get the opportunity to head a nation or society.

Another reason is that to prove they are strong, women sometimes follow a policy of more aggression than normal. History has examples of such leaders like Margaret Thatcher whose policies were very aggressive and not at all peace oriented. Thirdly, the policy a country follows depends upon the situation a country faces rather than the gender of the leader. For example, India and Pakistan have fought four wars and some wars have been under male leaderships while others have been under female leadership. The wars have not been due to gender of leadership, but because of conflicts like Kashmir and the past history of the countries.

Finally, if people want to really prove that women leaders would lead to less violence, firstly women should be given more opportunities in leadership positions. History has very few examples of women in leadership positions. Even a country like the US has never had a female President. Hence, without giving opportunities to women, we cannot form a judgement like this.

In conclusion, I cannot agree that women in leadership would lead to less violence than men in leadership positions.

Plan followed:
Intro: disagree
Para 1: Why female rulers are thought more peace loving, but then refute to prove your point
Para 2: Female rulers have also caused wars
Para 3: More reasons to support my view
Conclusion: Reiterate opinion

Written by: Indroop Singh

319. People are surrounded by advertising, which has an increasing effect on our lives. Do you think the positive effects of this outweigh the negative effects?

Whether it is on TV, internet, radio or hoardings at the side of the road, advertisements have become a part of our lives. While there are certain drawbacks, I believe that the beneficial effects of ads are far more.

The first benefit of advertisements is that they provide information on new products. If it were not for electronic and print advertising, many products would not be bought. In this way, advertising provides an important service to manufacturers and some consumers. Secondly, ads have a positive effect on the world economy as they help create more jobs. Advertising increases the demand for products and services, so more people are needed to manufacture, supply, ship and test them.

In addition, advertisements help make people make healthy choices and live a better life. For example, ads for pulse polio immunization, clean drinking water, nutritious diets and exercise etcetera have a positive effect on people's health and reduces their risk of diseases. Ads bring about many positive social changes like curbs on female foeticide, equal rights for women and reduction of child labour. Finally, advertisements have a positive effect on the environment as they educate consumers about serious threats like climate change and steps that can be taken to address it.

However, adverts also have some downsides. The main drawback is that sometimes consumers buy these tempting products without the insight of what they actually need. This impulsive buying can upset people's budgets and land them in debt. Another negative effect of advertisements is that they promote harmful products or misrepresent products and make false claims about them. For example, fast food ads have led to poor eating habits and an increase in problems like obesity and diabetes

To conclude, although there are certain drawbacks of adverts, I still consider their impact on society to be positive on the whole.

Plan followed:
Intro – Agree
Para 1 – Advantages
Para 2 – Advantages
Para 3 – negative effects
Conclusion: reiterate opinion

320. Advertising discourages people from being different individuals by making us all want to do the same and look the same. Do you agree or disagree?

It is believed by some that adverts dissuade people to have individual identity by promoting similar looks and lifestyles. While ads encourage people to buy similar things, I believe that wanting to look the same and do the same is a matter of personal choice and has nothing to do with ads.

Admittedly, when any advertisement bombards people with any new product, then people rush to buy it and it appears that all people are doing the same. However, this similarity is very short-lived, as sooner or later they realize that it is a huge waste of time and money to spend on something that is not really appropriate for them. Therefore, ads cannot suppress individuality permanently.

Secondly, all people cannot afford all things shown in the adverts. Even when ads use famous celebs to endorse their products, and people want to purchase those things, they have to consider their pocket and requirement. For instance, when it comes to luxury goods, solely a marginal number of purchasers can afford the financial cost. Therefore, no matter how attractive and persuasive an advertisement is, never can it tempt people to make the same purchase. Most people cannot afford to upset the whole monthly budget just because of certain alluring ads.

Furthermore, when we talk of the latest fashions, all people do not wear the similar clothes because of ads. If people wear jeans, it is because jeans are comfortable, and in today's fast life people need comfortable clothes. Nowadays, everyone knows that only that fashion should be followed which suits them. If adverts show celebs in flared pants, those who are not blessed with a good height would surely not follow them.

To sum up, from what has been analyzed above, it is concluded that advertisement cannot dominate the market trends as all people have different requirements, different material wealth and different choices. If at all there are any similarities, they are very short lived.

Plan followed:

Intro:

Para 1: Ads have short-term effects

Para 2: People have to see their pockets too

Para 3: Similarity is not because of ads. It is because of comfort.

Conclusion:

321. A large number of advertisements nowadays are targeted at children. Many people say this has negative effects on children and should therefore be banned. To what extent do you agree or disagree?

It is believed by some that adverts target vulnerable children and so should be barred. While ads do have some negatives, we cannot ban advertisements because they serve a lot of useful purposes as well.

Admittedly, in sensitive areas such as the toy industry, some censorship should be there to limit children's access to excess advertisement. This is because children under a certain age lack ability to make wise judgment as to what they really want. They are attracted by colourful pictures on advertisement and swayed by misleading information. So, they pester their parents to buy those things and this can upset the budget of many families. Even the advertisements of fast foods are bad for children. Children cannot understand that the slim-trim models advertising McDonalds burgers hardly ever eat such foods themselves. They are attracted to fast foods and these are very detrimental for their health. Finally, children try to copy the stunts, which can be disastrous for them.

However, advertising provides us with information on new products. If it were not for electronic and print advertising, many products would not be bought. In this way, advertising provides an important service to manufacturers and some consumers. Additionally, it fuels the advertising industry, creating jobs for thousands of people. In this respect it has become the backbone of many economies of the world.

Furthermore, advertisements touch social issues. For example, when Amitabh Bachchan tells people to bring their children for pulse polio immunization, people listen. Then there are ads against female foeticide which are very informative. Advertisements also teach a lot about the country from where the ads come. This is because through satellite TV we can see ads from all over the world. When we see a Japanese advert of a lady in a kimono, we come to know about the traditional clothes of Japan.

To conclude, although there are some negative effects of ads, these have much more positive effects on the society as a whole. So, we should not ban advertisements.

Plan followed:
Intro – We cannot ban adverts because they serve a lot of useful purposes as well.
Para 1 – Some people's view – bad ads
Para 2 – Good points
Para 3 – More good points
Conclusion:

322. There is an increasing amount of advertising directed at children, which encourages them to buy goods such as toys and snacks. Many parents are worried that these advertisements put too much pressure on children, while some advertisers claim that they provide useful information to children. Discuss both views and give your opinion.

Advertisements mostly target vulnerable children, and so many parents are worried that their children are being wrongly influenced by ads. However, advertisers claim that they provide beneficial information to children. In the following paragraphs I intend to discuss both perspectives. I believe that parents worry is justified.

There are reasons why parents' worry about the harmful effects of ads is justified. Children lack abilities to make wise judgments as to what they really want. They are attracted by colourful pictures on advertisements and swayed by misleading information. So, they pester their parents to buy those things, and this can upset the budget of many families. Even the advertisements of fast foods are bad for children. Children cannot understand that the slim-trim models advertising McDonalds burgers hardly ever eat such foods themselves. They are attracted to fast foods and these are very detrimental for their health.

What is more, some ads show some stunts, and although it is written that children should not copy these stunts, children hardly ever read that part. In their ignorance, they try to perform those stunts and get hurt. For example, in my neighbourhood, one child tried to jump from one rooftop to the other after seeing the ad of Thumbs Up and ended up with a plaster on his leg. Therefore, parents are rightly worried.

On the other hand, those who say that advertisements provide beneficial information to the children, give their reasons as follows. For example, the advert of Colgate toothpaste, which tells that we should brush our teeth twice daily, is good for children. Then there are ads about health drinks such as Complan and Bournvita, which are good for children. Furthermore, advertisements also touch important issues, such as ads against wastage of water, ads for tree plantation, ads against wastage of electricity and ads for keeping the surroundings clean. All these ads are good for children.

To conclude, even though adverts enlighten children in some ways by providing useful information, these have detrimental effects on children and should have some regulations.

Plan followed:

Intro – Discuss essay intro
Para 1 – Parents view
Para 2 – Parents view
Para 3 – advertisers view   *Conclusion*:

323. Consumers are faced with increasing numbers of advertisements from competing companies. To what extent do you think are consumers influenced by advertisements? What measures can be taken to protect them?

To survive in the competitive market of today, every product has to be advertised. There is a huge impact of these ads on the people, which is both positive, as well as negative. However, measures can be adopted to protect the people from the negative effects of adverts.

There are many ways in which these ads are helpful. First, ads tell people about the new products and about the working of these products. What is more, the advertising industry provides jobs to many. Many models and other people make a living through this industry. Ads also touch social issues. For example, there are ads which aware people that they can stand up against domestic violence and female foeticide. Another big positive influence of the ads of today is the entertainment they provide. They are made so hilarious that one feels like watching them again and again.

On the other hand, the main negative effect is that advertisements promote consumerism. These ads can cause people to be dissatisfied with what they already have and make them want more. This longing for more leads to workaholism. People are prepared to work long hours, or even turn to crime to get these goods. Finally, ads can be very irksome at times. This is especially true of Internet ads. Telephone ads are also very irritating. When a person is driving or in an important meeting, the bell rings and disturbs everyone.

The solutions are not simple, as advertising is a very persuasive medium. It would be unwise to ban ads, as this would cause more problems than it would solve. However, advertisements, which make false claims, should be banned. Advertisements for liquor and those ads, which show stunts, should also be banned. Then there should be consumer awareness programmes. Consumers should be warned against too much consumerism. Celebs have a big role in selecting what products they should endorse. People, who follow these celebs would buy anything they say even without needing it.

To conclude, today people are influenced a lot by adverts, both in positive and negative ways. However, many steps can be taken to mitigate the negative influence of ads.

Plan followed:
Intro –
Para 1 – positive effects
Para 2 – advertisements have negative points
Para 3 – solutions are not simple
Conclusion:
Written by: Indroop Singh

324. Research shows that overeating is as harmful to people's health as smoking. Therefore, the advertisements of certain food products should be banned, as the ads of cigarettes are banned. To what extent do you agree or disagree?

It is true that excessive consumption of certain types of food is bad for human health, just as smoking is. However, I disagree that adverts of these food items should be banned just as ads of smoking are. A number of arguments surround my opinion.

There are many reasons for having a ban on smoking. The main reason is that smoking causes harm to the smoker as well as the non-smoker, who is in the propinquity of the smoker. Studies have proven that the passive smoker is even more at risk of lung cancer than the active smoker. This is because he inhales the second-hand smoke, emitted by the smoker. A pregnant lady, who is continuously exposed to these passive fumes, may give birth to a child with congenital defects. So, smoking harms the innocent non-smoker even more than the smoker. Therefore a ban on advertisements of cigarettes is justified.

However, a prohibition on ads of foods is simply unjustified. To begin with, there is little relation between the over consumption of a kind of food and its advertising. Ads just tell us about the various choices we have. I believe that taking care of one's health is an individual's responsibility, and also is a right to freedom of choice. Also, it has been found through a research, that taste is the number one factor, when deciding what to eat. So banning ads of food will not make a considerable difference to the consumption of unhealthy foods.

Furthermore, advertising of food items should also not be banned, because ads are vital for any country's economy. Businesses thrive on ads, and if ads are banned they will go into bankruptcy. Another important reason against banning is that it would be very difficult to decide which food item to ban, and which not to.

To sum up, a ban on adverts of certain food items is not a good way to battle against overeating. Overeating can also not be likened to smoking, as overeating does not harm the bystanders, as smoking does.

Plan followed:
Intro: Disagree
Para 1: Reasons for ban on ads of smoking
Para 2: Reasons for not banning food items
Para 3: More reasons for not banning food items
Conclusion:

325. *Advertising encourages consumers to buy in quantity rather than promoting quality. To what extent do you agree or disagree?*

It is believed by some that adverts promote bulk buying and do not focus on the quality of products. While advertisements do lure people to do excessive purchasing, I believe that these commercials also promote quality.

Admittedly, advertisements make people pile up things in the home, which they may never ever use. For example, the one-on-one schemes, which those companies promote just to sell their old stock in bulk, lures us. For example, recently, I bought three pairs of jeans of Levis brand because there was a two-on-one offer. What I did not realize then was that the designs were outdated and defective. Now those jeans are just occupying space in my almirah.

Moreover, because of advertisements, sometimes people buy what tempts them without the insight of what they need actually. Impressive images, videos, or captions are bound to leave an imprint. For example, media is flooded with the advertisements of beauty products and they all claim to make the user fairer in a few days. Women, and these days, even men are crazy about these things and buy these things even without consulting their dermatologist.

However, advertisements aware people of all the latest facilities and trends and give them the chance and opportunity of choosing from the wide range of products available. Advertising links producers and consumers by providing relevant information of the latest products and services. Thanks to advertising, people know that there are so many nice things available. Moreover, an overwhelming majority of consumers are sensible enough to consider their options before they decide on a particular item.

To conclude, adverts promote quantity but they tell about quality too. The onus lies on people to look into our real needs and not be swayed by adverts.

Plan followed:
Intro – Agree with a concession
Para 1 – How ads promote quantity
Para 2 – How ads promote quantity
Para 3 – How ads give all good points of things and services
Conclusion: reiterate opinion

326. If a product is good or it meets people's needs, people will buy it. So advertising is unnecessary and no more than an entertainment. To what extent do you agree or disagree?

It is believed by some that advertising is not needed if the product is good, as people will automatically go for that thing. While it is true that a good product will sell even without any advertisement, I disagree that advertisements are unnecessary and just a form of entertainment.

It is irrefutable that advertising provides us with information on new products. If it were not for electronic and print advertising, many products would not be bought. This is because, there is a flood of consumer goods in the market and consumers ask for those products which they have heard of or seen in the market. Therefore in the initial stages, adverts are necessary but later on only those products will sustain in the market which are really good. In this way, advertising provides an important service to manufacturers and some consumers.

Additionally, the advertising industry creates jobs for thousands of people. In this respect it has become the backbone of many economies of the world. Jobs are also created in the manufacturing industries because of adverts. As demand increases, mass production has to be done and therefore more and more people are employed.

Furthermore, advertisements touch social issues. For example, when Amitabh Bachchan tells people to bring their children for pulse polio immunization, people listen. Then there are ads against female foeticide which are very informative. Advertisements also teach a lot about the country from where the ads come. This is because through satellite TV we can see ads from all over the world. When we see a Japanese advert of a lady in a kimono, we come to know about the clothes of Japan.

Summing up, adverts are not just a form of entertainment but they serve many other purposes as well. Even the good products need propaganda in today's competitive market.

Plan followed:

Intro – I disagree that advertisements are unnecessary and just a form of entertainment.
Para 1 – In the initial stages, adverts are necessary but later on only those products will sustain in the market, which are really good
Para 2 – Good points
Ads provide jobs
Para 3 – More good points
Ads touch social issues
Ads are educative at times
Conclusion: adverts are not just a form of entertainment but they serve many other purposes as well

327. Because of the global economy, many goods including what we use as daily basics produced by other countries have to be transported for a long distance. To what extent do the advantages outweigh the disadvantages?

Globalisation has revolutionized our world in many aspects. Now, we do not belong to a big planet Earth. We belong to a small global village. Everything is available everywhere. There are many advantages and disadvantages of transporting goods over a long distance. In my opinion, the pros outweigh the cons.

On the positive side, transporting goods over a long distance gives us a lot of choices. We can taste a variety of fruits and vegetables from all parts of the world. For example, about ten years ago, we hardly saw the kiwi fruit, which is from New Zealand. But, now it has a place on every fruit stand. Earlier, we had very few shoe brands like Bata and Carona, but now the market is flooded with Reeboks, Nike, Adidas and other foreign brands.

Secondly, many people get employment in the import and export field. Small businesses have a chance to expand globally and it increases the overall economy of the country. Finally, it helps in developing good relations between countries, which helps in international cooperation and peace. If countries are dependent upon one another for economic success, then they would not go against each other.

On the other hand, importing goods can have a negative effect on local culture. For instance, Indians used to give a lot of importance to the family meal, wherein all the members sat around the table and conversed with each other over dinner, but the young generation is going for fast foods and prefer to eat alone. Secondly, the diversity is being lost and everyone is wearing similar clothes, eating similar food, watching same TV programs and listening to same music. This is making the whole world dull and boring. Another major disadvantage is of pollution. When goods are transported thousands of miles by road, sea and air, it increases pollution from exhaust fumes.

To conclude, importing goods has both merits and demerits but the benefits outweigh the drawbacks.

Plan followed:
Intro: In my opinion, the advantages outweigh the disadvantages
Para 1: benefits
Para 2: More benefits
Para 3: Disadvantages – loss of culture and pollution
Conclusion: importing goods has both merits and demerits but the pros outweigh the cons.

328. Differences between countries are barely evident these days. Everyone in the world is wearing the same brands and watching the same TV channels and movies. Do you think it is a positive or a negative development?

It is irrefutable that because of globalization, similarities between countries are more obvious these days than in the past. In many ways people around the world are becoming more and more similar. While there are a few drawbacks of this similarity, the advantages are much more.

The main disadvantage of global similarities is that national identities are disappearing and diversity is being lost. People eat the same food, watch the same TV programmes, listen to the same music and wear the same clothes. For instance, the international outlets like Reebok, Nike and Levi's can be seen everywhere. Food outlets like MacDonald and Starbuck's etc. can be seen in almost all corners of the world. People have also started speaking one language, English, in many parts of the world. So, this lack of diversity is making the whole world dull and boring.

On the other hand, the main advantage of this change is that communication is much better nowadays, as people understand other cultures much better and have become more open in their outlook of life. This has resulted in more business and cultural contacts among different nations. Multinational companies have opened in many parts of the world providing jobs to thousands of people, thereby improving the economies of developing countries.

Moreover, I believe that nations are as different as they were ever in the past. Cultural identity is based on far more than just the films people watch or the clothes they wear. For example, in India people may wear any clothes, but they respect their elders and never call them by their name. In the west, it is acceptable to call anyone by name. In fact, after knowing about other cultures, people learn to respect their culture even more. So, some very deep-rooted national identities will always be there.

To conclude, similarities among people and their lifestyles cannot be denied. However, the similarities we see today are only on the surface. Total loss of national identities can never take place. Therefore, this situation is largely positive.

Plan followed:
Intro:
Para 1: Why it is negative
Para 2: Why it is positive
Para 3: Why the similarities are only superficial
Conclusion:
Similar: *Due to developments in science and technology, lifestyles of people across the world are becoming more and more similar to each other. Do you think this a positive or a negative development?*
Similar: *Many people go abroad to see what other countries look like. However, the places all around the world are looking more and more similar. What do you think is the cause of this similarity? Do you think the advantages of this effect outweigh the shortages of it?*

329. As we are facing more and more problems, which affect the whole planet, good relationships between different countries are becoming more important than ever before. To what extent do you agree or disagree?

It is irrefutable that nowadays the whole world is facing problems, such as environmental problem, terrorism, poverty and diseases. In my view, countries cannot solve these problems on their own and governments of different countries must cooperate to fight these problems.

To begin with, the environmental problems are affecting the whole world equally and need joint efforts to be ameliorated. It is a bitter truth that the Earth is facing the problem of global warming and if the whole world does not unite to fight this problem, then the day is not far when the whole Earth will become a boiling pot and life would not be possible here. The 2015 climate conference (COP21), was held in Paris in which many countries have pledged that they would take steps to bring down the global temperature by 2°C before 2025.

Furthermore, there are problems like terrorism, which are having a detrimental effect on our society. There are various global organizations, which are working towards eradicating these issues but it cannot be possible without trust and harmony between different nations. If all countries pledge not to shelter any terrorists, only then the terrorist activities will come to a halt and all societies will become pleasant places to live in.

What is more, the economic issues need to be dealt globally. The economic events in one region may affect many others. For example, the recession in the US in 2008, led many Indians to become jobless, as they were working for the US companies. Another befitting example would be the corona virus pandemic of 2019-20, which has shattered the economies worldwide. All nations had to work together to curb the situation. That is why all nations realize the importance of maintaining good relations.

Summing up, good relations between different countries are absolutely necessary nowadays to solve the critical issues, which the whole world is facing.

Plan followed:
Intro: Agree
Para 1: To begin with, take environmental problems – Kyoto protocol
Para 2: Talk of problems like terrorism, which cannot be handled alone
Para 3: In poor countries many people are suffering from starvation and poverty, which can harm the neighbouring richer nations – so cooperation needed
Conclusion: Reiterate opinion

Similar essay
Some people say that some urgent problems in modern society can only be solved with international cooperation. To what extent do you agree or disagree?

330. Many different countries have most shops and products as the same. Some consider it a positive development, whereas others consider it negative. Discuss both sides and give your opinion.

It is indubitable that globalization has ushered in an era of similarities. People are divided on whether these likenesses are good or bad. This essay intends to analyze both perspectives. I, personally side with the former view.

Those who say that the similarity in shops and products is negative, give their reasons as follows. Firstly, these similarities are diluting the national identities and diversity is disappearing. It is well known that diversity adds spice to life. Unfortunately, malls in any country have the same showrooms of the same brands that there is no charm of going anywhere for buying something unique. Another big demerit of all products being available everywhere is that the local businessman cannot compete with the international giants and is therefore going into oblivion.

On the other hand, the main reason why some people say that having similar shops and products is a positive development, is that people have more choices, as now everything is available everywhere. Earlier, only locally made products were available, but now people are able to enjoy things from all over the world. For instance, earlier there were only two popular brands of shoes available in India, which were Bata and Carona, but today there are Reebok, Nike, Adidas, Puma and so many more. Therefore, in this regard, having similar shops and products is a positive thing.

I believe that people are becoming aware of other cultures and lifestyles through these products. They are becoming tolerant of each other. They are adopting the best points of each culture, and as a consequence a global culture is emerging. Another benefit of this similar situation is that relations between countries are improving. For instance, India exports tea and iron ore to other countries, and imports automobiles, refrigerators and televisions etcetera. It is but obvious that countries, which are linked by trade, cannot afford to go against each other.

To sum up, similarity in shops and products has its dark and light side, but the pros definitely edge over the cons.

Plan followed:
Intro: Discuss essay intro
Para 1: One view
Para 2: Other view
Para 3: Our view
Conclusion:

331. Some developing countries invite large foreign companies to open offices and factories in order to help their economy. However, some people feel that foreign companies should be shut out and instead the government should help the local companies to contribute to the economic growth. To what extent do you agree or disagree?

Some people assert that the government should encourage local businesses and not invite Multinational Companies for developing the economy of the nation. However, I disagree with the given statement that MNC's should be shut out. I believe that the local companies alone cannot lead to sufficient development, and MNC's are indirectly benefiting the local companies also.

There are many advantages of MNC's. To begin with, these provide employment, which usually pays better than other available opportunities. What is more, they train local labour with more sophisticated techniques, which in the long run bring benefits to the host country. They also raise the growth rate of host nation by introducing new investment and new technology. To add to it, they promote efficient production and bring a broader range of products to the widest possible market.

Furthermore, such MNC's promote improvement or development of various supporting industries or complementary industries. For example, if an MNC opens in a place, then many businesses open in the neighbourhood, which cater to the workers working in these MNC's. In this way, these MNC's stabilize and stimulate local economies, and raise standards of living.

Another important advantage of MNC's is that they induce their local rivals to become more innovative and competitive. For instance, it is a well-known fact that Indian company Videocon has improved its standard to compete with MNC's such as Samsung and Sony. Finally, these companies promote positive values, such as diversity, and equality for women. They also create an environment of nonviolence and international cooperation.

To conclude, MNC's are very essential for the development of the developing countries. So, the governments of developing countries should promote them.

Plan followed:
Intro: I firmly believe that MNCs are good
Para 1: advantages of MNCs
Para 2: More advantages
Para 3: more advantages of
Conclusion:

332. Multicultural societies, in which there is a mixture of different ethnic peoples, bring more benefits than drawbacks to a country. To what extent do you agree or disagree?

Some people believe that multicultural communities with people from different ethnicities living together brings more benefits than drawbacks. I also agree that despite the few drawbacks of multicultural societies, these societies are better to live in.

Admittedly, there are a few drawbacks of multiculturalism. Firstly, multiculturalism may lead to conflicts and tensions as there are always a few who believe that their way of living is the only right way. When the government fails to control such outliers, it may lead to violence against certain communities. Secondly, if the communities in the society speak different languages, the language barrier may lead to social isolation. It is important to speak the same language to make friends and integrate into the society. If people do not have sufficient knowledge of the local language or are unwilling to learn it, they might find it impossible to become a part of the society.

However, the main benefit of multiculturalism is that it makes people broad minded. In other words, it makes people more accepting of other cultures. It is important to realise that there are different ways people can live their lives and living and growing up in a multicultural society brings that realisation. Another benefit of multicultural societies is the opportunity to learn and practice multiple languages. Schools in such regions offer multiple languages and children are also more likely to find partners to practice a language besides their mother tongue.

Finally, a multicultural society leads to increased confidence levels in minorities. Often, people belonging to minorities do not mix up with other communities because they fear getting attacked or discriminated against. In multicultural societies, minorities are more likely to feel more secure and confident and do not fear being prejudiced against. People of a multicultural society are cosmopolitan in their outlook and embrace each other's culture happily.

In conclusion, while there are certain downsides to living in a multicultural society, the benefits definitely outweigh the drawbacks.

Plan followed:
Intro: agree
Para 1: Disadvantages of multicultural societies
Para 2: Advantages
Para 3: More advantages
Conclusion: Reiterate opinion

Written by: Indroop Singh

333. These days the number of companies operating at multinational level has increased. To what extent are they responsible for the local communities in which they are located?

Multinational Companies have opened across the globe. These corporate houses are having environmental, social and economic impact on the host countries. Therefore, I firmly believe that they should give back something to the local communities in which they operate. I believe that only if they will do so, they will sustain in the long run.

To begin with, these MNC's should shoulder social responsibilities. All MNC's should abide by the law, and never make profit by unethical means. In times of natural disasters, business houses are supposed to make generous donations and set an example. This would be a win-win situation for the business houses and local communities. When any business house donates for charity, the media spreads a word about their efforts and they get advertisement for free. These business houses do not need to spend extra for their adverts.

Secondly, these businesses should also fulfil economic responsibilities. These can provide a number of job opportunities, which can greatly reduce the pressure of social unemployment. These corporate giants can also spend on the beautification of local areas. For example, in my hometown, many parks and roundabouts are maintained by the textile, sugar and starch mill in my hometown. Providing scholarships to poor, meritorious students is another way these enterprises can take social and economic responsibility.

Furthermore, MNC's should also bear environmental responsibility by doing waste minimization and pollution prevention. Indeed, it is argued that these corporate houses should go beyond this and embrace tomorrow's clean technology. For instance biofuels can be used in place of conventional fossil fuels.

To sum up, MNC's are thriving on the local communities. Therefore, these should bear the responsibilities of these communities.

Plan followed:
Intro
Para 1: Social responsibilities
Para 2: economic responsibilities
Para 3: Environmental responsibilities
Conclusion:

334. The spread of multinational companies and the increase in globalization produce positive effects for everyone. Do you agree or disagree?

It is believed by some that MNC's are beneficial for everyone around the globe. I strongly disagree with this viewpoint. I believe that MNC's are in fact damaging the quality of life.

My first argument relates to their products. Supporters of globalization would argue that multinational companies produce high quality goods available to most people. While this may be true to some extent, it also means we have less choice of products to buy. When powerful multinational companies invade local markets with their goods, they often force local companies with fewer resources to go out of business. In consequence, we are obliged to buy multinational products whether we like them or not.

Secondly, it is sometimes said that MNC's and globalization are making societies more open. This is true to some extent but the fact cannot be ignored that as a result the human race is losing its cultural diversity. If we consumed different products societies all over the world would be more varied. This can be seen by the fact that we all shop in similar multinational supermarkets and buy identical products wherever we live.

Thirdly, defenders of multinational companies often point out that they provide employment. Although this is undoubtedly true it also means we have become more dependent on them, which in turn makes us more vulnerable to their decisions. When, for example, a multinational company decides to move its production facility to another country, this has an adverse effect on its workers who lose their jobs. What is more, the jobs MNCs provide are not paid as much as they have to pay for similar jobs in their country. So, in fact they are exploiting workers of poor nations.

To summarise, multinational companies do have their benefits, but they also have their drawbacks, and they benefit not everyone.

Plan followed:
Intro: Disagree
Para 1: First point of the statement with my refutation – relating to more variety
Para 2: Second point of the statement with my refutation – relating to loss of cultural diversity
Para 3: Third point of the statement with my refutation – relating to Employment
Conclusion: multinational companies do have their benefits, but they also have their drawbacks and they benefit not everyone

335. The speeding up of life in many areas such as travel and communication has negative effects on society at all levels - individual, national and global. To what extent do you agree or disagree?

It is irrefutable that the IT revolution and faster means of travel have affected society at all levels. However, I disagree that all these effects are negative. The society has also benefited enormously from this speeding up of life which in other words we can say globalization.

At the individual level, we have more choices, more opportunities to travel, better job prospects and more awareness and tolerance of other cultures. Due to better communication, people are connected with their near and dear ones and distances are no longer a barrier. There has been a fall in face-to-face communication but the social network of friends that the young generation of today has is far more than ever before in the history of mankind.

At the national level, countries are getting closer and the boundaries are disappearing. Because of this fast era of today, nations are developing strong bonds doing successful trade with each other. The rich nations are opening Multi-National Companies in developing countries and thus providing job opportunities to millions. This is narrowing the gap between the rich and the poor. No doubt the people working in such companies are underpaid but it is definitely better than being unemployed. Because of this the economies of the poor countries are improving.

At the global level, nations are joining hands to fight evils such as poverty, disease, terrorism and global warming. Who has not heard of the Kyoto Protocol? The major feature of the Kyoto Protocol is that it sets binding targets for 37 industrialized countries and the European community for reducing greenhouse gas (GHG) emissions.

To conclude, the accelerating pace of life has both negative as well as positive effects. However, the positive effects are much more than negative effects.

Plan followed:
Intro: I disagree that all these effects are negative
Para 1: Benefits at individual level
Para 2: Benefits at national level
Para 3: Benefits at global level
Conclusion: the accelerating pace of life has both negative as well as positive effects. However, the positive effects are much more than negative effects

336. Some people think the increasing business and cultural contact between countries brings many positive effects. Others say it causes the loss of national identities. Discuss on both sides and give your opinion.

Globalisation has resulted in more business and cultural contacts among different nations. Some people hold the opinion that globalisation is advantageous, whereas others think it is diluting national identities. In this essay, I will discuss both perspectives. I believe that this connection between countries is very beneficial.

There are many reasons why some people see the good side of globalisation. To begin with there are more jobs because of globalisation. Multinational companies have opened in many parts of the world providing jobs to thousands of people. Secondly, there is more efficient trade between different countries around the globe thereby improving the economies of developing countries. What is more, today people have more choices of products because of globalisation.

On the other hand, those who say that national identities are being lost, give their reasons as follows. Firstly, people eat the same food, watch the same TV programmes, listen to the same music and wear the same clothes. They have also started speaking one language, English, in many parts of the world. In fact, English has become the lingua franca today. That is why they say that the whole world is looking similar and the diversity is being lost. They also say that weak cultures are on the verge of extinction.

I believe that cultural identity is based on far more than just the films people watch or the clothes they wear. For example, Indians may wear any clothes, but they never take the names of elders and always address them with respect. In the west, it is quite okay to call anyone by name. In fact, they appreciate it more. I believe that after knowing about other cultures, people learn to respect their culture even more. So, some very deep-rooted national identities will always be there.

To conclude, there are many advantages of increasing trade and cultural contact among nations. Whatever similarities seen today are only on the surface. Total loss of national identities can never take place.

Plan followed:
Intro: This situation has both pros and cons, which I shall discuss in the following paragraphs
Para 1: One view
Para 2: Other view
Para 3: Own view
Conclusion:

337. The food travels thousands of miles from farm to consumer. Some people think it would be better to our environment and economy if people ate only locally produced food. To what extent do the advantages of importing food outweigh the disadvantages?

Nowadays, supermarkets are stocked with food products from around the world. Some individuals are of the opinion that this imported food has detrimental effect on our economy and culture and it would be better if people ate only the local produce. Certainly, the disadvantages of imported food outweigh the advantages.

Admittedly, transporting food over a long distance gives us a lot of choices. We can taste a variety of fruits and vegetables from all parts of the world. For example, about ten years ago, we hardly saw kiwi fruit, which is from New Zealand. But, now it has a place on every fruit stand. Secondly, many people get employment in this field. Small farmers have a chance to expand globally and it increases the overall economy of the country. Finally, it helps in developing good relations between countries, which helps in international cooperation and peace.

However, importing food can have a negative effect on local culture. This can be seen in countries such as India where imported food has become more popular than traditional, local produce, eroding people's understanding of their own food traditions. Although some would claim that this is a natural part of economic development, in an increasingly global world, I feel strongly that any loss of regional culture would be detrimental.

A second major reason to reduce imports is the environmental cost. Currently, many food imports such as fruit, are transported thousands of miles by road, sea and air, making the produce more expensive to buy and increasing pollution from exhaust fumes. Despite the fact that trade in food exports has existed for many years, I am convinced that a reduction would bring significant financial and environmental gains.

In conclusion, I am certain that if people ate locally produced food, it would have environmental benefits. It would also benefit the local economy because, in time, people would prosper commercially as the demand for local and regional produce would remain high resisting the competition from overseas.

Plan followed:
Intro: Certainly, the disadvantages of imported food outweigh the advantages
Para 1: advantages of transporting goods
Para 2: Negative effects on local culture
Para 3: Negative effect on environment *Conclusion:*

Similar essays: *Air transport is increasingly used to export types of fruits and vegetables to countries where they cannot be grown or are out of season. Some people say it is a good thing, but other people think it cannot be justified. Discuss both views and give your own opinion.*

People can eat a wide variety of food of other regions. As a result they are eating a lot of foreign food instead of locally produced food. Do the advantages of eating foreign food outweigh its harms?

338. In many countries traditional foods are being replaced by international fast foods. This is having a negative effect on both families and societies. To what extent do you agree or disagree?

It is a fact that international fast foods and restaurants have eaten up traditional foods and cuisines. This has definitely had a detrimental effect on families and societies, which I will discuss in this essay.

There are a lot of damaging effects of international fast food on families. Firstly, the traditional art of cooking at home is taking a back seat. In this torrid pace of life, people are working till their death. They have no time to prepare and enjoy traditional home cooked food. Ultimately, they switch to an easy option of restaurants. Secondly, family bonds are getting weaker. For example, in earlier times all family members used to sit together and eat, and over the dining table they shared their happenings of the day. These fast foods are eaten alone mostly because they do not appeal to the palate of the older members.

Similarly, this trend has harmful effects on individuals. Undoubtedly, people are affected by health hazards like obesity and other diseases. Obesity is the root cause of many other diseases. Fast foods are rich in fats and salts which are not good for health. An obese person is more likely to suffer from diseases like hypertension and diabetes.

In addition, there are tangible consequences on society too. Broadly speaking, as people get inclined towards fast food and restaurants, local culture dies out. It is because traditional food is inextricably linked with culture. Also, if people are not healthy, the productivity of the nation will come to a standstill. Last but not least, fast foods promote use-and-throw culture, which adds to the problem of garbage dumps, contamination, pollution and eventually many diseases.

To summarise, it can be reiterated that international fast foods have carved their niche and traditional food has taken the backseat. Certainly, this has adverse effects on individuals, families and societies.

Plan followed:
Intro: I agree
Para 1: Effects on families
Para 2: Effects on individuals
Para 3: Effects on societies
Conclusion: reiterate opinion

339. Scientists say that junk food is harmful to people's health. Some say the way to ask people to eat less fast food is to educate them, while others say education does not work. Discuss both sides and give your own opinion.

It is believed by some individuals that people should be educated and made aware of the harmful effects of junk food, whereas others opine that education would not help in making people eat less junk food. In the following paragraphs I intend to discuss both viewpoints. I personally believe that educating people would be ineffective and so other methods should be employed.

The main reason why some opine that educating people about the harmful effects of junk food can help in reducing its use is that people do not actually know the negatives of fast food. So, if people are warned about their bad effects, they would eat less of it. Fast foods are rich in harmful substances such as fat, salt, sugar and preservatives. All these things can cause heart diseases, cancer, diabetes, and obesity. It is very important to reduce eating junk food for a healthy life.

On the other hand, those who say that educating people will not help, give their reasons as follows. Firstly, people would still consume junk food because it is very cheap, tasty and readily available. After a hectic day's work no one is in a mood to spend time in the kitchen . What is more, fast food outlets spend a lot to lure people with their ads. What people do not realize is that the celebs they use in these ads hardly ever eat such food themselves.

I believe that educating people would not help. It would be better if these fast food outlets were educated about making fast food healthier. Strict rules should be laid down against using trans-fatty acids and saturated fats. Whole wheat breads could be used instead of white breads. Use of preservatives should be lessened and juices should be served along with such foods instead of carbonated drinks.

To summarise, I would like to reiterate that educating people about the negatives of fast food would not help and thus, measures should be taken to improve the fast food and make it more nutritious.

Plan followed:
Intro: Discuss essay intro
Para 1: One view
Para 2: Other view
Para 3: Own opinion
Conclusion:

340. In many countries, people buy imported food rather than food produced locally. Why do people do that? How can people be encouraged to eat locally produced food?

It is true that the demand for imported food has increased over the past couple of decades. This essay intends to look into the reasons why people prefer imported over local produce, and also suggest ways to motivate people to eat local produce.

There are many reasons why people prefer imported food. First, when foods are imported, their quality is always checked, and only the best products end up in international markets. By contrast regulations on local food are less strict and quality control is ignored. Secondly, in some cases, overseas food imports are cheaper as compared to local food due to favourable growing conditions or foreign government support and subsidies.

In addition, globalization has created an awareness about exotic foods and thus created a demand that did not exist a few decades ago. For example, Italian pizza lovers prefer to buy imported cheese than local varieties to get the authentic taste. Importing food also gives people more choices as off seasonal fruits are also available. Finally, consumption of foreign foods has become a status symbol and people want to show off their wealth.

Many steps could be taken to encourage people to eat local produce. One step is to make people aware about the benefits of local food. For example, local food is fresher and more nutritious, as local food is harvested shortly after ripening. Government should also check the local produce for quality from time to time. If people get good quality local foods, they will be less likely to opt for foreign food. Last but not least, the government should subsidize the locally produced foods or impose taxes on imported foods, to make local options financially more attractive.

To sum up, there are many reasons why people opt for imported food, but some steps can be taken to reverse this trend.

Plan followed:
Intro:
Para 1: Reasons
Para 2: More reasons.
Para 3: Steps to make them like local food
Conclusion:

341. Demand for food is increasing worldwide. What are the causes of this? What measures can the international community take to make sure the supply of food is enough?

Meeting the food needs of billions of people is going to be a big challenge in the years to come. In this essay I will discuss the reasons for this growing demand for food and also suggest some steps, which can be taken at the global level to meet this requirement.

There are many reasons for the rising demand for food. The most prominent reason is the unprecedented growth in global population. The population was less than 2 billion in 1915, whereas today it is nearing 8 billion, and is expected to rise even further. The second major cause is the rising income of people in developing countries, which causes dietary changes such as eating more protein and meat. In addition, people do not care when they throw away food because it does not hit their pocket as much. However, increasing food waste does mean increasing food demand.

There are two main ways to address food shortage - decreasing food waste and increasing supply. To increase supply, farmers should be given assistance to produce more food on the land they currently operate, through intensive farming and use of technology like genetic modification and vertical farming. Similarly, through ethical factory farming, the production of milk and meat can be increased. The international community should ensure these expensive technologies are shared with the poor farmers in developing countries.

Food waste can be decreased through information campaigns to make people aware of the magnitude of food waste and the ways in which their food preparation and consumption habits can be changed. New technologies could be used to minimise food waste from storage and transportation. For example, genetic modification has been effective in increasing shelf life of vegetables and fruits and thus reducing their waste.

To sum up, there are many reasons for the increase in the demand of food all over the world, but many steps can be taken to meet the food needs of the world's population.

Written by: Kiranpreet Kaur

Plan followed:
Intro:
Para 1: Reasons
Para 2: Solutions
Para 3: Solutions
Conclusion

342. Some people support the development of agriculture, like factory farming and scientific creation of fruits and vegetables, while others oppose. Discuss both views and give your opinion.

Some individuals hold the opinion that factory farming and the creation of genetically modified foods are advantageous, whereas others assert that these are detrimental. In this essay I intend to discuss both perspectives. Despite the drawbacks of these modern agricultural developments, I support them as their advantages are far more.

There are numerous reasons why some people support scientifically created foods. First, there is greater yield in much less time. This is very important to meet the needs of the burgeoning population. Secondly, some genetically modified foods need little or no insecticides and chemical fertilizers and so genetically modified crops are beneficial for the environment as well. Similarly, some modifications increase the shelf life of fruits and vegetables and thus reduce waste and ultimately benefit the environment.

On the other hand, those who oppose genetically modified foods and factory farming, give their reasons as follows. The main reason is that genetic modification is considered unnatural and as it is relatively new, people are also concerned about its long-term harmful effects. Another reason is that only the rich countries can afford this technology and thus it is increasing the gap between the rich and the poor further. Factory farming is also considered inhumane as animals are tightly packed in cramped spaces and this may lead to many diseases.

In spite of harmful effects of recent agricultural advancements, I believe they are the need of the hour. Apart from the benefits mentioned above, by the addition of nutrients in food, genetic modification can lead to tackling issues like hidden hunger or deficiency of certain vitamins or minerals. Similarly, factory farming is necessary to meet the protein requirement in many developing countries. However, in both these technologies, there are risks involved like injections given to chicken in factory farming are building antibiotic resistance in people. So, measures should be taken to address these problems.

To summarise, scientific creation of crops and factory farming have their merits and demerits. I reiterate that genetic modification of food and factory farming are beneficial, but the conditions under which factory farming and genetic modification is done should be monitored nicely.

Plan followed:
Intro: This essay shall delve into the merits and demerits of these developments.
Para 1: One view
Para 2: Other view
Para 3: Own view
Conclusion:

343. It is known to all that the technological and scientific advances have made great changes to the range and quality of our food. Some people regard it as an improvement while others believe that the change is harmful. Discuss both views and give your own opinion.

Some individuals hold the opinion that changes in the range and quality of food brought about by technology are beneficial, whereas others assert that these are detrimental. In this essay I intend to discuss both perspectives. While I admit there are certain dangers associated with these new technologies, I consider their need to be far greater.

There are many reasons why some people say that these alterations in the range and quality of food are advantageous. Firstly, due to these technologies the yield of crops has increased substantially, and this increased yield is necessary as the land available for agriculture is ultimately limited. Secondly, these crops need little or no spraying with toxic insecticides, and as a consequence environmental damage like the contamination of soils and rivers is avoided.

On the other hand, those who assert that these changes are detrimental, give their reasons as follows. To begin with, they say that genetically modified crops are unnatural, and that by creating them their natural world is being altered. Another argument against scientifically modified foods is that these could constitute a health risk, for example by causing allergies or even by being toxic. The final objection is that crops, which are genetically modified to kill the pests, may also kill harmless insects.

I believe that genetic modification of foods is necessary despite the risks involved. My main argument is that these technologies are the only answer to our increasing food demand. The increasing population and growing land requirement for construction means that people have no option but to accept these modifications. Lastly, these technologies are the answer to many health problems like hidden hunger (deficiency in certain nutrients) since they can be used to add nutrients to food.

To conclude, although there are certain drawbacks associated with modern advancements in agriculture, I believe their benefits are far too many to disregard them.

Plan followed:
Intro: Discuss essay intro
Para 1: One view
Para 2: Other view
Para 3: Own view
Conclusion: GM foods should be encouraged
Similar essay: ***Food can be produced much more cheaply today because of improved fertilisers and better machinery. However, some of the methods used to do this may be dangerous to human health and may have negative effects on local communities. To what extent do you agree or disagree?***

344. Government needs to spend money to encourage the development of sport and art for school students, rather than to support professional sports and art events. Do you agree or disagree?

It is believed by some that the government should direct the funds allocated to professional sports and arts events towards encouraging sports and arts among school students. I believe that while promoting arts and sports in schools is important, it is as important to fund professionals in these fields.

On the one hand, there are reasons why the professionals sports events should be promoted by the government. Firstly, the professional sports bring name and fame to a country. When players bag medals in the Olympics, the World Cup and other such international competitions, it raises the name of the country in the whole world. Professional sports also boost the economy, as millions of spectators come to see and cheer for their favorite teams in the stadiums.

Similarly, government needs to spend on professional arts because these preserve and spread our culture in the whole world. If the governments do not support these artists, they look for other means of bread and butter, and so our art dies and with it our culture also dies. Furthermore, these cultural programs are recreational sources that help people relax and reduce stress after work. Entertainment is as important in human life as food, clothing and shelter.

On the other hand, it is necessary to motivate children to take up sports and arts. To begin with, children need to be fit and healthy, which can only be possible if they do sports. As it is children are leading sedentary lives, glued to the TV and computer screen in their free time. Moreover, future professional sportsmen can be recognised in their school time. Arts is also important as it brings out the creativity of children. Finally children are connected to the roots of their culture and tradition through the arts.

To sum up, it can be reiterated that spending on professional sports and cultural programs is as imperative for the governments as promoting sports and arts in schools.

Plan followed:
Intro: Disagree
Para 1: Reasons for promoting professional sports events
Para 2: Reasons for promoting arts events
Para 3: Reasons for promoting arts and sports in schools
Conclusion

345. Some people believe that to improve public health, governments should increase the number of sports facilities; others believe that it has little effect and need other measures to improve it. Discuss both views and give your opinion.

Some individuals hold the opinion that new sports facilities are needed to improve people's health, whereas others assert that governments have to come up with other ways to get people to live more healthily. I believe that the government should not only focus on sports facilities but also better nutrition to bring sizable improvement in public health.

The main reason given by people who think that the government should add more sports facilities is that the lack of sports facilities is the major reason for ill health and excessive weight nowadays. If a wider range of sports and fitness facilities (swimming pools, basketball courts and gymnasiums etc.) were available, then people would be more willing to spend time in these facilities to train their bodies and to improve their fitness, instead of living a sedentary life at home watching television, playing video games or using computers.

On the other hand, those who oppose the spending on sports activities, give their reasons as follows. They feel that such facilities may become a waste of time and taxpayers' money if people do not use them. They suggest that the government should take other measures like subsidizing healthier food and imposing a fat-tax on fast food. Food choices have a profound effect on health and poor diet has been linked to so many ailments like heart disease, diabetes, high blood pressure etc. People are less likely to buy fast food if healthier options are made cheaper or if a fat tax is imposed on processed food.

I believe that the government should do both – increase the number of sports facilities as well as ensure a good diet for its citizens. Exercise alone is not going to make people healthy if they keep eating highly processed junk food. Good nutrition coupled with exercise is an excellent recipe for good health.

To sum up, good health is a basic human need and healthy individuals lead to a healthy nation, and to promote good health it is important that the government focuses on increasing sports facilities as well as other measures like subsidizing healthy food.

Plan followed:
Intro: This essay shall discuss both views
Para 1: How the increase in sports facilities could help
Para 2: Why the government should be taking other measures like subsidizing healthy food
Para 3: Own opinion - should do both
Conclusion:

346. Some people think that the government should financially support national teams and individual men and women who represent their country. However, others argue that they should be funded by non-government sources (e.g. Business, scholarships, etc.). Discuss both views and give your opinion.

It is believed by some that the governments should fund the sports teams or sportsmen who represent their country, whereas others argue that they should be funded by the NGO's. In the following paragraphs, I intend to discuss both perspectives. Although there are some drawbacks of commercialisation, I consider that collaboration of business and governments is necessary.

There are many reasons why some people oppose the entry of businesses into sports. First, these sportsmen compete against opponents from all over the globe in international sports events for the whole nation. When they break a record or set up a new record in a world-class tournament, they inspire national pride and arouse patriotism among its citizens. Moreover, they also play a diplomatic function in competitions. They act as brand ambassadors for their country and their behaviour helps strengthen the relations between countries and also improve their nation's image.

On the other hand, those in favour of non-government sources funding the national sports teams argue that this would ease some burden off the government's shoulders. Moreover, these businesses are profit driven so they would provide the best coaching and facilities to their teams. Commercialisation also brings more exposure to the sport and if a major company sponsors a sporting event, it brings increased television coverage and in effect more viewership to the sport.

Despite the dangers of commercialisation, I consider that it is essential for the growth of sports. Besides the advantage mentioned above, commercialisation has opened new career opportunities for many youth and many of them now look at sports not just as a leisure activity but as a lucrative profession. The Indian Premier League, a commercial cricket venture is home to numerous rags to riches stories. It has brought recognition to many previously unknown players.

To sum up, the government and non-government organisations should both financially support teams and individual players to achieve the desired performance.

Plan followed:
Intro: In the following paragraphs I intend to delve into the advantages and disadvantages of both approaches.
Para 1: Why govt. should fund teams and individuals
Para 2: Why NGOs should fund
Para 3: Own view
Conclusion:

347. Nowadays, sport is becoming a business and more and more professionals and big companies are getting involved in sporting events. Do you think that it is a positive or a negative development?

It is irrefutable that today there is hardly any sporting event without a commercial venture or sponsorship. While there are some drawbacks of this trend, I consider the benefits to be far more.

There are many advantages of big businesses sponsoring sporting events. Firstly, commercialization brings media exposure for the sport. If a major company sponsors an event, it gets more television and news coverage. Besides increased viewership, it increases participation in sports among both children and youth. This increased participation is certainly beneficial from a health perspective as it reduces the risk of inactivity related illnesses like obesity and diabetes.

Secondly, commercialisation means better salaries for players and this has increased the viability of sports as a profession. In addition, because of increased funding, sporting teams and event organisers are able to provide better resources such as facilities, coaches and nutritionists to players. Finally, from the business perspective, sports can offer an excellent opportunity to popularise their product in front of a wider audience and in effect strengthen their brand image.

However, there are also a few drawbacks associated with commercialisation of sports. One major drawback is that it can affect performance as players get signed up to promote products and this takes away time from practice and training. In some cases players start focusing on their individual performance rather than the team victory to get better advertising contracts and deals. Furthermore, poor behaviour by players can also bring negative publicity for the brands and impact their sales.

In conclusion, while there can be some downsides of the entry of businesses into sports, I consider the benefits to be far greater.

Plan followed:

Intro: It is both – a positive as well as a negative development
Para 1: Positive effects –
Para 2: Negatives – match fixing – unethical means –
Para 3: non-glamorous games suffer
Conclusion: reiterate opinion

348. *Some people think sports and games are important for society, while others believe they should be taken as leisure activities. Discuss both views and give your opinion.*

It is believed by some that sports and games play a significant role in society, whereas others say that they should be just taken as playtime activities. This essay intends to delve into both views. I personally side with the former view.

On the one hand, there are many reasons why some people argue that sports are vital for society. Firstly, these draw people together. Playing together for a team against a common opponent brings people from different backgrounds together and their combined struggles and victories unify them. Even spectators gather and socialize while they watch events. Secondly, sports have a direct association with society's health and physical fitness. People belonging to societies where sports and physical activities are given more importance are more fit and agile.

On the other hand, those who assert that sports should only be taken as leisure activities give the following reasons. To begin with, they say that very few people actually play sports and majority only watch them. Watching sports for them is just like watching a TV show, a form of entertainment and nothing more. In addition, they believe that the role of sports in health and fitness is overstated. If sports did achieve the goal of making people fit and healthy, gyms and fitness centres would not have seen a substantial growth.

I believe that sports have a considerable role in today's world. Apart from their role in bringing together people and making people healthy, sportsmen are role models for the society. Youth are motivated by them to stay healthy and train harder. Sports events also generate revenue for the cities and many cities which have hosted sports events have seen considerable investment in public infrastructure and facilities.

To sum up, sports have a great role to play for societies apart from being just a source of recreation. In fact, the contribution of sports cannot be overstated.

Plan followed:
Intro:
Para 1: Importance of sports for society
Para 2: More importance
Para 3: Why some people say sports should be taken as recreational activities
Conclusion:
(Exam question 10/4/2021 1 pm BC)

349. Holding International games such as the Olympic Games is an exciting event. Some people think it has positive effects while others argue it is a waste of money. Discuss both sides and give your own opinion.

People are divided on the issue of hosting Olympic Games. Some individuals opine that it is advantageous to host such events, whereas others believe that there is nothing to be gained by hosting such events. This essay shall look into both arguments. Although hosting such grand sporting events can lead to certain problems, the immense benefits certainly make up for them.

Those who are in favour of hosting international sporting events, give their reasons as follows. To begin with, such events boost the economy. For example, during the Olympics many athletes, spectators, officials, sponsors and broadcasters come to the host country and spend money on hotels and restaurants. Additionally, many people get employment because of the jobs related to hosting such events. For instance, there are many new jobs in construction projects of stadiums and hotels and also in advertising related to such events.

On the other hand, there are many reasons why some people are opposed to hosting such events. The main reason is that the government of the host country usually allocates resources from other parts of the country to that part, because of which the development of the other parts suffers. Another disadvantage is that the tourism in the neighbouring area suffers, as all visitors are attracted towards the host city. Finally, cities or countries normally have to take considerable loans to pay for the expenses and many cities have fallen into endless cycles of debt as returns are not sufficient.

Despite the drawbacks of hosting such events, I believe that hosting such international events is beneficial in the long run. Firstly, the host country gets recognition in the whole world because of media exposure. It is also an opportunity for the host country and its people to know about the culture of other countries. Furthermore, the infrastructure of the host country develops at an accelerated pace. For example, when New Delhi hosted the Commonwealth Games, many flyovers and stadiums were built which are now being enjoyed by the local people of Delhi.

To sum up, it is clear that there are advantages as well as disadvantages of hosting such events, but the benefits far outweigh the drawbacks.

Plan followed:
Intro: Discuss essay
Para 1: - advantages
Para 2: advantage
Para 3: disadvantages
Conclusion: pros outweigh cons

350. Some people believe that sport competitions are a source of emotional stress for young people. Therefore, youth should be banned from participating in sport competitions. Do you agree or disagree?

It is believed by some that participation in competitive sports creates mental stress among the youth, and so they should be forbidden to take part in sports competitions. While competitive sports can cause some stress, I believe that sports competitions are very essential for young people and teach them important life skills.

Admittedly, there is a feeling of competitiveness that can cause some amount of emotional stress. Sometimes the pressures of winning are too demanding for the players and lead to deleterious consequences, like the win-at-all-cost attitude, not being able to accept failure, drug abuse for better performance, etc.

However, competition is not just limited to the field of sports. It is there in every aspect of life, starting with the school life, and continues onto when people start working. Sports competitions teach the youth how to overcome challenges, accept failures and keep trying to succeed, which helps them overcome other obstacles in their lives as well. Such competitions also promote skills like self-confidence, team spirit, developing strategies, overcoming obstacles, and so on.

To add to it, sport is a very popular career option for many youngsters. Through the state-level and national-level sporting competitions, the best of the talent can be identified. These youngsters can then move on to competing at an international level, and bring name and fame to the country. The government also provides job opportunities to the sport laureates. Furthermore, such competitions promote harmony, when people and teams from different cultures, countries and backgrounds compete with one another and strengthen relationships.

To sum up, the children and the youth should be encouraged to participate in sport competitions, to promote their overall development, and to inculcate in them the life skills, like self-confidence, sportsmanship spirit, feeling of fraternity and many more.

Plan followed:

Intro: Disagree with a concession
Para 1: Negatives of sporting competitions
Para 2: Benefits
Para 3: More benefits
Conclusion: Reiterate opinion

351. Some people think government should ban dangerous sports, such as skydiving and rock climbing. Do you agree or disagree?

It is believed by some that extreme sports should be prohibited. While sports such as bungee jumping, rock climbing and skydiving can be risky, I do not support a ban on these sports.

Admittedly, extreme sports can be highly risky and sometimes fatal. Firstly, people may not be aware of the risks involved and do such sports without preparation. For example, while performing bungee jumping, cases of back injuries, rope-burns and even retinal detachment have been reported. More than that, if the participants become disabled, their whole families suffer with them. Therefore, government should warn citizens about the risks involved in these sports.

However, banning such sports is not the answer. To begin with, participation in these sports should be a matter of personal choice. People should have the freedom to pursue the challenges which they set for themselves, even though this may involve a level of risk that others might find unacceptable. A further point is that in statistical terms there is a low probability of injury in many so-called dangerous sports, and people are at greater risk carrying out everyday activities such as crossing the road or cooking a meal.

Another argument against banning is that then people would play these sports in hiding, and then these sports would be even more risky. After all, it is well known that forbidden fruits taste sweeter. Finally, those sportsmen who excel in such sports bring name and fame to their country. They break records set by others, and when they do so, the name of their country shines in the whole world. Instead of banning, the government should ensure that the companies or centres, which provide the facilities for such sports should meet the required, legal safety standards.

To sum up, although I acknowledge the hazards associated with dangerous sports, laying a blanket prohibition on such sports is not the answer.

Plan followed

Intro: Disagree

Para 1: Concession that these sports are risky

Para 2: Arguments against banning

Para 3: Arguments against banning

Conclusion: should not be banned but regulated

352. Some people believe that the fittest and strongest individuals and teams always succeed in sports. Others think that success in sports depends on mental attitudes. Discuss both views and give your opinion.

Some individuals opine that only those who are physically fit succeed in sports. However, others believe that a positive mental attitude is required for succeeding in sports. Both sides will be discussed in this essay. I believe that at the professional level, physical fitness is really important, but so is mental tenacity and willpower.

The main reason why some people say that fitness and strength is very important for success is that being fitter and stronger enables a person to go the extra mile and gives him an edge over his competitors. In many sports, for example in boxing, a physically superior fighter can sometimes overcome a significantly more skilled opponent through sheer exertion. This is the reason coaches also give so much importance to physical training.

On the other hand, those who say that players can succeed with a positive mental attitude and good game plan give the following reasons. First, they cite the examples of players who have succeeded despite physical shortcomings like short height. Secondly, they believe, in most team sports like rugby and football, skill and decision making assume more importance and, in some cases, overwhelm fitness. For example, in football a player can outsmart a physically stronger player through a creative pass.

I believe it is true that at the elite or the professional level, physical fitness is extremely important. If two candidates with similar skills meet, it is generally the one with superior physical abilities that comes out on top. However, it is also true that most sports are more than a one on one physical fitness challenge. Many sports, for example, require long hours of concentration and even a second of complacency can cost the team a match. I do not think it would be correct to consider either physical strength or mental tenacity more important than the other.

To sum up, I think to excel in sports no doubt physical fitness and strength have a role, but mental attitude is also very important.

Plan followed:
Intro: Discuss essay intro
Para 1: One view
Para 2: Other view
Para 3: Own view
Conclusion:

Written by: Indroop Singh (12/9/2020)

353. In the society, male sports are given more attention than female sports. Why is it so? Does this trend have a positive or negative impact on society?

Though they are slowly dissipating, gender-based disparities are evident everywhere in society, including sports. In this essay, I will attempt to identify the reasons why we give more importance to men's sports as compared to women's, and why it is not good for society.

The first reason why men's sports are given more attention is rooted in the manner in which sporting events have evolved. In the early days, sports were all about brute strength, whether it was wrestling, or bull fighting or sports using weapons such as sword fighting. Because of their physical built and consequent strength, men were naturally more adept at such sports. Thus, the focus was on men and men alone.

The second reason is related to the slow and gradual increase in women's participation in sporting events. Initially, this began with women from the more affluent, western world. In the 1900 Olympics, of the 1000 odd participants, only 22 were women. African American women, who have dominated women's sports in the USA, had to wait for the abolition of slavery before they could freely compete with others. Thus, interest in women's sports was limited in scope and appeal.

Finally, sports administration has been dominated by men. These administrators pay more attention to men rather than women. As a result, there is more publicity, news coverage and live telecast of men's sporting events. Prize money offered for men and women have also differed, and it was only in 2007, after prolonged discussions that the world's premier tennis tournament, Wimbledon, offered equal prize money to men and women.

It is my view that such a bias in favour of men has a negative impact on society. Gender discrimination in any form is regressive and harmful. Women constitute half the population. A society that eschews itself the opportunity of celebrating their sporting successes and drawing inspiration from their achievements is undeniably creating a negative impact upon itself. There are innumerable examples of women who have come through most trying circumstances to excel and achieve success.

To sum up, it is easy to see why male sports has more coverage than female sports and this is certainly a negative situation.

Plan followed:

Intro:

Para 1: First Reason   *Para 2: Second Reason*

Para 3: Third Reason   *Para 4: Negative impact on society*

Conclusion

Written by: Sudipto Mukherjee

354. Some people prefer to go to health clubs and gyms for health care, but some say that walking and climbing stairs are more effective. Discuss both and give your opinion.

It is believed by some that working out in gyms and health centres is better for health, while others believe that walking and climbing stairs can lead to better results. In this essay, I will discuss both perspectives. I believe that working out in health clubs and gyms is not only better than just routine physical activities, but also a necessity.

There are many reasons why some people prefer to go to health clubs and gyms. Firstly, the instructors in such places guide people depending on their level of fitness and age, which reduces risks of injury. For example, they make them warm up properly and then do the more vigorous or demanding exercises. Secondly, the increasing consumption of fast foods and fats mean that walking and climbing stairs is just not enough.

On the other hand, those who believe that health can be maintained by just doing simple day-to-day physical activities, cite the following reasons. Their main argument is that it is impossible today to find special time for going to gyms. To add to it they believe that walking and taking stairs is enough for a healthy body. Health centres and gyms are only necessary for those who need a perfect physique and those who care about their appearance more than their health.

I believe that going to gyms and health clubs certainly has an edge over just walking or taking the stairs. Apart from the reasons mentioned above, working out in gyms provides a more holistic workout. For example walking and taking the stairs are mainly cardio exercises whereas in a gym one can also do strength training using weights. Strength training increases muscle mass and bone density. Finally, people's life is so sedentary now that just walking and climbing the stairs cannot burn the required calories to remain healthy.

In conclusion, I believe that one cannot depend on just routine physical activities. Our increasingly sedentary lifestyles have made joining a gym or a health care centre a necessity.

Plan followed:
Intro:
Para 1: One side view
Para 2: Other side view
Para 3: Own view
Conclusion:

355. Health experts believe that walking is a good exercise for health. However, people are walking less nowadays. Why is this happening? How can people be encouraged to walk more?

Regular physical exercise is a vital part of maintaining our health and wellbeing, yet people are walking less these days. There are several reasons why people are walking less, but this situation can be remedied through effective measures.

There are many reasons for a decrease in the walking trend among people. The first reason is that everything is spread out and people live far from the places they need to go to like offices, grocery stores, their children's schools etc. Driving to these places is more convenient, time saving, and sometimes the only option. In addition, even if the place is nearby, people prefer driving to walking as they are busy with their demanding careers. Secondly, today cars are a status symbol and driving expensive cars is a way for them to show off their position in society. Finally, many people walk less because it is not safe as modern cities are not pedestrian friendly. In other words, because of lack of pavements and footpaths in cities, people have to walk on roads along with vehicles, which is very dangerous.

There are certain steps that can be taken to encourage people to walk more. To begin with, governments should redesign the cities and have pavements on sides of the roads for pedestrians to make walking safer. Restricting traffic speeds in the city centres and at major intersections would also make people feel safe. Also, more parks and playgrounds need to be built inside city limits so people can walk as a leisure activity. In addition, people should be educated about the potential health benefits of regular walking through health apps. These apps can also help people track how much they should walk every day for staying healthy. Last but not least, businesses can incorporate a walking culture at work by having more walk and talk meetings, organising charity walks, setting up team walking challenges and rewarding employees on reaching steps or milestones.

In conclusion, there are many reasons why people are not walking enough but certain steps can be taken to motivate them to walk more.

Plan followed:
Intro:
Para 1: Why people do not walk
Para 2: Steps to encourage them
Para 3: More steps
Conclusion

356. Some people think health care should be free for everyone. Others think that people should pay for their medical costs themselves. Discuss both sides and give your opinion.

It is a highly debated issue as to who should pay for healthcare. There are those who argue that the government should pay for it, while others think individuals should shoulder the costs. This essay intends to analyse both perspectives. Personally, I think that primary health care should be on the government, but tertiary health care costs should be borne by the citizens themselves.

The main reason given by those who say that it is the government's responsibility to make health care accessible to everyone is that people pay taxes and so they are entitled to get something back in return. In addition, a nation's prosperity very much depends on the contribution made by its citizens who are in good health. So, it is the onus of the government to see to it that all people enjoy good health, and that no one suffers for want of health care.

On the other hand, those who say that individuals should be responsible for their health care argue that the advanced medical and surgical treatments are very expensive. In other words, it is impossible for the government to provide free quality healthcare for everyone. Instead of depending on the government, people should take some health insurance or save in any other way with the tomorrow in mind. Moreover, if healthcare is free, people might not pay much attention to their health.

I believe that free primary medical treatment should be there for all. However, it would not be possible or practical for the government to provide advanced and costly treatment for everyone. For example, in a country like India which has a population above 140 crores, providing free healthcare is a herculean task. Rather than providing free advanced health care, the government should spend on healthy living and prevention of diseases, so that there is less need for advanced health care.

To sum up, it can be reiterated that basic healthcare costs should be borne by the government, and individuals should bear the cost of advanced medical care.

Plan followed:

Intro:
Para 1: One view
Para 2: Other view
Para 3: Own view
Conclusion: Reiterate opinion

357. *Some people think the government should pay for health care and education, but other people claim that it is the individual's responsibility. Discuss both views and give your opinion?(Canada April 2022)*

It is argued by some that the government should pay for medical care and education, while others think individuals should shoulder the costs. In this essay, both views will be discussed. Personally, I think that primary and secondary health care and education should be paid by the government, but people should pay for higher education and tertiary medical care.

On the one hand, the main reason why some strongly profess that it is the government's responsibility to provide free health care and primary education is that a country's prosperity and development directly depend upon its productive workforce. If the people are healthy and educated, they can not only better their lives, but also drive the country's overall economy and development. Another reason is that it is the best utilization for government's resources as education and health care have a multiplier effect on the economy.

On the other hand, those who claim that individuals should be responsible for their health care and education say that free education and health care makes people complacent. When health care and education are free, people do not take care of their health to the same level and students are also not as serious in their studies. Secondly, they argue that free food, water, shelter, transportation is better for society than free education and health care.

I certainly believe that at the basic levels education and health care should be fully funded by the government, but it is financially impossible to do so at the tertiary level. For developing countries with limited resources, free primary education and healthcare is the best bet to free people from the cycle of endless poverty. In a sense, this would enable people to be independent and capable of funding their higher education or tertiary medical care if need arises, themselves.

To sum up, it can be reiterated that basic health care and primary education should be paid for by the government, but the individuals should pay for advanced health care and education from their pocket.

Plan followed:
Intro: I think that basic health care and primary education should be on the government but advanced health care and higher education should be borne by the individual.
Para 1: One view
Para 2: Other view
Para 3: Own view
Conclusion: Reiterate opinion

Written by: Indroop Singh (13/9/2020)

358. Some people say that the public funds should be spent on promoting healthy living than on the treatment of people who are ill. Do you agree or disagree?

It is believed by some that more resources should be put into promoting a healthy lifestyle than on treating those who are ill. While taking steps to improve the life style of people can save a lot of government budget, I believe that some funds should also be reserved for treatment, as not all diseases are dependent on lifestyle.

Admittedly, diverting public funds on promotion of healthy lifestyle is important because many modern diseases are a consequence of people's lifestyles. If people were educated about the demerits of a sedentary lifestyle, many expensive health problems such as diabetes or heart disease could be prevented. Unfortunately, most medical doctors today do not have the time to, nor are they paid to, teach patients how to make these changes to their lifestyle through diet or exercise. The government can take the help of pervasive media such as TV and radio to educate people.

Furthermore, there are many diseases, which if diagnosed early through proper screening tests can be treated very easily. For example, cancer of the cervix can be diagnosed with a very simple, inexpensive test called the Pap Smear. If the government spends a little amount to provide such screening tests free of cost, then a lot of money needed for expensive treatments could be saved later on.

However, some budget has to be reserved for treatment also, because there are some diseases, which are not dependent on lifestyles, such as some cancers. Then, people also suffer from accidents. The recent corona pandemic has made it clear that even a healthy lifestyle cannot save people from certain diseases. When people are sick they want the best medical treatment possible, with access to the latest diagnostic equipment and expensive MRI scans. Therefore, the governments have to spend on treatments also.

To conclude, it would be definitely worthwhile to divert the health budget towards prevention of diseases, but at the same time funds should also be reserved for treatment of ill patients.

Plan followed:
Intro: Agree.
Para 1: First argument
Para 2: more arguments
Para 3: Some areas, which would still require funds
Conclusion: Reiterate opinion

359. Nowadays, people are consuming more and more sugar-based drinks. Why do they do so? Suggest measures to solve the problem.

Sugar based drinks have become increasingly popular in the last few decades, and this has led to many health related problems like diabetes and obesity. There are many reasons why the consumption of such drinks has increased and steps have to be taken to ameliorate this problem.

There are a number of reasons for the popularity of sugar-based drinks. The main reason is the aggressive advertising of such products on TV and social media platforms. These ads target children and teenagers as they are easily swayed. Especially when people see famous celebrities endorsing these drinks, they do not think twice before consuming such drinks. Another reason is that these sugar laden drinks and sodas are cheaper than healthier options like fresh fruit juices, milk and bottled water.

In addition, these drinks also complement the fatty spicy fast foods very well and are more appealing than plain tasteless water. So just as consumption of fast foods is increasing, so is the consumption of sugar based drinks. Finally, sugar is very habit forming and some drinks contain caffeine that further increases their craving. People with overwhelming work schedules often skip meals and instead drive their energy from these conveniently available addictive drinks.

Steps need to be taken to stop the excessive consumption of sugar based drinks. Firstly, parents need to be good role models and change their grocery habits. For example, they can swap sodas and processed ready-made juices with healthier drinks like coconut water. Children mimic their parents and if they are guided right, they tend to make healthy choices even when they are not at home. Secondly, the government can help by imposing more taxes on such drinks, so that people are discouraged from buying them.

To sum up, there are several reasons why the sugary drinks have gained popularity among the people. However, many steps can be taken to mitigate the health problems that have arisen due to regular consumption of these drinks.

Plan followed:
Intro: Problem solution essay intro
Para 1: Reasons
Para 2: Reasons
Para 3: Solutions
Conclusion:

360. Some people think that the government should make laws regarding nutrition and healthy lifestyle, while others think that it is a matter of personal choice and personal responsibility. Discuss both views and give your opinion. (12 Feb 2022, India)

Some people opine that the government should make laws and policies to improve the health of its people, while others say that there should be no regulation on what they eat and how they live. This essay intends to analyze both perspectives. I believe that people should make decisions about their own health and the government's role should be limited, to actively promoting healthy food and exercise.

The main reason given by those who believe that the government should intervene to improve people's health is that not everyone has enough knowledge about health. Moreover, people go for easily and cheaply available fast foods, which provide calories, but are bereft of essential nutrients. This increases the risk of diseases and therefore the government should formulate strict policies such as heavily taxing such processed fast food and sugary carbonated drinks.

On the other hand, those who believe that the onus of having a healthy lifestyle should be left to the individuals, give their reasons as follows. They say that the government cannot and should not force anybody to follow a healthy diet and exercise daily. It is people's right to eat what they wish and follow any lifestyle they want. The government should just make people aware about the dangers of an unhealthy lifestyle, and then leave it on the people to do what they wish.

I believe that the government should not make harsh laws about nutrition and health. Instead the government should educate people about the benefits of healthy living and physical exercise through banners, TV advertisements etc. Government can also subsidize healthy foods and increase the number of parks and sports facilities for its citizens.

To conclude, there should be no laws on what people eat and how they live, but the government should create awareness about the importance of good nutrition and exercise and incentivise healthy living by subsidizing healthy food options.

Plan followed:
Intro: Discuss essay intro
Para 1: One opinion
Para 2: Other opinion
Para 3: Own opinion
Conclusion: No harsh laws but governments should promote healthy lifestyles

Similar essay: *Some people think the government should ensure the healthy lifestyle. of people, but others argue that it should be decided by individuals. Discuss both views and give your opinion.*

361. Science tells there are activities that are good for health. However, some people still continue doing unhealthy habits. Why is this so, and what changes can be done?

People of the modern world are ignoring their health and still doing things that are detrimental for their wellness. This essay intends to look into the causes of this phenomenon and suggest some solutions to mitigate this problem.

The main barrier to healthy living is the lack of time in this fast-paced competitive era of today. People are so busy with their work, their homes, their children and other day-to-day tasks that they find no time to exercise or cook a nutritious homemade meal. Another reason why people find it hard to break a bad habit is the stress and strain of life. People indulge in excessive drinking and smoking because they feel that it calms them down and relieves their stress.

The first solution to bring a change is to make individuals realise that hectic schedules are no excuse for unhealthy lifestyles. For example, people could incorporate activities like walking/biking to work, taking the stairs instead of the elevators and working out during lunch breaks, without needing extra time. Similarly, meal preps on weekends and planning out meals for the whole week would not only reduce fast food consumption but also give them more time to work out during the week.

In addition, the government can take some steps to help people lead a healthy lifestyle. For example, governments should impose a fat tax on fast foods and subsidize fruits and vegetables to encourage people to eat healthy. Similarly, building new parks and sports facilities inside cities would give people easy access to them and they might exercise more. Finally, there should be strict rules and regulations for food outlets to provide healthy food without trans-fats and excess salts.

To sum up, it is true that people are doing unhealthy activities even after knowing they are bad for them. However, self-motivation coupled with government intervention can change their sedentary lifestyle and encourage them to eat better.

Plan followed:
Intro:
Para 1: Reasons
Para 2: solutions
Para 3: solutions
Conclusion

362. *People should look after their health as a duty to the society they live in rather than personal benefits. To what extent do you agree or disagree?*

It is believed by some that people should look after their health as an obligation to the society and not think about their own benefits. I, however, feel that compliance would be much more if people were to look after their health for their own interest, and the benefits to the society would automatically ensue.

There are many benefits to the people if they look after their health. To begin with, if people eat healthy and do regular exercise, they would not have to spend on expensive medical treatment and have more productive life. They can work better and enjoy all the good things that life has to offer. Moreover, if a person suffers from any infectious disease and takes timely treatment then he does not spread it to others. Later on he does not stand the chance of getting re-infected by other people.

Furthermore, if people looked after their health for personal reasons, they would do it with more zeal. Selfishness is a basic human nature, and people would be more willing to do something if it benefits them. So, adopting a healthy lifestyle would be observed to a greater degree if people know it is for their benefit.

Finally, if all people are healthy then the society would also benefit involuntarily. People are inextricably linked to the society. A healthy society means a more energetic workforce, which would in turn raise the level of society. Finally, by looking after their health, a lot of government budget, which it has to spend on providing healthcare would be saved, which could be used in other areas, such as better roads and public transport.

To sum up, people should all look after their health. It does not matter whether it is for them or the society. If they do something good for themselves, the society is benefited and if they do something for society, they are benefitted, but they will do something for themselves with more enthusiasm.

Plan followed:
Intro: Disagree
Para 1: benefits to the individual if he/she looks after his/her health
Para 2: as a part of society, we all have an obligation to the society.
Para 3: more on the view
Conclusion:

363. Some people say that the government should give priority to health care, whereas others say they should spend on other important priorities. Discuss both views and give your opinion

It is believed by some that the government should pay more attention to healthcare, while others argue that the government should focus on other sectors. This essay intends to analyze both perspectives. I believe that the government must not only focus on healthcare but also on education, as both are crucial for the progress of the society.

The main reason why some people say that the government should focus on healthcare first is that the rising number of diseases has made quality healthcare critical. The corona pandemic is the biggest proof that better healthcare preparedness is a necessity today. In addition, the productivity of any society depends upon the health of its members. People cannot contribute to their fullest if they are suffering from any disease.

On the other hand, those who say that the government should prioritize other areas like education give their reasons as follows. Firstly, they believe that education is the basis of all professions. Without good education, there can be neither good doctors nor good innovations in healthcare. Secondly, they believe that the benefits of healthcare are reaped later on in life, while benefits of education and good infrastructure help people in their early years, which are the most crucial.

I believe that healthcare and education are equally important. Governments cannot look at them independently. Without health people cannot focus on education and without education, there can be no quality medical and paramedical professionals. Both education and healthcare are important in their own way. For example, for the older citizens, healthcare is paramount and for the youth, skills and education are second to none.

To sum up, the allotment of governments' funds should equally go to healthcare and education since both are crucial in their own way.

Plan followed:
Intro: Discuss essay intro
Para 1: Advantages of spending on healthcare
Para 2: Other important issues
Para 3: More important issues
Conclusion:

364. Nowadays the football supporters behave violently. What is the cause? How can we solve it?

It is irrefutable that there has been an increase in violence by football spectators and fans in recent years. Many reasons can be attributed for their violent behaviour, but some suitable steps can be taken to address the situation.

The main reason of violence by football supporters is that football is a competitive, physical sport and its audience is also young and aggressive. The supporters of the teams form gangs, and they have strong emotional ties with their teams. Their teams losing results in frustration and anger that leads to violence. Secondly, sometimes football players themselves show unsportsmanlike behaviour, and that sets the same tone for the fans.

In addition, the influence of alcohol is one of the major reasons for the disorderly behaviour of football fans. Binge drinking is common on game days and drunk fans are more prone to physical and verbal altercations with other fans. Finally, the media is also a culprit in football violence. The language of war and combat employed by the media in covering football incites the young supporters to indulge in violence.

There are many ways to put an end to this violent and destructive behaviour by football fans. One way to limit football hooliganism is to limit alcohol consumption at football events. This can also be achieved by changing the match time to earlier in the day. Scheduling the matches in the morning or early afternoon would mean less drinking, less violence and more visibility for police. Another step that can be taken is to segregate the rival team supporters, so as to limit any chance of altercation between them. Finally, the media should be wise enough to play its role in such a way that it does not give air to hooliganism.

To sum up, football violence is a problem, but many effective steps can be taken to address the issue and prevent further mishaps.

Plan followed:
Intro:
Para 1: reason
Para 2: More reasons
Para 3: Solutions
Conclusion

365. Everyone should become vegetarian because they do not need to eat meat to have a healthy diet. To what extent do you agree or disagree?

It is believed by some that diets containing meat are dispensable in today's time. While a wholesome vegetarian diet offers distinct advantages compared to meat, I disagree that everyone should adopt a meat-free diet to be healthy.

Undoubtedly, there are many benefits of a vegetarian diet. To begin with, vegetarian diets are easy to digest, whereas meats can be difficult to digest. The fats in meat are saturated, which means they are unhealthy and contribute to higher cholesterol levels. Plant sources of food, on the other hand, are rich in fiber, complex carbohydrates, magnesium, folic acid, vitamin C and E, carotenoids and other phytochemicals. Dietary fiber helps prevent colon cancer, which is more prevalent in meat-eaters.

However, a totally vegetarian diet can be deficient in several nutrients including protein, iron, zinc, calcium, vitamin B12 and A, n-3 fatty acids and iodine. Although vegetarians can consume protein through legumes and nuts, these protein sources are incomplete. A complete protein contains the essential amino acids that your body needs, and animal products provide a complete protein. Many animal products are also high in iron and vitamin B12. Iron found in animal products is easier for your body to absorb. A deficiency in iron or B12 can result in fatigue. For women, who lose iron through menstruation, getting enough iron through their diet is important.

Furthermore, people who go vegetarian may have to take a lot of supplements, and would definitely need to put in a lot of effort to have a balanced meal full of essential macro and micronutrients. A purely vegetarian diet, which is not planned well, may prove very bad for health. People, who are non-vegetarian, can easily have a mix of vegetarian and non-vegetarian diet to remain healthy. They can cut down their meat intake to avoid the detrimental effects of a non-veg diet.

To sum up, I reiterate that although a vegetarian diet has several benefits, I differ with those who say that everyone should turn vegetarian to be healthy.

Plan followed:
Intro: Disagree
Para 1: advantages of vegetarian diet
Para 2: Advantages of non-vegetarian diet
Para 3: More advantages of being a non-vegetarian
Conclusion

366. Some people think that the government should subsidize fruits and vegetables to make healthy food cheaper. Others argue that tax should be set on unhealthy food. Discuss both views and give your opinion.

It is believed by some individuals that the government should subsidize healthy foods, whereas others say that the solution is in levying a 'fat tax', which means a tax on fast food. This essay intends to delve into both perspectives. I believe that making healthy food options more affordable would yield better results.

The main argument given by those who support 'Fat tax' is that unhealthy food habits have led to an increase in health problems. The health of the general public is not only an individual's responsibility, but also the responsibility of the government. In addition, the prime reason for the growing popularity of the unhealthy fast foods is their affordability and levying a tax would definitely impact its consumption.

On the other hand, those who say that healthy food should be made cheaper, give their reasons as follows. Firstly, healthy food options are expensive and many people cannot afford them. For instance, a glass of sweetened soda is cheaper than a glass of milk. Therefore, instead of making fast food more expensive, subsidies should be provided for nutritious foods. Secondly, implementing the 'Fat Tax' would not affect consumption much as people can prepare such products at home also.

I believe that taxing fast food would not help as people would still consume it since it has been seen that taste is the number one factor, when deciding what to eat. In most cases, when the government levies taxes on some unhealthy foods, people do not start eating healthy but shift to other more affordable unhealthy options. Finally, most scientists claim that lack of healthy elements in the diet has more harmful effects than consumption of sugary drinks or fast food.

To conclude, to promote healthy living, the governments should consider subsidizing healthier options over taxing the unhealthy ones, since it would have a considerably larger impact.

Plan followed:
Intro: Discuss essay
Para1:One side view
Para 2: Other viewpoint
Para 3: Own opinion
Conclusion: Reiterate opinion.

367. New research has shown that overeating has become a bigger problem in the world than hunger. What are the reasons for this problem? How can you solve it?

A few decades ago a major problem in the world was malnutrition and hunger, but today more people are suffering from problems like diabetes and obesity because of overeating. This essay intends to analyse the causes of this phenomenon and suggest solutions to mitigate the problem.

One of the main reasons why over-eating has become a global health crisis is the change in diet pattern. People today consume more fast-foods and sugary drinks and these contain more calories than healthier options like fruits and vegetables. In addition, these foods do not create a feeling of fullness as they lack essential nutrients like proteins and amino acids. Thus, even after eating, people feel that they can eat more. The second reason is that there is more stress today because of competition and other factors and there is a direct link between stress and overeating.

A third reason for overeating is that nowadays people eat while doing other things like watching TV or sports. Thus, people are more distracted while eating and hence they fail to register when they become full. The final reason is the influence of fast food advertisements and offers like one on one. Thus, people order more than they can eat because they believe they are saving money by doing so.

The dangers of overeating can be much more severe than hunger and thus many measures need to be taken to control overeating. The first step could be to avoid ready-made unhealthy and fast food and eat a more balanced and healthy diet. A nutritious diet would create a feeling of fullness and reduce overeating to a large extent. Secondly, people should have a separate time for meals and they should avoid doing other things like watching TV while eating. Finally, the government can impose fat tax on the fast food outlets. This would increase the prices of such foods and people will be discouraged to buy and eat such foods.

To sum up, although there are several causes of overeating, it is not too late to tackle the problem of over-eating becoming a health crisis.

Plan followed:
Intro: Problem solution essay intro
Para 1: Reasons
Para 2: Reasons
Para 3: Solutions
Conclusion:

368. *Now the machine is very complex, and a lot of difficult work is automated. Does this machine automation have more pros than cons?*

It is true that in recent years there has been a considerable advancement in robotics and automation, and many challenging tasks are now done through machines. Although there are a few drawbacks of the growing usage of machines, I believe the advantages certainly outweigh them.

The first benefit of automation is that it saves human lives. There are many dangerous jobs like mining, bomb disposal, sewage cleaning, where they have made human involvement redundant. For instance, in Fukushima robots were employed and are still being used to clean the nuclear fusion disaster. Similarly, in health care, many complex surgeries, which were earlier considered too risky, have been made possible by robotics, saving precious human lives.

Secondly, automation saves time, enabling people to enjoy and relax. For instance, many monotonous and repetitive works like washing, cleaning etcetera can be done by machines, thus saving people time, which they can spend with friends or family or on their hobbies. Finally, automation enables higher productivity and efficiency by reducing labour costs and errors. This not only benefits employers by increasing profits, but also consumers by providing cheaper, quality products.

On the other hand, the main drawback of automation is that it can displace human labour and lead to unemployment. In a way, this also leads to income inequality, benefitting the industry owners and hurting the employees. Another negative of machines is that they lead to dehumanization. Interacting with machines can never provide the same sense of satisfaction as talking to a human, as machines cannot empathise and understand our feelings.

To summarize, I would like to reiterate that while the increasing dependence on automation has some disadvantages, I believe that advantages are far more.

Plan followed:
Intro: Overall the pros outweigh the cons
Para 1: Advantages of machines
Para 2: More advantages
Para 3: Disadvantages
Conclusion: pros more than cons
Written by: Indroop Singh (example essay in video)

Similar: Some people think that robots are very important to human's future development, while others think they are dangerous and have negative effects on society. Discuss both views and give your opinion.

369. *Scientists believe that computers will become more intelligent than human beings. Some people find it a positive development while others think it is a negative development. Discuss both points and give your own opinion.*

Artificial intelligence is about designing machines that can think. Some take it as a blessing, whereas others take it as a curse. In the following paragraphs I shall discuss both viewpoints. I believe that machines turning more intelligent can be disastrous for the human race.

On the one hand, there are many reasons why some people think that intelligent machines will be a boon for humanity. Firstly, intelligent robots can be used where humans have limitations and find solutions to problems which have eluded human beings till now. To cite some examples, intelligent machines could find cures for diseases like cancer and AIDS. They can hasten our development and progress to unimaginable levels. What we see in science-fiction movies can become a reality in no time, if true artificial intelligence comes to life.

On the other hand, those who say that the development of AI is negative, give their reasons as follows. To begin with, if intelligent machine-robots replace human being's work then this would cause many to go out of work. Already machines have replaced humans in laborious and time-consuming work, but if machines become more intelligent, they might make human beings redundant. An implication of this can be seen in the form of driverless cars. Also, artificial intelligence systems like autonomous weapons in the hands of the wrong people can cause mass casualties.

Although AI may revolutionize life on earth, I hold the opinion that artificial intelligence can be very detrimental for our race. I believe that intelligence needs emotions and temperance to be good and it is impossible for AI to have emotions. Without feelings, it is very hard to predict what kind of future AI would bring and I am against leaving our destiny in the hands of machines.

In conclusion, I believe it is highly possible that an advanced AI may create a utopia, a perfect world, but it is also possible that it may lead human beings to their extinction. Hence, I am strongly opposed to the idea of human beings trying to create highly intelligent machines.

Plan followed:
Intro: Discuss essay intro
Para 1: Positive view
Para 2: Negative view
Para 3: Own view
Conclusion with own view.

370. There are social, medical and technical problems associated with the use of mobile phones. What forms do they take? Do the problems of mobile phones outweigh the benefits?

Mobile phone is one of the most important inventions that has brought people tremendous convenience and efficiency. Admittedly, if misused or overused, it may cause some social, medical and technical problems. However, if used judiciously, its pros far outnumber its cons.

The social problems of cell phones cannot be understated. People are busy on their apps and social contact is going down. Spending time with friends, family and stranger can strengthen the social bond, but smartphone apps and games are somehow making the social distances larger. Cell phones also keep people connected to their work, as a consequence of which, people fail to draw a line between their personal and professional lives, which causes stress and strain within the family, leading to spoilt children and broken homes.

There are many medical and technical problems concomitant with the use of cell phones. First, they emit radio frequency waves, which although are of very low frequency, can still have negative effects. Second, excessive use of cell phone can increase stress levels and affect the mental health of young adults. Moreover, the increased touching of the cell phones can harbour germs on the handset, which can lead to diseases. Network coverage may not be there at some places, which may cause too much stress. Charging issues, battery life and unwanted calls are some other technical glitches faced by the cell phone users.

However, despite all these negative issues, the advantages of cell phones have an edge over the disadvantages. Mobiles have helped people remain connected with the world from wherever they are. At the time of emergencies and calamities, they are one of the most used tools for supplying immediate help. Mobile phones also provide facilities like messaging, camera, recording and the Internet. Business transactions can also take place at any time of the day and family commitments can also be fulfilled while at work. Cell phones also serve as entertainment tools as many games can now be played and some phones have FM radio connection too.

To sum up, the advantages of the mobile phone far outweigh its disadvantages. Mobile technology definitely has brought a revolution and changed the way to work, to socialize and to entertain, but we must be more wise and responsible in using it.

Plan followed:

Intro: its pros far outnumber its cons.
Para 1: Social problems
Para 2: Medical and technical problems
Para 3: Advantages
Conclusion: the advantages of the mobile phone far outweigh its disadvantages.

371. Mobile phones have made life easier: anyone can use a mobile phone to answer/make work calls or home calls at any place 7 days a week. Do you think this development has more positive effects or negative effects on the individual and society?

Mobile phones have revolutionised the concept of communication. They have a big role in transforming the society into a 24/7 society. This development has its pros and cons but the advantages definitely outweigh the disadvantages.

On the positive side, mobile phones have simplified people's lives. Today, people are well connected with their family and friends all the time. Earlier, if a person was late from work, his family would be worried about him till he returned home safe and sound. Today, a person can inform his family of his/her whereabouts. Today, if something goes wrong with anyone's vehicle and he is stranded on the road then he can immediately call someone for help.

Nowadays, the shopkeeper does not miss an important customer just because he had to go home for five minutes for some urgent work. Even in offices which require fieldwork, a person can take advice from his seniors any time and from anywhere. Some businesses, in fact, thrive on the mobile phone.

On the other hand, cell phones can take away your calm and quiet. A person with a mobile phone cannot draw the line between work and leisure. If he does not answer the mobile phone or keep it switched off in his off-duty hours, then he is considered rude and if he answers, then his family life is in jeopardy. What is more, if he listens to a mobile phone while driving then he can cause accidents. Finally, the ads, which are shown on cell phones, can be very bugging especially when the person is in the middle of an important meeting.

Summing up, mobile phones actually make life simpler and more convenient. It is in our hands to know where to draw the line and use them to our benefit only.

Plan followed:
Intro: This development has its pros and cons but the advantages definitely outweigh the disadvantages.
Para 1: Positive effects on family
Para 2: Positive effects on business
Para 3: Negative effects
Conclusion: Reiterate opinion

372. The use of mobile phone is as antisocial as smoking. Smoking is banned in certain places and so mobile phones should also be banned. To what extent do you agree or disagree with this statement?

Although smoking and the nuisance of mobile phones are both antisocial activities, I disagree with a ban on cell phones. I believe that smoking does not have any good side to it and therefore, its ban is justified, whereas the cell phone has its own set of advantages and so should not be banned.

To begin with, smoking causes harm to the smoker as well as the non-smoker who is in the propinquity of the smoker. Studies have proven that the passive smoker is even more at risk of lung cancer than the active smoker. This is because he inhales the second-hand smoke, emitted by the smoker. Similarly, in public places, the cell phone can distract other people and divert their attention. For instance, in libraries, people can be easily distracted through ringtones of incoming calls or people talking over the phone loudly with their loved ones. Even in public places like hospitals, cell phones can easily interfere with the medical equipment and also irritate the patients waiting to see the doctor. Moreover, its usage in religious places can spoil the peace of those paying obeisance.

However, despite all the abuses of cell phones, one cannot deny the uses of mobiles. They are one's easily available help in case of an emergency. They also keep loved and near ones well connected. No matter where one goes, cell phones are the only hope of keeping families connected without any hassle. The SMS is also a convenient way to keep in touch with your loved ones when no one has the time for writing long letters. Mobiles are also a great source of entertainment. You can listen to songs, play games, get live cricket scores, market-updates and even the headlines. They are convenient, easily accessible and of great use.

Moreover, these modern devices are very important in this commercial and financial society. Therefore, the total banning of pagers and mobile phones in public places is not practical. It will cause inconvenience and the people would not be able to catch up with the modern trend of communication. Cell phones have become vital tools in today's world and blocking them in public places will result in a gross violation of personal freedom.

To sum up, mobiles were invented for our convenience and not to create nuisance. If used judiciously, wisely and with public etiquette, mobiles can be of great use. Comparing the cell phone to smoking and banning the cell phone would not be practical.

Plan followed:
Intro: Disagree
Para 1: why ban
Para 2: Why not ban
Para 3: Why not ban
Conclusion: reiterate opinion

373. The use of mobile phones should be banned in public spaces such as libraries, transportations, and shops. To what extent do you agree or disagree?

Mobile phone etiquette has become an important issue, with mobiles ringing at funerals, weddings, movies and plays. Therefore, some people advocate their prohibition in public places. Although cell phones can be a nuisance if used in public places, I disagree with a ban on these gadgets as they have many advantages.

Undoubtedly, using mobile phones in public places can distract other people and divert their attention. For instance, in libraries, people can be easily distracted through ringtones of incoming calls or people talking over the phone loudly with their loved ones. Even in public places like hospitals, cell phones can easily interfere with the medical equipment and also irritate the patients waiting to see the doctor. Moreover, its usage in religious places can spoil the peace of those paying obeisance.

However, despite all the abuses of cell phones, one cannot deny the usefulness of mobiles. They are very helpful in case of an emergency. They also keep loved and near ones well connected. No matter where one goes, cell phones are the only hope of keeping families connected without any hassle. The SMS is also a convenient way to keep in touch with your loved ones, when no one has the time for writing long letters. Mobiles are also a great source of entertainment. You can listen to songs, play games, get live cricket scores, market-updates and even the headlines. They are convenient, easily accessible and of great use.

Moreover, these modern devices are very important in this commercial and financial society. Therefore, the total banning of pagers and mobile phones in public places is not at all practical. It will cause inconvenience and the people would not be able to catch up with the modern trend of communication. Cell phones have become vital tools in today's world and blocking them in public places will result in a gross violation of personal freedom.

To sum up, mobiles were invented for our convenience and not to create nuisance. If used judiciously, wisely and with public etiquette, mobiles can be of great use. Banning the cell phone would not be practical.

Plan followed:
Intro: Disagree
Para 1: why ban
Para 2: Why not ban
Para 3: Why not ban
Conclusion: reiterate opinion

374. Leisure is a growing industry, but people no longer entertain themselves as much as they used to because the use of modern technology has made them less creative. Do you agree or disagree?

It is believed by some that despite the growth of leisure industry, people do not enjoy as much as they did in the past because modern technology has taken away their creativity. I believe that modern technology has not made people less artistic. In fact it has changed the definition of leisure and the lifestyle of people, and has also given people more options for creativity.

To begin with, modern technology has changed our definition of leisure. Earlier, leisure meant going out and meeting people, playing outdoor games, going to cinema to watch movies and so on. However, today, leisure time is full of choices. We have so many things to do within the four walls of our house. We can watch countless programs on national and international channels; we can play online games; we can chat with friends and relatives in any corner of the world; we can do armchair tourism by which we can visit any historical place or museum sitting in our armchair. That is why perhaps it looks as if we people do not entertain ourselves as much as we used to in yesteryears.

Another reason why people do not entertain as much as before, is also not because of technology. Technology has, in fact, given us more time to enjoy but we cannot strike a balance between work and leisure. We have become workaholics. Life in the past was simpler. People worked for basic needs. Now work is not just a way of life. It is for personal fulfilment. We set goals for ourselves such as a house or a car. We choose this way of life. Now we have improved standard of living but this has come at a very high cost.

Finally, I would like to state that the given statement is flawed, because nowadays people specially take out time to entertain themselves. This can be evident from the mushroom growth of leisure centres such as hotels, restaurants, fun parks and spas. Tourist places are full of people, and train and air reservations have to be done well in advance.

To sum up, technology has not made us less creative. We entertain ourselves more than earlier times but the ways of entertainment are different and technology has given us more choices than before.

Plan followed:
Intro: Disagree.
Para 1: How modern technology has changed our definition of leisure.
Para 2: Another reason why people do not entertain as much as before is also not because of technology.
Para 3: the given statement is flawed because nowadays people specially take out time to entertain themselves.
Conclusion:

375. The rapid development of communication technology, such as smart phones, tablets and other mobile devices, has more disadvantages than advantages. To what extent do you agree or disagree?

It is believed by some that the speedy advance in communication technology has more negative effects than positive. While these communication gadgets have a downside, I believe that without them human life would not be the same and the society would not be as prosperous as it is today.

Admittedly, the disadvantages of mobile communication technology cannot be overlooked. First, these are not very reliable, as a person cannot be sure whom he is talking to, unless it is a video call. While texting or emailing, there's no vocal tone and one cannot see facial expressions. So, there is an increased chance that the message will be misunderstood. Additionally, there is the issue of cyber-crime. Anyone can become the victim of cyber bullying. The wrong people could gain access anyone's personal details, which could result in loss of money or reputation.

However, the modern gadgets have accelerated the pace of communication, and now people are able to communicate with anyone in any corner of the world. Long distance communication has also become much cheaper than before. Newer jobs have been created because of these technologies. Many people work in the programming field, as systems analysts and as web designers. Furthermore, businesses can expand globally, with very little investment. They can develop a network of customers and get instant feedbacks on their products or services. Payments can be sent and received by online transactions.

Another big advantage is to the students. Students can create documents and immediately upload them to a teacher's electronic folder. Similarly, teachers can upload assignments, links, or feedback for students via these shared resources or folders. Finally, these gadgets have proved an asset in healthcare also. One survey in 2013 discovered that 86% of physicians used smartphones. In one handheld device, doctors can access patient information, research medical literature, and securely communicate with patients and colleagues.

To sum up, the pros of modern communication technologies are far more than their cons. The onus is on us to use these gadgets judiciously, so that the negative side can be minimised.

Plan followed:
Intro: Disagree
Para 1: Disadvantages
Para 2:Advantages
Para 3: Advantages
Conclusion:

Similar: Some people have benefited from modern communications technology, but some people have not benefited from it at all. To what extent do you agree or disagree?

376. Today, people can work and live anywhere they want, because of the improvement of communication technology and transport. Do advantages of this development outweigh the disadvantages?

It is irrefutable that because of the advances in telecommunication technology and travel, today's person can live and work in any part of the globe. While there are a few disadvantages of this trend, the advantages definitely supersede them.

There are many advantages of being able to live and work from anywhere. First of all, people have more choices of jobs because of technological advances. Not only can you work in any part of your home country, you can work for any company in any part of the world by telecommuting. Secondly, modern wireless technology has made work easier and created more time for self and family. What is more, people can lessen their work hours and still do their work more efficiently. Another advantage is that people can manage more than one work at a time. This is the need of the day as inflation is touching the sky and people need to earn more and more.

Furthermore, the modern transportation modes like the metro and light rail have lessened the travel time and also made it more convenient for commuters. This has also decreased the need for people to live in the cities to do jobs because now it is possible to work in cities and come back to peaceful countryside in the evenings because of modern transport systems. This has decreased the overcrowding of cities, which was making cities unbearable to live in.

On the downside, this is leading to a sedentary lifestyle, as people do not need to travel. Another disadvantage is that people become so dependent on technology that any network failure may lead life to come to a standstill. Nevertheless, I still believe that these minor disadvantages are of no importance if we look at the plethora of advantages this situation has to offer.

Summing up, people can live and work anywhere today and this situation is more of a boon than a bane.

Plan followed:
Intro: Advantages more than disadvantages
Para 1: Advantages
Para 2: More advantages
Para 3: Disadvantages
Conclusion: The situation is more of a boon than a bane

377. More and more people work at home and study at home with the development of computer technology. Do you think it is a positive or negative development?

It is true that the Internet has become an important part of modern life and telework and online education have become very common. Although there are a few drawbacks of this trend, I believe working or studying from home is a positive development.

On the one hand, the most important benefit of working or studying from home is that it saves time and money. People do not waste time commuting back and forth from work or college and this allows them to spend more time on their hobbies and families. They also have less expenses as they save money on public transport, gas, lunch etc. The companies and colleges also save money as they do not have to bear huge rents and other utility costs for the building premises.

In addition, telecommuting has many environmental benefits. Less car travel reduces carbon emissions and leads to better air quality. Fewer people in offices and colleges saves resources like paper, energy, power and thus is an effective way to combat climate change. Finally, technology has given birth to opportunities for many people for whom none existed earlier. For example, physically challenged or people living in remote areas can now get online education from any university in any part of the world and can work for any office in any corner of the world.

On the other hand there are also a few negatives of telework and online education. Firstly, there is a decrease in face-to-face communication, which is isolating people socially and can be very depressing and demotivating at times. Face to face interaction also enhances learning and productivity. Secondly, teachers and employers cannot control how students or employees use their time. For example, employees might be tending to family commitments during work hours.

To sum up, although there are a few disadvantages of online work and education, on the whole the positives outweigh the negatives.

Plan followed:
Intro: telecommuting has more advantages
Para 1: Advantages
Para 2: Advantages
Para 3: Disadvantages
Conclusion: on the whole the positive side outweighs the negative side.

378. More and more people are using mobile phones and the Internet to communicate. Therefore, people are losing the ability to communicate face to face. To what extent do you agree or disagree?

It is believed by some that the modern communication gadgets have snatched away people's ability to communicate in-person. Although, people are communicating less in-person, I disagree that their ability of face-to-face communication has been lost because of technology.

Undoubtedly, the excessive use of smart phones and the Internet has weakened people's offline relationships, including face-to-face interaction. The sight of people looking at their cell phones, ignoring their friends and family sitting next to them, has become common. People would rather text or call someone than take time out to meet in person. This has made people lead isolated lives despite the fact that they have the largest circle of online friends than ever in the history of mankind.

However, technology is not snatching their ability of direct communication; it is just giving them other options, which they find more interesting and beneficial. It has become exceptionally easy to contact each other electronically and share information instantaneously in a community. Furthermore, people are not having face-to-face communication because they have become workaholics. They cannot, and should not blame technology. They have the ability to communicate, but they are themselves choosing not to.

Face-to-face communication also has become possible because of technology. Video calling and video conferencing have become very affordable and very easy. Messages are not misunderstood because facial expression and the body language which is needed for good communication is not masked anymore. Grandparents can virtually see and talk to their grandchildren every day even if they are sitting miles away.

To conclude, I reiterate my view that even though, the smart phones and the Internet have reduced the face-to-face communication, these gadgets have not reduced our ability to do so. The onus is on us to keep the face-to-face communication alive.

Plan followed:
Intro: Disagree
Para 1: How technology has affected communication.
Para 2: How technology is not to be blamed
Para 3: Another reason why technology cannot be blamed for less face-to-face interaction.
Conclusion: Reiterate opinion

Similar: Mobile phones and the Internet play an important part in the way, which people relate to one another socially. Is this a positive or a negative development?
Similar: The development of technology changes the way people connect with each other. In which way does the development of technology change the types of relationships that people make? Does it have positive or negative effect on the relationships?

379. Some people think that the development of technology has made our life more complex, and the solution is to live a life without that technology. To what extent do you agree or disagree?

It is believed by some that modern technology has made our lives more complicated and it would be wiser to revert to the older and simpler ways of life. I believe that while there are a few downsides of technology, it has in fact simplified our lives, and life without technology is unimaginable.

On the one hand, there are plenty of examples of how life is now much simpler. Firstly, online shopping has made it possible for people to sit at home and buy almost everything they want with just a few clicks. There are other examples such as teleconferences, which save the trouble to bring people from different parts of the world together, and software like Skype and Face-time, which allow users in different places to communicate "face-to-face". In fact, the goal of new technologies is to simplify people's life instead of complicating it.

Moreover, because of technology people enjoy every device imaginable to assist them in conducting their everyday affairs, from baby strollers to life-support machines. In fact, people are flooded with technological gadgets in this modern world and there is no sign of a reversal in this trend occurring. Imagine for a moment, if there were no television or computers. How would we know who had won the latest cricket match? Or what was going on in the world? What would the weather be like tomorrow?

On the other hand, the problem with modern technology is our increasing inability to tune out from an overload in information and our growing reliance on machines that perform mindless tasks, which we could simply do for ourselves. It is not rare to see people who choose to get away from the online social network for some time. Their feedbacks are generally positive but eventually they all come back because simply living without the technology is not the solution.

In conclusion, it seems to me that the purpose of technology is not to make life complex, but quite the opposite, to solve problems in our life and make life easier. Therefore, giving up technology is not the way to have a simpler life. Instead, we should know where to draw the line so that this technology does not take over our life completely.

Plan followed:
Intro: Disagree
Para 1: Examples of how technology has simplified our lives
Para 2: More examples
Para 3: Reasons for the opposite view but still the solution is not to live without technology.
Conclusion:

380. Earlier technological developments brought more benefits and changed the lives of ordinary people more than recent technological developments. To what extent do you agree or disagree?

It is commonly believed that the technological advancements of the past had a bigger contribution in people's life than the advancements of recent times. I disagree with this notion and I believe the developments of today have influenced people's life more.

The first reason why the recent developments have made more impact is the rapid speed at which technology is progressing nowadays. Earlier it took years before another breakthrough in technology could be noticed, whereas now every now and then we hear of new gadgets with new features in the market. For example, radio came as early as 1920's, but it took two decades for the TV to make its presence. However, the cell phone technology has developed much faster with the onset of video calling features now.

Another reason is that recent developments like the Internet have had an impact in nearly every field of life. By contrast, none of the previous developments had such a remarkable or widespread impact. Nowadays, because of the internet, education can be reached to the remotest corners of the world and even many jobs can be done sitting at home. All types of travel tickets can be bought online and even banking and shopping can be done at home. By contrast, no earlier technology had such a widespread impact.

Last but not least, because of the fast pace of communication, the spread of technology is also much faster than before. For example, in the past, if a type of development took place in the US, it took months or even years to make its presence in India. However, now every technological gadget makes its presence almost simultaneously in the whole world.

In conclusion, I would like to reiterate that the technological gadgets and advancements of recent times have influenced our life much more significantly than the developments of previous times.

Plan followed:
Intro: Disagree
Para 1: Compare the speed of the progress of recent technology with past technology
Para 2: Compare the effect of recent technology on all spheres of life
Para 3: Compare the spread of recent technology with the past
Conclusion: recent developments of technology have certainly benefited and changed our lives more than the earlier ones did
Written by: Indroop Singh

381. Technological progress in the past century has its negative effect, despite its remarkable contribution. To what extent do you agree or disagree?

Technological progress began in the late 19th century and the 20th century but that brought about more benefits than harms but the technological progress of the 21st century has crossed all boundaries that human beings could ever envisage. I believe that technological progress has its dark side, despite its stupendous contribution.

The most significant progress in the 21stcentury is in the field of Information Technology. It has brought a revolution in the field of communication. Distances are no longer a barrier and the whole big planet Earth has become a global village. However, the same technology when used by terrorists can cause havoc in the life of humans. For example, who has not heard of the 26th November terrorist attacks in Mumbai, India? Terrorist with the help of the latest communication technology did all the planning.

In the field of transport, there are superfast jet planes and international tourism has become the backbone of many economies of the world, but this has also lead to environmental pollution and excessive consumption of fossil fuels, which is a non-renewable energy source. It has been rightly said that, "Modern technology, owes ecology, an apology." What is more, in the quest for an unending source of energy, progress has been made in the field of nuclear technology but the construction of a nuclear power plant can also cause major threat to human life if a radiation leak occurred.

Technological progress has left no place untouched. Even in homes, people have the microwave ovens, dishwashers and washing machines to make life simpler but what is seen is that people have lost moral values and face-to-face communication has taken a back seat. In offices, computers finish work in minutes, which earlier took days to complete, but it has been seen that the expectation for work has also risen and men have had to become workaholics. Automation has made possible mass production but unemployment has also risen.

Summing up, technological progress has both pros and cons and the onus lies on us to use it for our benefit only otherwise it can become a boomerang for humanity and ultimately destroy our planet.

Plan followed:
Intro: Agree.
Para 1: One positive and negative
Para 2: Another positive and negative
Para 3: Final positive and negative
Conclusion:

382. *People living in the 21st Century generally have a better quality of life than the previous centuries. Do you agree or disagree?*

It is commonly believed that today the quality of life is better than the past. While I consider that life is certainly more comfortable than the past in many areas, in some areas life has become more stressful than before.

There is no doubt that life quality has improved in many ways. Firstly, many of the issues that people faced in the past centuries such as hunger and epidemics like plague etcetera are non-existent today. Due to the agricultural revolution, there is enough food supply for everyone. Similarly, cures of many diseases have been found and today the life expectancy is considerably higher than the past centuries.

Secondly, human effort and labour has been reduced substantially owing to improvements in machines. Automation has meant that people can relax, instead of spending hours on chores after work. Another area in which life has progressed a lot is transportation. Cars, trains and aeroplanes have not only made travelling comfortable but also much faster. Travelling overseas takes hours instead of days. Finally, people today have more freedoms and rights than before. Many of the nations are democratic and people are free to live their life in the way they want.

On the other hand, people also face many problems that did not exist before. To begin with, there is more stress due to increased competition and inflation. People have to work longer hours to make ends meet. This also means that they cannot spend as much time with family as in the past. It is not surprising that more marriages end up in divorce than ever before. Furthermore, although the transportation has improved, the level of pollution has also risen, and it is becoming worse day by day. As a result, today many people die of diseases like cancers.

In conclusion, I would like to reiterate that though life is more comfortable due to improvements in health care, agriculture and more freedoms, people are also facing issues that did not exist before like pollution, competition and so on.

Plan followed:
Intro: Partial view
Para 1: How life is better
Para 2: How life is better
Para 3: How life is worse
Conclusion: Reiterate opinion

Written by: Indroop Singh

383. Mobile phones and the internet could have many benefits for old people. However, this age group uses technology the least. What are the benefits for old people of using mobile phones and the internet? How can we encourage them to use this new technology?

It is irrefutable that the young generation of today is technophile and is very comfortable with mobile phones and the internet, whereas the elderly are uneasy with the latest technological devices. This essay shall delve into how the mobile phone and the Internet could be useful for the senior citizens, and also discuss ways to motivate them to use such technology.

Mobile phones and the Internet could be beneficial to old people in various ways. Firstly, technology is the answer to one of the biggest problems elderly face today, which is social isolation. This is mainly because nuclear families predominate these days, and even in nuclear families, children have to leave their parents to seek greener pastures abroad. However, through these technologies the elderly can connect with their kith and kin that live far away from them. They can also connect and reignite their friendships with their college friends through social networking sites like Facebook.

Secondly, the elderly face a lot of health problems, for which they can use the technology to get timely help. Through the Internet they can get consultation from any doctor in any part of the world by showing their digital x-ray or MRI scan. Another advantage is that they can entertain themselves through these gadgets. They have a lot of free time and they can listen to religious hymns, visit sacred and holy places on the net, which they cannot otherwise visit because of failing health.

There are a lot of ways to motivate the elderly to use these gadgets. One way to encourage them is to make them comfortable with technology. For example, the government and NGOs can open free training centres to apprise them about technology. Family members and especially children can also play a role by teaching their grandparents about these gadgets. Finally, too many features on mobile phones deter the elderly from using them. So, user-friendly models could be made especially for them.

To sum up, there is an unending list of how mobile phones and the internet could help the elderly, but a little effort is required to make them comfortable with technology.

Plan followed:
Intro:
Para 1: How mobile phones and Internet could be useful to the elderly
Para 2: More uses
Para 3: How the elderly can be motivated to use these technologies
Conclusion:

Written by: Indroop Singh

384. Some people think that access to Internet is necessary to live a full life? Do you agree or disagree?

With growing presence of Internet in our lives, questions about its importance in life have also arisen. In this context, some people are of the opinion that to enjoy a full life, we need Internet. While life is possible without the internet, to enjoy life to the fullest, the internet has become a necessity.

There is no dearth of examples, which depict that Internet usage, is more than just a luxury today, and has become a basic human need. The first and foremost area where the Internet has become indispensable is employment. Internet know-how is not merely a job requirement today but also pivotal in getting jobs, as a lot of companies nowadays only advertise job opportunities online. Moreover, some of the application forms for the exams have to be filled online.

The second area where Internet access is paramount is social networking. Social networking does not mean making friends online, as it still happens offline, but it is about maintaining friendships, which seems almost impossible without Internet today. To cite a personal example, I have lost touch with many of my friends who do not have a presence online or are not active online. On the other hand, some of my friends who are active online are closer to me than they were when we became friends. Furthermore, the governments have also started acknowledging Internet as a basic need today and this is evident by the inclusion of Internet in basic consumption baskets that is used to determine poverty line in developing countries like India.

Admittedly, just a few years back when Internet's presence wasn't so all encompassing, people still lived without any issues. And there are still many countries in the world, where people do not have Internet access. Rather than thinking of Internet as a necessity many individuals believe Internet to be nuisance, which has actually made us selfish and more self-absorbed. Similarly, some consider its use to be an addiction. News about children acting out and committing suicides due to the issues like cyber bullying, etcetera does add weight to their argument.

In conclusion, it can be said that the Internet has become key to succeeding in this integrated world of today. As for the downsides of this development, it is an individual's responsibility to use the Internet wisely and mitigate the associated problems.

Plan followed:
Intro: Paraphrase, Agree
Para 1: Internet a necessity for employment
Para 2: Role of internet in everyday life
Para 3: Negative aspects of Internet
Conclusion:

385. Most people today prefer to socialize online rather than spending time with their friends in the local community. Do the advantages outweigh the disadvantages?

It is irrefutable that an increasing number of people today like to chat and make friends online instead of socializing with their friends and neighbors in person. Although there are certain advantages of this trend, I believe the drawbacks certainly outweigh the benefits.

The main advantage of people spending time on social networking sites is that it helps them to keep in contact with a lot more people than they could in person. It is easy to maintain contacts, keep links with friends from high school and college even if they are living miles away. Moreover, socializing online helps to form friendships with people with similar likes and dislikes. For example, if a person likes knitting, playing chess, reading books or discussing politics, he or she can chat or discuss them online. People are not limited to interests based on their location.

Despite these benefits of online networking and socializing, I believe it far more detrimental for the individuals and the society. Firstly, it has impacted the quality of friendship. People have many friends online, but the number of friends people can rely on in case of adversities has fallen. This is because social networking has reduced the emotional connection, the thoughtfulness that develops when people actually spend time with each other. Secondly, the preference for spending time online has also adversely affected people's health. Earlier people used to go out and spend time with friends doing outdoor activities, visiting malls and so on. All of these entailed some walking or physical exercise.

Finally, I believe the biggest impact of social networking has been the increase in cyber bullying and online harassment. It is easier for people to be rude on the internet as they can hide behind the anonymity that the Internet offers. In a sense, social networking sites have given people the license to be hurtful as there are no apparent consequences of being hurtful or bashful on the internet.

To conclude, although socializing online rather than spending time with friends and neighbors in person has certain benefits, I consider it to be negative development overall.

Plan followed:

Intro: I believe that the drawbacks are more
Para 1: Advantages
Para 2: Disadvantages
Para 3: Disadvantages
Conclusion

Written by: Indroop Singh

386. Spoken communication is always more powerful than written communication. Do you agree or disagree?

It is commonly believed that oral communication has a greater impact than written communication. While I believe that spoken communication can be better than written in some situations, I cannot agree that this holds true in every situation.

Spoken communication has an edge over written communication in many ways. Firstly, oral communication is more effective when instant response is required as it establishes a direct contact between the sender and the receiver. In other words, the person can clarify their questions or doubts immediately and start working on them. In addition, unlike written communication, verbal communication does not require any pen, paper or computer.

Another benefit is that in face-to-face spoken communication, besides words, gestures, body language and variations in the intensity of voice can be used to convey meaning to an audience. Because this, there are less chances of misunderstanding in case of verbal communication. To be specific, a speaker has significantly more control over what the listener will hear than the writer has over what the reader will read.

On the other hand, written communication is also better than oral communication in some situations. Firstly, written words can be chosen with great deliberation and thought. One can write and rewrite to get the message perfect, but spoken words cannot be retracted, although one can apologise for a mistake. So, for introverts or those who have difficulty in speaking out their minds, written communication is a boon.

Furthermore, written communication is preferred where a permanent record is needed for future reference. For example, in case of business dealings, it is better to communicate in writing from the legal perspective. What is more, complex information can be conveyed better in written communication as the reader can read and re-read till he understands the context.

To sum up, both written and oral communication are more influential than each other in different situations, so it would be wrong to say that spoken communication is always better than written communication.

Plan followed:
Intro: Disagree
Para 1: Where spoken is better than written
Para 2: Where spoken is better than written
Para 3: Where written is better than spoken
Para 4: Where written is better than spoken
Conclusion:

387. In the last century when a human astronaut first arrived on the Moon he said: "It is a big step for mankind". But some people think it makes little difference to our daily life. To what extent do you agree or disagree?

Many people are of the view that all the money and energy spent on space exploration and research is a complete waste because it has no effect on our daily life. I strongly disagree with this view. In the following paragraphs I shall discuss how space research has touched our lives in more ways than one.

Space research has touched the life of the common man in myriad ways. The secondary uses of space research are called spin-offs. The common smoke detector used in homes was first prepared for spacecrafts as a warning system. Computer bar codes in retail stores, shock absorbing shoes used by tennis players and athletes, lightweight materials used for helmets and sporting materials and non-stick coating used in pans, were all first developed as part of space research.

Space technology has provided many benefits to the medical field as well. Pace makers used to treat cardiac ailments, remote monitoring devices for intensive care patients, and portable medical equipment carried aboard ambulances are but a few applications of space technology providing daily benefits in hospitals, offices and homes. Artificial limbs of less weight are also a by-product of space research, and these are a blessing for the physically challenged.

Not only that, it is well known that global warming will soon transform our Earth into a boiling pot. Then it would be very essential to find alternative places to live. If we were able to find signs of life elsewhere in space, it would be a jackpot for mankind.

To sum up, space exploration and research has touched our everyday lives in numerous ways. So, it definitely is a big step for mankind.

Plan followed:
Intro: Disagree.
Para 1: Some spin-offs of space research, which have touched the common man
Para 2: More ways in which space research has touched the common man – in medical field
Para 3: Why it is necessary to see possibilities of life in space
Conclusion: So, it definitely is a big step for mankind.

388. *In the future, it seems it would be more difficult to live on Earth. Some people think more money should be spent researching on other planet to live such as Mars. To what extent do you agree or disagree?*

Global warming is occurring at an unprecedented speed, and if the present trends continue, it will become increasingly difficult to sustain life on Earth. While space research is important, I disagree that we should waste our resources in finding a new planet to live. I firmly believe that some other more practical solutions should be researched upon.

Admittedly, space research is important for benefiting the life of humans on Earth. The spin-offs of space research such as the satellite TV, the featherlight artificial limbs for the physically challenged, the pace maker used for heart problems, light weight sports shoes are just a few examples of how space research is touching the lives of common men.

However, spending money on finding another home in space for all people on Earth would not be an effective measure. First, there is little hope of seeking a planet that has favourable conditions for life. In addition, the cost of researching such a planet would be exorbitant. At a time when millions of people are suffering from poverty, homelessness and illiteracy, it would be better to spend on the present problems and leave the future in the bucket list.

I believe that instead of spending on research on space, a much better solution would be to invest in environmental projects and encourage people to lead a more environmentally friendly lifestyle. For example, green energy should be harnessed and made more available to replace our dependence on fossil fuels. People should also opt for public transport rather than driving their vehicles. Such actions can cut exhaust emissions and slow down the effects of global warming, making the earth a more desirable place for us all.

To conclude, I reiterate that although global warming is making Earth uninhabitable, researching outer planets for scope of life is not the plausible solution. It would be more worthwhile to spend those resources on improving life on Earth.

Plan followed:
Intro: Disagree with a concession
Para 1: Importance of space research
Para 2: Why spending money on other planets is not the right solution
Para 3: What can be done instead
Conclusion:

389. Animals are in danger of extinction. Some people say that we should protect only those animals, which are useful to humans. Do you agree or disagree?

It is believed by some that out of all the endangered animals, only those should be conserved which are beneficial for humans. I believe that all animals have direct or indirect effect on mankind, and so steps should be taken to protect all animals.

The most important reason for saving all animals is that they are part of our ecosystem. Every species of wildlife plays a role to maintain the balance of life on Earth. Thus, the loss of any species can affect us directly or indirectly. For example, there are many bat species that are becoming extinct. Such bats help keep the insect population in control. If these bats die then the insects will increase a lot and destroy our crops. So, we will have nothing to eat. In addition, many animals, like rodents, help in the dispersal of plant seeds and in the pollination of plants. By protecting endangered animals we ensure not only their survival but also the biodiversity that is necessary for the ecological health of the planet.

Secondly, wild animals provide many valuable substances such as medicine and fur. The horn of the rhinoceros has medicinal value and the fur of the mink is very valuable. The recreational viewing of animals at zoos is also a source of revenue. Thus, the financial value of wild species is important to the economies of many nations.

Furthermore, wild animals have aesthetic appeal. They are beautiful creatures of nature and are a part of our bio-diversity. Their beautiful and mysterious life has enchanted mankind since the dawn of evolution. Scientists have been awed, by observing their behaviour. Such study has helped scientists understand how the human body functions and why people behave as they do. Scientists have also gained medical knowledge by studying the effect of many drugs on these animals.

To sum up, it can be reiterated that saving all the animal species on the verge of extinction is well justified. All animals have direct or indirect relation to humans. So we should not work to save only those few species, which have a visible effect on humans.

Plan followed:
Intro: Disagree
Para 1: Part of ecological chain – interconnected
Para 2: Provide us many things
Para 3: Aesthetic appeal
Conclusion:

Similar: ***Some animal species, such as the dinosaurs and dodos, became extinct as a result of natural causes. Thus, extinction is a normal part the world's evolution and actions should not be taken to prevent the disappearance of today's endangered animals. Do you agree or disagree?***

390. Many animal species in the world are becoming extinct nowadays. Some people say that countries and individuals should protect these animals from dying out, while others say we should concentrate more on problems of human beings. Discuss both views and give your opinion.

It is believed by some people that the animal species which are on the verge of extinction should be conserved, whereas others argue that human problems should be given priority. In this essay I will discuss both perspectives. I believe that animal conservation is very important for humans.

The main reason why some people are in favour of saving endangered species is that these species are part of our ecological chain. The removal of a single species can set off a chain reaction affecting many others. For example, the gray wolf was once on the verge of extinction but has now been restored to Yellowstone National Park. Because of that all other animals which were dying have come back and so saving one species has led to benefit many other species, which would have otherwise also gone into extinction.

On the other hand, those who say that the governments should focus on other more pressing issues instead of endangered species, argue that in many countries, human beings are still suffering from poverty, famine, epidemics and natural disasters. If the limited government budget is allocated to animal conservation, many people will face huge difficulty making a living. Therefore, many people believe that protecting basic human rights should be the top priority of these countries.

I believe that animal conservation is not an option but a necessity. Not only are animals vital to the ecosystem they also directly benefit humans. For example, in the field of medicine the venom of cobra is being used in some anticancer drugs. Furthermore, small animals like butterflies, bees and birds aid in pollination, so conservation of these animals is vital for food production.

In conclusion, protecting wildlife is of great significance, as it is a vital cornerstone of the survival and future development of mankind. It is a well-known adage that - Animals gone, plants gone, humans gone.

Plan followed:
Intro: Discuss essay intro
Para 1: One side view
Para 2: Other side view
Para 3: Own view
Conclusion:

Similar: ***Some people hold the view that we should spend money and time on the protection of wild animals, while others suggest that the money should be spent on populations living in the poorest areas of the world. Discuss both views and give your opinion?***

391. Some people say that too much attention and resources are given to protect wild animals and birds. To what extent do you agree or disagree with this statement?

In recent times, there has been a great hue and cry over the money and efforts being spent on conservation of wild animals and birds. However, I disagree with the given statement that 'a lot' is being done for them. I believe that whatever is done for them can never be 'too much'. It has been rightly said that – "Animals gone, Trees gone, Humans gone".

The most important reason for saving wild animals and birds is that they are part of our ecosystem. Every species of wildlife plays a role to maintain the balance of life on Earth. Thus, the loss of any species can affect us directly or indirectly. For example, there are many bat species that are becoming extinct. Such bats help keep the insect population in control. If these bats die then the insects will increase a lot and destroy our crops. So, we will have nothing to eat. In addition, many animals, like rodents, help in the dispersal of plant seeds and in the pollination of plants. By protecting endangered animals we ensure not only their survival but also the biodiversity that is necessary for the ecological health of the planet.

Secondly, wild animals provide many valuable substances such as medicine and fur. The horn of the rhinoceros has medicinal value, and the fur of the mink is very valuable. Moreover, the recreational viewing of animals at zoos is also a source of revenue. Thus, the financial value of wild species is important to the economies of many nations.

Furthermore, wild animals have aesthetic appeal. They are beautiful creatures of nature and are a part of our bio-diversity. Their beautiful and mysterious life has enchanted mankind since the dawn of evolution. Scientists have been awed, by observing their behaviour. Such study has helped scientists understand how the human body functions and why people behave as they do. Scientists have also gained medical knowledge by studying the effect of many drugs on these animals.

To sum up, the resources spent on these animals and plants, are well justified. Wildlife is Mother Nature's greatest treasure. To protect it, we must take every measure.

Plan followed:
Intro: Disagree
Para 1: Part of ecological chain – interconnected
Para 2: Provide us many things *Para 3: Aesthetic appeal*
Para 4: We humans responsible for the damage to them
Conclusion:

Similar Essay: ***Wild animals have no place in the 21st century, and their protection is a waste of resources. To what extent do you agree or disagree?***

392. Human activities have negative effects on plant and animal species. Some people think it is too late to do anything about this problem. Others believe that effective measures can be taken to improve this situation. Discuss both views and give your opinion.

Some people believe that damage done by humans to some animals and plant species is irreversible and so we can do nothing, whereas others persist that effective measures can alleviate the current situation. This essay intends to examine both perspectives. However, I believe a difference can still be made if actions are taken immediately.

One of the arguments given by people who think that it is too late to save the animal and plant species is that human activities like deforestation, pollution and overpopulation have already accelerated out of control. This has resulted in climate change which has led to the extinction of many animal and plant species. They further claim that thousands of endangered animals have already died because of poaching. Ever increasing demand for animal products like elephant tusks and rhino horns has made the situation even worse and uncontrollable.

On the other hand many believe that humans can take simple steps to minimize their impact on plants and animals. Afforestation can help reverse the effects of global warming and also restore natural wildlife habitats. Heavier penalties on wildlife traffickers and poachers is another way to save the endangered species. For example, Indian government was able to save the Royal Bengal Tiger from extinction by banning hunting and setting up wildlife preserves throughout the country.

I believe that saving these animals and plants may seem like an overwhelming task, but if everyone pitches in, the situation can still be reversed. For example, air pollution, another contributor to climate change, can be controlled if people take simple steps like walking or taking public transportation instead of driving. Using plastic-free alternatives can help save our oceans and the marine animals and plants. Going paperless can save our trees and forests.

To sum up, although human activities have done a lot of harm to the animal and plant species, it is still not too late to make a difference.

Plan followed:

Intro:

Para 1: First perspective – why it is too late

Para 2: Second perspective – we can still do a lot

Para 3: Own view

Conclusion: There is still time and it is never too late to begin.

393. Far too little has been done to prevent animals and plants from dying out, although people have been aware of this problem for a long time. Why do people do so little about it? Give your suggestions on how to solve this problem.

It is irrefutable that people know about the endangered animal and plant species but do not take enough efforts to save them. In the following paragraphs I will discuss the reasons why people are so indifferent towards this problem and suggest some methods to address the issue.

There are many reasons why people are doing so little for the protection of animals and plants. The first reason is that people believe that individual action cannot make a big difference. People feel that these problems are too big and only action at the government level or national level can improve the situation. Secondly, people have become so accustomed to luxuries that they feel incapable of living without them. Although they know that these luxuries like cars, air conditioners etcetera are damaging for the environment, they find themselves helpless.

In addition, although people are aware about animals and plants dying, they are unaware about how dangerous the consequences of the extinction of animal and plant species can be for humankind. For instance there are many bat species that are becoming extinct and bats help keep the pests in control. If these bats die, the insect population would increase and this would impact agriculture considerably. Many people are also not aware that human beings are directly or indirectly responsible for the extinction of many plants and animals.

The solutions need to be taken at the government level as well as the individual level. At the individual level, there should be awareness of how individual actions can go a long way in bringing a change. For example, people can be told about the difference, recycling and reducing their carbon footprint can bring. In addition, the government can force a change in behaviour by making strict laws and their strict implementation. For example, plastic use in India has fallen considerably after the government levied heavy fines on plastic use.

Summing up, there are many reasons for the lackadaisical attitude about animal extinction issues, but actions can be taken to address this situation.

Plan followed:
Intro: I shall discuss why people do not do enough and suggest solutions
Para 1: People have no time
Para 2: People do not know the consequences
Para 3: Solutions
Conclusions:

394. Some people think people can exploit animals for any purpose they need, while others do not think so. Discuss both sides and give your opinion.

Some individuals are of the opinion that we can exploit animals for our benefit, while others hold the opposite view. In this essay I intend to look at both sides. I personally believe that technology has provided us enough alternatives that animal exploitation can never be justified.

Those who say that it is acceptable if humans exploit animals argue that humans are at the top of the food chain and killing animals for food adheres to the law of nature. Also, they say that animals are vital in the medical field. By conducting experiments on animals, researchers have developed treatments to remedy fatal diseases like diabetes, cancer, heart attack and saved so many human lives. Research on mice, rats and other animals has led to vaccines for polio, tetanus, measles etc.

On the other hand, there are many reasons why some people argue that it is wrong to cause suffering to animals for the benefit of humans. Firstly, humans do not need to eat animals to survive. Research shows a plant based diet contains all the necessary vitamins and nutrients that a human body needs to thrive. Secondly, they say that animals should not be exploited for products like wool, fur, leather as humans do not require these products and nowadays a lot of synthetic substitutes are available. Finally, they argue that using animals for cosmetic testing is inhumane. There are many non-animal testing alternatives like in vitro testing using human tissue cell cultures, computer models and human volunteers.

I believe that it is unacceptable to harm innocent animals as they are sentient beings. People can survive on a vegetarian diet and there are so many faux meat options available for those who really crave meat. Also, our vanity is not worth the suffering of innocent animals. There are a multitude of cruelty-free cosmetics and household products that are not tested on animals.

In conclusion, the lack of alternatives cannot be used as an excuse to justify animal exploitation. It is inhumane and it can certainly be avoided today.

Plan followed:
Intro: It is necessary to look at both sides of the argument before forming an opinion.
Para 1:: Why animal exploitation is justified
Para 2: Why animal experimentation is not justified
Conclusion:

395. In the modern world, it is no longer necessary to use animals for food or use animal products, for instance, clothing and medicines. To what extent do you agree or disagree?

Trying to live without exploiting animals for food, clothing or medicine can certainly be done nowadays, and people in the modern world seem to agree that it is not at all justified to eat meat, clothe in leather, or use animals as medical research subjects. Therefore, I agree with the given statement that we can do without animal products.

To begin with, a vegetarian diet has proven to be a healthy choice. The earlier beliefs that vegetarian diet is deficient in proteins and other micronutrients, such as vitamins and minerals, have been proved wrong. On top of that, a vegetarian diet, is rich in fiber, prevents cancer of the colon, which is the most prevalent cancer in the West, where people mostly eat non-vegetarian food. Even the vegans, the very strict vegetarians, who do not even use animal products such as milk and eggs, have not been seen to be suffering from any malnutrition. So, we can safely spare the animals from becoming our source of such nutrition.

Talking about clothes, today pure leather shoes and garments can be easily replaced by faux leather, which is just like pure leather and only a true connoisseur can tell the difference. Such products have the added advantage of being easier on the pocket, as their initial cost is also less, and the maintenance cost is also less than that of pure leather products. So, even for clothing, animals can be left alone.

It is true that animals have been used for experimenting new drugs and are also the source of many medicines, but for that too today we have computer-simulated experiments, which give better results than those done on animals. Medicines can also be obtained from plant sources or can be prepared by using chemicals. Therefore, animals are not needed anymore in this field also. We must not abuse or exploit the animal kingdom because preserving them is good for humans in the long term.

To sum up, it can be reiterated that it is definitely possible to lead a good life without depending on animal products, and so we have no right to exploit animals.

Plan followed:
Intro: Agree
Para 1: no need to use them for food
Para 2: no need to use them for clothes
Para 3: no need to use them for medicines
Conclusion:

396. Some people think that using animals for experimentation purpose is cruel, but other people think that it is necessary for the development of science. Discuss both views and give your opinion.

It is believed by some people that experimentation on animals is not justified, whereas others believe that laboratory animals perform a great service for humans. This essay intends to analyze both perspectives. I personally believe that experiments done on animals can save many human lives.

Those who are against animal experimentation, give their reasons as follows. Firstly, animals are also sentient beings, and people have no right to exploit them for their selfish motives. Secondly, animals are very different from humans and so what is tested on animals cannot be applied to humans. Finally, unnecessary experiments are done just for new cosmetics, which are not even needed, which is bad.

On the other hand, the main reason given by those who say that animal experimentation is needed is that new medicines and drugs should be first tested on animals and only if found safe should be given to humans. If any drug is not tested, it can create havoc. For example, in 1952, a drug, Thalidomide, was used for vomiting of pregnancy. All the children born had seal-like limbs. By the time it was known that thalidomide was responsible, it was too late.

I believe that animal experimentation is acceptable as the effect of any drug can be seen over generations. It is known that the lifespan of guinea pigs used for experimentation is very small, only 3-4 years, and so the effect of drugs can be tested over generations. Even if humans volunteered for testing, it would take many years to test whether the effect passed from one generation to the other.

Summing up, the human need must always come first, and the use of laboratory animals in testing new products made today, would help humans enjoy a better tomorrow.

Plan followed:
Intro: Discuss essay intro
Para1: One view
Para 2: Other view
Para 3: Other view
Conclusion: Animal experimentation is justified

397. Some people think that the government should provide assistance to all kinds of artists including painters, musicians and poets, etc. However, other people think that it is a waste of money. Discuss both views and give your opinion.

It is believed by some that it is important to support the artists, whereas others are opposed to government funding of artists. This essay intends to analyse both perspectives. I believe that it is necessary to support all types of artists.

There are many reasons why some people say that the government should fund artists. To begin with, artists are the ambassadors of culture. Art is a means of communication and of diffusing tradition. For example, people learn about their history, traditions and culture through movies, songs and paintings made by artists. Another important reason is that artists entertain us. Finally, the government should fund artists because earning a livelihood from art is difficult, especially in the budding stages.

On the other hand, those who say that money should not be spent on artists and should be used for more vital purposes, give their reasons as follows. Firstly, when people are suffering from disease, then the spending on art is plainly immoral. In addition to health concerns, there are also more deserving social causes such as homelessness and unemployment. These deserve to be addressed before money is spent on art and entertainment. Also, enough funding should be reserved for the education sector.

I believe that spending on art is as important as spending on other areas, as art is also a basic human need. Art is what differentiates humans from animals and makes humans the most superior of all animals. Art gives people a reason to live their life. So, spending on art can never be a waste of money.

To sum up, I reiterate that spending on artists is not a waste of money as art is as important as healthcare and education.

Plan followed:
Intro:
Para 1: One side view
Para 2: Other side view
Para 3: Own view
Conclusion:
Similar essay: *Many countries spend a lot of money in art. Some people think investment in art is necessary, but others say money is better spent on improving health and education. Discuss both views and give your opinion?*

398. Some people say that the government should not put money on building theatres and sports stadiums. They should spend more money on medical care and education. Do you agree or disagree?

It is believed by some that the government should spend money on healthcare and education rather than on theatres and sports stadiums. In my opinion, all these things are important for the people and therefore, the government should allocate equal resources for both.

On the one hand, basic medical care is very important for the general public. If people are healthy, there will be more productivity of work and the country will prosper as a whole. There are many people who live below the poverty line and it is the government's responsibility that they should receive medical aid whenever needed. There are also the elderly who have paid taxes throughout their working life and now need good medical care.

Moreover, good education facilities are also the duty of the government. Today, there are a number of children from deprived backgrounds who get substandard education. They would definitely require a high quality of education if they were to succeed in later life. What is more, an educated society has less crime and violence and the country gets good recognition in the whole world if its people are educated.

On the other hand, theatres and sports stadiums are equally essential for people. Art and entertainment is also a basic human need. Theatrical shows provide entertainment and at the same time preserve our culture and tradition. Our artists earn name and fame for our country. Sports stadiums, similarly, attract millions of spectators to watch matches every year. Many more millions watch games on television, read about them in newspapers, and discuss them with their friends. Therefore, we cannot say that these are unnecessary expenditures and therefore the government should ignore them.

Summing up, medicine and education are needs that we recognize, but theatrical or sports events are also basic needs. Therefore, governments should allocate resources for both these things.

Plan followed:
Intro: The government should allocate equal funds for both
Para 1: Importance of spending on health
Para 2: Importance of spending on education
Para 3: Importance of spending on theatres and sports stadiums
Conclusion: Reiterate opinion

399. *Today, the advanced science and technology have made great changes to people's life, but artists such as musicians, painters and writers are still highly valued. What can arts tell us about life that science and technology cannot?*

It is irrefutable that artists as well as scientists bring many benefits to society. The role of art as well as science is different, yet inextricably linked. In the following paragraphs I intend to delve into the role of both in our lives. What is certain is that both types are valuable, priceless and irreplaceable for every society.

The contributions of artists to the society are very essential. Art can bring out people's creativity, views and personalities. For example, people learn about history, traditions and culture through movies, songs and paintings made by artists. Art also entertains people. Another important aspect of this is that art is an ancient means of communication. Language is a result of people's need to communicate. Appreciation of art is what differentiates human beings from animals.

On the other hand, the contribution of scientists also cannot be overstated. Scientists make life easier. People have cars and aeroplanes to move fast from one place to another. They have microwaves and ready-to-eat foods to make cooking much easier. They have different devices that simplify all that is done. Finally, scientists are making great achievements in medicines that make life longer and happier. For example, during the Covid19 pandemic, all humanity relied on scientists to come up with a vaccine to prevent its spread.

Science and technology give us better life but arts tell us how to live that life. In Science truths are proved and phenomena are explained, while in art they are interpreted. However, what people want most is the emotion from their deep hearts, which can only be obtained from art. Art cannot be valued as certain amount of money, not like the productions of science. Take the painting of Mona Lisa for instance. It cannot be rated by the value of dyes and canvas. The sensation in mankind's heart is priceless. That's why art isn't equal to science. Art makes people enjoy life, gives people the pleasure of living from the mental level. That's where art differs from science.

To conclude, artists nourish our souls, whereas scientists and technologists feed our needs. So, it would be wrong to underestimate any one of them.

Plan followed:
Intro: In the following paragraphs I intend to delve into the role of both in our lives.
Para 1: Contribution of artists
Para 2: Contribution of scientists
Para 3: comparisons (a beautiful paragraph)
Conclusion:

Written by: Indroop Singh

400. Governments should focus their spending on public services rather than on arts such as Music and Painting. To what extent do you agree or disagree?

Some people argue that arts like painting and music fail to directly improve people's quality of life and consequently government should allocate money on other things like infrastructures to promote people's quality of life. While spending on essential public services is important, spending on arts, such as music and painting, is as important.

Admittedly, the government should spend money only on certain things, such as defense, health and education. Basic medical care is very important for the general public. If people are healthy, there will be more productivity of work and the country will prosper as a whole. Similarly, good education facilities are also the duty of the government. An educated society has less crime and violence and the country gets good recognition in the whole world if its people are educated.

However, the advantages of spending money on arts cannot be overlooked. The arts clearly make people's lives better. To begin with, the arts give us immense joy and relaxation. Consider listening to a beautiful song sitting on the sofa after a whole day's work; it really relieves the tiredness and we feel rejuvenated. Paintings, photographs and other pictures add color to our lives and often inspire people to create works of art of their own. I am not only thinking of artistic works produced by renowned artists, but also those produced by children for their parents to attach to refrigerators using magnets.

Furthermore, the arts like music and painting are part of our culture and give identity to the country. Arts also bring people together. By appreciating arts, individuals from different parts of the nation could feel connected and related. Moreover, arts like music and painting can help us express our emotions. It is a basic human need to be able to express themselves. Art is what differentiates us from animals. As humans, most of us need an outlet for our creative and emotional needs and the best way to express this is through arts like music and painting.

To sum up, our government is responsible for improving the quality of people's lives both physically and spiritually, therefore proper amount of money should be allocated wisely on arts along with expenditure on other essential services.

Plan followed:
Intro: Disagree
Para 1: why spending on essential services is needed
Para 2: Why spending on arts should be done
Para 3: More points for spending on arts
Conclusion: Reiterate opinion

401. Some people think music plays an important role in society. Others think it is simply a form of entertainment. Discuss both sides of this argument and give your own opinion.

It is believed by some people that music is purely for amusement, whereas others opine that it has many other functions. This essay intends to analyse both perspectives. I believe that music has numerous other roles apart from providing entertainment.

The main reason why some people say that music is just a type of amusement, is that it helps to cheer everyone up. When people come home after a hectic day's work and they need some entertainment, they play music and it calms them and they feel relaxed. Music is also played in parties and ceremonies to entertain everyone. Young people dance to the beat of music and release their pent-up energy.

On the other hand, those who say that music plays a vital role in society, give their reasons as follows. Firstly, music links people to their culture and tradition. For example, the folk songs sung by great artists like Gurdas Mann are on everyone's lips. His lyrics contain many things of Punjabi culture, which are alive today because of these folk songs. Moreover, music is a lucrative profession these days. Famous singers and musicians of India, like Lata Mangeshkar and A.R. Rehman have earned millions from music.

Another role that music plays is of connecting people. When people go to a musical concert, they are with those people who share their musical tastes. Together, they feel the emotions that the music evokes. Music has always been a part of ceremonies because it has the ability to make people feel connected. To add to it, music improves concentration. Students can concentrate better if light music is played in the background because it kills the other disturbing noises.

To sum up, music is not just for entertainment. It has many other roles in society such as connecting people to each other and to their culture, making them rich and famous and also relaxing them.

Plan followed:
Intro: I shall put forth both sides of the argument
Para 1: One view
Para 2: Other view
Para 3: Other view
Conclusion:

402. Towns and cities are attractive places. Some people suggest that the government should spend money putting in more works of art like paintings and statues to make them better to live in. Do you agree or disagree?

It is believed by some that a part of the national budget should be spent on the beautification of towns and cities through works of art, like statues and paintings. I believe that it should be done, and in the following essay I will put forth my arguments in support of my views.

The main reason why it is important to beautify towns and cities is that art instils happy feelings among people and acts as a stress buster. Putting up statues or sculptures in open areas, gives an opportunity to people to enjoy it and acts as a distraction from the monotony of everyday activities. Research has proved that appreciating art helps people relieve stress. Having sculptures, statues or murals in public places, gives an access to people from all strata of society to enjoy art and refresh their mind.

Moreover, installing statues in public places is not only a way to commemorate a famous historical figure, but also is an interesting way for children to learn about the history or the accomplishments of that person. For example, in my hometown, there is a statue of Dr. B.R Ambedkar. Everyone who passes by that statue reads about him and children are fascinated by it and know all about Dr. Ambedkar.

Another added advantage is that statues become a tourist attraction and people like to visit places, which have a rich history, art and culture. This helps the local business and thus, helps make the economy of the place better. For example, the Rock Garden in Chandigarh has modern sculptures made of trash, which attract a lot of tourists from all over the world. Artworks make the cities and the country more beautiful and attractive, for the residents and for those who visit.

In conclusion, I would reiterate that art cannot be separated from our lives and importance should be given to making a place more appealing, by installing works of art, like sculptures, statues and paintings in public places.

Plan followed:
Intro: Agree
Para 1: Reasons
Para 2: More reasons
Para 3: More reasons
Conclusion: Reiterate opinion

403. Some people say that museums should be free, whereas others opine that some entry fee should be there. Discuss both sides and give your opinion.

It is believed by some that there should be no entry fee for museums, while others opine that an entry fee should be charged from visitors. In this essay both views will be discussed. I believe that there should be an entry fee for museums, but it should be reasonable.

On the one hand, the main reason why some believe that museums should charge people is that museums require huge amount of funds for maintenance, and it would be difficult to run museums without any income. Another reason is that museums need to invest a lot of money to bring in new exhibits and art pieces, which again would not be possible without a source of money.

On the other hand, those who believe that entry to museums should be free, give their reasons as follows. Firstly, the main purpose of museums is to educate people and education is a public service. In other words, charging people for visiting museums would be unreasonable as it is a public service. The second reason is that museums play a valuable role in transmitting knowledge about a country's culture and traditions to its new generations and charging people would deter many youngsters from visiting museums and in effect from learning about their history.

I believe that museums should certainly have some entry prices, but they should be within the reach of the common man. Today, the interest in museums is decreasing worldwide and if the ticket prices are very high, it would further discourage people from visiting museums. Moreover, high prices would mean that only the wealthy are able to view the exhibitions, which would be unfair.

In conclusion, I would like to reiterate that although there should be some entry charges for museums, they should not be exorbitantly high.

Plan followed:
Intro:
Para 1: One view
Para 2: Other view
Para 3: Personal opinion
Conclusion:

Indroop Singh: 22/12/2021

404. Some people claim that public museums and art galleries will not be needed because people can see historical objects and works of art by using a computer. Do you agree or disagree with this opinion?

It is irrefutable that nowadays, because of technology, armchair tourism through which we can see historical objects and works of art on a computer, has gained popularity. However, I disagree, that public museums and art galleries will no longer be needed. In fact, I believe that their popularity will grow even further.

First of all, computers can never replace real public museums and art galleries. No matter how real and vivid computer images are, they are only images and can never be likened to the historical objects and works of art that we see in real or even might be allowed to touch with our fingertips. The difference can be compared to seeing the picture of a mango rather than actually eating it.

Secondly, visiting real museums and art galleries is a rewarding experience in many respects. For one thing, it is a good exercise. While people make the trip to a museum or art gallery and then stroll about on site, they get some exercise, which does a lot of good to their health. People generally go with family and friends and enjoy a lot. They also learn about the culture and tradition of the place. All this broadens their horizons, which can never be done by the passive activity of seeing something on the computer screen.

Finally, I believe that after seeing these objects and museums, our craving to actually see these increases even more and so we make efforts to go and see these places. The overwhelming number of tourists to these places that has been increasing year after year can prove this. At certain times, especially when it is temporarily impossible for us to visit museums and art galleries in person, we can get a rough picture of what is on display on site. However, what we see from a computer screen is, after all, not exactly the same as what we see and feel with our own eyes on site.

In conclusion, armchair tourism is there today but museums and art galleries will still be needed

---

Plan followed:

Intro: I disagree, that public museums and art galleries will no longer be needed. In fact, I believe that their popularity will grow even further.

Para 1: computers can never replace real public museums and art galleries - The difference can be compared to seeing the picture of a mango rather than actually eating it

Para 2: Why visiting real museums and art galleries is a rewarding experience in many respects.

Para 3: I believe that after seeing these objects and museums, our craving to actually see these increases even more

Conclusion: armchair tourism is there today but museums and art galleries will still be needed

405. Some people think museums should be enjoyable places to attract and entertain young people, while others think the purpose of museums should be to educate, not entertain. Discuss both sides and give your own opinion.

It is believed by some people that the role of museums should be only to amuse, whereas others opine that the function of museums should be only to educate. In this essay I will discuss both perspectives. In my opinion, museums can and should be both - entertaining and educational.

On the one hand, the main reason given by those in favour of museums being entertainment sources is that the average visitor may become bored if there is too much educational content. Museums are tourist attractions, and their aim is to exhibit a collection of interesting objects that many people will want to see. So museums should put more of an emphasis on enjoyment rather than learning. Such museums may have interactive activities or even games as part of its exhibitions.

On the other hand, the reason given by those who opine that the main role of a museum is to educate, is that the majority of those who visit museums expect to know more about the pieces of art and antiquities. Therefore, museums should focus on providing all that information in a nice and easy manner. Some museums employ professional guides to talk to their visitors, while other museums offer headsets so that visitors can listen to detailed commentary about the exhibition. In this way, museums can play an important role in teaching people about history, culture, science and many other aspects of life.

I believe museums should do both – educate as well as entertain. If museums will be fun places to visit, then young people would be encouraged to learn more about history and culture from the various things that museums display. Museums such as the Salarjung Museum in Hyderabad, the Houston Museum of Natural Science, the Louver, and the National Palace Museum are eye-opening experiences.

In conclusion, it seems to me that a good museum should be able to offer an interesting, enjoyable and educational experience so that people can have fun and learn something at the same time.

Plan followed:
Intro: Discuss essay
Para 1: One view
Para 2: Other view
Para 3: Own view
Conclusion:

406. Museums and art galleries should concentrate on local works, not showing the cultures or artworks from other countries. To what extent do you agree or disagree?

Today many local artists and painters are not finding patrons and the recognition they deserve. In this context it is considered that museums and art galleries should focus only on indigenous art and culture instead of foreign art. While I do feel local artists need support, I cannot agree that museums should restrict themselves to just local artwork.

The main reason why local art and paintings needs more stimulus is that it is very hard for local artists to compete with global artists, who have already established their name and have a huge following. Moreover, art is a field, which is not very lucrative unless the artist is famous. Many artists with incredible talent are forced to leave their passions and dreams just because of financial reasons.

However, I believe that museums only showcasing local culture would be much more detrimental. If museums and art galleries were only limited to local artwork, then local people would lose a reason to visit such places. Local people get a chance to know about foreign cultures, history, and foreign artwork by visiting museums and art galleries, which promote global artwork.

My second argument for promoting global art is that if there were not enough local art, museums might be forced to also show some lacklustre work, which might fail to attract visitors. Finally, the fears about local artists not finding platforms can be addressed in other ways, as in my opinion if the art is good, it would definitely find patronage and recognition. Rather than forcing museums to showcase only indigenous artwork, governments can organize special competitions and have award for new and upcoming artists with special skill and talent.

In conclusion, although I do agree that there is a need to support new and upcoming local artists, I also believe that museums and artwork should showcase all art, local as well as global.

Plan followed:
Intro: Disagree, but with some concession to the statement
Para 1: Why local art should be shown
Para 2: In favour of global art
Para 3: In favour of global art
Conclusion: Reiterate opinion
Written by: Indroop Singh (Exam question 19/9/2020, India)

407. Many countries construct modern buildings to give a good view of towns and cities. Some people say that countries should make new buildings with traditional style to preserve their culture as part of their identity. Do you agree or disagree?

Some people believe that the new buildings should be made with traditional design to preserve the country's cultural identity instead of the currently preferred modern buildings. I also believe that benefits of traditional architecture certainly warrant a change in government's inclination towards modern architecture.

There are many reasons why traditional buildings should be preferred. Firstly, they are undoubtedly a representation of a country's past culture and its people's identity. Globalisation is making us similar in every possible way. People are wearing the same clothes, enjoying the same foods and even watching the same TV shows across the world. If people's houses are also built in a similar pattern, there would truly be no diversity left in the world. Traditional architecture is one of the last remaining methods to stay connected to our past history and culture.

Secondly, traditional architecture through its diversity and uniqueness would attract tourism. When the whole world is similar, except a few countries, there is no question that people would prefer to visit these few exceptions much more. In a few years, these countries would become tourist hotspots and the benefits of tourism to the economy would more than cover the additional costs of using expensive traditional materials.

The final advantage of traditional architecture is its longevity. There is a reason why great historical buildings have lasted centuries or even millennia but the modern buildings barely last a few decades before needing maintenance. The reason is simple - the traditional buildings materials like stone, marble and lime mortar are superior to today's modern materials like glass, plastic and reinforced concrete and steel. They do not expand or shrink due to temperature changes like modern materials. So, in the long run traditional buildings would require much less maintenance and renovation costs.

To conclude, I think there needs to be some serious rethinking about how new buildings should be constructed, as modern buildings cannot be compared to traditional architecture.

Plan followed:
Intro: Agree
Para 1: Traditional buildings represent identity.
Para 2: Traditional buildings attract tourism
Para 3: Traditional materials are better.
Conclusion:

408. There are more new towns being built nowadays. It is more important to include public parks and sports facilities than shopping centres for individuals to spend their free time. To what extent do you agree or disagree?

Some people believe that new town designs should include more parks and stadiums than shopping centres. I believe that having gardens and sports complexes inside town boundaries is more beneficial for the residents and ecommerce has made shopping stores expendable.

There are numerous reasons why public parks and sports facilities should be an essential part of new towns. Firstly, these facilities have a major role in improving the overall health and wellness of the individuals and the community. People with easy access to these facilities are physically more active and tend to spend more time outdoors breathing the fresh air. They create a healthy environment as plants and trees reduce pollution and improve air quality. In addition, these green spaces in the middle of a congested urban landscape provides a connection to nature which relieves stress and improves mental health.

Secondly, these facilities create safe neighbourhoods with fewer violent and property crimes as more people are out on the street and neighbors tend to support and protect one another. Youth also have the opportunity to use their endless energies in sports and so are less likely to be involved in delinquent acts. Finally, these parks and sports stadiums can generate revenue for the town later on as they can be used to host art and music shows or local games.

On the other hand, towns and cities can do without shopping malls inside their boundaries. People are embracing the convenience offered by online shopping and this has made retail stores inside the city centres redundant. Having a few shopping centres in the suburban areas are enough for any shopping needs that virtual stores cannot fulfil.

To sum up, sports facilities and parks have an important role in improving the life of urban residents so their abundance inside city boundaries is a must.

Plan followed:
Intro: Agree
Para 1: why parks and sports facilities are important inside cities
Para 2: more reasons
Para 3: why shopping centres are less important
Conclusion:

409. It is more important for a building to serve a purpose than to look beautiful. Architects should not worry about producing a building as a work of art. Do you agree or disagree?

It is believed by some that the purpose for which a building is made is more important than its outward appearance or façade. I believe that while utility is important, looks of the building are as important. I also believe that today's architects have the capability of designing buildings which serve the purpose as well as appeal to the eye.

On the one hand, the main reason why buildings need to have aesthetic appeal is that beauty in architecture brings joy and happiness, and happiness is a fundamental human need. The emotional impact of beautiful buildings can improve the communities people live in. When buildings look good outside and feel good inside, the whole world of people is improved. Secondly, beautiful buildings also enhance the utility. For example, well-designed hospitals ensure that patients are treated quickly, well-designed schools create better learning environments, and workplaces with good architecture experience higher productivity.

On the other hand, there are many reasons why a building should give importance to its functionality. Firstly, todays buildings need to address the burgeoning population, and the main purpose of building should be to accommodate more people in less space. In addition, a building meant for the elderly, such as an old-age home should have a lot of railings and slopes for their ease. For instance, if a five storey old-age home is made without elevators, it will fail to serve the very purpose for which it is designed. Finally, todays architects need to focus on green buildings, which means that the energy use and carbon footprints of the buildings need to be looked into.

To summarise, the utility and aesthetic appeal of a building are equally important, and it is possible for architects to incorporate function, and aesthetics both in their architectural design.

Plan followed:
Intro: Disagree.
Para 1: Why a building should be beautiful
Para 2: Why it should be utilitarian
Conclusion: It is a big responsibility to have buildings, which are both useful and beautiful and architects of today have the capability to do so

410. *Some people say that vertical city is best where people live and work in tall buildings. Others say that horizontal city is better where there are few tall buildings. Discuss both sides and give your own opinion.*

Some people believe that cities should have more tall buildings, whereas others are in favour of a more traditional and horizontal spread. In this essay, I will discuss both perspectives. I personally believe that horizontal cities are better for a good quality of life, but vertical cities are the need of the hour.

On the one hand, there are many reasons given by those who favour vertical cities. Firstly vertical cities have environmental benefits as they help reduce air pollution. Having numerous services and amenities in these tall buildings would reduce the need for driving and thus reduce emissions associated with cars. Secondly, these buildings foster social connectedness by making it easier for individuals to socialize in common areas and with their next door neighbors. These buildings also save energy as water supply, central heating and cooling, waste disposal etcetera are more efficient when done in small spaces.

On the other hand, supporters of horizontal spread of cities cite a host of benefits. To begin with, horizontal cities in which most buildings are low-rise are safer than high rise buildings. For example, these buildings are better in case of natural calamities such as earthquakes and other disasters like building fires are also more containable in a horizontal spread. Finally, people who live in horizontal cities can enjoy a better quality of life. These buildings have better ventilation, more natural light and individual gardens or open backyards.

I believe that even though horizontal cities are better, people's only option is to go upwards because of rising population and land scarcity. Population is burgeoning, and it is estimated that by 2050, more than 75% of the population will be in cities. Land is scarce and to prevent the loss of farmland and allow green spaces for parks, vertical cities are the only realistic option.

To conclude, even though horizontal cities offer a better quality of life, the increasing population and land scarcity have left people no option but to go for vertical cities.

Plan followed:
Intro: Discuss essay intro
Para 1: One view
Para 2: Other view
Para 3: Own view
Conclusion

411. Some people believe that the government should spend on new public buildings, such as libraries and museums, rather than renovating old buildings. To what extent do you agree or disagree?

It is believed by some that government resources should be spent on constructing new public buildings rather than restoring the old ones. I believe that there are numerous benefits of developing new buildings from scratch and following this direction is justified.

The main reason the government needs to spend on constructing new buildings rather than renovating older ones is the environmental and health benefits. Old buildings produce a vast amount of emissions and waste that has a negative effect on both human and ecological health. By contrast, new buildings built using green methods in design and construction consume less energy, conserve water, lower greenhouse gas emission and generate less waste. The improved indoor air quality and environment is also beneficial for people's health.

Secondly, renovation can be a lot more complicated and expensive than just building from scratch. It is much easier to design a building with a specific purpose in mind than to convert a building intended for a different use. Renovation is expensive as some of the materials used in traditional buildings like marble and stone are much more costlier than currently used materials like concrete and reinforced steel in modern buildings. New buildings would also require less maintenance and thus save money in the long term as well.

Finally, due to increasing natural disasters, many countries have come up with very strict building codes. For some old or outdated existing buildings, it may be impossible to bring the entire building up to the current code. For example flood prone areas require buildings to be elevated but for some old buildings, it is not feasible.

To sum up, I believe that building new buildings is cheaper, simpler and more environment friendly than restoring old ones and the government should take that direction.

Plan followed:
Intro: Agree
Para1: Main Reason
Para2: Another reason
Para 3: Final reason
Conclusion

The restoration of old buildings in major cities in the world involves a lot of government expenditures. This money should be used in new housing and road development. To what extent do you agree or disagree?(AC 411)
Some people think that too much money has been spent looking after and repairing old buildings, so we should knock down old buildings and build modern ones instead. To what extent do you agree or disagree? (Similar)

412. Some people believe that living in big cities is becoming more difficult. Others believe that it is getting easier. Discuss both views and give your own opinion.

Some people say it is getting easier to live in cities, whereas other people say that cities have become unsuitable to live in. In this essay I will discuss both viewpoints. I personally believe that while cities have a lot of issues, they are being controlled and city life is getting better.

On the one hand, those who believe that living in big cities is becoming easier, give their reasons as follows. Firstly, basics like healthcare, education, and transportation are better than ever before in cities. For example, metro trains in Delhi have made travelling both comfortable and safer. Secondly, cities now have even better WiFi and telecommunication coverage so many people are able to work from the comforts of their home. Finally, many new restaurants, theatres and cinemas have opened in big cities which gives city dwellers more options for fun nights out with family and friends.

On the other hand, there are many reasons why some people say that living in big cities is becoming more difficult. The most common cause of declining life quality in cities is environmental pollution caused by cars and construction activities. Poor air quality is detrimental to the health of city dwellers and leads to many respiratory ailments. Secondly, people are not able to maintain their living standards as housing has become very expensive. Finally, crime rate is high in large cities as criminals have greater access to the wealthy, a denser victim population and more chances to escape in urban areas.

I believe all the above problems with metropolises are not new and in the last few years cities have been putting an effort to address these issues. For example, city authorities have been able to control road traffic by providing better public transport and incentivising ride sharing and electric vehicles. Crime rates have been controlled by installing surveillance cameras all over the cities. Governments have taken a series of steps to provide affordable housing options to city residents. These controlling measures along with city comforts have made cities more liveable.

To conclude, cities are becoming better and problems associated with city living are gradually decreasing.

Plan followed:
Introduction
Para 1: One view
Para 2: Other view
Para 3: Own view
Conclusion

413. In many countries, the quality of life in the large cities is becoming worse. What causes this problem? What measures can be taken to solve it?

It is irrefutable that the quality of life in metropolitan cities is deteriorating. There are many reasons why this is happening, but effective steps can be taken to alleviate the problems.

The most common cause of declining life quality in many cities is environmental pollution. Increasing traffic has led to poor air quality which is detrimental to the health of city dwellers and leads to many respiratory ailments. Secondly, large cities have a greater crime rate than rural areas. This is because criminals have greater access to the wealthy, a denser victim population and more chances to escape in urban areas. Finally, cities are no longer affordable as overpopulation has led to the increase in demand and so housing has become very expensive.

There are many ways to improve the quality of life in cities. Firstly, air contamination can be significantly reduced if the public transport system is improved and there are higher taxes on the use of private vehicles. Secondly, the government should promote bicycles in city centres by making separate bike lanes so cities are suitable for bicyclists.

In addition, crime rates can be controlled by installing surveillance cameras all over the cities. Funding for police and other law and order personnel should also be increased so that they have the best technology for keeping the crimes in check. Last but not least, population in cities can be controlled if connectivity between urban and suburban areas is improved. People can commute to cities for work rather than live there which will also bring down the housing demand in cities.

In conclusion, poor air quality, increasing crime and higher cost of living have impacted the quality of life in large cities. However, these problems can be addressed by taking appropriate measures.

Plan followed:
Intro:
Para 1: causes
Para 2: Solutions
Para 3: Solutions
Conclusion:

Similar essay: Some people think the standard of living only benefit cities more than rural areas. What problems might this situation cause and how to reduce the problems?

414. An increasing number of people choose to live in big cities. What problems will this bring about? Should the government encourage people to live in small towns?

Cities act as magnets to many from rural areas, as a consequence of which, many problems arise in the cities and rural areas. While I believe that one way to address these problems is to encourage people to live in small towns, I do not agree that it is a practical approach.

There are many negative consequences owing to rapid urbanization in cities. A major problem is the pressure on the cities' infrastructure. For example, as more and more people crowd into cities, water delivery and sewerage disposal systems are often found to be inadequate to cope with demand. Urbanization is also leading to an increase in the number of vehicles plying on city roads. As a result, cities are getting congested and there is a rise in noise and air pollution. Villages also have to bear the brunt of urbanization as migration of young people leads to shortage of agricultural labour impacting agricultural productivity.

Admittedly, if the government encourages people to live in small towns, it would have a positive impact on the overcrowding of some cities. There would be less traffic, less people in the city centre, and this would obviously be highly desirable. In addition, there would be less strain on the services offered by the city like banks, public transportation and restaurants. This would mean a reduction in queues and faster customer service.

However, the problem would be that a dramatic reduction in numbers of people in the cities would mean that many businesses would go broke. Restaurants, cafes and other service areas would suffer tremendously and overcrowding would occur in the small towns. Restaurants, shopping centres and other businesses would open in small towns. So, although the idea seems good in theory, it would be very impractical. The better solution to the problem would be a careful planning of the city keeping in mind the future population predictions.

Summing up, because of migration of people from rural to urban areas, many problems arise in cities. However, the solution is not in encouraging people to live in small towns, as this would be a short-sighted approach.

Plan followed:

Intro: This essay will discuss these problems and also give opinion on whether or not the government should encourage people to live in small towns.
Para 1: A major problem is the pressure on the cities' infrastructure.
Para 2: Some benefits of asking people to relocate
Para 3: Problems that would arise because of relocation
Conclusion: encouraging people to live in small towns as this would be a short-sighted approach.

415. The movement of people from agricultural areas to cities to work can cause serious problems in both places. What are the serious problems and what measures can be taken to solve this problem?

The world is steadily becoming more urban, as people move to cities and towns in search of employment, educational opportunities and higher standards of living. This situation can cause serious problems in both villages and cities, but measures can be taken to reverse this trend.

The first negative consequence of the rapid urbanization in cities is that the cost of living is going up day by day. For example, there is an increased need for housing, which pushes the property prices and rents. In addition, as people are not able to afford basic necessities, crime also goes up. Secondly, urbanization is leading to an increase in the number of vehicles plying on city roads. As a result, cities are getting congested and there is a rise in noise and air pollution.

Villages also have to bear the brunt of urbanization. To begin with, it affects the demographics of rural areas as most of the people who migrate belong to the young working age category. Consequently, the older people face isolation and depression. Secondly, migration of young people leads to shortage of agricultural labour impacting agricultural productivity.

There are three main ways to address this issue. One step could be for the government to increase the quality of life in rural areas by providing urban facilities like hospitals, schools, shopping complexes and entertainment facilities in rural areas. Another step could be to create employment in villages by promoting industries to shift there through tax and other incentives. Finally, governments should try to provide high speed connectivity between large cities and neighbouring villages, so that people prefer to commute rather than migrate to cities.

Summing up, urbanization per se is not bad but it can have some serious consequences if it is not managed well. Steps must be taken to regulate so that the negative impacts can be minimized.

Plan followed:

Intro:
Para 1: Problems in cities
Para 2: Problems in villages
Para 3: Solutions
Conclusion:

Similar essay: The major cities in the world are growing fast, as well as their problems. What are the problems that young people living in cities are facing with? Give solutions to these problems.
Similar essay: Young people are leaving their homes in the rural areas to go and work in the cities. Why do they do so? What are the consequences? How to solve the problem?

Written by: Indroop Singh

416. Housing shortage in big cities can cause severe social consequences. Some people think only government action can solve this problem. To what extent do you agree or disagree?

Rapid urbanisation in big cities is leading to lack of affordable housing. It is believed by some that only government has the power to solve this problem. While I agree that the government can play a major role to mitigate the problem of housing shortage, I believe that the people in the real estate sector and ordinary people can also help in this regard.

There is no doubt that the government has a major role in alleviating the problem of housing shortage. The government has land banks in city centres where the housing shortage is the most pronounced. Secondly, housing goes hand in hand with other government objectives, such as poverty reduction and employment generation. Thus the resources for one scheme can be shared with those of other schemes. For example, in India, the government promotes both housing and employment by giving jobs to local masons and construction workers.

However, government is not solely responsible to address the issue of housing. The real estate companies can also address the issue of housing shortage in many ways. They are experts in the building and construction sector, and they can assist the government in providing low cost housing. For instance, in places where the houses made by the government have not proved upto the mark, there these companies can step in and fill the void. In this way they can improve their image and also fulfil the housing deficit. In places where these housing companies have provided low cost housing, slum areas have stopped developing further and this has improved the situation considerably.

People also have a responsibility to help the government in addressing the problem of housing shortage. They must see to it that if government is taking steps, then they also proactively back the government. For instance, when governments come out with housing schemes, people should come forward and invest in those. As governments do not have the financial capital to address the housing requirement completely, so if people come forward then the problem can be addressed faster and better.

To conclude, it is irrefutable that governments have a major role in providing low cost housing, but the real estate companies and people themselves can definitely back them. So, it would be wrong to say that only governments can solve the issue.

Plan followed:
Intro: Disagree
Para 1: Role of governments
Para 2: Role of real estate companies
Para 3: Role of people
Conclusion: Reiterate opinion.

417. In many cities, planners tend to arrange shops, schools, offices, and homes in specific areas and separate them from each other. Do you think the advantages of this policy outweigh the disadvantages?

In recent years, many city planners tend to segregate commercial areas, residential areas and educational institutes. While I agree that there are certain drawbacks to land zoning, the benefits are significantly more.

Admittedly, there are some disadvantages of zoning of land according to use. To begin with, it encourages the use of cars because people have to cover long distances. This also means children and people spend more time travelling and this limits the time they can spend with family. Furthermore, mixed use enhances the vitality and security of an area by increasing the number and activity of people on the street. In other words, there might be increased house robberies and burglaries, when residential areas are isolated.

However, there are many benefits of segregation of residential and commercial areas. Firstly, it ensures that there is less noise nuisance in residential areas. There is a certain level of noise and traffic associated with the running of businesses and shops and this can significantly impact the quality of life of the residents living in the vicinity. For example, their sleep might be disturbed and this may lead to irritability. Home owners also lose their privacy as it is nearly impossible to track visitors in mixed land use areas.

Secondly, land use zoning also helps to control land prices for residential areas. When there is mixed land use, residents might be forced to pay significantly higher rents since landowners have the option to switch to commercial usage. In addition, if all shopping is confined to one area, such places can also attract tourism. For example, sector 17 Chandigarh is a well-known shopping centre and is an attraction for tourists. Finally, segregation allows local authorities to better manage parking and traffic.

Summing up, while land use zoning has certain downsides, it is certainly worthwhile considering the innumerable benefits.

Plan followed:
Intro: There are advantages and disadvantages of this policy but overall the advantages are much more
Para 1: Disadvantages
Para 2: Advantages
Para 3: Advantages
Conclusion: Overall, the pros of city planning outweigh the cons.

418. In some cities, there are few controls on the design, construction of homes, office buildings, and the owners can decide on the styles of their houses. Do the advantages of this outweigh its drawbacks?

In some parts of the world, the government does not have any regulations and rules for building design and construction. While there are a few advantages of freedom to design buildings, I believe that there are far more disadvantages.

Admittedly, there are a few benefits to freedom in building design. The main benefit is that it gives owners an opportunity to design houses according to their personal preferences which may vary significantly from person to person. For example, people who prefer spending time with nature might want a bigger lawn and less built up space. Furthermore, eclectic neighbourhoods with diverse building designs have their own charm and beauty.

However, there are a number of drawbacks of lack of regulations on building design. Primarily, it may affect the uniformity of the community or the city. For example, if a street is known for its traditionally designed houses, a modern house may reduce the aesthetics of the whole neighbourhood. Secondly, lack of design regulations can compromise the safety of the residents as home designers might not be aware of the area's vulnerability to potential natural disasters. For instance, some regions are prone to natural calamities like earthquakes, and construction of multiple storeyed houses might increase the risk of collapse during such disasters.

In addition, having design restrictions is necessary because new constructions may obstruct the light and ventilation of the older houses, which may lead to bitterness among societies. Rules ensure that everyone can enjoy decent living conditions. Lack of design requirements can also lead to encroachments onto public property. To cite an example, many people in India have extended their front porches and gardens onto roads, constricting traffic flow.

In conclusion, although liberty in constructing homes according to one's preference can bring about certain benefits, its downsides are much more.

Plan followed:
Intro: Disadvantages are more
Para 1: Advantages
Para 2:Disadvantages
Para 3: Disadvantages
Conclusion:

419. *It is important for all towns and cities to have large public outdoor places like squares and parks. To what extent do you agree or disagree?*

It is believed by some that public spaces such as squares and parks inside urban areas are very much needed in today's era. I think it is imperative for all urban areas to have such outdoor places as they improve the nation's health, boost social cohesion and improve economies.

There are many advantages of having outdoor places such as squares and parks inside cities and towns. Firstly, these facilities have a major role in improving the overall health and wellness of the individuals and the community. People with easy access to these facilities are physically more active and tend to spend more time outdoors breathing the fresh air. They create a healthy environment as plants and trees reduce pollution and improve air quality. In addition, these green spaces in the middle of a congested urban landscape provide a connection to nature which relieves stress and improves mental health.

Secondly, these parks and squares boost the economy of the towns and cities. These spaces can earn revenue for the town by hosting musical concerts, farmer's markets, art shows etc. They also add identity to a place and tend to attract tourists from all over the world. Tourism in turn increases incomc for the businesses surrounding these spaces like hotels and restaurants. This is the reason why neighborhoods in the vicinity of these places are the most sought after business locations.

Finally, parks and open spaces facilitate social interaction and increase the solidarity within communities. People get to know one another, learn about one another's cultures, and discuss common interests, concerns, and goals. More people outside their homes also makes neighborhoods safer.

To conclude, large open spaces such as parks and squares are absolutely essential for all towns and cities, as they serve many important purposes.

Plan followed:
Intro: Agree
Para 1: Reason 1 – health
Para 2: Reason 2 – economy
Para 3: Neighbourhood interactions
Conclusion:

420. Nowadays, some buildings, such as offices and schools have open-space design instead of separate rooms. Why is it so? Do you think it is a positive or a negative development?

A comfortable environment in classrooms and at the workplace is very essential as we spend a lot of time there. Contemporary architecture is promoting open layout in such places. This essay intends to analyse the reasons for this. While this has a few drawbacks, the benefits are far more.

Considering the advantages (which are also the reasons) of having open plans for schools, the most obvious advantage is the cost. The cost of land has increased a lot in recent years especially in urban areas. Having an open design is a lot cheaper. In addition, without doors and walls, a lot more students and staff can be accommodated in the same space.

Secondly, openness promotes sharing and this in effect promotes cooperation and productivity. In open offices, employees have to share equipment like stationery, which leads to more communication. Additionally, there is better collaboration in open spaces. Furthermore, in open classrooms, children can see each other's progress and help each other. For example, children who are strong in mathematics can help other students with the difficult concepts like calculus, algebra etc. All these above-mentioned pros explain why such architecture is becoming popular.

On the other hand, open offices have some negatives too. The high levels of noise in open offices can be very distracting. Teachers may have to shout to express themselves. Moreover, the lack of privacy can decrease comfort levels and impact performance. Saying this, it is also true that comfort is also dependent upon interaction between employees, which is certainly higher in open offices and classrooms.

To sum up, the clamor for open office and school design is certainly justified owing to their umpteen advantages like reduced costs and increased cooperation. Although this open layout has some disadvantages as well, I still consider the growing trend of open offices and classrooms as a positive development.

Plan followed:

Intro:
Para 1: Advantages and reasons
Para 2: Advantages and reasons
Para 3: Disadvantages
Conclusion

421. As transport and accommodation problems are increasing in many cities, some governments are encouraging businesses to move to rural areas. Do you think the advantages outweigh the disadvantages?

In recent years, government has taken steps to encourage businesses to shift from urban areas to rural areas. Although this would have certain benefits, I believe it would be a negative development overall.

Admittedly, there are a few advantages of business shifting from cities to villages. Firstly, running a business in a rural area would be a lot less expensive. This is because land prices are cheaper, raw materials are located closer and workers can be hired for comparatively lower salaries. The second benefit is that the problems faced in urban areas like pollution, traffic and crime etcetera would fall as less people would move to urban areas in search of jobs.

Despite the advantages mentioned above, I believe that businesses relocating to villages would be detrimental for the following reasons. One drawback would be that businesses might find it difficult to find skilled or experienced workers in villages and they might be forced to hire city dwellers to shift to rural areas. For this, they might need to pay extra, thus increasing their costs.

Additionally, villages might face problems like pollution and waste dumping due to opening of industries. Thus, opening of industries in villages can adversely impact their environment and health of people. Finally, businesses might not be able to sustain themselves as they will shift away from city centres, which are their main market. In other words, they might not find enough customers to buy their products in such areas.

In conclusion, I would like to reiterate that while there might be certain benefits of businesses moving to rural areas, I believe its drawbacks would be far more.

Plan followed:

Intro: the disadvantages would be far more than the advantages.
Para 1: Disadvantages of relocating
Para 2: Advantages
Para 3: More advantages
Conclusion: Reiterate opinion

Written by: Indroop Singh (13/5/2022)

422. "Tomorrow is the most important thing in our life." However, some people think that the present time is more important. How important is it for individuals and the country to think and do something for the future?

It is a fact that people keep saving for the future and not enjoy the present. Therefore, some people opine that it is more important to live for the present and not keep thinking about the future. I believe that while the present is important, it is definitely worthwhile for individuals and nations to save for the future.

Admittedly, it is important that the present life should be comfortable. People should not live the present in a miserly way and save everything for the future. A person should spend on the basic necessities of life and provide good education and healthcare to his family. Spending extravagantly is bad, but a frugal life can be led, which will definitely not spoil the present.

However, the most important reason for the nations to keep the future in mind is that the mortality rate is coming down and the span of life is increasing. So, population is going to increase, especially that of the elderly, who would need support from the government. Another reason why countries should plan for the future is that if wise spending is done today it may save a lot later on. For example, if countries do screening tests for early detection of certain cancers such as breast cancer and cervical cancer, then it may save a lot on very expensive treatment later on.

Similarly, individuals should also always save for the future. Lifespan is increasing but the period of earning is comparatively limited. Nobody knows how long he would live, but the age of retirement is generally fixed. One cannot work indefinitely. Therefore, during one's earning span, one has to put aside enough money for the later years, when it will be impossible to work anymore. Further, the requirements in old age are sometimes more than a person's needs during the period of his youth. Deteriorating health translates into higher medical bills and hospital charges. Being weak and infirm, one needs to spend more on commuting. People will need to hire assistants to help in the house.

To sum up, it is imperative that people and countries plan wisely for the future. If one has saved enough, one can sit back and enjoy peace and comfort in one's later years and even witness the smile of joy on the faces of one's children. If countries plan well for the future, everyone would have a better tomorrow.

Plan followed:
Intro: Agree
Para 1: Why the present is important
Para 2: Why nations should think about the future
Para 3: Why peoples should think about tomorrow
Conclusion: Reiterate opinion

423. As housing is a basic need for people, governments should provide free housing for everyone who cannot afford it. To what extent do you agree or disagree?

It is believed by some that to tackle homelessness, governments have the obligation to provide free homes to everyone. While it is the onus of the government to ease the life of people, I disagree that it should provide free housing to all as it would not be a practical and sustainable solution to homelessness and would annoy the taxpayers.

First of all, if government started providing homes to all the people, it would imbalance the economy. The government has so much on its shoulders. Providing basic education and healthcare and maintaining other infrastructure of the country, is also the onus of the government. Moreover, the taxpayers would not be happy about it as their money, which they pay as taxes, would be helping some people who may be unemployed just to get government benefits. Finally, if people knew they would get free housing, they would stop working hard and become complacent. Such a policy would not be good for the economy of any country.

Undoubtedly, it is the responsibility of the governments to improve the living standards of the poorer sections of the society. For example, it can offer low cost housing to people below the poverty line. In India, for example, the government has launched several schemes to provide housing and employment to people. Although the country still faces these problems, the situation has improved considerably in recent years. This is a clear indication that political willpower and proper governance can improve the economic status of a country and its people.

To sum up, it is difficult for governments to provide free housing to all its citizens. Of course, the governments have a role to play in easing the problem of homelessness, but cannot, and should not provide free housing to all.

Plan followed:
Intro: I do not agree
Para 1: Reasons
Para 2: how good governance can help ease the situation
Conclusion:

424. People's shopping habits depend more on the age group they belong to than other factors. To what extent do you agree or disagree?

It is believed by some that age of a person determines the shopping habits of a person. I believe that besides age, there are numerous other factors, which have equal impact on how and why people buy things.

Undoubtedly, age is an important factor affecting people's shopping. A consumer does not buy the same products or services at 20 years and at 50 years. His lifestyle, activities, hobbies and habits evolve throughout his life. Accordingly, his shopping needs also change. For example, during his life, a consumer could change his diet from unhealthy products, such as fast foods, to a healthier diet to avoid health problems. His clothing preferences also would change with age. Therefore, age does affect the shopping habits.

Another factor, which is as important as age, is the socioeconomic status of the person. The upper strata of society, is very brand conscious. The middle and lower income groups have to see their pocket. Brands are like sour grapes for them. Peer pressure is another important element, which controls purchasing choices. If one friend has an I-phone, the other also buys the same. Advertisements, which keep bombarding people with info about any product, also affect consumerism.

Furthermore, gender is another factor which determines the shopping habits. In general, men have a different attitude about shopping than women do. Their personal needs are also different. The clothes, toiletries, accessories etcetera, all requirements are different. Finally, there are individual differences. Two consumers can be similar in age, personality, gender, and so on but still purchase very different products.

To conclude, it can be reiterated that shopping habits depend on age, gender, financial status, family, friends and many other factors equally. To label any one of these factors, as the most important would be wrong.

Plan followed:
Intro: Disagree
Para 1: Influence of age
Para 2: Socio-economic status
Para 3: Gender
Conclusion: Reiterate opinion

425. *There are an increasing number of people who do not know their neighbours. What causes this situation? How to solve it?*

It is undeniable that in today's contemporary society, more and more people are leading self-centred lives, unaware of who their neighbours are. There are many reasons why people are not acquainted with their neighbours, but this situation can be rectified with suitable measures.

The first reason for people not knowing others in their community is longer working hours, which is due to materialism and the pressures of the highly competitive era of today. The result is that people get very little time after work and therefore socializing with neighbours is out of question. The second reason is that our dependence on neighbours has decreased because of technology. Today through technology people can interact with their family and friends, so they do not feel the need to interact with neighbours.

The final reason is the change in people's entertainment sources and leisure activities. Earlier, neighbours used to meet after work hours and chat and play with each other, but now all the recreational activities are at home only such as watching TV and surfing the net. Similarly, earlier, people did shopping from local small shops where one could accidentally bump into neighbours, but now online shopping has even deprived people of such accidental collisions.

The solutions are not simple but the onus is largely on people themselves. To begin with, people should try to achieve a work life balance. For example, they should take time off on festivals and celebrate them together with their neighbours. In addition, technology itself can provide a solution, as neighbours can use social networking apps to connect with each other. However, again people have to make an effort to use these apps to connect. Lastly, local authorities should make sure that every community has places like parks, gyms and pools, where neighbours can meet and spend time together.

To summarise, the decrease in neighbourliness can be attributed to a range of factors like longer working hours, technology and change in people's leisure choices and this trend can only change if people make a conscious effort to do so.

Plan followed:
Intro:
Para 1: Reasons
Para 2: Reasons
Para 3: Solutions
Conclusion:

426. Intelligence is the most important quality for a leader. Do you agree or disagree?

There are several qualities a good leader must have, and intelligence is just one of those virtues. While intelligence is an important characteristic of a good leader, I disagree that it is the most essential quality.

Admittedly, intelligence is needed to be good at any work, and in any field. People need to have good knowledge and awareness for any work they specialize in. However, intelligence is not the most important quality needed by a good leader because any single trait is not enough to be a good leader. It has to be a blend of many traits. For instance, an analyst in any field has an immense knowledge about his field of work and can work very well with data to improve processes. However, all the analysts cannot become leaders.

To further add to it, there are many other characteristics that make someone a front-runner. Some abilities like good interpersonal skills, communication and oratorical skills are essential, as it is only through these abilities that a leader can inspire, motivate and encourage his/her team or followers on the path of success or progress. In addition, people seek honesty, integrity and positivity in leaders, be it a politician, a team manager or a project leader. If any of these attributes is missing in a person, he/she cannot be an effective leader. A very good example of such a leader is late Dr. Abdul Kalam, who was not only a genius in his field of work, but also a very good orator. He was honest and inspires the youth of India, even after his demise.

To conclude, it can be reiterated that intelligence alone cannot be deemed as the most important attribute of a good leader. It is an amalgamation of several characteristics that make and define a virtuous and respectable leader.

Plan followed:
Intro – Disagree
Para 1 – Any single trait is not enough. A blend of many traits is
Para 2 – Other traits required
Conclusion:

427. The tendency of human beings to copy one another is shown in the popularity of fashions in clothes and other consumer goods. Do you agree or disagree?

Undoubtedly, in the contemporary society most people are following the same fashions and buying the same consumer goods. While people do want to be part of a group, following similar fashion and using similar things is not solely a reflection of people wanting to imitate one another

To begin with, widespread purchase of the popular consumer products is not just because people want to imitate one another, but because they have the knowledge of the best things available around the globe. They can compare things and check the reviews and then choose to buy anything if it suits their pocket or needs. People do not buy anything just because the other person has it. For example, the Apple I-phone is widely accepted and used by an increasing number of people around the world due to its extraordinary functions and ease of use.

Secondly, people wear similar clothes because these are comfortable and not just because they want to imitate others. Even after watching the fashion shows on TV, people do not rush out to wear all that stuff. They buy and wear only what is comfortable to them and suits them and not because others are wearing the same clothes. For instance, jeans and T-shirts are worn all over because they are the most comfortable clothes for casual wear. So, even though it looks as if everyone is wearing similar clothes because of a tendency to copy one another, it is actually not so.

It cannot also be denied, that there is a tendency among people to feel wanted and a part of a group. This is because man is, after all, a social animal and so he does what everyone else does. If he does not wear what is the fashion of the day, he feels out of place, or may even be ridiculed by others. Therefore, to some extent it can be said that people imitate each other, which can be reflected in what they wear or do.

To sum up, I reiterate my opinion that the popularity of fashion is the irreversible tendency brought about by advanced technology, which has led to the economic and cultural integration and only partly due to the so-called tendency to copy.

Plan followed:
Intro: Disagree
Para 1: first reason
Para 2: second reason
Para 3: Final reason
Conclusion:

428. Ambition is an important character for people who want to be successful in life. How important is it? Is it a positive or negative characteristic?

One of the most important qualities associated with success is ambition. Although some people see it is as a negative attribute, I believe that ambition is an extremely important quality.

There are many reasons why being ambitious is important. Firstly, ambition provides the energy required to achieve goals. Life is full of challenges and things are not handed out, but rather require significant hard work and efforts. In other words, ambitious people do not lose spirit when facing challenges, and remain motivated even during tough times. Secondly, ambition makes people confident. When people achieve goals, they gain the confidence to take on even more difficult tasks. Every time they fulfil their goals, they are inspired to achieve more. In fact, I believe that nothing great in life can happen without ambition. Finally, ambitious people are happier. There is no greater joy or happiness in life than the satisfaction of achieving goals and ambition makes this possible.

Admittedly, many people mistrust and fear ambition. Ambitious people are seen as manipulative and willing to harm others to achieve their goals. However, I think it is not ambition and instead lack of moral values and ethics, which is the culprit. Ambition can lead to both good and bad and it all depends on whether people are able to rein-in their negative tendencies. On the other hand, people without ambition take very little risk in life and as a result achieve nothing. They have no dreams, no vision, no direction and, therefore, they get nowhere. Thus, I believe it is better to be ambitious.

In conclusion, I would like to reiterate that ambition is one of the most important qualities in life and it doesn't deserve the negative image that it frequently gets.

Plan followed:
Intro:
Para 1: importance of ambition
Para 2: when ambition can be bad
Conclusion:

429. Some people think that politicians have the greatest influence on the world. Other people, however, believe that scientists have the greatest influence. Discuss both views and give your opinion.

Some individuals hold the opinion that politicians have more influence on people's lives, whereas others say the scientists have made a bigger contribution than politicians. In this essay both perspectives will be discussed. I believe that the role of both is equal, albeit different.

Those who say that government office-bearers have more effect on people, give their reasons as follows. Firstly, politicians enforce laws to maintain social harmony in the country. These legislators represent the common man and do their best so that no one is devoid of their fundamental rights. Secondly, they represent their countries in matters where global co-operation is needed. They have the power to change the standing of their nation in the whole world.

On the other hand, the main reason why some people say that scientists have played a great role is that they have bettered our life through research in different fields like medicine, electricity, automobiles. It would not be not wrong to say that today, the impact of scientists is there in every field. The contribution of scientists in the field of communication has shrunk the whole planet Earth into a global village. Because of scientists, education has reached the remotest corners of the world.

I believe that the role of scientists and politicians cannot be compared. Both have had a profound influence on the lives of people in their own respective ways. To do their jobs well, scientists and politicians must operate in very different settings, but it is also important that they act together to improve the lives of people. In many ways their roles are interdependent. Scientists may not have been able to achieve all that much without the funding by the governments. Similarly, the politicians decide which research should be funded more than others. So, the roles of both are equally important and incomparable.

To sum up, politics and science are two endeavours that have fundamentally different aims. Both have equivalent and profound impact on the lives of the common man.

Plan followed:
Intro: Equal roles
Para 1: Role of politicians
Para 2: Role of scientists
Para 3: Own view
Conclusion: Both have equivalent and profound impact

Written by: Indroop Singh (Task seen in India 26/9/2020)

430. *A hundred years ago, people thought that human race was steadily improving in every area of life. Now it seems this is not certain in all situations. In which areas do you think we have made important progress nowadays? In which areas do you think we still need to make progress?*

Due to the growth of science and technology the world we live in today has changed beyond recognizable limits, to what it was a hundred years ago. This essay shall look into some areas in which we have made progress, and the areas in which we still have a lot to do.

On the one hand, the two main areas where the world has made important progress is transport and communication, and agriculture. In the field of communication, distance is no longer a barrier and people can connect with anyone living in any part of the world through mobile phones and the internet. Similarly, air travel has made it possible to travel around the world in a matter of hours instead of days or months. In agriculture, the recent technologies like genetic modification, vertical farming have ensured that there is no shortage of food. In addition, the quality of food grown is better today because of reduction in the use of pesticides and harmful chemicals(organic farming).

On the other hand, the two main areas where a lot of progress is still needed are environmental protection and healthcare. Today, the air in cities is a lot more polluted than before and the landfills are overflowing with plastic and other harmful wastes. Furthermore, many plants and animals are becoming extinct because of human activities like deforestation. In healthcare, although scientists have found cures for many diseases, there are still treatments for many ailments like cancer and AIDS that still evade us. The recent COVID pandemic has also highlighted our shortcomings and how much progress still needs to be made. Even developed countries like the US and Italy have lost precious lives despite having the best medical facilities.

To conclude, the human race has made a lot of progress in the last hundred years, but there are still many areas in which further work is needed.

Plan followed:
Intro:
Para 1: The growth in medical science
Para 2: Revolutionary developments in the transport and communication sector
Para 3: There are still many sectors where we have to work further
Conclusion:

431. Most countries want to improve standard of living through economic development. However, others think social values are lost as a result. Do you think the advantages of economic development outweigh the disadvantages?

It is irrefutable that most countries focus on economic development for raising the living standard of its citizens, but it is also true that there is social cost to this development. Although there are a few drawbacks to economic development, the benefits are far more.

Admittedly, economic development can lead to loss of social values. Primarily, in the quest for raising their living standard, people fail to maintain work life balance and this not only affects family relationships but also social harmony. Economic development is also associated with a rise in materialism and consumerism. In effect, people start defining success from a financial standpoint and material possessions rather than one's impact on society. This means that people stop caring about social welfare or helping the poor and focus only on getting rich.

However, there are many benefits of economic development. Firstly, due to economic development businesses earn more revenues and profits and they also pay higher taxes to the government. In effect, the government is able to spend more on services like healthcare and education and thus it raises literacy rates and increases people's life expectancy. More tax revenues also mean that the government is able to spend more on social welfare measures and bring more people out of poverty.

Secondly, as people become more affluent, they consume more products and services and this directly enhances their quality of life. In addition, as people buy more products, firms also hire more employees to meet the increased demands. This leads to reduction in unemployment. Finally, economic development increases the status of the country, in terms of its political clout and trading power. A good example is the rise of China in the past two decades.

Summing up, there is no doubt that economic development comes with its own share of problems, but its advantages certainly outweigh the disadvantages.

Plan followed:
Intro: the cons of economic advancement outweigh its pros
Para 1: Disadvantages
Para 2: Advantages of economic development
Para 3: Advantages of economic development
Conclusion:

432. *Many people believe that scientific research should be carried out and controlled by the governments rather than private companies. To what extent do you agree or disagree with this opinion?*

Scientific research is very important for the economic and social development of any country. While I agree that some critical areas of research like health and defence should be only in the hands of the government, in all other areas private companies should be handed over the research.

There are many reasons why research into critical areas should be publicly funded. To begin with, private companies are profit-oriented. In other words, they invest in research with the main aim of making money on their investment even if it goes against the general public interest. To cite an example, many drug manufacturers have been caught creating artificial medicine shortages even at the cost of public health to earn a premium.

Furthermore, there are some other areas, which are better left off in the hands of the government like defense, atomic energy etcetera because these areas are pivotal to a country's security. Research only in the hands of private organizations could be detrimental for the country. Private companies tend to neglect certain areas, which are not so lucrative. A case in point being Ebola vaccination. As Ebola is third world disease with people lacking the financial capacity to pay huge prices, research on it was neglected for a very long time. Compare this with potentially less threatening, developed world diseases like diabetes and obesity, where considerable amount of money has been spent.

I believe that to expect government to be solely responsible for research would be wrong too. To begin with, private companies do researches more efficiently because they are profit driven. Every dollar is spent wisely to ensure maximum benefits and every resource is used effectively to avoid waste. Also, government has so many priorities like healthcare, education and so on. Thus, it is financially constrained. Barring private companies from research would slow down innovation and ultimately progress. Governments can invest more in critical and neglected areas and also subsidize the final products like medicines even if private companies do the research. India has recently done so for stents bringing down their cost considerably.

To conclude, governments and private companies should be active in scientific research. However, some critical areas should only be reserved for the government.

Plan followed:
Intro: Both the governments and private companies should be involved in scientific researches.
Para 1: Why scientific researches should be done by the government
Para 2: Another reason why the government should do scientific research
Para 3: Why private companies should also do the research
Conclusion: *Written by: Indroop Singh*

433. Many people are optimistic of the 21st century and see it as an opportunity to make positive changes to the world. To what extent do you share their optimism? What changes would you like to see in the new century?

Although there are several serious problems affecting the world today, many people are positive about mankind's future. There are many changes I would like to see. While I think they will not be easy, I am hopeful and optimistic that they can be brought about.

The first change I would like to see in this century is that everyone should be treated equally irrespective of their race, religion, caste, background or physicality. People should not be judged or discriminated against on the basis of their appearance or their financial status. Secondly, the environment should also be clean and free from pollution. This includes everything from the air people breathe, the water people drink and soil people grow their crops in.

In addition, basic necessities like clean drinking water, electricity, a good education and a quality healthcare should be available to all the people. I believe that only when all these basic needs are met, individuals can reach their full potential. Finally, I would like to see advancements in healthcare like treatments and cures for cancers and other fatal diseases such as AIDS. In fact, the recent Covid pandemic has made it abundantly clear that medical innovations are the need of the hour.

Achieving all this might seem overoptimistic and it would be challenging to bring about these changes, but they are possible. The biggest proof for this is the past century's achievements. A century ago, no one could have imagined air travel, computers, internet communication or even household appliances like televisions and microwaves, but now people take all these things for granted. Despite the magnitude of the problems today and the enormity of change required, I trust human ingenuity and capacity for innovation to deliver.

To sum up, there are many developments I envision for the 21st century and I am positive in mankind's ability to achieve them despite the hurdles.

Plan followed:

Intro: I am an optimistic person and I believe there will be many beneficial changes which I would like to see in the 21st century.
Para 1: Changes I would like to see
Para 2: More Changes
Para 3: why I am optimistic that changes can be made
Conclusion: Reiterate

434. The number of people interested in cosmetic surgery is increasing in order to improve their physical appearance. Why do people go for operations to change the way they look? Do you think it is a positive or a negative development?

Cosmetic procedures are becoming increasingly popular among people all across the world as everyone desires to look perfect. There are several reasons for people undergoing cosmetic surgery. While there are certain advantages of this trend, I consider it to be a negative development on the whole.

One of the most common reasons why more and more people are undergoing cosmetic surgery is the influence of the media. Movies and celebrities have set impossible beauty standards, and these are nearly impossible to achieve without plastic surgery. Another reason for causing people and especially adolescents to go for such surgeries is bullying and body-shaming by peers. Bullying has an effect on the psychological functioning of people and this in turn increases their desire for cosmetic surgeries.

There are definitely a few advantages of growing popularity of such surgeries. To begin with, it increases people's self-confidence and esteem. In other words, when individuals think they look good, they become more outgoing and social. Furthermore, cosmetic surgery can have health benefits as well. For example, there are circumstances where rhinoplasty not only improves the appearance of a patient's nose, but also makes it much easier for the individual to breathe by clearing the air passages of the nasal cavity.

However, I also believe that the drawbacks of cosmetic surgery can be much more severe. Firstly, cosmetic surgeries are expensive, and this means that they are unaffordable for many people. In effect, this leads to people taking loans for such surgeries and going into debt. Secondly, cosmetic surgeries are addictive, and some people go for multiple surgeries in a quest to achieve their perfect body shape. Multiple procedures can have negative effects on an individual's muscles and skin. Finally, such surgeries are creating a culture of vanity. The young generation today has a very limited perception of beauty, and they forget that the inner beauty is what actually matters.

To sum up, although there are some upsides to the increasing popularity of cosmetic surgeries, I consider its downsides far too many to consider it a positive development.

Plan followed:
Intro: largely positive
Para 1: Reasons
Para 2: How it is positive
Para 3: How it is negative
Conclusion: Reiterate opinion

435. Today, many people rely on the internet to diagnose and cure their own health problems instead of seeing a doctor. Why is this happening? Is it a positive or negative development?

Nowadays people use the internet to self-diagnose their ailments instead of seeing a doctor. I think cost, time and convenience are the main reasons for this change. I believe web diagnosis can be inaccurate and relying on it for curing health problems is dangerous.

The main reason why people have turned to the internet for curing their health problems is that it's a much cheaper way of getting a diagnosis. Doctor appointments cost more money than what millions of people can afford and may involve unnecessary tests which are also very expensive. The second reason is that seeing a doctor is time-consuming, so people prefer finding information on the internet rather than waiting hours in clinics and hospitals. Finally, modern technologies like search engines, smartphones, social networks, etc. have made it very convenient to get this information.

I believe relying on the internet for health advice and reaching a medical diagnosis based on that is a negative development. To begin with, information on internet is not regulated and some websites can have inaccurate or outdated information. Not only that, some people intentionally post manipulative information on the internet for their benefit. Vulnerable people can trust these misleading sites and adopt beliefs that not only conflict with regular medical practices but do nothing to improve their health.

Another drawback of web diagnosis is that after researching their symptoms online people may develop unnecessary fears which is not good for their mental health. Sometimes symptoms can be due to a minor passing illness, but people tend to latch on to the worst-case scenario and think that it's something serious. Moreover, improper self-treatment or wrong diagnosis can aggravate the situation and people may get even sicker.

To conclude, there are many reasons why people have turned to the web to diagnose and cure health problems but there are a lot of downsides to this that can be hazardous for their health.

Plan followed
Intro:
Para 1: Reasons
Para 2: Negatives
Para 3: More negatives
Conclusion:

436. Music has been and will continue to be the universal language of mankind. To what extent do you agree or disagree?

It is believed by some that music is universally understood across cultural and linguistic boundaries. I completely agree that music is one language that everybody understands no matter what tongue they speak.

The main reason why I believe that music is the universal language of mankind is that music expresses feelings that everyone understands. People can understand the emotion conveyed in the music even if they do not understand the lyrics. The components that makeup music like pitch, tempo, and rhythm are present in all cultures. Humans can easily interpret the two basic emotions happiness and sadness by analyzing a song's acoustic features. For instance, higher pitches and a faster tempo convey happiness. Songs like the Korean Gangnam song, Spanish Despacito have been hits globally. This is a testament to the universality of music that regardless of the language, people appreciate and interpret music in the same way.

Moreover, music is universal because it's an important part of all cultures, all over the world. In all the different types of music, one common attribute is that it brings people together, whether it's by dancing to the music, singing to the music, or just celebrating the music. It is a vital part of religious ceremonies, weddings, birthday parties, and other social activities. It is also therapy for many as it can help with anxiety, depression, and stress and uplift one's mood.

Finally, because of technological advancements music has had the opportunity to blend with music of other countries and transcend cultural differences. As such, music is in a unique position where it contains bits and pieces from every place on Earth. For example, Bollywood songs contain, English, Japanese and Spanish words. Therefore, music is one way that people are able to communicate with each other when words fail.

In conclusion, music is universal because it exists in all societies and people can understand its meaning regardless of the cultural background.

Plan followed
Intro: Strongly agree
Para 1: Reason
Para 2: Reason
Para 3: Reason
Conclusion:

437. Some people think that children should aim to be the best at what they are doing, while others believe it is not necessary for them. Discuss both views and give your opinion.

It is believed by some that children should strive to be perfectionists, whereas others say that it is not needed to excel at everything. In this essay, I will discuss both viewpoints. I believe that children should set achievable goals according to their ability and not run after perfection.

On the one hand, the main reason why some people opine that children should aim to do everything perfectly well is that it develops the habit of perseverance. Such children take pleasure in doing difficult tasks, and set high standards for themselves. Children who have perfectionist tendencies demonstrate good focus and attention to detail, and produce high quality work.

On the other hand, those who say that perfection is not essential in everything, give their reasons as follows. To begin with, when such children perform below their own expectations, they experience mental problems. They have strong feelings of inadequacy and lose their confidence. They exhibit persistent anxiety about making mistakes. When behavior of this type affects normal development and social relationships, these children need assistance.

I believe that perfectionism is good only upto a certain limit. If children work hard to achieve a goal, then it is good. Such perfectionist tendency is an asset. However, extreme perfectionism can lead to eating disorders, migraine headaches, obsessive-compulsive disorder, depression, and even suicide. Counselling of these children may be needed. Such unhealthy perfectionism can be detrimental for the children.

To sum up, it can be said that running after perfection is not needed and in fact can be detrimental for children.

Plan followed
Intro: Discuss essay
Para 1: One view
Para 2: Other view
Para 3: Own view
Conclusion

438. Nowadays, it is not only large companies that are able to make films as digital technology enables anyone to produce films. Do you think this is a positive or negative development?

The improvement in digital technology has made it possible for even ordinary people to create movies and it is not just the domain of a few big movie production houses. Although there are certain drawbacks of this development, I believe the benefits are far more.

The main issue of the digital technologies is the lack of regulation on the content produced. Some people create and post videos which can be culturally insensitive, and promote racism and violence. Because anyone can post videos online, it is nearly impossible to keep track of what is being posted and to take it down if it is inappropriate. By contrast, earlier, the videos were being produced by a few big companies and thus it was easier for governments to regulate them and give them a rating defining their suitability according to age.

However, despite the drawback mentioned above, I believe that these technologies are beneficial for the following reasons. Firstly, people can show their talent as directors and actors by creating and performing in self-shot films. If they are talented, they may get noticed and get a chance to work with a big production house as well. In a way, this is also ending nepotism, as earlier in film industries like Bollywood, it was very difficult for newcomers to get roles as most movie producers reserved roles for their family members, even if they were not as talented.

The second benefit is that the people have options to watch from. The increased competition has also led to an improvement in the quality of movies and especially their storylines. Film makers know that people are not going to watch films with cliched storylines since they have so many options available. Finally, it has promoted creativity since creators have the freedom to create the kind of story they want. They can take the plot to directions that they envision because there is no executive or a higher person that can restrict them from doing what they want.

In conclusion, while digital technologies have made it challenging to regulate content, I believe their benefits certainly make them a positive development.

Plan followed
Intro: A few drawbacks, more benefits
Para 1: Negatives
Para 2: Positives
Para 3: Positives
Conclusion

439. Some people think that it is good for a country's culture to show imported foreign films and TV programmes. Others think that it is better to produce these locally. Discuss both views and give your opinion.

Some people believe that broadcasting foreign TV programs and movies is better for a country's culture, whereas others believe that it is beneficial to make movies and TV shows locally. In this essay I will discuss both perspectives, but I agree with the latter side.

On the one hand, the main reason why some people think that foreign movies and tv soaps help a county's culture is that such media promotes awareness, curiosity, and interest in other cultures. People start respecting diversity and understand why people from different countries do some things that they themselves do not value. Furthermore, people can learn a lot from other cultures and try to adopt the good values of other cultures.

On the other hand, there are many reasons why some people believe that it is better to create films locally. Firstly, films and TV serials are the carriers of a country's culture. The local film and TV industry enables a country to spread its culture and be recognized worldwide. Secondly, the film industry promotes economic growth by creating so many jobs for thousands of people like actors, directors, choreographers, editors, cinematographers, makeup artists, etc.

I also believe that a country benefits by keeping cinema production in-house. Revenue earned from local movies and TV series boosts a country's economy. For example, Indian films like 'RRR, ''Bahubali,' 'Dabang,' 'Lagaan' etc., have done business worth crores not only in India but abroad as well. Local movies can also highlight social issues and problems relevant to the country. Thus, they influence citizens to address these issues and improve their country.

To sum up, I would like to reiterate that creating TV programmes and movies domestically is better for the cultural and economic growth of a country.

Plan followed
Intro: Paraphrase, Opinion
Para 1: how foreign films help local culture
Para 2: why it is better to promote local films
Para 3: Opinion – more points for producing local films
Conclusion – reiterate opinion.